Towards Organizational Knowledge

The Nonaka Series on Knowledge and Innovation

The Nonaka Series on Knowledge and Innovation is designed to honour Professor Ikujiro Nonaka for his scholarly achievements. Through his intellectual contributions, Professor Nonaka has achieved a remarkable advancement in our academic understanding of management and organization as well as the very practice of management.

After decades of conceptual and empirical work, many scholars and managers alike have come to see good leadership as an essential means to unleash individual and organizational potential to create knowledge. We recognise such leadership in Professor Nonaka, who, like all great scholars, deserves an academic tribute. The reader of this series will find many novel and inspiring ideas, interesting historical nuggets, critical thinking, and unusual perspectives.

The series will be composed of research-based books on knowledge and innovation in management. It will centre on the discussion and study of knowledge and innovation from a wider perspective including philosophical, epistemological, psychological, linguistic, semiological, cognitive founding in lieu of focusing on IT-related social network, intranet angles.

Titles include:

Kimio Kase, Ying Ying Zhang and Alesia Slocum
ASIAN VERSUS WESTERN MANAGEMENT THINKING
Its Culture-Bound Nature

Georg von Krogh, Hirotaka Takeuchi, Kimio Kase and César González Cantón (*editors*)
TOWARDS ORGANIZATIONAL KNOWLEDGE
The Pioneering Work of Ikujiro Nonaka

The Nonaka Series on Knowledge and Innovation
Series Standing Order ISBN 978–1–137–30919–8

You can receive future title in this series as they are published by placing a standing order. Please contact your bookseller or, in case of difficulty, write to us at the address below with your name and address, the title of the series and the ISBN quoted above.

Customer Services Department, Macmillan Distribution Ltd, Houndmills, Basingstoke, Hampshire RG21 6XS, England.

Towards Organizational Knowledge

The Pioneering Work of Ikujiro Nonaka

Edited by

Georg von Krogh
ETH Zurich, Switzerland

Hirotaka Takeuchi
Harvard Business School, USA

Kimio Kase
IESE Business School and International University of Japan

and

César González Cantón
CUNEF (Universidad Complutense de Madrid), Spain

palgrave
macmillan

First published 2013 by
PALGRAVE MACMILLAN

Palgrave Macmillan in the UK is an imprint of Macmillan Publishers Limited, registered in England, company number 785998, of Houndmills, Basingstoke, Hampshire RG21 6XS.

Palgrave Macmillan in the US is a division of St Martin's Press LLC, 175 Fifth Avenue, New York, NY 10010.

Palgrave Macmillan is the global academic imprint of the above companies and has companies and representatives throughout the world.

Palgrave® and Macmillan® are registered trademarks in the United States, the United Kingdom, Europe and other countries

ISBN: 978–1–137–02495–4

This book is printed on paper suitable for recycling and made from fully managed and sustained forest sources. Logging, pulping and manufacturing processes are expected to conform to the environmental regulations of the country of origin.

A catalogue record for this book is available from the British Library.

A catalog record for this book is available from the Library of Congress.

To my wonderful family, for all your support

– *GvK*

To Sachiko, Ikujiro Nonaka's better half, who made him who he is today

– *HT*

To Mercedes and in tender memory of Gabriel, my beloved son

– *KK*

To Sonia and Elías

– *CGC*

Contents

List of Tables

List of Figures

Notes on Contributors

Stefano Brusoni is Professor of Technology and Innovation Management at the Swiss Federal Institute of Technology (ETH) Zurich. Previously, he was Associate Professor in Applied Economics at Bocconi University, Milan. He has received his a PhD in Science and Technology from SPRU, University of Sussex (UK). His research focuses on the strategic implications of product design strategies. Brusoni has published in various journals such as *Administrative Science Quarterly, Organization Science, Research Policy, Organization Studies* and *Industrial and Corporate Change.*

Andrew Campbell is Director of Ashridge Strategic Management Centre at Ashridge Business School. Previously he was a Fellow of the Centre for Business Strategy at London Business School and a consultant at Mckinsey & Co. Andrew specializes in corporate-level strategy, business strategy, organization design, the role of the corporate centre, capability building and acquisitions. He has co-authored several books including *Corporate Level Strategy* (1994), *Core Competency-Based Strategy* (1997) and *The Collaborative Enterprise: Why Links between Business Units Often Fail and How to Make Them Work* (2000).

Rodolfo G. Campos is an Assistant Professor in the Economics Department at IESE Business School, University of Navarra. His research interests are include applied theory, macroeconomics, financial economics and banking. He has published 'Risk-sharing and Crises. Global Games of Regime Change with Endogenous Wealth', forthcoming in the *Journal of Economic Theory.*

César G. Cantón is Professor of Management at CUNEF (Universidad Complutense de Madrid), Spain. In the past, he worked with University of Navarra, Pompeu Fabra University and IESE Business School. His main interests include corporate responsibility and human rights, global business ethics, and gender issues. He has published in journals such as *Journal of Business Ethics and Management Revue.*

Jorge Cruz González is Research Fellow at Universidad Complutense de Madrid (CUNEF), and also Researcher at CUNEF Centre for Knowledge and Innovation. He has been visiting student at Copenhagen Business School (2011) when he was working on his PhD. His research interests are focused on organizational learning and innovation management, covering the topics on dynamic capabilities, exploration-exploitation, absorptive capacity, open innovation and combinative capabilities. His work has been published in journals such as *Technological Forecasting and Social Change* and *Journal of Knowledge Management*.

Thomas H. Davenport is President of the Information Technology Management Division and co-directs the Working Knowledge Research Center at Babson College. He has been the first to write about business process reengineering, knowledge management and the business use of enterprise systems. He has co-authored and edited twelve books and several articles. In 2003, he was named one of the top 25 consultants in the world by *Consulting* magazine; in 2005, he was rated the third most influential business and technology analyst in the world and in 2007, he was the highest-ranking business academic in Ziff-Davis' listing of the 100 most influential people in the IT industry.

Guillermo Fariñas Contreras is Business Ethics Professor at Universidad Monteávila. He has been also General Director of the Centro de Desarrollo Ejecutivo (Venezuela). His studies focus on values and humanistic management. He has a PhD in organization, government and culture from the University of Navarra, with a dissertation on Ikujiro Nonaka's thought and 'Theory of the Firm'.

Robert M. Grant is ENI Professor of Strategic Management at Bocconi University in Milan, and Visiting Professor at Georgetown University and at City University, London. He has also joined the McDonough School of Business. He specializes in organizational capability and strategic planning processes. The eighth edition of *Contemporary Strategy Analysis* is forthcoming.

Nigel J. Holden is Visiting Research Fellow at Leeds University Business School, having previously held professorial appointments in the UK, Germany and Denmark. An internationally active management researcher and educator, he is best known for his pioneering work *Cross-Cultural Management: A Knowledge Management Perspective*. He is leading consultant editor to the *Routledge Companion to Cross-Cultural Management*, due to be published in 2014.

Kimio Kase is Professor of Strategic Management at IESE Business School and International University of Japan. He has received his doctoral degree in business administration from Manchester University, worked for Price Waterhouse European Firm, Inter-American Development Bank, etc., and has previously taught at International University of Japan and ESADE. He has been teaching strategy, corporate-level strategy and Asian management. Kase has published articles and books including, as co-author, *Asian versus Western Management Thinking: Its Culture-Bound Nature* (2011) and is currently on the editorial board of: *The Nonaka Series on Knowledge Management and Innovation*, Palgrave Macmillan, UK; *Cross Cultural*

Management: An International Journal, and *Academia: Revista Latinoamericana de Administración*.

Florian Kohlbacher is a senior research fellow and head of the Business & Economics Section at the German Institute for Japanese Studies (DIJ) Tokyo. He holds both a master's degree and a doctorate from the Vienna University of Economics and Business (WU Vienna). His research interests focus on marketing and innovation management, sustainable business and the business implications of demographic change. Kohlbacher is also an adjunct professor at Temple University, Japan Campus, and a research fellow at the Sloan Center on Aging & Work at Boston College. He is the author of *International Marketing in the Network Economy: A Knowledge-Based Approach* (2007), and co-editor of *The Silver Market Phenomenon: Marketing and Innovation in the Aging Society* (2nd edition, 2011).

Noboru Konno is Professor at Tama Graduate School of Business, Tama University and president of KIRO (Knowledge Innovation Research Organization). His recent studies and projects include knowledge innovation, design thinking, and workplace for knowledge creation. He has consulted knowledge firms and design organizations based on his approach. His most recent books include *Dynamic Knowledge Asset* (2007), *Knowledge Design Company* (2008), *Virtue-based Management* (2008, co-author with I. Nonaka), *The Grammar of Knowledge Creating Management for Prudent Capitalism* (2012, co-author with I. Nonaka) and others.

Pedro López Sáez is Associate Professor at Universidad Complutense de Madrid (CUNEF), and also Researcher at CUNEF Centre for Knowledge and Innovation. He has been visiting scholar and Fellow at Harvard University (2004–2005). His research interests are focused on organizational learning, dynamic capabilities, strategy and innovation. His publications have appeared in SSCI journals such as *Technovation, International Journal of Technology Management, Journal of Business Ethics* and *Journal of Intellectual Capital*.

Gregorio Martín de Castro is Associate Professor and Researcher at the CUNEF Centre for Knowledge and Innovation, CUNEF Business School, Complutense University of Madrid. He has been visiting scholar and fellow at Harvard University (2004–2005), the University of Manchester (2009) and the University of Southern California (2011). His numerous works regarding intellectual capital, knowledge management, innovation and strategic management appeared in academic journals as *Technovation, Journal of Business Ethics* and *Knowledge Management Research and Practice*.

Jane McKenzie is Professor of Management Knowledge and Learning at Henley Business School, University of Reading. She became Director of the Henley KM Forum in 2009. Her research interests centre on the role of knowledge and learning in organizational development the contribution of leadership and decision making behaviour in that process. Much of her thinking builds on theories of learning, complexity, paradox and dilemmas. She has written three books and many papers.

José Emilio Navas López is Business Administration Professor at Universidad Complutense de Madrid. His research interests are Business Administration and Technology & Knowledge Management. He is author and co-author of several books and papers published in *Technovation, International Journal of Technology Management, Technological Forecasting and Social Change, Journal of Knowledge Management, Journal of Business Ethics* and *Journal of High Technology Management Research.*

Vesa Peltokorpi is Associate Professor at the Japan Advanced Institute of Science and Technology. His research interests include international business, international human resource management and group cognition. He has published numerous articles in peer-reviewed journals, such as *Journal of International Business Studies, Journal of Management Studies,* and *Review of General Psychology.*

Laurence Prusak is an independent consultant. Currently he is a senior advisor on knowledge issues to NASA, the Gates Foundation, and the World Bank. He was the founder of the IBM Institute for Knowledge Management and has extensive teaching and consulting experience on issues of knowledge and learning in organizations. He has co-edited *Knowledge Management and Organizational Learning* (2005), and co-authored *Storytelling in Organizations* (2004). He has been awarded many honours such as Simmons College Distinguished Alumni Award in 2002 and the Lewin Award from *Organization Science* in 2000.

Patrick Reinmoeller is Professor of Strategic Management at Cranfield University and Visiting Professor at Erasmus University. He is the Director of the 'Breakthrough Strategic Thinking' and 'Directors as Strategic Leaders' programmes at Cranfield School of Management. As the first Academic Director, he led University of Pretoria's Centre for Japanese Studies at the Gordon Institute of Business Science, and he established the Executive Program in Strategic Management at the Rotterdam School of Management. He has won several awards for excellence in teaching and programme delivery. Reinmoeller specializes in knowledge creation, organizational resilience, management innovation and international business. He has published in leading Asian, European and US journals. Following *Strategy Management: Competitiveness and Globalization* (with Volberda, Morgan, Hitt, Ireland, Hoskisson) in 2011, his book on *Ambidextrous Organization* is forthcoming.

Florian Rittiner is a PhD student at the Chair of Technology and Innovation Management at the ETH Zurich. His research interest is in the field of organizational learning, routines and framing processes. He has specialized in R&D management, process optimization, knowledge management, innovation management and change management.

John-Christopher Spender is a visiting professor at ESADE and Lund University School of Economics and Management. He was also Dean of the School of Business and Technology at FIT (State University of New York). He specializes in theory of the firm, strategy, history of management and management education and he has written numerous journal articles and books.

David J. Teece is the director of the Institute for Business Innovation, Haas School of Business, University of California, Berkeley. Between 1989 and 2007, he was Mitsubishi Bank Chair in International Business and Finance. He has published six books in which he has studied the role of product, process development and intellectual property in the competitive performance of the business enterprise. In 2011, he received the Herbert Simon award and he has been identified by Accenture as one of the World's Top 50 Living Business Intellectuals.

Fangqi Xu is Director of the Institute for Creative Management and Innovation at Kinki University. In the past, he has been president of the Japan Creativity Society. His main research topics are creative management and the source of Chinese enterprises' competitive power. Fangqi has been the editor of the *Kindai Management Review* journal; he has published *Comparative Research between Japanese and Chinese Enterprises* and *Liu Chuanzhi: The Founder of Lenovo.*

Yingying Zhang is Associate Professor of Management and Organization at Complutense University of Madrid (CUNEF). Before this appointment, she was visiting research scholar at Rutgers University. She also serves at Editorial Review Board of *Management and Organization Review*. Her research interests include dynamic strategic management, knowledge and innovation, learning, people management, and Chinese management. She has published numerous books, books chapters and scientific journal articles in English, Spanish and Chinese.

Yu Zhou is Assistant Professor at the School of Business, Renmin University of China. His research interests include strategic HRM, HRM-innovation/creativity linkages, HRM effectiveness within the Chinese context, and HRM–leadership interaction. He has been publishing on these themes in different international reputed scientific journals.

Scholarship with Wisdom: An Introduction

Georg von Krogh, Hirotaka Takeuchi, Kimio Kase and César G. Cantón

This chapter is composed of five sections:

1. Introduction: The purpose of this Festschrift and its significance in an academic context is explained.
2. Biographical notes on Ikujiro Nonaka: Some landmark events in Professor Ikujiro Nonaka's trajectory are highlighted.
3. A Panoramic view of Professor Ikujiro Nonaka's contributions: Professor Nonaka's contributions to the study of management is provided.
4. An overview of the chapters: By way of orientation for the readers, an outline of the book with a brief summary of each article is given.
5. Annex: A list of some of the major works by Professor I Nonaka.

Introduction

This book is designed to honour Professor Ikujiro Nonaka for his scholarly achievements. Through his intellectual contributions, Ikujiro Nonaka has achieved a remarkable advancement in our academic understanding of management and organization as well as the very practice of management. After decades of conceptual and empirical work, many scholars and managers alike have come to see good leadership as an essential means to unleash individual and organizational potential to create knowledge. We recognize such leadership in Professor Ikujiro Nonaka, who, like all great scholars, deserves a tribute in the academic tradition of a Festschrift in which colleagues are given the opportunity to express their admiration and gratitude in the way they know best: to write a paper in his honour. Compared to academic volumes and journal papers, a Festschrift has few set standards of rigour and relevance, and its contributors write what they feel serves the celebratory purpose best. Papers in such books are therefore often unconventional and daring, venturing in new strings of thought. The reader of this book will find many novel and inspiring ideas, interesting historical nuggets, critical thinking, and unusual perspectives. This is perhaps not so surprising given that it celebrates the work of a man whose greatest achievements have been to show how we may develop and deploy more creativity and innovation.

For those readers who know Ikujiro Nonaka personally, the motivation behind this undertaking should be obvious. Not only do the authors celebrate an outstanding scholar, but also a person of great integrity, kindness, intellectual virtue, open mindedness and inquisitiveness. Nonaka has been the mentor of dozens of students and young scholars who under his guidance have moved on to produce their own academic achievements. His willingness to listen, share and explore new ideas with co-researchers is unparalleled and a gift to our academic community. Knowledge is of a fragile construction often left in shambles by people's thirst for solid justification. Yet what will eventually become new knowledge of great value to those who created it and beyond starts with an insight, intuition, hunch, feeling or idea that must be allowed to emerge and take wing. Ikujiro Nonaka not only knows and writes about this, but also so clearly demonstrates it in his own behaviour. To paraphrase from his writings: He knows how to walk the talk. It takes patience and tolerance to hold back tough criticism and resort to conventional solutions and easy answers, so that such fragile knowledge can be allowed to emerge. In his lifelong contributions, it is very clear that from many small fragments of hunches and ideas, a perspective eventually emerged that had the power to alter the way we think about management and organization. If he and his co-workers had resorted to quick theoretical fixes early on, the chances are the world would not have seen the importance that knowledge creation plays in modern business. There is therefore a remarkably consistency in Nonaka's writings and personal conduct, and perhaps this consistency is the mark of true scholarship with wisdom.

This introductory chapter is organized as follows: In the first section, we briefly present the biography of Ikujiro Nonaka; the second section serves as an introduction to some select contributions in Nonaka's work; and the third section provides an overview of the invited chapters in the book.

Biographical notes on Ikujiro Nonaka

Ikujiro Nonaka was born in Tokyo in 1935 and received his B.A. from Waseda University in Political Science. Right after graduation, he started working for Fuji Electric, where he spent nine years in various departments, including corporate planning, marketing and human resources. He and his wife Sachiko, who worked together with him at Fuji Electric, quit their jobs and moved to the US, arriving in San Francisco on a cargo vessel. Ikujiro enrolled in the MBA program at University of California Berkeley and then moved on to its PhD program. The Nonaka's made ends meet during their Berkeley days by working as a gardener and a waitress. Just before finishing up his

PhD degree, Ikujiro met a young MBA from Japan, Hirotaka Takeuchi, who would become his lifetime colleague.

After returning to Japan in 1972, Ikujiro Nonaka held a number of academic positions at Nanzan University (1972–1979), National Defence Academy of Japan (1979–1982), Hitotsubashi University (1982–1995), Japan Advanced Institute of Science and Technology (1995–2000) and finally at Hitotsubashi University's newly established business school, Graduate School of International Corporate Strategy (2000–). Since 2006, he is a Professor Emeritus of Hitotsubashi University. Outside of Japan, he is the Xerox Distinguished Faculty Scholar of the University of California, Berkeley (1997–) and the first Distinguished Drucker Scholar in Residence at the Peter Drucker School of Management, Claremont Graduate University (2007–), among others.

Professor Nonaka has been distinguished with many awards and honours throughout his career. To mention a few, his co-authored books *The Knowledge-Creating Company* and *Enabling Knowledge Creation* each received the Best Book of the Year Award in business and management from the Association of American Publishers in 1996 and 2000, respectively. In 2002, he was conferred with a Purple Ribbon Medal by the Japanese government and was elected a member of the Fellows Group of the Academy of Management in the US. In 2007, he received the Booz Allen Hamilton Eminent Scholar in International Management Award at the annual meeting of the Academy of Management. In 2008, he was chosen as one of the 20 most influential business thinkers by *Wall Street Journal*. In 2010, he was conferred The Order of the Sacred Treasure, Gold Rays with Neck Ribbon from the Japanese government for his outstanding achievement, long service, and contribution to education. In 2012, he received the Eminent Scholar Award by the Academy of International Business.

A Panoramic view of Professor Ikujiro Nonaka's contributions

To most readers, Ikujiro Nonaka will probably be best known for his discussions on the distinction between tacit and explicit knowledge in management and organization studies, the idea of knowledge conversion, and the development of the SECI model for knowledge creation. Taken together, these are central elements of what has come to be known as organizational knowledge creation theory (See Annex for some of the major works by Professor I. Nonaka). This theory seeks to explain the why, when, what and how of individual and organizational entanglement in creating new knowledge (see Nonaka, von Krogh, & Voelpel, 2006 for a full review).

In the late 1980s and early 1990s, a growing worldwide community of scholars began to question some of the fundamental assumptions behind individual cognition, information processing, and organization structure that had dominated the academic debate in the field of management and organization since the 1950s (Kogut & Zander, 1992; Nonaka, 1987; 1988; 1994; Grant, 1996; Spender, 1996; Tsoukas, 2005; von Krogh et al., 1994; SMJ). These scholars were uneasy with the idea that information as a unit of analysis was encompassing enough to describe, and perhaps even predict, decisions and actions of individuals and the structuring of organizations to optimize information processing (March & Simon, 1958; Galbraith, 1973). Their interest shifted from information to knowledge, which opened for a broader understanding of what individuals do and how they shape and are shaped by the organizations in which they work and live. In the early 1990s, many concepts of knowledge were offered in the literature, but one rather encompassing and convenient, but not necessarily complete, definition got increasingly adopted: Knowledge is justified true belief, a potential to act, and ranges between the tacit and explicit ends on a continuum (Nonaka, 1994; Nonaka & Takeuchi, 1995; Nonaka, 1991; von Krogh, Ichijo, & Nonaka, 2000; Nonaka & von Krogh, 2009). When people believe something to be true, they typically need a justification, which is private or social. Nonaka never stops emphasizing that belief and justification are more important than 'truth' in this definition, because he is uncomfortable with the notion that knowledge should be judged by its correspondence to an external environment (Nonaka & Takeuchi, 1995).

Knowledge is also what enables people to act and should therefore be thought of as potential rather than actuality. People may not only know more than they can tell, but also more than they *will* tell. Inspired by the work of Michael Polanyi, a Hungarian polymath, Nonaka distinguished knowledge in tacit and explicit dimensions. Explicit knowledge can be captured in symbols, codes, statements, figures, drawing, heuristics, criteria and so forth, whereas tacit knowledge is tied to the body, senses, movement, physical experiences, mental practice, intuition etc. Tacit knowledge is difficult or oftentimes impossible to express to others. Knowledge was also considered a feature of team and organizations, with some of the same characteristics (Nonaka & Takeuchi, 1995). This tripartite definition inspired generations of scholars in management and organization studies to investigate antecedents and effects of knowledge at multiple levels in organizations. Perhaps one of the reasons was that the definition remained broad rather than specific that allowed more precision over time coupled with increasing expansions.

During the past decade as new empirical studies of knowledge creation followed and advancements were made in neuroscience and cognitive psychology, knowledge was increasingly redefined as dynamic construct in constant flux on a tacit-explicit continuum. For individuals, knowledge conversion describes this flux. As knowledge moves towards the explicit end of the continuum, physical experience, mental practice, and movement are put to use to articulate, overtly reason or argue, draw, shape, calculate and so on. However, when knowledge moves towards the explicit end, it also simultaneously changes the basis in the senses, physical experiences, imagery, movements, and memory. Therefore, knowledge at the explicit side is neither static nor a representation of tacit insight, a sort of incomplete image of what you have experienced or thought. Knowledge towards the tacit end is not some private recollection of what had been seen or heard that has yet to be articulated. Rather, knowledge is made up of this relentless high-frequency dynamic between physically experiencing the world and the expressing to shape it, and as such a crucial element in our biological condition as humans (Nonaka & von Krogh, 2009). To management and organization scholars, this condition is more than a fanciful notion: It is in fact the source of new knowledge, creativity, and innovation for organizations and thus should be handled with care.

A third major contribution by Ikujiro Nonaka is the so-called SECI-model of how knowledge is created in organizations. SECI is an acronym for socialization, externalization, combination, and internationalization. Socialization describes the sharing of tacit knowledge between individuals through their close and repeated interaction. Sharing of tacit knowledge presupposes coordinated activities that give rise to joint experiences. Externalization is the articulation and expression of knowledge. Combination is a process whereby pieces of data, information and knowledge at the explicit side, are reassembled in novel ways. Internalization describes a process where external stimuli enter the knowledge conversion process of individuals. Often described as 'learning by doing' (Nonaka & Takeuchi, 1995), internalization is thought to describe a process of building up the capacity to perform tasks through repeated practice. The SECI process is located in teams of individuals who are work in Ba/spaces throughout the organization. A good Ba has qualities that inspire people to interact intensively and share ideas and experiences. Teams also retrieve and access predefined knowledge assets that help them augment their knowledge. As an outcome of SECI, people also capture knowledge assets that become a resource for the organization to create new knowledge and innovate across time and space (Nonaka & Konno, 1998). A metaphor of an upward knowledge spiral is often used to illustrate how this process enables organizations to continuously create new knowledge at many levels.

A brilliant departure of Ikujiro Nonaka was to tie in the definition of knowledge, the idea of knowledge conversion, and the SECI model with innovation in organizations. By so doing he and his co-workers could explain in novel ways how firms bring process and product innovations to the market. Nonaka and Takeuchi (1995) and von Krogh, Ichijo, and Nonaka (2000) show many cases of innovation in firms, and how this process can be understood by applying organizational knowledge creation theory. An important contribution was to illustrate that many new and highly successful products or categories, such as a bread-baking machine, a meat-processing plant, a cosmetic series, a digital hearing-aid, or a compact car all could be traced back to surprising and unconventional experiences – at the tacit end of the knowledge continuum – that people made with work, technology, customers, processes and sites. The advice to managers was that rather than heavily planning and streamlining an inward-looking innovation process, they needed to ensure that developers get exposed to unfamiliar situations that lie beyond the boundaries of the firm. For example, a pharmaceutical company sent their scientists to work as orderlies in a hospital for geriatric care for them to learn how their patients lived their lives and responded to the firm's medication. Their new experiences led scientists to develop entirely new ways of administering drugs to patients with Alzheimer's disease.

One of the important academic and practical implications of organizational knowledge creation theory is that we have come to understand that a broad set of factors are required to enable the flow of knowledge in organizations (Toyama, Nonaka, etc., Knowledge Flow book). Some of these factors are a strong organizational culture, a multi-layered organizational structure, a vision of what knowledge the organization should create, autonomy of teams, redundancy in work processes, slack resources, collaboration between talent from different organizational practices, and the development and use of dedicated information and communication technology. Recent work has argued that one of the critical factors to enable knowledge creation is a strong, positive, multi-level leadership sensitive to the intricacies of knowledge creation (von Krogh, Nonaka, & Rechsteiner, 2012). For example, as previously mentioned, there are many social barriers such as justification that hinder people from sharing knowledge. People often face a belief by fellow team members that what they may want to share is of lesser relevance to the problem at hand, and the process may be broken off prematurely. Good leadership may mitigate such problems, by dampening early criticism in the stage of externalization.

What characterizes such leadership? First of all, it is clear that teams themselves need a capacity for 'distributed leadership', whereby leadership and followership activities are spread across team members depending on the tasks at hand. People rise to leadership depending on expertise and experience, which is needed at different times. Knowledge creation is dynamic and so are tasks, leaving leadership as emergent and distributed throughout the process. Second, more centralized leadership is needed in order to support local knowledge creation processes. People in formal organizational positions exercise such leadership. They hold the authority to formulate knowledge visions, allocate resources to build Ba, incentivize team members, secure access to knowledge assets and bridge between different teams. Negotiations between people who exercise distributed and centralized leadership are crucial in order to provide some direction to knowledge creation, coupled with sufficient autonomy, in order to mobilize the creativity of teams members.

The implications for academic research of this new view of leadership in knowledge creation are worthwhile thinking about. For example, future work should study how the factors that impact on the transition between leadership and followership, and the effects such transitions have on team performance. Likewise, management practice can also learn from this view: When judging good leadership, one should ask to what extent an individual has supported the creation of new knowledge in the organization and with what results. The capacity for distributed leadership is not a precondition, but must be built through systematic investments. New training programs on leadership need to be developed and offered broadly as part of corporate development activities. Overall, this contemplation on the role of leadership shows the generative power of Nonaka's work. You can use it to find new theoretical strains and research problems, it never seems entirely conclusive.

An overview of the chapters

Professor Nonaka has been distinguished with many honours throughout his career. To mention some, he has been recognized as the First Distinguished Drucker Scholar in Residence at the Drucker School and Institute, Claremont Graduate University; Professor Emeritus, Hitotsubashi University Graduate School of International Corporate Strategy; Xerox Distinguished Faculty Scholar, IMIO, University of California, Berkeley; and Xerox Distinguished Professor in Knowledge, Walter A. Haas School of Business, University of California, Berkeley.

Professor I. Nonaka was born in 1935 in Tokyo, starting his professional life by joining Fuji Electric in 1958. Following his urge to learn, he moved to the US to pursue PhD studies at the University of California, Berkeley, where he obtained his doctoral degree in 1972. From then on, Professor Nonaka would never abandon the academic approach to work and organizations, and would exercise as a management professor at universities both inside and outside Japan including Nanzan University, National Defence Academy of Japan, Hitotsubashi University and Japan Advanced Institute of Science and Technology.

Part I A historical perspective

Teece (1–1) analyses Nonaka's contribution to the understanding of knowledge creation as well as its codification and decodification. He places emphasis on a crucial aspect of Nonaka's theory: What is the make-up of a leader, or the role of managers, in fostering, leading and bringing to fruition the knowledge creation process within their companies. In particular, the important role played by middle managers, in the justly famous Nonaka's 'middle-up-down' flow of information and decision-making, is seen as one of the greatest contributions by Nonaka.

Spender (1–2) sets the frame in terms of time by reviewing Nonaka and KM's past, present and future. Spender makes an interesting case for Nonaka regarding the latter's contribution to the theory of the firm, i.e., a response to the long-standing and unresolved question about *what is a firm?*

Xu (1–3) carries out, based on a thorough perusal of Nonaka's documented background, a sort of 'cleaning up' work in order to explain away some misinterpretations and bring into light the true spirit and contents of Nonaka's proposition, supporting all along his argument with pieces from Nonaka's own biographical records. A number of concepts stand out in the process, such as *ba*, tacit knowledge, the SECI model, or middle-up-down management.

Part II Contemporary development

Grant (2–1) offers some reflections on a key theme: The role of organization in the production and deployment of knowledge by examining its epistemological and ontological dimensions. The comparison with the concept of organizational capability allows Grant to shed light upon the limitations of this promising notion and how Nonaka's perspective can make a substantial contribution to it. He also points to the absence of a clearly defined notion of knowledge, to suggest that Nonaka's work is more of a model than a theory.

Fariñas (2–2) delves into the metaphysics of Nonaka's world. Fariñas's work represents a determined intent in clarifying Nonaka's philosophical assumptions. He stresses the debt Nonaka owes to Aristotle concerning the idea of practical reasoning, or phronesis, as well as Nonaka's adroit use of the idea for the understanding of managerial judgment. At the same time, the author also marks the limits of Nonaka's interpretation of Aristotle clearly and points to a number of shortcomings in the structure of Nonaka's philosophical building.

Brusoni and Rittiner (2–3) attempt to expand Nonaka's SECI model, making a threefold contribution; first, showing that the starting point of Nonaka's learning spiral varies with the knowledge content; second, that the learning spirals of process knowledge and improvement knowledge are connected; and finally, that this link is established by specific organizational roles, called *continuous improvement facilitators*, who match, in a 'garbage can' logic, the solutions embedded in the improvement knowledge to the problems identified through process knowledge.

Much in Spender's vein, but with a different focus, Cruz, López, Martín and Navas (2–4) explore Nonaka's explanatory power to define the boundaries of the firm. The authors venture a joint interpretation by reading Nonaka within the transaction costs theory framework. In doing that, they review key concepts of the resource-based view of the firm, clarifying its differences with Nonaka's theory.

Noting that authors Nonaka and Takeuchi in *The Knowledge-Creating Company* touch upon the relationship between KM and the Japanese language, Holden (2–5) examines Russian as a language of KM. With reference to Russia's first authoritative book in KM, he finds that Russian is heavily indebted to English for its core concepts, but that the vague and casual nature of its basic working terminology in the English language – characterized as an awkward confection of sociological discourse, the management-functional, the folksy and the modish – present translators with exceptional challenges. Holden uses back-translation and contextual analysis to reveal unexpected semantic asymmetries between English and Russian. His approach hints at future fertile work on the topic of language and KM.

Zhang, Zhou, and McKenzie (2–6) take on a new perspective to highlight the spirit that animates Nonaka's theory: the centrality of persons in organizations, or its human-centric character. The concept of Ba speaks for itself in this regard and is accordingly examined by the authors in relation to the process of innovation. Organizational aspects strongly based on personal characteristics, such as the company's culture, work climate, and human resources management, have merited their analysis.

Reinmoeller (2–7) focuses his attention on how the behavioural theory clarifies the mechanism of knowledge creation, since, similar to the Behavioral Theory of the Firm, after 20 years Knowledge Creation Theory has become a major influence to many theoretical and empirical studies focused on knowledge based phenomena in organizations. In the belief that, given the centrifugal forces in management research it is time to attend to the neglected relationship between these two theories. Acknowledging a range of distances between Cyert and March (1963) and Nonaka's seminal work (1994), he focuses on similarities and analyse the 'best of both worlds' to advance a deeper understanding of their complementarities. A joint appreciation of the theories is especially meaningful because searching for the 'first best solution' by making small steps is different from leaping to the 'best solution first' and both theories are essential for explaining success of organizations. The chapter points to an agenda of a shared quest, accentuated insights and an emergent complementary relationship.

Konno (2–8) turns to the intellectual environment asking how well Nonaka's theory can contribute to the development of a theory of knowledge's economic value in a post-capitalist society, along the lines of Drucker's reflection. This 'revisit' of Drucker's thinking turns out to be necessary because Japanese firms, once pioneers of a knowledge-based approach to competition, have forgotten their initial thrust along the way. The author focuses, then, on the exploration of two basic Nonakian concepts: 'tacit knowledge' and its relationship to innovation, drawing also upon ideas by Hayek and Schumpeter; and '*Ba*', quite a complex notion that demands a renewed attention. The concept of 'purpose reengineering', meaning by that the organization's capability to aggregating individual's desires and actions into a knowledge ecosystem, is the outcome contribution of this analysis.

Part III Perspective for further development

Campbell's chapter (3–1) shares a common ground of themes and interests with Nonaka's thinking, notwithstanding this not coming to the fore. His work, as one of the most prominent thinkers of corporate-level strategy, concerns how corporate headquarters can help build capabilities across business divisions in a decentralized organization structure. Its main contribution is a language for describing capabilities in divisionalized organizations and a typology of different roles corporate headquarters can play in building core capabilities.

Campos (3–2) makes an inroad into the theme of game theory. The chapter is a nontechnical account of how recent developments in game theory have shaped the way economists think about coordination failures. Nonaka's theory can be brought in for a better understanding of the process by which the players' information about payoffs is shaped as result of an interaction with the world and among the players.

Prusak and Davenport (3–3) bring in a practitioner's interpretation of knowledge and its role management. They present us with a short but intense piece of work about the revolutionary appearance of Nonaka's *The Knowledge-Creating Company* in the knowledge literature, when the field had seemingly run out of new ideas. Stranded in an understanding of knowledge as information, the field welcomed the Nonaka's SECI model and, particularly, the thought-provoking idea of tacit knowledge as a way out of a reductionist account of KM and into the nature of innovation. A blend of history and forecasting, of conceptual analysis and personal anecdote, of theory and practitioner's perspective, this chapter makes for a delightful and informative reading.

Peltokorpi (3–4), on his part, focuses on the challenges of locating and sharing knowledge across projects in project-based organizations. He proposes a more balanced account of knowledge processes in project-based organizations by integrating two different – and sometimes opposite – streams of literature on knowledge governance: the 'hard' dimensions of compensation systems and the 'soft' dimensions of trust and community-based aspects. A non-exhaustive set of governance mechanisms, complementary to and substitutable for each other, is further displayed: consensus-based hierarchy, shared human resource management (HRM) practices, and performance and output control. This conceptual framework is tested through the case study of Mayekawa Manufacturing, Ltd., currently one of the world's leading industrial refrigeration system manufacturers.

Kohlbacher (3–5) views KM from the viewpoint of marketing centred on innovation through marketing knowledge co-creation. Finally, Kase and Cantón's work (3–6) is a daring leap into the philosophical assumptions of the process of decision-making in excellent managers as part of knowledge creation and innovation. Their reflection combines a highly abstract account of the concept of contingency from a philosophical perspective and the attempt to show that excellent managers are characterized by their ability to convert possibility in necessity, i.e., a business idea in an actual successful project. A case study of innovative product development in Japan confers strength and concretization to their argument.

Synthesising the contributions

On the basis of the foregoing sections as well as the overview of the contributed chapters we may point out the fertility of soil opened up by Professor Nonaka. That Nonaka's contributions to management thinking and practice are wide and varied is shown in the fact that the Festschrift deals with a wide gamut of issues: leadership, the theory of the firm revisited, the role of organization regarding knowledge creation and deployment, phronesis, the process of knowledge creation through the SECI model, the question of firm boundary, the involvement of language in knowledge management, the centrality of person in organization, the economic value creation through knowledge, the role of the corporate centre in capability-building, the game theory and knowledge management, the question of fortuity and knowledge and so on.

The amplitude of research topics is not the only characteristic of Professor Nonaka's contributions. He calls into question the prevailing profit maximization paradigm (Grant, 2010, p. 35). Nonakian proposition of knowledge-based management (Nonaka, Toyama, & Hirata, 2008, p. 2; Grant, 2010, pp. 159–165) leads ultimately to Knowledge School (Nonaka & Konno, 2012) that aspires to 'build a theory that grasps the essential reality of life in the firm' (Nonaka et al., 2008, p. 3).

Thus, we are convinced that by studying Professor Ikujiro Nonaka's theories and ideas we are witnessing the opening of a new horizon in management, both in theory and practice.

References

Cyert, R. M., & March, J. G. (1963). *A Behavioral Theory of the Firm*. Englewood Cliffs NJ: Prentice-Hall.

Galbraith, J. R. (1973). *Designing Complex Organizations*. Reading: Addison-Wesley.

Grant, R. M. (1996). 'Toward a knowledge-based theory of the firm'. *Strategic Management Journal*. *17*, 109–122.

Grant, M. G. (2010). *Contemporary Strategy Analysis: Text & Cases* (7th ed.). Oxford: John Wiley & Sons.

Kogut, B., & Zander, U. (1992). 'Knowledge of the firm, combinative capabilities, and the replication of technology'. *Organization Science*. 3 (3), 383–397.

March, J. G., & Simon, H. A. (1958). *Organizations*. New York: Wiley.

Nonaka, I. (1987). 'Managing the firm as information creation process'. *Working Paper*. Institute of Business Research, Hitotsubashi University.

Nonaka, I. (1988). 'Toward middle-up-down management – accelerating information creation'. *MIT Sloan Management Review*. 29 (3), 9–18.

Nonaka, I. (1991). 'The knowledge-creating company'. *Harvard Business Review*. November–December, 96–104.

Nonaka, I. (1994). 'A dynamic theory of organizational knowledge creation'. *Organization Science.* 5 (1), 14–37.
Nonaka, I., & Takeuchi, H. (1995). *The Knowledge-creating Company.* New York: Oxford University Press.
Nonaka, I., & von Krogh, G. (2009). 'Tacit knowledge and knowledge conversion: controversy and advancement in organizational knowledge creation theory'. *Organization Science.* 20 (3), 635–652.
Nonaka, I., von Krogh, G., & Voelpel, S. (2006). 'Organizational knowledge creation theory: evolutionary paths and future advances'. *Organization Studies.* 27 (8), 1179–1208.
Nonaka, I., & Konno, N. (2012). *The Grammar of Knowledge Creating Management for Prudent Capitalism (chishiki sozo keiei no principles: kenryo shihonshugi no jissenron).* Tokyo: Toyo Keizai.
Spender, J. C. (1996). 'Making knowledge the basis of a dynamic theory of the firm'. *Strategic Management Journal.* 17, 45–62.
Tsoukas, H. (2005). *Complex Knowledge: Studies in Organizational Epistemology.* New York: Oxford University Press.
von Krogh, G., Ichjio, K., & Nonaka, I. (2000). *Enabling Knowledge Creation: How to Unlock the Mystery of Tacit Knowledge and Release the Power of Innovation.* New York: Oxford University Press.
von Krogh, G., Roos, J., & Slocum, K. (1994). 'An essay on corporate epistemology'. *Strategic Management Journal.* 15 (S2), 53–71.

Annex to Introduction: some of the major works by Professor Ikujiro Nonaka

Johansson, J. K., & Nonaka, I. (1996). *Relentless: The Japanese Way of Marketing.* New York: HarperCollins Publishers.

Kagono, T., Nonaka, I., Okumura, A., Sakakibara, K., Komatsu, Y., & Sakashita, A. (1981). 'Mechanistic vs organic management systems: A comparative study of adaptive patterns of US and Japanese firms'. *The Annals of the School of Business Administration, Kobe University.* 25, 115–145.

Kagono, T., Nonaka, I., Sakakibara, K., & Okumura, A. (1985). *Evolutionary Management: A US-Japan Comparison of Strategy and Organization.* Amsterdam: Elsevier Science Publishers B. V.

Kase, K., G. Cantón, C., & Nonaka, I. (Forthcoming). *Phronesis and Quiddity in Management: A School of Knowledge Approach.* Hampshire, UK: Palgrave Macmillan.

Nonaka, I. (1988). 'Self-renewal of the Japanese firm and the human resource strategy'. *Human Resource Management.* 27 (1), 45–62.

Nonaka, I. (1988). 'Toward middle-up-down management: accelerating information creation'. *Sloan management review.* 9 (Spring), 9–18.

Nonaka, I. (1990). 'Redundant, overlapping organization: a Japanese approach to managing the innovation process'. *California Management Review.* (Spring), 27–38.

Nonaka, I. (1991). 'The knowledge-creating company'. *Harvard Business Review.* November–December, 96–104.

Nonaka, I. (1992). 'Watakushino shin shihon shugi ron: Nihon kigyo no chi no saiko-chikuwo (Restructuring of the knowledge at Japanese enterprises)'. *Nippon Keizan Shimbun,* 27 June, 22.

Nonaka, I. (1994). 'A dynamic theory of organizational knowledge creation'. *Organization Science.* 5 (1), 14–37.

Nonaka, I. (1995). 'Kigyo to chishiki sozo (Firms and knowledge creation)'. *Nihon Keizai Shimbun*, 27 April–2 May.

Nonaka, I. (1996). 'The vitality of agile companies (Agile company de katsuryoku)'. *Nihon Keizai Shimbun.*, 22 April, 18.

Nonaka, I., Kagono, T., Komatsu, Y., Okumura, A., & Sakashita, A. (1978). *Theories of Organizational Phenomena and Their Measurement (Soshiki gensho no riron to sokutei).* Tokyo: Chikura Shobo.

Nonaka, I., & Konno, N. (1998). 'The concept of "ba": building a foundation for knowledge creation'. *California Management Review.* 40 (3), 40–54.

Nonaka, I., & Konno, N. (2012). *The Grammar of Knowledge Creating Management for Prudent Capitalism (chishiki sozo keiei no principles: kenryo shihonshugi no jissenron).* Tokyo: Toyo Keizai.

Nonaka, I., Konno, N., & Kase, K. (Forthcoming). *Prudent Capitalism.* London: Palgrave Macmillan.

Nonaka, I., & Okumura, A. (1984). 'A comparison of management in American, Japanese and European firms (I)'. *Management Japan.* 17 (1), 23–39.

Nonaka, I., & Okumura, A. (1984). 'A comparison of management in American, Japanese and European firms (II)'. *Management Japan.* 17 (2), 20–27.

Nonaka, I., & Takeuchi, H. (1995). *The Knowledge-Creating Company: How Japanese Companies Create the Dynamics of Innovation*, New York: Oxford University Press.

Nonaka, I., & Takeuchi, H. (2011). 'The wise leader'. *Harvard Business Review.* May, Reprint RT1058.

Nonaka, I., & Toyama, R. (2003). 'The knowledge-creating theory revisited: knowledge creation as a synthesizing process'. *Knowledge Management Research & Practice.* 1 (1), 2–10.

Nonaka, I., & Toyama, R. (2003). 'The knowledge-creating theory revisited: knowledge creation as a synthesizing process'. *Knowledge Management Research &# 38; Practice.* 1 (1), 2–10.

Nonaka, I., & Toyama, R. (2007). 'Strategic management as distributed practical wisdom (phronesis)'. *Industrial and Corporate Change.* 16 (3), 371–394.

Nonaka, I., Toyama, R., & Hirata, T. (2008). *Managing Flow: A Process Theory of the Knowledge-Based Firm.* London: Palgrave Macmillan.

Nonaka, I., Toyama, R., & Hirata, T. (2010). *Managing Flow: the Dynamic Theory of Knowledge-Based Firm (Nagare wo keiei suru: jizokuteki innovation kigyo no dotai riron).* Tokyo: Toyo Keizai Shimposha.

Nonaka, I., Toyama, R., & Konno, N. (2000). 'SECI, Ba and leadership: a unified model of dynamic knowledge creation'. *Long Range Planning.* 33 (1), 5–34.

Nonaka, I., Toyama, R., & Nagata, A. (2000). 'A firm as a knowledge-creating entity: a new perspective on the theory of the firm'. *Industrial and Corporate Change.* 9 (1), 1.

Nonaka, I., & von Krogh, G. (2003). 'Tacit knowledge and knowledge creation: controversy and advancement in organizational knowledge creation theory'. *Organization Science.* 20 (3), 635–652.

Sullivan, J. J., & Nonaka, I. (1986). 'The application of organizational learning theory to Japanese and American management'. *Journal of International Business Studies.* (Fall). 127–147.

Takeuchi, H., Sakakibara, K., Kagono, T., Okumura, A., & Nonaka, I. (1986). *Self-Renewal of Enterprise – The Management of Chaos and Creativity (Kigyo no Jiko Kakushin – Chaos to Sozo no Management).* Tokyo: Chuo Koron.

Tobe, R., Teramoto, Y., Kamata, S., Suginoo, Y., Murai, T., & Nonaka, I. (1991). *The Essence of Failure: An Organizational Study of the Japanese Army (Shippai no honshitsu: nihongun no soshikironteki kenkyu).* Tokyo: Chuko Shinsho.

von Krogh, G., Ichijo, K., & Nonaka, I. (2000). *Enabling Knowledge Creation: How to Unlock the Mystery of Tacit Knowledge and Release the Power of Innovation.* Oxford: Oxford University Press.

von Krogh, G., Nonaka, I., & Nishiguchi, T. (eds). (2000). *Knowledge Creation: A Source of Value,* New York: Palgrave Macmillan.

Von Krogh, G., Nonaka, I., & Rechsteiner, L. (2010). 'Leadership in organizational knowledge creation: a review and framework'. *Journal of Management Studies, Accepted article.*

von Krogh, G., Nonaka, I., & Rechsteiner, L. (2012). 'Leadership in organizational knowledge creation: a review and framework'. *Journal of Management Studies.* 49 (1), 240–277. doi: 10.1111/j.1467–6486.2010.00978.x

Part I

1

Nonaka's Contribution to the Understanding of Knowledge Creation, Codification and Capture

David J. Teece

Introduction

The work of Ikujiro Nonaka has been very influential, both in theory development and in management practice. His deep insights into the process of new product development have shed light on the roles of leaders and middle managers in the knowledge creation process.

Before the 1980s, academic research on knowledge creation was largely limited to studies of industrial research and development, such as the pioneering work of Edwin Mansfield (1968) and others. Strong economic growth in Asia, particularly Japan, demanded a new view of the innovation process. The Japan challenge made clear that organizational and innovation systems very different from those employed by US multinationals could achieve noteworthy results, particularly in terms of incremental innovation.

At the same time, increased technological activity in the newly industrialized countries in Asia and elsewhere created even greater dispersion in the sources of new knowledge and manufacturing excellence. Large companies needed new ways to access and manage knowledge assets residing in different corners of the globe. Whereas some of the offshore knowledge and capability could be tapped through arm's-length purchases of components, cross-border strategic alliances and offshore R&D were also needed, and their use grew steadily.

In the midst of this global economic transformation, Ikujiro Nonaka provided new frameworks to help managers think about how to share knowledge within the enterprise and develop intellectual capital. His approach was informed by his study of the process of new product development, especially in Japan. Japanese firms, particularly in autos and electronics, had by this time established themselves as formidable competitors in product development and manufacturing.

Nonaka's contributions to the field of strategic management have helped deliver improvements to management practice in Japan, the United States, and Europe. Although practitioners have not always fully appreciated the profundity of his recommendations, his writings provide valuable insights and his intellectual currency continues to advance.

Knowledge creation

Perhaps most fundamentally, Nonaka (1991) critiqued the view of the firm as an information-processing machine. Instead, the firm should be seen as a knowledge creating entity that reshapes the environment and itself by applying its knowledge.

In this knowledge-centric conception of the firm, individuals matter. They interact with each other to transcend their own limits. Subjective tacit knowledge held by individuals is externalized and shared. New knowledge is socially created through the synthesis of different views. The resulting knowledge can still have tacit elements; in fact, tacit/explicit is best understood as a continuum rather than two opposing states (Nonaka & von Krogh, 2009).

Through Nonaka's SECI (socialization, externalization, combination, internalization) process, knowledge keeps expanding. The company's vision for what it wants to become and for the products it wants to produce inspires the passions of employees. This vision of the future must go beyond goals defined by financial metrics alone.

Knowledge creation begins with intuitive metaphors that link contradictory concepts. New knowledge is created by logically working out the contradictions (Nonaka, 1991). In this way, organizations create and define problems that they then solve by generating new knowledge (Nonaka, Toyama, & Nagate, 2000, p. 3). Breakthroughs occur by exploiting and managing what Kuhn (1963) would call 'creative tensions' between the old paradigms and the new.

The SECI process is a routine, but it is a routine with a difference. It is a 'kata' (way of doing things), a set of practices and interactions (Nonaka & Toyama, 2005). Most routines become calcified and, over time, out of line with changing circumstances. A complete break is then required, so that Nonaka's routines tend to morph over time. A company's kata is a creative routine that leads to continuous self-renewal. Each time a pattern is mastered, the process of looking for a better alternative begins.

The SECI process is not mechanical or deterministic. Vision, organizational structure, incentives, and corporate culture are all implicated. Nonaka recognizes that employees, if they don't identify with the organization, will not necessarily help convert their collective store of tacit and explicit knowledge into something of value. Leadership matters. Good leaders can accelerate the SECI process and make it more productive.

Knowledge codification and capture

At the heart of the SECI process is the conversion of personal tacit knowledge to new, collectively constructed concepts. This is different from codification as conventionally understood, that is, the simple documentation of personal knowledge.

In the SECI process, individual knowledge is shared within a team that has taken the time to build trust. Together, the team develops 'new perspectives created from shared tacit knowledge' (Nonaka, 1994, p. 25), which it then 'crystallizes' into some kind of output. At this point, upper management must screen the output (for example, a product concept) for consistency with corporate strategy and other standards of evaluation.

Attempts at implementing SECI have been most likely to go astray in their misconception of the externalization phase, that is, the conversion of knowledge from tacit to explicit. Most early knowledge management efforts limited externalization to the generation of 'discrete declarative knowledge' (ibid., p. 22) that could be stored in databases or on intranets. But this converts it to 'information' rather than 'knowledge' (Nonaka & Konno, 1998, p. 41).

Nonaka's conception of knowledge is less explicit, more deeply rooted in individual experience, and more oriented toward pursuing the firm's differentiated vision than the information to be found in best practice databases and the like. Shards of knowledge cannot be isolated in a database and later recombined into something useful; the knowledge must be made available in the 'shared spaces' in which joint knowledge creation is to take place (ibid., p. 40). These spaces exist within an environment created by managers to foster the goal-directed sharing of knowledge between individuals, within teams and across corporate intranets.

In other words, individual knowledge, to be made useful to the enterprise, cannot be simply captured through documentation requirements. It must be captured by building a collaborative commitment to a shared vision. This is at odds with the claims of many so-called knowledge management software tools.

Management's role in the knowledge creation process is critical. Nonaka advanced the proposition that firms differ because each firm's managers are pursuing distinct visions (Nonaka & Toyama, 2005).

Nonaka's view places an emphasis on the critical entrepreneurial role of managers, which is also at the heart of creating competitive advantage (Augier & Teece, 2009). Good leaders provide a vision and help the organization to synthesize and resolve contradictions that arise in the pursuit of a vision.

Managers and knowledge creation

Nonaka also restored the middle manager to an important role in management theory. In his framework, middle managers provide the vital linkage in knowledge creation inside the organization by bridging the visionary ideals of top management and the chaotic realities of front line workers. Once top managers create a concept of the organization's future, middle managers bear responsibility for solving the tensions between things as they are and the changes required for top management's vision to be realized.

This model, which Nonaka (1988) calls 'middle-up-down management', puts middle managers in the most entrepreneurial role. The task of top management in this model is to challenge and inspire. It is then up to middle managers to lead teams whose members are drawn from different functional perspectives to engage in the give-and-take of knowledge creation, such as product development. The teams that they lead must be given autonomy to achieve their goals within the limitations imposed by time-to-market constraints and other requirements (Nonaka, 1988).

A team breaks into sub-units that concurrently tackle different elements (or, sometimes, alternative approaches to a single element) of the task (Takeuchi & Nonaka, 1986). The managers leading the team must foster an atmosphere that encourages open information sharing and debate. They are also responsible for conveying progress and results to top management.

This model places middle managers in the primary position of converting raw information and technology developed by employees into new product and business concepts that meet the goals enunciated by top management (Nonaka, 1991). Nevertheless, it is the employees working on the middle manager's team who are the 'most important knowledge creating individuals' in this approach (Nonaka, 1994, p. 32).

Nonaka considers this management approach to be particularly vital in times of crisis. While search must be enabled in many directions in order to consider as many options as possible, it is up to managers to 'orient this chaos toward purposeful knowledge creation' (Nonaka, 1991, p. 103). The ability to handle crises creatively rather than destructively must be built into the company's structure and routines (Nonaka, 1994, p. 28). This ability to channel crises into new opportunities is a key dynamic capability of an enterprise (Teece, Pisano, & Shuen, 1990, 1997).

In Nonaka's view, the necessary flexibility is ensured by information 'redundancy' (Nonaka, 1994, p. 29). The more that information about the knowledge of employees is widely available, the more likely that an employee will find a new combination that can address a challenge. This is where database-driven approaches to knowledge management fit into Nonaka's framework, and he provides a clear example when discussing the use of information technology at Seven-Eleven Japan (Nonaka & Toyama, 2007, p. 390). Information overload at the individual level is avoided by limiting the number of employees with whom any single employee interacts (Nonaka, 1994, p. 29).

Although this approach may not be valid in all contexts, it provides an apt description and normative framework for how the enterprise can exploit new opportunities and transform itself in response to challenges. In that sense, it is also a useful elaboration of how a large organization can build and maintain dynamic capabilities.

Nonaka's middle managers are far from the useless drones that we often caricature in the management literature. Moreover, they haven't been made obsolete by information technology and movements to empower front-line employees. Indeed, information technology allows middle managers to command more information and data in executing their role of guiding the active collaboration and healthy conflict of the company's knowledge-creating workers.

Conclusion

Nonaka's conception of the knowledge-creating firm and the SECI process is firmly rooted in his deep knowledge of the experience of Japanese firms. The emphasis is very much on group creativity and consensus-based decision making. This raises the question of whether the SECI process is fully transferable to US and European contexts.

The stagnation of Japan's economy over the past two decades has shifted the world's focus from the value creation ability of Japan's major firms to their relatively poor record of transformation. In this context, it is important to note that Japan's value creation record remains strong. According to the annual list of top US patent assignees compiled by IFI CLAIMS® Patent Services for 2011, Japanese companies held six of the top ten places and 19 of the top 50 (IFI CLAIMS, 2012).

Nevertheless, from a strategic management perspective, it is fair to note that companies do not live by knowledge creation alone. To serve as a basis for competitive advantage, Nonaka's knowledge creation framework must be married to good strategy and strong dynamic capabilities. Knowledge creation without a suitable strategy, timely resource re-allocation, and a viable business model is of little value.

Nonaka implies the presence of good strategy by referring to the vision of top management and the development of new business concepts by middle managers, but the strategic side of his theory is underdeveloped. A vision is not a strategy. Nonaka and Toyama (2007) specifically address strategic management, but their framework of 'phronesis' (which involves, among other things, subjective judgments about what constitutes a 'good' solution in a given context) still largely revolves around the management of 'knowledge' within the organization. The key elements of strategy, such as diagnosis, guiding policy and coherent action (Rumelt, 2011), are not emphasized.

I am in agreement with Nonaka that it is foolish to search for a general theory of management rather than a framework that relies in part on intuition skilfully applied in each context (Nonaka & Toyama, 2007, p. 373). However, that does not eliminate the need for an analytic understanding of strategic variables such as network effects, entry timing, the role of industry architecture, complementarities, coherence, and cospecialization – all of which are important for capturing value from new products (Teece, 1986, 2006).

One attribute of Nonaka's work is that it has a deep philosophical bent, which makes it hard in some cases to operationalize. At the same time, this philosophical patina helps us better appreciate that management is not just about the numbers. Much of what Nonaka has written, based on his own observations about the benefits of healthy conflict within teams, has been substantiated by empirical studies (for example, Dooley & Fryxell, 1999; see Nemeth, 2012, for an overview).

Nonaka's achievements are manifest. His work helps us understand how great companies are able to create great products, and how management matters to this process – not just the top management team, but also middle managers. He has illuminated our understanding of new product development and inspired countless scholars and practitioners to develop new approaches to creating and managing knowledge.

Acknowledgement

I would like to thank Dr Greg Linden for his helpful comments and assistance.

References

Augier, M., & Teece, D. J. (2009). Dynamic capabilities and the role of managers in business strategy and economic performance. *Organization Science*. 20 (2), 410–421.

Dooley, R. S., & Fryxell, G. E. (1999). Attaining decision quality and commitment from dissent: The moderating effects of loyalty and competence in strategic decision-making teams. *Academy of Management Journal*. 42 (4), 389–402.

IFI CLAIMS. (2012). IFI CLAIMS® 2011 Top 50 US patent assignees. Retrieved from http://www.ificlaims.com/index.php?page=misc_Top_50_2011.

Kuhn, T. S. (1963). The essential tension: tradition and innovation in scientific research. In C. W. Taylor, & F. Barron (eds), *Scientific Creativity: Its Recognition and Development* (pp. 341–354). New York: John Wiley & Sons.

Mansfield, E. (1968). *Industrial Research and Technological Innovation*. New York: WW Norton.

Nemeth, C. J. (2012). Minority influence theory. In P. Van Lange, A. Kruglanski, & T. Higgins (eds), *Handbook of Theories of Social Psychology, Volume Two* (pp. 362–378). New York: Sage.

Nonaka, I. (1988). Toward middle-up-down management: accelerating information creation. *Sloan Management Review*. 29 (3), 9–18.

Nonaka, I. (1991). The knowledge-creating company. *Harvard Business Review*. 69 (6), 96–104.

Nonaka, I. (1994). A dynamic theory of organizational knowledge creation. *Organization Science*. 5 (1), 14–37.

Nonaka, I., & Konno, N. (1998). The concept of "*Ba*": building a foundation for knowledge creation. *California Management Review*. 40 (3), 40–54.

Nonaka, I., & Toyama, R. (2005). The theory of the knowledge creating firm: subjectivity, objectivity and synthesis. *Industrial and Corporate Change.* 14 (3), 419–436.

Nonaka, I., & Toyama, R. (2007). Strategic management as distributed practical wisdom (phronesis). *Industrial and Corporate Change.* 16(3), 372–394.

Nonaka, I., Toyama, R., & Nagate, A. (2000). A firm as a knowledge creating entity: A new perspective on the theory of the firm. *Industrial and Corporate Change.* 9 (1), 1–20.

Nonaka, I., & von Krogh, G. (2009). Tacit knowledge and knowledge conversion: Controversy and advancement in organizational knowledge creation theory. *Organization Science.* 20 (3), 635–652.

Rumelt, R. P. (2011). *Good Strategy, Bad Strategy: The Difference and Why It Matters.* New York: Crown Business.

Takeuchi, H., & Nonaka, I. (1986). The new new product development game. *Harvard Business Review.* 64 (1), 137–146.

Teece, D. J. (1986). Profiting from technological innovation. *Research Policy.* 15 (6), 285–305.

Teece, D. J. (2006). Reflections on profiting from technological innovation. *Research Policy.* 35 (8), 1131–1146.

Teece, D. J., Pisano, G., & Shuen, A. (1990). *Firm Capabilities, Resources, and the Concept of Strategy.* Working Paper 90–8. Center for Research in Management. University of California, Berkeley, CCC.

Teece, D. J., Pisano, G., & Shuen, A. (1997). Dynamic capabilities and strategic management. *Strategic Management Journal.* 18 (7), 509–533.

2

Nonaka and KM's Past, Present and Future

J.-C. Spender

Introduction

Our *Festschrift* is dedicated to lauding and explicating Professor Nonaka's thinking, contributions and influence. His impact has been especially notable in the field of knowledge management (KM). Clearly KM began long ago as the ancient activity of developing, codifying, testing, storing, transmitting and applying human knowledge – or, as Nonaka and Takeuchi put it in the Preface to their *The Knowledge-Creating Company* (hereinafter *KCC*), 'it is as old as human history'. In this chapter, I argue that Professor Nonaka's work, along with that of his colleague Hirotaka Takeuchi and others, intersected this ancient project and changed its course irrevocably. Nonaka is still highly active in the field and continues to contribute. His impact is already widely recognized and appreciated. Along with his extensive bibliography, many honorary doctorates, academic awards and associations, the Emperor of Japan awarded him the Order of the Sacred Treasure in 2010 for his contributions to education in Japan, having previously awarded him the Medal of Honor in 2002 for his academic contributions.

In the first and second sections, I do some of the groundwork necessary to assessing Nonaka's contributions, framed as a discussion of KM's past and present. They demand the reader's patience because KM presents researchers and commentators with challenges that are not widely understood but are germane to Nonaka's achievement. KM is not only about managing the knowledge we have already, storing it, moving it around, securing ownership and so on. Nor is it only about creating it – because our knowledge seems to increase, as through the processes of scientific research, as well as decrease as we forget how to do things our forebears did. But KM actually turns on the curious nature of 'knowledge' – a notion that continues to puzzle us today as much as it has throughout history. As a result, the KM field is marked by confusion and sharp divides about what, precisely, is being discussed – especially between those who attempt to address 'knowledge' with science's methods versus those who see this as a flawed endeavour and propose something different. The interchanges between the groups are marked by mutual incomprehension, one of the reasons the KM field is dismissed by some, regarded as a passing fad by others, a new bottle for old wine, but of enormous potential by a somewhat embattled group that includes this author. Professor Nonaka's work has sustained our wavering spirits as we contest louder voices, especially from information technology.

The first step is to explain the fundamental differences between KM's various camps. At bottom this is a philosophical or epistemological matter, so it is no surprise to see Nonaka's own interest in philosophy, for his *oeuvre* is the patient articulation, explication, and exploration of a unique philosophy of the organization as a knowledge-creating apparatus or social institution. His position is grounded in Japanese philosophy, especially that of Kitaro Nishida (1870–1945), the most influential Japanese philosopher of the twentieth century. It rejects many Western presumptions about an organization's nature, especially the view of an organization as an information-processing system. As Nonaka's work goes to the heart of our assumptions about firms, it has major implications for (a) microeconomics, given that a 'theory of the firm' is one of its core projects; and (b) for organization theory, work that inevitably turns on a view of organizations.

In the third section, Nonaka's theory of the organization is sketched against KM's present condition. Knowledge-creation is at core of Nonaka's thinking – what some economists see as the kernel of 'endogenous growth'. Necessarily, and appropriately, a view of knowledge itself is fundamental to KM as an intellectual discipline. Some writers are tempted to approach it from the classical literature – from epistemology, the theory of knowledge. Others subsume it under 'information technology' – whatever IT systems move around. Yet others treat it as a human capability, perhaps labelled human or economic capital, and held at either the organizational or individual level. Nonaka takes a different line. He proposes a dynamic process view encompassing all these levels and bound up with a notion of organizational learning, but always presuming the organization is comprised of value holding individuals who are acting knowledgeably (mindfully). Note his view of organizational learning diverges from Western theories of individual learning that derive from developmental psychology, machine learning or evolutionary biology. The people in his theory are engaged in the value-laden purposive or intentional interactions that bring the organization to life. His theory is profoundly humanist and (a) political, for it deals with collective interaction and group relations; and (b) economic, because its purposes and consequences lie in competitive markets. So it reaches behind neoclassical economics and into political economy, especially in his most recent work.

Given the KM field's interest in learning within organizational contexts Nonaka's thinking runs close by and helps explain its impact. But his is a unique way of thinking about organizations and managing, a paradigm to itself, with impacts in many other areas. So it is far more than the sum of its impacts on KM. At the same time the KM discourse has been complicated by expanding rapidly without being constrained by any clearly agreed problematics, fragmenting from the divergent views KM writers have of 'knowledge' and the possibilities and consequences of managing it. Those that think of knowledge as capital are looking for insights into managing its acquisition and allocation. Those that think of knowledge as information focus on systems design and, in the case of the MIS researchers, managing the impact of IT systems on organizational behaviour and performance. Those that think knowledge production can be shaped by rewards and encouragement are looking for ways to manage the firm's intangible resources and at the nature of social organization. In short, KM is a fragmented and poorly defined discipline comprising many different agendas.

The distinctions selected and made axiomatic to the discourse are key to every analysis. These appear as the basic terms and relationships in the analytic language. Data, bandwidth and storage capacity implies one language; individuals, information, and behaviour imply another. My emphasis is on the languages the KM field has developed and deployed to frame its problematics. I argue Nonaka's project is about developing a language that defines KM in a way that engages fundamental questions that have escaped others' framing. What are organizations? How are they bounded? How do they persist? What is 'knowledge-work'? The traditional KM questions, and KM's main camps, are around (a) the acquisition, deployment or safeguarding of non-financial capital or (b) the efficient movement of information. These questions are important, of course, but subordinated in Nonaka's theory of the firm. So this chapter proceeds by surfacing the language/s that the Nonaka paradigm contests and displaces on the way to establishing his own paradigm. His language stands on distinctive axioms. Microeconomics, for instance, distinguishes supply from demand, valuable assets from worthless assets, scarce goods from public goods, perfect from imperfect markets, rational from irrational behaviour and so on. The microeconomics discourse arises from the interplay of these distinctions. While economics has many powerful visual images and graphs – supply curves crossing demand curves, for instance – the graph's meaning depends on the supporting discourse. Organization theory contrasts with economics because its distinctive axioms, illustrated in diagrams such as organization charts. These distinguish structure from process, superiors from subordinates, the division of labour from its coordination and so on.

In the fourth section of this chapter, the analysis of *The Knowledge-Creating Company* (*KCC*), published in 1995, shows how Nonaka's language reflects distinctions between knowledge-creating and (a) knowledge-processing, IT's specialism; (b) knowledge-possessing, the microeconomic and IC accounting concern at the organizational level; (c) knowledge-possessing and IC accounting at the individual level, the skill-oriented HRM approach; and (d) knowledge for command and control, the OT or administrative theory problematic. Nonaka's language leads towards a novel knowledge-based theory of the firm, so his work suggests new ways forward for (p) microeconomists of entrepreneurship and growth, and (q) organization theorists of innovation and adaptation. Being dynamic at its axiomatic level, Nonaka's work is of great relevance to our present economic, social, educational and political challenges, and whatever policies we adopt to deal with them. In Section 5, I offer a complementary interpretation of *KCC* and relate the SECI model to a tentative 'thermodynamics of knowledge'. Section 6 looks at Nonaka's post-*KCC* extensions and additional language. Section 7 comments on the future of KM.

KM's past

Scientia potentia est (knowledge is power) is the 16th century maxim incorrectly attributed to Francis Bacon, though findable in Thomas Hobbes and others who gave us the Enlightenment and our concept of scientific knowledge. Knowledge management – the creation, storage, distribution and application of human knowledge – goes back to ancient times. By the 8th century, we see it already in full flow with the Abbasid project to collect and translate all the world's knowledge into Arabic. This enabled the 12th century translations from Arabic into Latin that gave European scholars access to the work of the Ancient Greek authors and facilitated Europe's emergence from the Dark Ages. Diderot and d'Alembert's *Encyclopedie* (1751) was similarly conceived to memorialize the body of knowledge on which the Enlightenment's 'Republic of Letters' rested. Knowledge is power because it can be used to shape human practice towards greater effect, not simply telling us what our enemies are up to. KM axiomatizes Adam Smith's 1776 thesis contradicting the primitive idea that the wealth of the nation was the amount of bullion stored in its strong-rooms and that the national debt should be reduced. A hundred years before him, Sir William Petty, following Aristotle, argued the nation's wealth lay in its peoples' abilities, what we now call its human capital (HC), and the future lay in increasing this as rapidly as possible. This idea was recovered by Gary Becker and has had some impact on the field of knowledge management (Burton-Jones & Spender, 2011).

While KM has deep roots and broad scope, its modern story is framed narrowly in terms of the private sector economic and organizational impacts of knowledge (or knowing) and its management. KM thinking is segmented thereby, for economics and organization theory are different disciplines with different axioms and so theories of the private sector firm – and any connections or differences are not well understood. There is no generally accepted theory of the firm in conventional economics, certainly no theory of the firm in which knowledge has a central place. The knowledge-based view (KBV) is an aspiration at best, certainly not an achievement, and it has yet to be articulated or accepted by microeconomists (see this volume). Nor are there any generally accepted theories of organization or its knowledge production, storage or application. We have a handful of mutually inconsistent theories such as bureaucracy, stakeholder theory, cultural or political theory, systems theory and so on (Morgan, 1986). KM is likewise fractured with different camps claiming ownership. Many organizational theorists presume KM springs from the notion that knowledge is a form of organizational capital. But insofar as organization is the rigorous allocation and administration of the organization's resource bundle, managing its knowledge can be adequately handled by the discipline's current notions of administration, right along with the management of its tangible resources and accountable capital. The point being that no new theory of administration is called for, it is simply a matter of reshaping current theory to handle 'knowledge capital', an unusual asset. This group's agenda revolves around the inefficiencies that follow from inadequate attention to or ignorance about the firm's existing 'stock of knowledge' or intangible capital (IC). The KM agenda is then to help managers find the IC 'lying around' and put it to better use, perhaps moving it from where it is not needed to where it is of higher value. Aspects of this agenda can be thought of as creating and managing an internal market (clearing house) for the organization's knowledge assets where none exists. It presumes today's competitive situation demands closer attention to IC and its management, and that more efficient knowledge markets yield additional returns and profits. Note there is no theory about the generation or acquisition of these assets, nor is there a theory relating increased knowledge to improved organizational performance. Lacking a theory of the firm we also lack a theory of inter-firm competition.

Some economists, especially those in the Penrosian tradition, are working on a theory of the firm to which knowledge is axiomatic (Pitelis, 2002). The neoclassical theory of the firm presumes processes that use productive resources, assets or factors of production to meet demand; so productive, demand-related or market knowledge already have a place in the theory. But such knowledge carry no special theoretical implications because neoclassical theory presumes all resources, including knowledge, are commensurate. These are costly in comparable ways, with cost being the only relevant attribute. Hence economists see nothing special about knowledge that would differentiate it from the firm's other assets. It is already covered, right along with other costly resources such as land and labour. Recollect the discussion about entrepreneurship as an additional factor of production beyond land, labour and capital, and whether that too might be tradable. Under equilibrium conditions the value of any type of resource, including knowledge, is also equivalent to its cost, and does not differ from its use-value. There is no long-run concept of or place for economic profit beyond defining it as the return to investors, the cost of the firm's economic capital to be contrasted with wages as the return to its human capital. 'Real profit' is added value; something new that did not exist before the transaction or production process took place. It cannot arise in a neoclassical equilibrium analysis (Knight, 1965). Where 'real' profits occur, they are transient, quasi-monopolistic, and arise from varieties of 'market power', market imperfections, asymmetric information, barriers to entry, patents and so on. While knowledge fits in, it does not do so axiomatically because equally beneficial consequences can be obtained from the asymmetric ownership of any of the firm's resources, especially land, as Ricardo argued. The point being that knowledge can indeed be a source of market power but is not its only source – temptation, gullibility, seizure, and theft work equally well. Asymmetric knowledge is one source of 'market imperfection', asymmetric power is another. The neoclassical theory of 'rents' turns on quasi-monopoly and market power derived from any source, not only from knowledge assets or asymmetries.

Organization theory's agenda is to absorb organizational knowledge and individuals' IC into its existing concepts of organizational resource or asset by supplementing the inventory of established administrative techniques with those appropriate to managing intangible resources, accepting that such different resources might need to be managed differently. Labour cannot be managed in the same way as land; they are different in substance and require the correct metrics if their management is to be rational. Hence the efforts to create IC accounting, for HR managers desire to bring knowledge into their existing administrative methodology. In this direction lie ways to measure the cost of creating intangible resources and estimate their profit contribution, to bring the firm's resource accounting and managing together into a coherent administrative system. In contrast, the agenda of those seeking a knowledge-based theory of the firm turns on differentiating IC from conventional economic resources, and exploring how the differences might lead to a theory of imperfect markets, value appropriation, and thus to sustainable economic rents (Rumelt, Schendel, & Teece, 1991).

Economic theory is primarily about markets not firms; the firm is a 'black box'. So the emphasis is on the market failures precipitated by difficulties with trading resources, with knowledge especially problematic in this respect. The problems of trading land, which is fixed in space but persists across time, differ from those of trading labour, which is fixed in time but movable in space, and from those of trading financial capital, the ultimate liquid resource, movable across time and space and transformable into every other type of resource anytime, anywhere. Given this space-time-value matrix of resource management issues, some fit knowledge in by presuming it can be objectified and so rendered tradable across both space and time without loss of value. But this makes nothing of how knowledge is not valuable if it is entirely liquid and of the same value to everyone (like money) or that it does not behave as an object with sustained value (like land). Others see knowledge as an objectified potentiality or capability (like the energy stored in a battery or the worker waiting to start work), persisting across time but, like labour and energy, valueless until activated, only realized when embraced through practice or process. However resources are brought into the analysis, the Ricardian position is that rents arise from the possession and application of scarce, valuable, objectifiable, own-able and manageable resources. But objects and knowledge differ in many significant ways. Most importantly, knowledge is 'non-rivalrous' and can be in two places at once – when I tell you something you gain knowledge but I have no less of it. In contrast, whatever their form and nature, rent-earning resources must be explicit, manageable and rivalrous – when I give you an apple I no longer have it. The scarcity requirement supports the impression that IC-based rents have become especially important because of the explosion of scientific and technological knowledge that erodes such scarcity and makes the asset more liquid. Likewise, the increasing efficiency of global markets, regulation and transferability of knowledge and financial capital has lessened the profit potential of monopolies, such as those that constituted the core of the nineteenth century 'robber-baron' Trusts or the core of Coca-Cola's business model. These ideas come together in the view that unshared and ownable technologies now offer the best 'windows of opportunity' to pursue quasi-monopoly rents, a view that animates much of the KM discourse about managing intellectual assets (Teece, 2000).

In spite of offering no theory of knowledge generation or acquisition, nor showing much anxiety about its absence, both the economic and the administrative KM agendas show interest in innovation, especially technological. Those familiar with Penrose's 'theory of the growth of the firm' might see this as symptomatic of KM's parlous condition because a technology is more of a potential than a resource and even then more of a resource than a service, which is what generates economic value. Nonetheless many think of innovation as the profit-yielding production of resource-like objects rather than the production of new practices or services. For organization theorists innovation produces additional resources to be administered and managed as they 'bulk-up' the firm's bundle, and maybe these additions imply new modes of administration. The new resources' impact can be immediate, altering production efficiency and the division of labour and thus demanding new organizational structures. For economists, innovation offers new ways of creating and responding to competition by deliberately 'imperfecting' markets, opening up new sources of market power and rents. In this case, there is little interest in innovations whose rent-stream cannot be 'appropriated' or secured. Both agendas lack crucial connecting links at their core. At the same time organization theorists have proliferated the subcategories of capital that might need to be administered such as structural, relational, organizational, social and so on. But without any overarching theory of organizational capital that explicates these sub-categories' nature, differences or relationships to the organization or its economic activity, there is little clarity about how these new capitals' administrative procedures might differ from those inherited from classical organization theory.

Likewise, in the expanding discourse around innovation there is no generally accepted theory about how it should be generated or managed (see this volume). While economists have long argued for an 'information economy', there is no clear 'economics of information' that might illuminate the differences presumed between knowledge and other forms of economic resource, a distinction that could spring KM free of microeconomics.

KM's present

The past of KM is still pretty much with us in that the previous issues have not been much clarified over the last two centuries, especially when we add in the unresolved debate over whether social sciences such as economics and administrative theory (and their forms of knowing) are the same as or different from natural science and its way of knowing. Despite these lingering questions, KM has achieved a certain academic identity, even notoriety; there are KM professors (including our own Dr Know, *sensei*), researchers, courses, texts, journals and conferences – all the paraphernalia of an academic discipline. There is a huge parallel industry of KM consultants, publications and conferences, servicing a goodly number of KM executives, departments, projects and budgets. Wiig points to KM's long historical roots (Wiig, 2000). As Prusak tells the story, KM's rise was due to (a) the rapid improvement in computers' cost-effectiveness and range of application, (b) increasing academic interest in the economic value of knowledge, and (c) managerial interest in the value and complex nature of practical skills, all in the context of globalization, increasing professionalism and the rapid diffusion of all kinds of knowledge (Prusak, 2001). Prusak led IBM's KM initiative. In contrast, Teece, an academic economist, argues KM was precipitated by increased academic interest in knowledge's impact on innovation and competitiveness, globalization of knowledge's originators and users and IT developments (Teece, 2008). Clearly, computer improvements are (a) the leading explanation for KM's growth and the vast bulk of KM's commercial and academic activity is still related to IT and systems theorizing. But this speaks to only one of the KM camps. It may be an unfair assessment but the IT camp seems to have made little use of KM's theorizing beyond co-opting its terminology to relabel their existing products and services and goose-up their already vigorous markets. This is an over-simplification, of course, given that new computing techniques are transforming the strategic, economic and political significance of information, data collection and surveillance (to say nothing of warfare).

But insofar as the KM literature engages non-IT issues, the insights that touch the previously described (b) and (c) agendas turn most often on the distinction between intangible and tangible resources. It leads to literatures that embrace innovation, learning, accounting and communication. But note none of these topics are exclusive to KM. The research into innovation, organizational learning, accounting and organizational communication is often done in other disciplines, and also typically without any discussion of or reference to any specific concept of knowledge. The key point being that we can research these topics without addressing the puzzling nature of knowledge. In contrast, KM must come to grips with this. Its demarcating characteristic must be that it treats knowledge as both axiomatic and problematic, even as many other disciplines take it for granted and focus only on its absence. Scientific research deals with its chosen knowledge-absences by seeking knowledge that is presumed findable and logical – reality exists and is logical,- so unproblematic in principle. IT deals with knowledge as stuff in the wrong place; unproblematic to the extent it is presumed moveable without loss or corruption. In contrast, KM's intellectual identity hinges on a concept of knowledge that is problematic in some fundamental manner, not simply a yet-to-be-discovered logical representation of reality or one misplaced.

Most of the academic KM discourse is dominated by positivist epistemology, the natural science concept of knowledge as 'true, justified belief' (JTB), wherein justification is bound up with the scientific method. One positivist axiom is that JTB is a tentative representation of the reality that lies beyond our minds. All other notions of knowledge are subordinated to this one. Revealingly, the 'received view' of the scientific method addresses knowledge's absence without making much of what is already known; for instance Popperian falsification puts hypothesis formation in the dark, beyond consideration. Yet the possibilities of coming up a new idea clearly revolve around what you know already. Those in the Popperian tradition admit 'temporary' or 'tentative' knowledge that is useful and survives until it is falsified and displaced by better-justified knowledge but are less interested in where the knowledge comes from in the first place. It follows that if there is only one form of knowledge or mode of knowing, as positivists argue, there can be no distinction between KM and science generally. At best, KM identifies a sub-group of scientists who engage a particular topic or type of science, inviting the accusation that KM is an insubstantial label or terminological fad that ignores the accepted language of science without offering a replacement that is more informing; indeed, it may be more confusing for people clearly attach their own meanings to 'knowledge'. In complementary manner the systems theorists' problematics tend to be about knowledge's mislocation, what they promise to correct without any consideration of (a) the nature of what is to be moved; (b) how one might identify the need for something one does not know or (c) the value issues around moving it. Systems theorists also share the positivist idea of a single form of knowledge – what is computable. All in all, adopting a positivist epistemology means the KM field has no distinctive or fundamental intellectual identity. One can test this empirically by taking a KM text, doing a 'find and replace' of 'knowledge' by 'information', and seeing if any insights are lost.

Positivism is not our only epistemology, nor is it that ancient. Its origins lie in eighteenth century 'modernism' as the evolving techniques of the natural sciences began to be drawn into theorizing social, economic and organizational life. Natural science probes for the truths of the natural universe, those that lie beyond us, our condition and our thinking. Social scientists who adopt positivism presume there are similar truths to be discovered about the social, economic and organizational universe(s). There many interpretations of positivism, but the concept of the logically constructed, knowable and rational reality that lies beyond our minds remains central. In contrast, most ancient epistemologies regard 'knowledge' as an extremely problematic concept, perhaps the most puzzling concept we are capable of conceiving – itself a corollary of our awareness or consciousness (perhaps the only viable definition of knowledge is 'consciousness', making for a tautology). Many ancients presumed that it may not be given to Man to have certain knowledge of reality, that the human condition is one of inescapable ignorance, perhaps transcended in death. Philosophers allude to this by contrasting the human condition with the 'God's Eye view', how everything would look from the Archimedean fulcrum from where we would 'know' all things 'as they really are', as well as how everything is connected to everything else. The ancients presumed Man could not enter into God's mind to know such truths. Positivism claims to colonize God's Eye. Man and his knowing then lie at the centre of everything knowable, proposing that what is knowable is objective, object-like, and lies beyond us, but also asserting Man can approach knowing it step by step, by applying the objectifying and rigorous methods of science. In contrast, many earlier epistemologies were more humble and defined knowledge as about Man and his modes of knowing rather than about 'things as they are' or the 'essential truths' they manifest. In such epistemologies, many see the possibility of knowledge as inherently subjective and reflexive, more to do with us and how our minds and languages work rather than with what might be known. This 'humanism' turns discussion of the way we think into an enquiry into who we are, addressing the originating philosophical question, What is Man? This presumes we are more like Rodin's *Penseur*, lost in thought about our condition, than like Newton or Galileo contemplating the eternal non-human truths with their mathematical and experimental tools – as illustrated in William Blake's "The Ancient of Days" (1794). The positivist approach to organizations and markets so evident in our A-journals presumes that they are discoverable truth-objects, or more specifically, objects that manifest eternal truths in the same way that a nebula manifests the eternal laws of astrophysics.

Problematizing knowledge is the radical originating step for any form of KM that steps away from the positivist tradition to seek its own intellectual identity. In this respect, Nonaka's work cannot be comprehended without appreciating how he stepped away from the US tradition of administrative and economic theorizing, and into a more subjective epistemology. This was in part a result of his interest in Japanese philosophy, a critical response to his studies at UC Berkeley and because of his own early business experience and his intuitions about the dynamic nature of organizational work. Again, any type of KM that denies this objective/subjective distinction remains a captive of positivist science – not 'real' KM. So researchers in this camp think the other camps trash the full potential of KM. 'Real' KM begins by adopting an us-centered notion of knowledge that starts out from the way we humans 'really know' – subjectively rather than objectively. If we ignore the ancients' thinking and focus on contemporary thought, we can say the non-positivist notion of KM is articulated in Kant's observations that time and space are *a-priori* intuitions, and that we look out at the world we experience through these *a-priori* structures and capabilities of the human mind. Kant distinguished analytic from synthetic propositions, so identifying two differing modes of human knowing rather than the single representational mode of knowing positivists presume and privilege. Knowledge management is then the human activity of confronting (a) the irremediable lack of total knowledge or certainty about reality (the impossibility of achieving the God's Eye view) and (b) the struggle to make as much as we can of how we know 'faultily'. The implication is that the notion of knowledge must be approached obliquely, abandoning the idea that it can ever be 'total', 'certain' or a true representation of reality beyond us. Instead, it suggests all human knowing hinges on how we deal with our experience and resulting sense of knowledge absence – seeing all human knowing as contingent on our experience of pursuing an intention and discovering how reality allows or disallows that – which, under these circumstances, is the only way we ever know reality. To exist knowingly (or mindfully, as Weick puts it), is not so much *cogito ergo sum* as 'agentic', to have chosen 'my intention' or 'my project in the lived world' that determines from where we look at it.

The subtler point is that subjective human knowing is something unlike the positivist notion of partial certainty and is more to do with how the human mind deals with what must lie forever beyond it in space and time. To know in this manner is to construe part of what can be known as a practice that turns on deliberately ignoring something else, a method is familiar to us from the ancient story of the blind men and the elephant. Descartes knew this story as he pondered the nature of our knowing and gave us the concept of knowledge as representation of the real. Another metaphor is that to know is to abridge or distort reality's un-know-ability so as to render it knowable; implying the concept of knowledge hinges on our not-knowing something that could be known, on our knowing ignorance. If we knew any one thing 'for certain', our concept of knowledge would cascade off that touchstone and evaporate because without ignorance there can be no knowledge. Our knowledge is only realized and secured by our not-knowing. Or, put differently, to know is to hold some aspects constant even though unknown – assumed – while allowing others to vary and be researched, a methodological trick.

What follows is that by necessity and definition all human knowing embraces multiple knowledge types and so indicates a typology; this is my chapter's most fundamental point and the purpose of my initial sections – for without it we cannot grasp the nature of Nonaka's achievement. Each type of knowledge addresses some of what can be known or some way of human knowing, by presuming its absence. With a suitable knowledge-typology in hand the deeper aspects of our knowing and not-knowing can be captured in the interactions between the knowledge types chosen. This 'trick' or 'knowing practice' is thoroughly familiar to us from the interplay of hypothesis and evidence. These are two different ways of knowing the phenomena of interest, our experience of the experimental event. To think these are the same way of knowing and that the evidence gathered is able to falsify a hypothesis about the nature of the event, as a matter of logic, is to misunderstand the contingent nature of experiment, of observation, and of what we might ever learn about an event. Popper's idea of falsification is actually a philosophical error, embedded in the positivist method, but one he should have known about before he advanced his thesis. A philosophical statement of this point is implicit in the Duhem-Quine thesis (see Wikipedia on this). It explains how it is impossible to separate the hypothesis being tested from the complex of background assumptions, any of which could equally well 'explain' the event. Popper's pallid attempts to justify falsification after being obliged to recognize the Duhem-Quine thesis are interesting.

The knowledge-type (KT) methodology stands in contrast to the positivist methodology of truth (PT), directly approaching reality with a single notion of knowledge. KT offers a study of experiencing the interplay of whatever modes of knowing we are able to achieve as an alternative to the failure of PT and to our thinking whatever we know is falsifiable. The KT approach has aesthetic dimensions that allow us to see all human knowledge as a human artifact, and imperfect on that account. It opens up knowing as an interaction of knowledge types and defines KM as the practice of directing and benefiting from the management of the multi-mode human way of knowing. As soon as we step away from PT and engage the more tractable KT universe, we have several completely different concepts of KM available. Each knowledge typology implies a different kind of KM. So we can actually fold PT into this approach by seeing it as a curiously weak single type of knowledge, namely scientific. Today's KM adopts many other knowledge typologies, among which Polanyi's explicit/tacit dichotomy obviously looms large. There is also the DIKW typology variously credited to Mortimer Adler, Frank Zappa or Milan Zeleny, and popularized by Russ Ackoff. Other KTs include 'individual' versus 'team' knowledge, William James's 'knowledge of' and 'knowledge about', Gilbert Ryle's 'know how, know what', Håkanson's 'theory, codes and tools', or even Spender's 'scientific, conscious, communal, automatic' (Spender, 1996). It is worth noting the KT strategy was fundamental to most Greek epistemologies with their distinctions between *episteme, metis, phronesis, sophia, techne* and so on. This brings us to Nonaka's work, of course.

Before getting into his work, however, it is worth noting Fritz Machlup's knowledge typology. He drew on typologies advanced earlier by Anthony Downs – information for edification, information for decision-making – and by Max Scheler – instrumental knowledge, intellectual knowledge, spiritual knowledge. Machlup also distinguished basic and applied science, enduring and transitory knowledge, and general-systematic knowledge from that which is particular-concrete. He began his analysis of the economic consequences of the application of knowledge with a complex fivefold typology: practical, intellectual, pastime, spiritual and unwanted (Machlup, 1962, p. 22). Along similar KT lines, Freud distinguished the personal unconscious and Jung the collective unconscious. The general point is that all human knowing stands on knowledge typologies, on the interaction between the types framed in the typology rather than on the quasi-photographic representations of the real that positivism suggests as it contrasts our knowing against the real – even though that is unknowable. Given that we have not even one single representation of the real that we can be certain about, the representations we are comfortable with are exploitations of a knowledge typology that is implicit in our distinctions between truth and falsehood (implicit in JTB). The nature of the knowledge claimed lies less in the definitions of the knowledge type, such as truth or falsehood, than in their interplay, and this is always contingent on the practical use to which the resulting knowing is to be placed. We gain enormously from Polanyi's distinction between explicit and tacit without asking for, or getting, positivist-style definitions of either. It is not even necessary to settle the debate between those that think of tacit as categorically distinct, versus those that see it as explicit-in-waiting (Håkanson, 2007). It follows that attempts to 'define' knowledge are deeply illogical. Indeed, if we had such a definition would it be a part of knowledge, as defined, or some 'meta-knowledge' that stands outside what we call knowledge? Would the definition be more real than the reality being represented?

Epistemology's history provides a rich variety of knowledge typologies, and wherever we look we can find more. It is easy to presume, given our positivist tendencies, that one typology might be 'closer to reality' than some other. This again misses the essence of the Greeks' insight and their strategy for engaging the questions of how we humans know and what might count as our knowledge. A knowledge typology is an epistemological toolkit for examining the relationship between our thinking and our lived projects; it cannot ever illuminate the gap between our knowledge and a real that is unknowable. Thus knowledge's practical value lies in how it illuminates our life-world of intentions, projects and practice, and opens up action options otherwise hidden. For instance, the conscious-unconscious distinction opens up a psychological discourse that differs from a healthy/sick distinction on which some medical practice might be based. The ice / water distinction informs our discourse about global warming, just as the unfreezing-refreezing distinction gives us a Lewinian model of learning.

We can assess the present state of 'real' KM by examining the degree to which the knowledge typologies chosen have facilitated KM theorizing and practice as it relates to the projects we have in hand. Polanyi's explicit-tacit distinction has proved remarkably useful to many scholars. Economists have cited it to leverage the distinction between tangible and intangible assets. For example, Teece (2000) starts from Polanyi's distinction, moves on to distinguish observable and not-observable knowledge, positive and negative knowledge, autonomous and systemic knowledge, tight versus loose appropriation regimes and so on. Along similar lines, capabilities are distinguished from priced and tradable assets, and dynamic capabilities from static knowledge assets. Once Teece has adopted his chosen KT to generate an analytic language, his focus shifts to using that language to discuss the arrangements, institutional and otherwise, that might enable firms to control these differing forms of knowledge, most particularly those of the non-tradable type. They are often non-tradable because they lack clear title and hence are sometimes leaky – transferred without full exchange – or sometimes sticky – an exchange not followed by full transfer. Especially when assets are non-rivalrous (able to be in two or more places at once) they escape both the economists' theoretical scarcity requirements and the laws of property and clear title.

The point here is that Polanyi's knowledge typology opens up its own particular KM discourse around modes of human knowing that are ignored in the positivist discourse. As the analyst steps away from positivism's assumptions an immense variety of possible KTs open up. There is no 'one best way'. It is a matter of choosing a knowledge typology well adapted to one's intention – drawing attention to the practice-based contingency between the actor's project and her/his knowing. The DIKW typology opens up an equally specific discourse, unrelated to the economist's but pertinent to the organizational theorist's, especially handy for IT and MIS professionals interested in the organization's data plumbing and the problems created when data is mistaken for information. Different KTs illuminate the differing problems managers have when (a) an organization's economically valuable assets are not restricted to those that can be clearly owned and disposed; or (b) an organization's communications are not restricted to the unambiguous instructions presupposed in bureaucratic theory. Economists are especially interested in the flow of poorly titled assets between competing firms, whereas organization theorists are interested in the non-explicit human capital necessary to translate plans and instructions into added value in an uncertain world.

Nonaka's contributions

Over the last few decades, in spite of KM's messy condition, it has cast a certain amount of light onto these issues and had a significant impact on managers, economists and administrative theorists. Again, part of KM's impact comes from the staggering advances in computing cost-effectiveness and in the economy-transforming ability of modern organizations to gather and compute vast amounts of data. Huge amounts of money are being spent on cloud computing, data-mining, data-reduction, real-time modelling, high speed trading, surveillance and so on; clearly the lights shine bright in at least one of the KM camps. Somewhat darker are those parts of the field where we look for a KM-based or knowledge-based theory of the firm or theory of managing. Not all recognize this part of the field proposes an escape from or a critique of the positivist approach, rejecting its single knowledge-type epistemology. In its place would be theorizing a multiple KT context with the process of knowledge-creation or organizational learning as a managed KT interplay.

Much of whatever light there is here derives from the work of Nonaka and his colleagues. It is appropriate to note they were not the first to define the firm as an epistemological knowledge creating or 'learning' entity. This chapter is not the place to delve into the history of economics, but Penrose's *Theory of the Growth of the Firm* certainly defined the firm along these lines (Penrose, 1959). Penrose's book was derived from her PhD, supervised by Machlup. The research project was initially joint but Machlup dropped out because he had too much else to attend to, being active in the field of international financial policy as well as popularizing the concept of the 'information society'. Hayek had earlier published an influential paper on the use of knowledge in society from the economist's point of view (Hayek, 1945). Nonaka and Takeuchi also note Marshall's interest in an economics of knowledge (Nonaka & Takeuchi, 1995, p. 33). Nor were Nonaka and his colleagues the first to look at the problems of administering the generation, flow and application of knowledge within the firm. That project goes back at least to Adam Smith and two centuries of pre-positivist administrative theorizing. But there is a good case to be made that Nonaka and his colleagues were in the forefront of (a) combining the modern economists' interest in knowledge's value with the organization theorists' interest in its creation and flow; and (b) bringing that discourse to the attention of the corporate community via articles in the *Sloan Management Review*, the *Harvard Business Review*, and most spectacularly, the successful and influential *The Knowledge-Creating Company*. Note that many of these ideas had already been widely published and circulated in Japan.

Nonaka's interest in bringing these threads together sprang from his WWII and post-war work background (Helgesen, 2008). As a young Waseda University-trained political scientist working for Fuji Electric, he became involved in creating a management-training scheme. In collaboration with Keio University, the program spread to many Japanese companies at a time when they were expanding rapidly, establishing the basis of the Japanese industrial miracle, and beginning its export led growth into the world's second economy. Nonaka enrolled at UC Berkeley, worked as a gardener while his wife waited tables, gained an MBA in 1967 followed by a PhD awarded in 1972. His thesis was published in Japanese in 1974. His Berkeley studies familiarized him with US notions of organization theory, sociology, and economics – and with the US academic journals and their approach to research. His PhD thesis was on centralization versus decentralization, a hot topic at the time given Chandler's work and McKinsey's successes with divisionalization (Nonaka, 1972). He took a contingency view, with structure being driven by environmental circumstance, somewhat in the Burns and Stalker or Lawrence and Lorsch tradition. Dr Nonaka returned to Japan to Nanzan University and later the National Defence Academy. Starting in 1976, he took part in a large-scale empirical study of Japanese companies and their management practices. This expanded into an international study when Tadao Kagono, the study team's leader, visited Harvard for a year in 1979. The team then mailed the questionnaire developed for the 1031 Japanese companies in their sample to all of the Fortune 1000 companies, receiving an astonishing response rate around 25 per cent in both countries. They followed up with in-depth interviews. As the quantitative analysis and theorizing proceeded, it drew the team's attention to deeper differences beyond structure and strategy, towards what some called differences in organizational culture between the Japanese and US companies. The team published their findings in Japanese in 1984 and in English in 1985 (Kagono, Nonaka, Sakakibara, & Omura, 1985). The challenge that loomed largest was to explain how Japanese companies held together, given the absence of the command and control administrative technologies so evident in US companies.

In addition, the Japanese economic miracle was already high on organizational researchers' list of topics. Kenichi Ohmae, then head of McKinsey's Tokyo office, published *The Mind of the Strategist* in Japanese in 1975 and English in 1982. Both Ouchi's *Theory Z* and Pascale and Athos's *Art of Japanese Management* appeared in English in 1981, with Ouchi and Pascale on the faculty at Stanford whereas Nonaka was at Berkeley. A common thread was the view that American management techniques were overly analytical ('hard'). Ohmae and Pascale and Athos related the Japanese firms' success to their 'softer' management techniques. Peters and Waterman, two McKinsey consultants collaborated with Pascale, set up a wide-ranging empirical program, interviewing managers in 62 'excellently performing' companies around the world. Their conclusions were published in 1982 as *In Search of Excellence*, still the best-selling management book of all time. It articulated a broad eight knowledge-type approach that proved immensely popular with managers. But these books were largely anecdotal and none proposed a testable theory of the organization or, as necessarily entailed, theory of managing it. Ouchi, a Hawaiian working at Stanford, took a more academic Durkheimian view that stressed 'group culture', implying the Japanese firms' advantage was 'in the miso soup'. Nonaka and his colleagues found Ouchi's work profoundly flawed, lacking in theory, empirical content, validity and humanism. They began to search for a theory of the organization that could be stood up against the classical organization theorizing of Weber, Fayol, Taylor and Parsons, and publishable in the US journals.

One of Nonaka's Berkeley mentors was Francesco Nicosia. In a joint paper, Nonaka drew on his PhD (Nonaka, 1972) and explored an information-based theory of the organization, taking special note of Ashby's notions of requisite variety (Nonaka & Nicosia, 1979). The paper turns on the distinction between environmental homogeneity and environmental uncertainty. From the intellectual archaeology point of view, the matrix offered is interesting as a forerunner to the later SECI matrix (Figure 2.1).

The 1979 paper's distinctions are organization-environment, centralization-decentralization, homogeneity-heterogeneity and certainty-uncertainty. The language generated was essentially static. Nonaka's next major English language paper was co-authored with Johny Johansson, one of the team who had worked on the Kagono-led survey mentioned earlier. It was a direct rebuttal of Ouchi's work, helped along by Sullivan's earlier critique (Sullivan, 1983). Nonaka and Johansson proposed an information-based approach to superior performance, facilitated by Japanese managers' superior 'soft skills' (Nonaka & Johansson, 1985). These ensured more information of higher quality was shared in Japanese firms and that far from presuming Japanese managers were less able than their Western peers, offered evidence to the contrary. Nonaka, still far from satisfied, realized the language he was creating was not yet capable of grasping his intuitions about the dynamic nature of organizations and organizational work.

In 1982, Ken-Ichi Imai, later Dean, recruited Nonaka to Hitotsubashi University. He also recruited Nonaka's Berkeley friend and fellow student Hirotaka Takeuchi in 1983. The three co-authored a chapter in *An Uneasy*

		Environment	
		Homogeneous	**Heterogeneous**
Environment	**Certain**	Centralization (1)	? (2)
	Uncertain	? (3)	Decentralization (4)

Figure 2.1 Forerunner to the later SECI matrix

Source: Nonaka and Nicosia (1979).

Alliance, edited by Clark, Hayes and Lorenz in 1985, that dealt with how Japanese firms 'learn and unlearn'. Co-authoring again with Takeuchi, Nonaka published *The New New Product Development Game* in HBR 1986, remembered for its introduction of the 'rugby scrum' approach to new product development – the multi-channel parallel approach that denied the serial model then the norm (Takeuchi & Nonaka, 1986). Again, these papers failed to provide a theory of the dynamic information-based organization. But change was coming. In 1985, came – in Japanese – *Corporate Evolution: Managing Organizational Information Creation*, based on an earlier Hitotsubashi working paper titled *Towards a Self-Organization Paradigm: Managing the Creation of Information*. A year later in 1986, a jointly authored book in Japanese titled *Managing Self-Renewal of the Firm* was published. In 1987, Nonaka completed another Hitotsubashi working paper *Managing the Firm as an Information Creation Process*. At the same time, Nonaka was collaborating again with Sullivan on a 1986 paper that made a new attack on Ouchi's work (Sullivan & Nonaka, 1986). This showed Nonaka drawning again on the American literature, especially that on organizational learning (Nonaka & Sato, 1981). Stepping further forward he proposed completely new language that reflected back to his earlier appreciation of Ashby's work – the idea that managing the firm as an information absorbing and managing apparatus meant alternately amplifying and reducing its variety in the dynamic manner suggested in Klapp's 1975 classic but uncited paper, (Klapp, 1975). By now, Herb Simon had become the whipping boy or information processing 'straw man' that Nonaka's information creating was contesting, suggesting a Nonaka-Simon dichotomy. But this is a curious reading of Simon's complex *oeuvre*, for the problematic that drove his career-long project – 'How do human beings make decisions when the prerequisites for rational decision-making are absent?' – lay closer to Nonaka's than he seemed prepared to admit, as Simon's paper in Kato and Iino (1986) confirms (Simon, 1986; Spender, 2013).

At this point, Nonaka's search was clear, impelled by an sustained critique of his own work's failure to capture the dynamics of organizational knowledge-creation as he wished. This kind of casting-around groundwork is seldom discussed in the social sciences, though is typical in the arts, famously evident, for example, in the transitional periods of artists like Arshile Gorky or Jackson Pollock as each evolved entirely new visual language. Unmistakable signs of Nonaka's impending breakthrough, like Pollock's first 'drip paintings' of 1947, appeared in two sole-authored 1988 papers. One, a California Management Review paper *Creating Organizational Order Out of Chaos: Self-Renewal in Japanese Firms* brought some of Nonaka's mid-1980s Japanese writing into the American literature (Nonaka, 1988a). The paper draws again on the Ashby-based variety-amplification and variety-reduction (or fluctuation) distinction. The other was the *Sloan Management Review* paper *Towards Middle-Up-Down Management: Accelerating Information Creation* (Nonaka, 1988b). This turns on two new distinctions (actually trichotomies) one structural or 'ontological' – organization, group, and individual – the other 'epistemological' – deductive, inductive, compressive. The SMR paper posits a new role for middle management; not simply the interlinking communication role written into the US literature, rather a newly identified central middle-up-down coordinating and language management role. This paper's two diagrams (Figures 2 and 3) were clearly parents to the SECI model. Most importantly, in these two papers Polanyi's explicit/tacit distinction appeared in Nonaka's work, perhaps for the first time, though it is mentioned in passing rather than made central to his analysis.

But Nonaka's language was still insufficient for grasping the creation of organizational knowledge, his target. Nonaka and Yamanouchi (1989) reworked the self-renewal argument as an analysis of the development of Canon's Mini Copier, illustrating empirically the gap between information-processing and information-creating and the task of 'fluctuation management' (Nonaka & Yamanouchi, 1989). It was reminiscent of Ashby and the Lewinian 'un-freezing, re-freezing' model. A 1990 CMR paper *Redundant, Overlapping Organization: A Japanese Approach to Managing the Innovation Process* pushed further forward, with Polanyi's distinction bearing more of the weight (Nonaka, 1990a). Nonaka introduced yet another new distinction between sufficient and redundant information, meaning that dynamism requires that the different organizational (ontological) levels must all have information beyond that which is strictly necessary for them to perform their appointed tasks and on which they can draw when anomalies arise and thus generate 'new knowledge'. There is an echo of Selznick's definition of institutionalization as 'the infusion of meaning beyond that technically necessary to the practice' (Selznick, 1957). The sense of the work group's compression was carried in from the 1988 SMR paper as the precondition for the transfer of tacit knowledge between the group's members. Nonaka wrote: 'Meaningful information arises as a result of the conversion of tacit knowledge into articulable knowledge. Redundancy of information facilitates this process' (Nonaka, 1990b, p. 33). A series of 1991 papers, such as *Managing the Firm as an Information Creation Process*, re-explored the territory (Nonaka, 1991b).

Finally, in the 1991 *Knowledge-Creating Company* HBR paper, the language came together in a way that enabled Nonaka to grasp the problematic he had chosen – the organization as a managed dynamic knowledge-creating apparatus (Nonaka, 1991a). While there were no diagrams, neither a SECI matrix nor a knowledge-creation spiral, both were spelled out. Nonaka's new language was also significantly reshaped by a period in Stockholm working with Gunnar Hedlund (Hedlund & Nonaka, 1991, 1993). Polanyi's explicit-tacit distinction became the 'epistemological' axiom, along with the 1988 SMR paper's 'ontological' axiom of organizational levels, with the mid-level being pivotally self-organizing and self-renewing. Nonaka identified two background distinctions (a) organic-mechanical – recalling Burns and

Stalker's distinction – and (b) committed-uncommitted, defined in terms of the employees' sense of identity with the enterprise and its mission. He set the knowledge-creating spiral spinning by asserting 'new knowledge always begins with the individual' (Nonaka, 1991, p. 97). The point of managing the knowledge-creation process is to transform the individual knowledge created (predominantly tacit) into organizational knowledge (predominantly explicit) in ways that make it available to inform the firm's value-adding practice (tacit again).

The analysis was thoroughly re-worked – and the SECI matrix and a version of the knowledge-spiral presented – in the 1994 Organization Science paper *A Dynamic Theory of Organizational Knowledge Creation* (Nonaka, 1994). Founding Editor Arie Lewin commended the paper to his readers saying he felt it had 'the potential to stimulate the next wave of research on organization learning'. The two fundamental distinctions – epistemological and ontological – were foundational, with personal commitment as the spiral's driver and organizational performance as its intention or goal. In the background hovered Nonaka's earlier thoughts about the quality of the knowledge being generated and circulated, and the nature of the inter-ontological interactions that comprise the knowledge loops or flows, implying the managerial task differed at each ontological level, the middle level being crucial to the knowledge process. A co-authored 1992 Japanese paper *Hypertext Organization for Accelerating Knowledge Creation* was cited to show how the multi-tiered approach worked, that the organization's language was layered. By now Nonaka was also drawing on Anderson's ACT model, autopoietic theory, and radical constructivism to support his notions of learning, self-organization, and self-renewal. A 1994 paper co-authored with Philippe Byosiere, Chester Borucki and Noboru Konno explored the empirical validity of the SECI categories and processes proposed in the Organization Science paper, finding good confirmation (Nonaka, Byosiere, Borucki, & Konno, 1994).

The Knowledge Creating Company (KCC)

The groundwork for *KCC* was complete. Eleanor Westney, who had published a 1987 book on the transfer of innovations to Meiji Japan, had been following Nonaka's writings, considered the 1994 HBR article promising and mentioned it to Herbert J. Addison, a Senior Commissioning Editor with Oxford University Press (OUP)[1]. With the two *KCC* authors at Hitotsubashi, Addison alerted OUP's Tokyo office and a contract was soon arranged. The rest, as they say, is history. *KCC* was published to critical acclaim from both academics and business people, many awards, and quickly climbed to the top of OUP's bestseller list. As I write, Google Scholar reports *KCC* with 30,600 hits – comparing favourably with Porter's *Competitive Strategy* at 28,000 hits, Williamson's *Markets and Hierarchies* at 25,000, or Simon's *Administrative Behavior* at 16,600.

This is not the place for a thorough analysis or critique of *KCC*, a rich and complex masterwork. But it is worth looking briefly at its impact, which was large among organization theorists, KM authors, and managers interested in innovation and related strategic issues. It was less in economics in spite of the book's potential as a theory of 'endogenous growth'. Indeed, there is not a single mention of Nonaka's work in Aghion and Howitt's compendium of endogenous growth theory (Aghion & Howitt, 1998). Economics differs from organization and management theory in how new literature is taken up. In economics, the critical tradition is alive and well, and new work attracts criticism of its concepts, methods and findings – which encompasses the whole project. Work that survives these challenges gradually makes its way into the body of the economic discipline where it begins to change the conversation. Lekachman, an economist with Keynes in mind, argued 'it is reasonable to term a book truly significant if, after its appearance, economists think differently, students are presented with a fresh set of textbooks, politicians hear unexpected voices, and perhaps most important of all, the public at large comes to expect a different set of government policies and a transformed attitude' (Lekachman, 1968, p. 8). By this measure, *KCC*'s impact on management practice was considerable. The book created new managerial language, popularized the term 'tacit knowledge', provided new insight into the strategic significance of 'tacit knowledge', and gave CEOs a new way to assert 'our people are the firm's most important resource'. Aside from the difficulty of defining or analyzing tacit knowledge (Håkanson, 2007), the difficulty of communicating it illuminated every business's 'communication problem' in a wholly new manner, revealing why IT's promise should be rethought around the distinction between tacit and explicit knowledge-flows. The classic 'innovation management problem', with R&D 'throwing their stuff over the wall' to production and marketing was also reframed. Without question, *KCC* significantly changed how business people talked about their firms' internal processes. It also significantly restored business peoples' interest in KM, altering relevance-seeking academics to its possibilities.

But the intellectual impact on management academics is less easy to identify. In spite of the high number of Google Scholar hits it was not easy to see how, or even if, *KCC*'s achievement as a completely new paradigm, language or theory of the firm was understood. Indeed it was often unclear whether the citing author had read the book cited. The notations were typically uncritical and comment-free, simply reporting the writer's awareness of the SECI model – a nod in its direction rather than something to be used or built on. There was little appreciation for the new up-down middle management role, for the model's dynamic mechanisms, or the closed paradigmatic nature of its language. Critiques are regrettably rare in our discipline; Håkanson's 2007 critique of tacit knowledge is already noted. Gourlay's 2006 critique of *KCC* was another. His summary of the previous critiques of *KCC* showed two principal lines of argument (Gourlay, 2006). First, there was concern about

KCC's founding 'epistemological' axiom, and about Nonaka and Takeuchi's handling of Polanyi's tacit/explicit distinction. There was less comment on their 'ontological' axiom, the separation of middle, up, down or their three-tier cross-levelling structure (Nonaka & Takeuchi, 1995, p. 111). Second, there was some criticism of *KCC*'s five-phase process: sharing tacit knowledge, creating concepts, justifying concepts, building an archetype, cross-levelling knowledge – the five phases embraced in the SECI matrix's four moves (Nonaka & Takeuchi, 1995, p. 84).

Essers and Schreinemakers's 1997 paper was a careful and in-depth analysis of *KCC*'s epistemological grounding, securely seizing the essential point that *KCC* rejected a positivist approach and proposed a subjective epistemology (Essers & Schreinemakers, 1997). But the authors also pointed to the logical entailment – the challenge to cope with several knowledge-types. They concluded *KCC* failed to address the knowledge-types' incommensurability. Any model that adopts a multiple KT strategy must deal with their incommensurability. Essers and Schreinemakers leveraged on the second argument too and pointed out that if the 'ontological' separation holds then *KCC* failed to explain the absence of inter-level misunderstanding and conflict. They concluded *KCC* proposed a closed paradigm, assumed to come into existence unproblematically as a result of choosing a strategic goal or intention. Gourlay's critique took the previous points into account but drew extensively on Dewey's notions of learning to raise doubts about *KCC*'s underlying assumption that the production of knowledge arose as an interaction of different knowledge-types (Gourlay, 2006; Gourlay & Nurse, 2005). Nonaka and von Krogh addressed some of these points in a careful restatement of the 'epistemological' axiom, avoiding a direct rebuttal of the previous criticisms (Nonaka & von Krogh, 2009). They also laid emphasis on the need for the interplay of the tacit and explicit knowledge types to be in a social context, to be a social practice rather than an individual one. There was no discussion of inter-level conflict management.

An interpretation of KCC's proposals

While there is much more to be said along these lines, in this section I move in a different direction, taking off from a widespread misunderstanding of *KCC*'s proposals. With this clarified it may be possible to restate *KCC*'s achievements and limitations in non-Nonakian language – and thereby lay the groundwork for assessing Nonaka and his colleagues' later moves to extend *KCC* by adding further new language – specifically the terms *ba*, 'flow', and *phronesis*. At the same time, bearing KM's future in mind, we see Nonaka's post-*KCC* work diverging from KM's main track, for its problematics are not much illuminated by these new terms. This reinforces my earlier point that Nonaka's work 'intersected' KM and perhaps now moves away – having opened up a unique language that has not much impacted mainstream KM beyond introducing Polanyi's tacit-explicit distinction – leaving mainstream KM half in and half out of positivism, puzzled about how to handle it or where to go next.

There is a certain ambiguity throughout the Nonaka *oeuvre* in its alternating language of knowledge-creation and knowledge-conversion. *Strictu sensu KCC* offers a humanist theory of the company as a knowledge-conversion apparatus. It is perfectly up-front about this, for firms cannot and do not create knowledge. In parenthesis is 'only individuals can do this', something stated over and over throughout the *oeuvre*. My switch from organization to firm is to highlight that while firms are goal-oriented, organizations are less clearly so, as Simon's 1964 paper on organizational goals showed (Simon, 1964). In Nonakian terms organizations are pretty coherent, having ontology, boundaries, missions, values and goals. In the background is the specific 'ontological' axiom of the *KCC* model, distinguishing individual, group and organization levels in a typology of 'work units', each fundamentally different from the other.

Some of the ontological critique previously noted springs from Western theorists' doubts about this. They see more heterogeneity, permeability, dysfunctionality, confusion and conflict. Indeed it can be argued that, post-Weber, organization theorists' principal problematics are around the effectiveness of various ways to generate, promote, or sustain organizational order in the face of divergent knowledge. In fact, some see Nonaka as taking coherence very much for granted, given rather than created by management. Notwithstanding these gaps, *KCC* is about the conversion of knowledge generated by individuals into knowledge made available to the organization's goal seeking activities. In retrospect it might have been useful to restate *KCC* as providing a 'theory of the conversion of individual knowledge into organizational knowledge', stressing the differences between these two types of knowledge and leaving the mysterious term 'creation' out. The unremarked possibility – or probability, given the ontology – that individual-type knowledge might differ from organizational-type knowledge runs throughout the *oeuvre* but is neither rejected, nor admitted. *KCC* embraces the commonly held view that all knowledge is created by individuals – both positivists and non-positivists go along with this, only arch-Durkheimians or Jungians would object. Then there is practice. Nonaka's intuitions about knowledge-creation or learning were shaped by Nishida's action-based epistemology that stands against the Western view that knowledge is created by thinking alone. Polanyi, of course, stood up for a 'practice-based' epistemology against the pure ratiocination of the logical positivist model of hypothesis statement and falsification. In this case, the evolution of *KCC*'s language can be thought of as the project to meld axiom (a), that individuals in action develop individual knowledge, together with axiom (b), that organizations are internally heterogeneous with structures and interacting layers of activity.

The bottom line here is that *KCC* offers no original or well-formed theory of knowledge-creation, yet the title of the book and the alternation of terminology leads many to think that it does – even though Nonaka and Takeuchi actually make no such claim. The intuition running throughout is that with several types of knowledge in mind and to hand, individuals 'create' in the circumstances of 'compression' and 'goal-oriented action' that seem conducive to invention. Necessity is the mother of invention or what US business people call 'stretch goals'. There is also some distance between *KCC*'s five phases of the organizational process and the four moves in the SECI matrix. The first of the five phases involves sharing the tacit knowledge the individual already has available. Socialization is marked by articulation, capturing this knowledge in concepts that are eventually shared non-tacitly as explication and explanation kicks in. Creation does enter into this analysis at all so the book's title has a measure of bait-and-switch.

Recalling my earlier comment about the matrix in Nonaka and Nicosia (1979), there is a profoundly illuminating difference between it and the SECI matrix. Matrices are of at least two types (Spender, 1979). One type is static, the matrix being a classification scheme (bunch of pigeon-holes). The SWOT matrix is of this type. Another type of matrix is dynamic, a way of illustrating interaction between its boxes. The BCG matrix is of this type as funds flow from 'cash-cows' into 'questions-marks' to transform the survivors into the 'stars' that mature into the next generation of 'cash-cows'. Dogs, incidentally, are not necessarily failures; they may be perfectly viable businesses, it is just that they cannot be fitted into the funds flow around the other three boxes. Both matrices propose a particular language to grasp a specific universe of phenomena, implicitly admitting the existence of other phenomena that they cannot capture and which have been consigned to *'ceteris paribus'* clauses. The boundaries around the matrices are crucial. As they become porous, the matrix's message (implicit theory) is undercut. It is well known that one weakness of the BCG matrix is its assumption that internal operations are the only source of funds for question marks – for if the deal is good enough to fund internally, why not go to the bank or capital market, and why make so much of the difference? In the background, here is the debt-equity and funds management debate, expressly excised from the matrix.

In this sense Nonaka's 1979 and 1994 matrices are of different types illustrating, among other things, that his Nishida-based intuition of knowledge's dynamic nature was kept out of his early work, reframing his later *oeuvre* as the project to bring it back in, challenging him to fit a non-positivist Japanese philosophical concept into an inherently positivist American intellectual tradition. Second, the boundary around the SECI matrix remains impermeable, which brings us back to the oft-criticized assumption of organizational homogeneity. At the same time presuming such a boundary opens up conceptual connections to thermodynamic thinking and to information entropy – and to the work of Max Boisot. One of the curious non-events in KM's history is that, as far as I know, Nonaka and Boisot never met or collaborated on their projects even though they were startlingly similar. This becomes even more curious when we appreciate Boisot's conceptual breakthrough to his codification–diffusion or C–D matrix occurred while he was in Japan. His 1982 paper was published at Keio University just as Nonaka was moving to Hitotsubashi (Boisot, 1982). Boisot's model of knowledge conversion was also cyclical and social, what he ultimately named the Social Learning Cycle (Boisot, 1998). Boisot's concept of knowledge combined explicit and tacit types; his cycle arguing that both are convertible and communicable. His ultimate point being to show codification improved knowledge's transferability while leaving the informed recipient the task of reoperationalizing it. The benefits of relocating the valuable information had to be set against the work required to operationalize abstractions. Boisot also appealed to Polanyi's knowledge-types. Boisot was not familiar with Japanese philosophy, though he later became a China expert, and his thinking was based on the work of the nineteenth century French engineer-economists, plus Carnot and Maupertius (Spender, forthcoming). He also adopted Ashby's notions of requisite variety. The C–D cycle reflected the thermodynamic principle of conservation of energy, the information-conversion taking place in a closed system with no leakage across its boundaries. If the SECI matrix is equally bounded, there may be a conservation principle at work as the knowledge-conversion process moves knowledge between the different types contained in the language – both explicit/tact and individual/organizational – while keeping the total amount of knowledge constant.

This suggests a 'thermodynamics of knowledge' and reinforces Nonaka's powerful metaphor of the SECI matrix as the 'engine' of the knowledge-creation process (Nonaka & Takeuchi, 1995, p. 57), more correctly the knowledge-conversion process. Engineers know that engines are devices for converting heat into mechanical energy (power). They illustrate the process with pressure-volume diagrams that distinguish, for instance, the Stirling cycle from the Diesel cycle (Figure 2.2). Work means something specific, more or less defined as the area within the cycle. This is a metric of the 'work' the heat engine does during the conversion. Note the heat source is exogenous to the analysis; thus heat enters from outside, the mechanical energy is delivered outside as the engine 'performs'. The engine does not create heat (it actually loses a fair amount, which is why perpetual motion is impossible). Neither does the engine 'create' power; only those ignorant of the conversion process would think so.

These graphs show the pressure and volume changes in the combustion chamber as heat or fuel enters and the engine 'works'. In an analogy to the multiple knowledge types addressed earlier, these (and several other) engine cycles differ as engineers' different implementations of the 'perfect' cycle Carnot identified,which is impossible to implement.

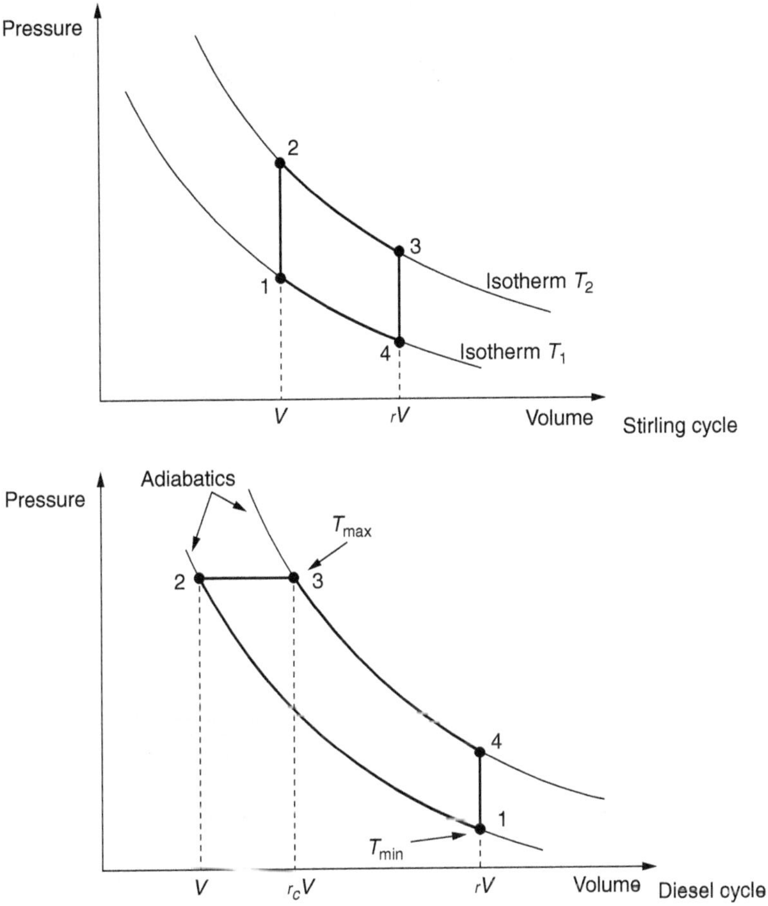

Figure 2.2 The process with pressure-volume diagrams that distinguish, for instance, the Stirling cycle from the Diesel cycle

Source: Ferreira da Silva (2012).

With this kind of graph in mind we can draw a thermodynamic interpretation of the *KCC* model as an equivalent work cycle (Figure 2.3). The energy source, the imagining or knowledge creating we presume is done only by individuals, is exogenous, as in the engineers' heat engines. Fresh 'knowledge energy' is delivered to the SECI engine that converts it into organizational performance (market power). It enters as individual tacit knowledge at the bottom of the cycle. In the first 'sharing' phase, it is not yet explicit and cannot be shared beyond close co-workers. The second 'creating concepts'

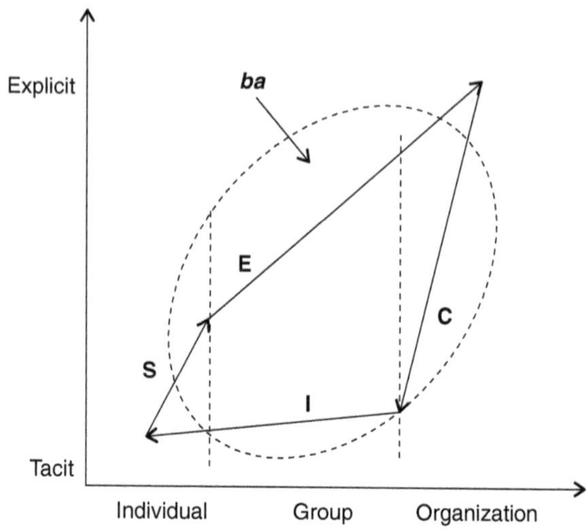

Figure 2.3 Thermodynamic interpretation of the KCC model as an equivalent work cycle

Source: The author.

phase carries the partially converted knowledge towards the condition in which it can be widely shared with 'justified' concepts. Eventually it arrives at the top of the cycle. Here it becomes available to be integrated with other knowledge into the firm's business model (archetype) and then, through 'cross levelling', the appropriate projects and work groups can be instructed. As they transform the now strategically structured knowledge into practice, the knowing becomes increasingly tacit. Eventually each operator develops her/his own practice-based take, perhaps refuelling the individual knowledge creation process that lies outside the cycle.

The central space, *ba*, to be examined further later, indicates a totality of what can be known that might also be brought into the knowledge-engine, given the organization's people, resources and goals. The diagram frames the strategic challenge as that of capturing as much of the *ba* as possible in the SECI cycle. Against this, any portions of the SECI cycle that fall outside the *ba* suggest dys-functionalities management should avoid – to the bottom left, individuals who cannot convey their tacit knowledge to their work-group, to the upper right managers too ready to instruct the work-groups without considering the tacit knowledge necessary to transform their instructions into value-adding practice. The analogy to a heat engine suggests the area within the SECI cycle is the 'knowledge-work' necessary to make the conversion of individual level tacit knowledge into organizationally effective practice. This should be as large as possible consistent with avoiding dysfunctionality. Note there is no apparent relationship between the quantity, or quality, of the knowledge-work, purely internal to the organization, and its economic costs or consequences in the world beyond its boundaries. Using this metaphor of a humanly populated knowledge-engine that does a specific amount of contextualized knowledge-work gets around the knowledge-creation/knowledge-conversion ambiguity noted at the start of this section. It is also inherently modelable and computable, and could broaden *KCC*'s impact, especially among academics.

Expanding the model with new language

Takeuchi and Nonaka wrote expressly about extending their model with three additional concepts: *ba*, dialectical thinking, and Giddens's 'structuration' theory (Takeuchi & Nonaka, 2004, p. xi). Nonaka, Toyama and Hirata brought in the concepts of 'flow' from Csiksentmihalyi and, from Greek epistemology, *phronesis* (Nonaka, Toyama, & Hirata, 2008). These new terms imply a large project, too large for to be analyzed here, although some comment might be useful. First, expanding the analysis seems a natural sequel to *KCC*, reflecting Nonaka's intellectual restlessness, vigour, and self-critique, the need to keep pushing ahead to capture his deeper intuitions of human dynamism. But a case could be made that the 'expansion project' is a response to the critics, such as those previously mentioned, especially those advancing the ontological critique. In this case, *ba* is a means to break free of the naïve notions of organizational homogeneity that are almost certainly no part of *KCC* even though it proposes a secure boundary around the knowledge-engine. *Ba* derives from Nishida's notion of *Basho*, and is defined as 'shared context in motion'. This must be bounded. Note it is not a 'space' in which individuals create knowledge that lies outside the cycle.

The 'shared context in motion' evokes an analogy to the 'working fluid' of the heat engine – the steam in a steam engine, the hot gases in a diesel. Knowledge of the 'shared context in motion' is what flows in the SECI knowledge-engine but as we know, knowledge is tricky stuff. Perhaps the analogy is orthogonal to the knowledge-types Nonaka introduced with his paradigm/language. To explain this, just as water changes state in a steam engine, so knowledge changes its state (type) in a knowledge-engine – from tacit to explicit and then the other way around (not back again directly, only through practice). The knowledge gets merged, synthesized, and reconstructed at every point in the cycle. The cycle is not reversible, just as those of engineers' heat engines are not. Likewise boundaries are crucial to the knowledge-engine. The boundary implied by *ba* identifies that specific subjective knowledge-context in which the knowledge content is meaningful, manageable, convertible, and relevant to the organization's project

(Nonaka & Reinmoeller, 2000). The positivist tendency would be to try and identify this as a space-time context, thus missing the subjective nature of Nonaka's work and philosophizing.

There is a sense in which *ba* points towards 'everything that can be known intentionally and subjectively by the actors involved'. As such it may be the same as *phronesis*, or allude to another knowledge type, a more social and intuitive mode of shared knowing that contrasts with individual knowing. Instead of being differentiated and heterogeneous, as are the knowledge-types that derive from (a) the epistemological distinctions or (b) the ontological distinctions, *ba*-type knowledge is homogenous and holistic, like the feeling of utter absorption in proficient social practice (equally a state of flow) or the remembered feeling of community in the village or locality where you grew up. The term 'place' does not illuminate the nature of *ba* any more than 'place' illuminates the concept of consciousness. Being conscious means, as Kant advised, appreciating being space-time aware and so in a place and moment. *Ba* points to the essence of human knowing, to what is knowable, rather than to a place in which to construct knowing. It is diametrically opposed to the Cartesian concept of individualistic knowing with its isolation and enclosed-ness of private language. *Ba* reflects the Japanese aesthetic that all human knowing is fundamentally social and collective, active, and time-full, with the awareness of past knowing as a constraint on as well as an impulse towards future knowing.

Inasmuch as the exploration of *ba* reconstitutes the ontological dimension of the *KCC* paradigm, the adoption of *phronesis* reconstitutes its epistemological dimension. It dismisses the easy dichotomy of tacit and explicit and moves into the more complex tradition of Greek epistemology. There are two points to be made. First, the power of the multi-KT method lies in the implications of the contrasts between knowledge types, not in their definition. It sidesteps the positivist obligation to define or axiomatize things before analysis can begin for everything must be derived logically, deductively or inductively, from these axioms. The method of KT contrasts renders definitions of the knowledge types contrasted rather peripheral. Without having to define either explicit or tacit knowledge, Polanyi's approach enabled him to relate analysis to synthesis and to practice, and break through the boundaries the logical positivists placed on their 'philosophy of science'. Polanyi, a major inorganic chemist, knew his science was simply not done the way they suggested, that the positivist's philosophy of science transformed his crucial in-the-lab skills into a barren mind-game. The meaning embedded in the interplay of knowledge types was bound up in his skilled laboratory practice. It is moved from there at some risk of being ignored or becoming incoherent or hopelessly subjective.

Put differently, the tacit meanings that hold scientific projects together are embedded in the scientist's practices and form of life – in Polanyi's case, chemistry-lab life. Transporting the distinction from the lab to organizational life may not seem excessively risky because both contexts are made tractable by the concept of purposive or goal seeking – presuming all human action is towards definite ends. To go beyond this and pick up the broader Greek tradition is (a) to exchange a tractable dichotomy for the greater complexity of the knowledge-types in Greek epistemology – *techne, nous, thymos, eros, metis, episteme, sophia* and so on. These are grounded in Greek life at large, not all of which is purposive. Equally a focus on *phronesis* alone abandons the method of contrasting knowledge-types; and (b) slides into the trap of trying to define *phronesis* (Nonaka, Toyama, & Peltoporpi, 2011). Extracting *phronesis* from the philosophical discourse and using it to illuminate our form of life is to presume the Greek form of life bears some reasonable relation to ours. This must be doubted. 'What is the purpose of life?' is as tricky a question for us as it was for the Greeks in their pursuit of the 'good life'. The Greeks' complex epistemological apparatus enabled them to consider such questions about life – much of which may have had no 'purpose' that we can comprehend today. Economist and organization theorists depend on purpose and intention, especially self-maximization, and need an epistemological apparatus well adapted to examining the problems of purposive organizations. In short, the Greeks' concepts can only be imported into today's organizational context at great risk of incoherence, as teachers of business ethics sometimes discover.

KM's future

Given the non-positivist moves Nonaka is still making, not much of the future of KM seems to lie in his direction. Yet recall KM comprises many different camps. The IT camp is blazing ahead with new technologies and techniques for acquiring, digesting and delivering data. Society is clearly hungry for more data and more analysis in every quarter and for every trade. There is no limit in sight, no hint of overshoot or strategic failure. In spite of the stream of complaint about the corrupting influence of quantification the answer is clearly not to have less of it. The philosophical and pedagogical challenge is to recapture what gets lost in our enthusiasm for data. *KCC* probes this and Nonaka's later moves towards an aesthetic of organizing, *ba*, and dialectics reopen the search for a more balanced and philosophically mature methodology – always the real agenda behind comparing US and Japanese management methods. Beyond KM's IT agenda, the ancillary KM applications like intellectual property and human capital management are equally vigorous, divergent specialisms directed towards different goals. But they have little to do with 'real' KM, the search for knowledge-based theories of the firm/organization and its management. *KCC* is a stunning achievement in this program, clearly a thorough and operational articulation of a knowledge-dependent theory of the organization and its administration. But it suffers the inevitable consequences of the assumptions on which it stands.

As Essers and Schreinemakers argued, like most rich theories *KCC* offers a paradigm, a closed island of mutually sustaining and defining language, relatively tightly bounded and consequently cut off from the broader socio-economy. The firm is defined as a bounded dynamic context of action-knowledge. *KCC* delves into its internal processes in ways that connect well to how the managers who inhabit the organization might set about shaping them. It is a surprisingly practical manual as the many cases show (Nonaka & Reinmoeller, 2000). But the firm's existence is presumed and logically prior to the analysis. Thus *KCC* does not engage the Coasian microeconomists' problematics, 'Why do firms exist? How do they come into existence?' versions of the question 'What is entrepreneurship?' that many think *KCC* engaged. In this direction, of course, lie further questions about individual or collective knowledge-creation, issues that *KCC* does not, in fact, address. Sprinkled through Nonaka's writings are mentions of the ability of the organization to absorb and convert knowledge that has not been created by its own members, that the organization must have some 'absorptive capacity' to supplement its five-step process in ways that logically complement the requirement for redundancy at each ontological level. Meanwhile the Coasian agenda is being pursued vigorously elsewhere (see Foss & Klein, 2012 for recent work) and might eventually merge with theorizing endogenous growth. As this agenda moves forward, there may well be major advances in 'real' KM.

Those who write about KM's future tend to ignore *KCC* and focus on the KM's other initiatives and intellectual artefacts: communities of practice, dynamic capabilities, innovation management, knowledge-sharing and so on (Renzl, Matzler, & Hinterhuber, 2006, p. 1). There are many interesting methodological challenges here, given 'real' KM starts out by rejecting positivist methods. There is increasing interest in moving beyond our often-trivial notions of learning through 'experience alone' or by knowledge-aggregation, a discussion led by a reappreciation of Dewey's work or that of Vygotsky and Piaget. There is increasing attention to narrative, reframing the firm as a body of discourse (language-use) rather than as a body of knowledge or bundle of resources (Putnam & Nicotera, 2009). There is increasing interest in theories of practice, with the usual references to Bourdieu, Turner, de Certeau, Foucault, and Schatzki (Schatzki, Knorr Cetina, & von Savigny, 2001). There is increasing interest in self-organization and self-regulation, drawing on the same sources as Nonaka, such as in the work of Maturana and Varela, Ashby, Mingers, and von Glasersfeld.

Each of these research programs offers a distinctive notion of KM, reiterating variety, the most basic point about KM and its future. There is not much evidence of an overarching theory of organization creation. Neither 'effectuation', a rearticulation of Kirzner's approach to entrepreneurship, nor Schumpeterian approaches seem to have grasped the nettle that entrepreneurship is, at bottom, the process of socio-economic knowledge-creation. Yet if a substantive theory of knowledge-creation could ever be found it would spell the end of knowledge itself, for it would have broken through the boundary indicated by the question, what is the knowledge status of a theory of its own creation? It would be a bootstrapping 'theory of everything' that would mark the end of knowledge as presently conceived for the notion of knowledge as a human artrefact hinges on its incompleteness. The more likely circumstance is that KM will remain a vigorous plurality of enquiries, their agendas differentiated by differing axioms and resulting paradigms. They are post-positivist methodology's children, a flourishing diaspora of those who have escaped positivism. Nonaka's take is especially informed by Japanese aesthetics and philosophy, and so inevitably disjoint from the US discourse and equally from the European 'continental philosophy' fuelled discourse. In the US, in particular, and in English-language management theorizing generally we are in the evening of the positivist or modernist dream of a form of knowledge of reality that would be objective and insulated against our subjectivity and human weaknesses such as bounded rationality, decision bias or emotion. This dream is exhausted and disappearing into our intellectual history. In this respect, the non-positivist types of KM have enormous potential and Nonaka and his colleagues have shown us one way to make them work.

When it comes to a greater appreciation of *KCC* and exploration of the uses to which the Nonaka paradigm might be put, Teece's commentary was suggestive (Teece, 2008, p. xiv; see this volume). He implied more than he said about *KCC*'s inattention to resource allocation. While *KCC* locates the company in a competitive economy, there are few connections between its five-step process and the resulting economic performance. In the *KCC* paradigm, organizational knowledge tends to become an end in itself, a demonstration of knowledge management as an art form. Precisely how or why it leads to competitive advantage is not addressed. Yet of all people, academics should be most suspicious of the idea that more knowledge leads ineluctably to economic success. This points towards the *KCC* paradigm's closed nature. Explaining economic growth requires starting off with some kind of openness at an axiomatic level – perhaps a crucial uncertainty such as Knight or Penrose suggested. An analysis of how the growing firm engages its markets can then follow – turning on their asymmetries, imperfections and so on – as well as an analysis of its knowledge-conversion engine. As Teece suggested, there is an empirical program of testing the links between good *KCC* practice and firm performance, and he itemized some specifics for the forthcoming 'battalions of doctoral students' (Teece, 2008, p. xv).

Conclusion

This chapter explores and lauds the substantial intellectual achievements of Professor Nonaka and his colleagues, Hirotaka Takeuchi especially. It shows the outcome is academically substantial, widely applicable and the result of patient and persistent labour over many years. Notable was the gradual evolution of an idiosyncratic language as Nonaka probed this way and that seeking to capture his intuitions in ways that would make them accessible to his colleagues, clients and students. It is an achievement with lessons for any social scientist thinking of moving on from our positivist heritage, abandoning its empty promise of objectivity and so entering – or reentering – the post-modern world of human subjectivity. Here all knowledge is human artefact, not a representation of Nature's doings. Its creation is a collective art form for which we must take moral, ethical, political and aesthetic responsibility. Too few can show us how to engage these issues and so recover social science's founding agenda, which is to improve the human condition. Nonaka is surely one of them.

Acknowledgements

The author thanks several readers for their insightful comments on earlier drafts of this piece, especially Herb Addison, Lars Håkanson, Stephen Gourlay, and Tim Ray.

Note

1. Personal communication, September 2012.

References

Aghion, Philippe, & Howitt, Peter. (1998). *Endogenous Growth Theory*. Cambridge, MA: MIT Press.

Boisot, Max. (1982). The codification and diffusion of knowledge in the transactional strategy of firms. *Keio Economic Studies*. 19 (1).

Boisot, Max. (1998). *Knowledge Assets: Securing Competitive Advantage in the Information Economy*. Oxford: Oxford University Press.

Burton-Jones, Alan, & Spender, J.-C. (eds). (2011). *Oxford Handbook of Human Capital*. Oxford: Oxford University Press.

Essers, Juup, & Schreinemakers, Jos. (1997). Nonaka's subjectivist conception of knowledge in corporate knowledge management. *Knowledge Organization*. 24 (1), 24–32.

Ferreira da Silva, M. F. (2012) Some considerations about thermodynamic cycles, *European Journal of Physics*. 33 (13), 13–42.

Foss, Nicolai J., & Klein, Peter G. (2012). *Organizing Entrepreneurial Judgment: A New Approach to the Firm*. Cambridge: Cambridge University Press.

Gourlay, Stephen. (2006). Conceptualizing knowledge creation: a critique of Nonaka's theory. *Journal of Management Studies*. 43 (7), 1415–1436.

Gourlay, Stephen, & Nurse, Andrew. (2005). Flaws in the "Engine" of knowledge creation: a critique of Nonaka's theory. In Anthony F. Buono & F Poulfelt (eds), *Challenges and Issues in Knowledge Management Research* (Vol. 5, pp. 293–315). Greenwich, CT: Information Age Publishing.

Håkanson, Lars. (2007). Creating knowledge: the power and logic of articulation. *Industrial & Corporate Change*. 16 (1), 51–88.

Hayek, Friedrich A. (1945). The use of knowledge in society. *American Economic Review.* 35 (4), 519–530.

Hedlund, Gunnar, & Nonaka, Ikujiro. (1991). *Models of Knowledge Management in the West and in Japan*. Institute of International Business, School of Economics Working Paper RP 91/9.

Hedlund, Gunnar, & Nonaka, Ikujiro. (1993). Models of knowledge management in the west and Japan. In Peter Lorange, Bala Chakravarty, Johan Roos, & Andrew Van de Ven (eds), *Implementing Strategic Processes: Change, Learning and Cooperation* (pp. 117–144). Oxford: Basil Blackwell.

Helgesen, Sally. (2008). The practical wisdom of Ikujiro Nonaka. *Strategy+Business.* 53.

Kagono, Tadao, Nonaka, Ikujiro, Sakakibara, Kiyonori, & Omura, Akihiro. (1985). *Strategic vs Evolutionary Management: A US-Japan Comparison of Strategy and Organization*. Amsterdam: North-Holland.

Klapp, Orrin. (1975). Opening and closing of systems. *Behavioral Science.* 20, 251–257.

Knight, Frank Hyneman. (1965). *Risk, Uncertainty and Profit*. New York: Harper & Row.

Lekachman, Robert. (1968). *The Age of Keynes*. New York: Vintage Books.

Machlup, Fritz. (1962). *The Production and Distribution of Knowledge in the United States*. Princeton, NJ: Princeton University Press.

Morgan, Gareth. (1986). *Images of Organization*. Newbury Park, CA: Sage Publications.

Nonaka, Ikujiro. (1972). Organization and Market: Exploratory Study of Centralization vs. Decentralization. *Unpublished PhD Thesis Graduate School of Business Administration, University of California Berkeley*.

Nonaka, Ikujiro. (1988a). Creating organizational order out of chaos: self-renewal in Japanese firms. *California Management Review* (Spring). 57–73.

Nonaka, Ikujiro. (1988b). Toward middle-up-down management: accelerating information creation. *Sloan Management Review.* 29 (3), 9–18.

Nonaka, Ikujiro. (1990a). Redundant, overlapping organization: a Japanese approach to innovation. *California Management Review.* 32 (3), 27–38.

Nonaka, Ikujiro. (1990b). Redundant, overlapping organization: a Japanese approach to managing the innovation process. *California Management Review.* 32 (3), 27–38.

Nonaka, Ikujiro. (1991a). The knowledge-creating company. *Harvard Business Review.* 69 (6), 96–104.

Nonaka, Ikujiro. (1991b). Managing the firm as an information creation process. In J. Meindl, R. L. Cardy, & Sheila M Puffer (eds), *Advances in Information Processing in Organizations* (Vol. 4, pp. 239–275). Greenwich, CT: JAI Press.

Nonaka, Ikujiro. (1994). A dynamic theory of organizational knowledge creation. [Article]. *Organization Science.* 5 (1), 14–37.

Nonaka, Ikujiro, Byosiere, Philippe, Borucki, Chester C., & Konno, Noboru. (1994). Organizational knowledge creation theory: a first comprehensive test. *International Business Review.* 3 (4), 337–351.

Nonaka, Ikujiro, & Johansson, Johny K. (1985). Japanese management: what about the "Hard" skills?' *Academy of Management Review.* 10 (2), 181–191.

Nonaka, Ikujiro, & Nicosia, Francesco M. (1979). Marketing management, its environment and information processing: a problem in organizational design. *Journal of Business Research.* 7, 277–300.

Nonaka, Ikujiro, & Reinmoeller, Patrick. (2000). Dynamic business systems for knowledge creation and utilization. In Charles Despres, & Daniele Chauvel (eds), *Knowledge Horizons: The Present and the Promise of Knowledge Management* (pp. 89–112). Boston, MA: Butterworth Heinemann.

Nonaka, Ikujiro, & Sato, T. (1981). Corporate strategy and organizational learning (in Japanese). *Diamond Harvard Business Review, July–August*. 89–102.

Nonaka, Ikujiro, & Takeuchi, Hirotaka. (1995). *The Knowledge-Creating Company: How Japanese Companies Create the Dynamics of Innovation*. New York: Oxford University Press.

Nonaka, Ikujiro, Toyama, Ryoko, & Hirata, Toru. (2008). *Managing Flow: A Process Theory of the Knowledge-Based Firm*. Basingstoke: Palgrave Macmillan.

Nonaka, Ikujiro, Toyama, Ryoko, & Peltoporpi, Vesa. (2011). The distributed and dynamic dimensions of human capital. In Alan Burton-Jones & J.-C. Spender (eds), *Oxford Handbook of Human Capital* (pp. 459–476).Oxford University Press.

Nonaka, Ikujiro, & von Krogh, Georg. (2009). Tacit knowledge and knowledge conversion: controversy and advancement in organizational knowledge creation theory. *Organisation Science*. 20 (3), 635–652.

Nonaka, Ikujiro, & Yamanouchi, Teruo. (1989). Managing innovation as a self-renewing process. *Journal of Business Venturing*. 4, 299–315.

Penrose, Edith T. (1959). *The Theory of the Growth of the Firm*. New York: John Wiley & Sons.

Pitelis, Christos N. (ed.). (2002). *The Growth of the Firm: The Legacy of Edith Penrose*. Oxford: Oxford University Press.

Prusak, Larry. (2001). Where did knowledge management come from? *IBM Systems Journal*. 40 (4), 1002–1006.

Putnam, Linda L., & Nicotera, Anne Maydan (eds). (2009). *Building Theories of Organization: The Constitutive Role of Communication*. New York: Routledge.

Renzl, Birgit, Matzler, Kurt, & Hinterhuber, Hans. (2006). Introduction. In Birgit Renzl, Kurt Matzler & Hans Hinterhuber (eds), *The Future of Knowledge Management* (pp. 1–4). Basingstoke, Hants: Palgrave Macmillan.

Rumelt, Richard P., Schendel, Dan, & Teece, David J. (1991). Strategic management and economics. *Strategic Management Journal*. 12 (Winter Special Issue), 5–29.

Schatzki, Theodore R., Knorr Cetina, Karin, & von Savigny, Eike (eds). (2001). *The Practice Turn in Contemporary Theory*. London: Routledge.

Selznick, Philip. (1957). *Leadership in Administration: A Sociological Interpretation*. New York: Harper & Row.

Simon, Herbert A. (1964). On the concept of organizational goal. *Administrative Science Quarterly*. 9 (1), 1–22.

Simon, Herbert A. (1986). Keieisha no Yakuwari Saihomon (The Functions of the Executive). In K Kato, & H Iino (eds), *Banado (Barnard)* (pp. 3–17). Tokyo: Bunshindo.

Spender, J.-C. (1979). Theory building and theory testing in strategic management. In Dan Schendel, & Chuck Hofer (eds), *Strategic Management: A New View of Business Policy and Planning* (pp. 394–404). Boston, MA: Little, Brown.

Spender, J.-C. (1996). Competitive advantage from tacit knowledge? Unpacking the concept and its strategic implications. In Bertrand Moingeon, & Amy Edmondson (eds), *Organizational Learning and Competitive Advantage* (pp. 56–73). Thousand Oaks, CA: Sage Publications.

Spender, J.-C. (2013). Herbert Alexander Simon: philosopher of the organizational life-world. In Morgen Witzel, & Malcolm Warner (eds), *Oxford Handbook of Management Thinkers* (pp. 297–357). Oxford: Oxford University Press.

Spender, J.-C. (forthcoming). Max Boisot's theorizing. In John Child, & Martin Ihrig (eds), *Knowledge and the Study of Organization and Management – Building on the work of Max Boisot*. Oxford: Oxford University Press.

Sullivan, Jeremiah J. (1983). A critique of theory Z. *Academy of Management Review.* 8 (1), 122–142.

Sullivan, Jeremiah J., & Nonaka, Ikujiro. (1986). The application of organizational learning theory to Japanese and American management. *Journal of International Business Studies.* 17 (3, Autumn), 127–147.

Takeuchi, Hirotaka, & Nonaka, Ikujiro. (1986). The new new product development game. *Harvard Business Review, Jan–Feb,* 64 (1), 137–146.

Takeuchi, Hirotaka, & Nonaka, Ikujiro. (2004). *Hitotsubashi on Knowledge Management.* Singapore: John Wiley & Sons.

Teece, David J. (2000). *Managing Intellectual Capital: Organizational, Strategic, and Policy Dimensions.* Oxford: Oxford University Press.

Teece, David J. (2008). Foreword: from the management of R&D to knowledge management: some contributions of Ikujio Nonaka to the field of strategic mangement. In Ikujiro Nonaka, Ryoko Toyama, & Ryoko Hirata (eds), *Managing Flow: A Process Theory of the Knowledge-Based Firm* (pp. ix–xvii).

Wiig, Karl M. (2000). Knowledge management: an emergent discipline rooted in a long history. In Charles Despres, & Daniele Chauvel (eds), *Knowledge Horizons* (pp. 3–26). Woburn MA: Butterworth-Heinemann.

3

The Formation and Development of Ikujiro Nonaka's Knowledge Creation Theory

Fangqi Xu

Introduction

After the 1970s, Japanese enterprises drew attention because of their increase in competitive power in the world. However, this phenomenon hit a peak by the end of the 1980s, concluding the heyday of Japanese enterprises. In the United States, many organizations – not only those in the public, but also private sectors – dedicated no end of human and financial resources to research why Japanese enterprises were so much stronger. As a result, Total Quality Control (TQC) and Lean Product System (LPS), based on the Toyota Production System, became widely known in the world. However, this is only a manufacturing method, not a managerial theory. Does Japan not have any original management theory? It is undoubtedly a fact that almost no Japanese name was recorded in the text of management in the 20th century. From Scientific Management (Frederick W. Taylor) in the 1910s to Core Competence (Gary Hamel & C.K. Prahalad) in the 1990s, almost the entire corpus of theories was devised by Westerners. Even if some Japanese names (Juji Misumi & Kenichi Ohmae) were referred to in a management text, the references are limited to a few lines and never form an entire chapter.

Against this backdrop Ikujiro Nonaka (Professor Emeritus of Hitotsubashi University) stands out because he has become the first person who disproved the belief that Japan research on management has been only following a Western direction since the Meiji era (1868–1910). In 1995, he published *The Knowledge-Creating Company: How Japanese Companies Create the Dynamics of Innovation* (Oxford University Press) with Hirotaka Takeuchi, a Harvard Business School professor. The book won the 1995 Best New Book of the Year Award in the business and management category by the Association of American Publishers. In 2007, Nonaka won the 2007 Booz Allen Hamilton Strategy+Business Eminent Scholar Award at the Annual Conference of Academy of Management. Also, Nonaka was ranked among the top twenty most influential business thinkers by the *Wall Street Journal* in 2008. Therefore, he is the only Japanese scholar among the top twenty business thinkers. Nowadays, the number of management textbooks that include Ikujiro Nonaka and Knowledge Creation Theory have continuously grown not only in Japan but also overseas.

How did Nonaka's Knowledge Creation Theory (hereafter referred to as Nonaka Theory) form and develop? This chapter focuses on the trajectory of Nonaka Theory with a view to answering this question.

Building the academic foundation

In 1958, Nonaka joined Fuji Electric Co., Ltd. which was created in 1928 and the parenting company of Fujitsu, after graduating from the Department of Political Science, School of Political Science and Economy at Waseda University. Originally, he worked at a factory, in a personnel section, a labour union and so on. The knowledge he acquired at the operational level came to offer a solid background for his theoretical research several years later. In 1967, Nonaka left Fuji Electric and enrolled as a student at Haas School of Business at University of California, Berkeley.

Nonaka chose marketing as his first major at the school. He also registered at Professor Francesco M. Nicosia's laboratory. Professor Nicosia was the pioneer of Consumer Decision theory and known for being strict with his graduate students as to the cogency of their reasoning. If a student made a logical mistake, the student would have Professor Nicosia conscientiously refute it. In 1979, Professor Nicosia's his book *Consumer Decision Processes*, translated into Japanese by Ikujiro Nonaka and Komatsugu Haneji, was published by Toyo Keizai, Inc. in Japan.

Professor Herbert A. Simon (1916–2001) was another person who provided great intellectual stimulation to Nonaka at Berkeley. Simon was well known as one of the fathers of "Barnard=Simon theory" on management research, and had produced distinguished works in Economics, Management, Information processing, Psychology, Recognition science and Cognitive science. Accordingly, Simon was awarded the Nobel Economics Prize in 1978. Simon's conviction of management as science stimulated researchers' drive and enhanced their self-confidence. But Simon's thought deemed management as being equivalent to decision-making[1], which for us is only a partial view of the field. Simon carried out the decision-making analysis of organization development, dealt with human thinking process as information processing and developed a theory about artificial intelligence. He also proposed an individual decision-making model.

Nonaka presented his doctoral dissertation, *Organization and Market: Exploratory Study of Centralization vs. Decentralization* in 1972. We discern Simon's influence within it. In fact, Nonaka commented to the author of this chapter that, "When I wrote the dissertation, I was influenced by Hebert A. Simon who was the pioneer of modern management."[2]

According to Berkeley's curriculum, graduate students had to choose either Economics, Sociology, Psychology or Operations Research as their second major; Nonaka chose Sociology and studied with Professor Arthur L. Stinchcombe and Professor Neil J. Smelser. The former was a well-known scholar of Sociology; the latter was a pupil of Talcott Parsons, a professor at Harvard University and widely recognized for Structural-functionalism on Sociology. Nonaka's knowledge was greatly enriched under the supervision of these famous professors. Nonaka focused on ten representative theories on sociology and conducted case studies on their theoretical structure. Further, Nonaka learned fundamental theories on sociology and method, and understood how they were formed. Berkeley's sociology department was, and remains, at the top level in the United States, so Nonaka benefited from such an optimal environment, and produced as a term paper a piece of work called *The Centralization and Decentralization of Organization* which would become the basis of his doctoral dissertation.

University of California, Berkeley is reputed to be "Athens of the Pacific." Its founders wanted to resurrect the Athens of Plato, Aristotle and Periguresu at Berkeley. Therefore, students at the university consciously or unconsciously were instilled with Greek Philosophy. Needless to say, Nonaka was one such student. He wrote in the preface of *The Knowledge-Creating Company* as follows, "We inherited this philosophical tradition, as evidenced from the ample references made to Greek philosophy and epistemology throughout the book."[3]

Such substantial study most likely served as the solid academic foundation that led to the birth of Nonaka Theory.

Starting as an organization researcher

The 1960s saw a new impulse in management organization theory thanks to the focus on organization-environment research that considers organization as the unit of analysis. The dominant trend until then had been the motivation theory that had considered individual or a collective of people as an analytical unit based on classic management theory. With increasing environmental change, the survival of an organization became the key problem, which pushed the theory of organization-structure that considered organization as an analytical unit to the forefront. The subject of the correspondence between organization and the environment became the focus of organization research. Vis-à-vis this new development, Nonaka conjectured as follows: "the market seems to exert the most important influence on organization in the organization-environment dyad. So, I will attempt to advance a theoretical model on the undeveloped organization-market relations area."[4] Thus, Nonaka challenged the newest subject in organization theory. For Nonaka, it was the first step towards academic research as an organization researcher.

Nonaka, aware of organization as a positive science, insisted on the method of explaining organizational phenomena, based on scientific method.[5] He stressed, as the essence of scientific method, the cycle was made up of theoretical model-building → deduction → handling of concept → verification → amendment of the theoretical model.[6]

Motivation and organization-structure were then typical areas in organization research. The former was a theory, the same as human relations, that dealt with the motivation of organization members; the latter was a theory that analysed the organization structure. Nonaka endeavoured to categorize the patterns of organization theory findings by comparing motivation and structure approaches. For that purpose, he directed his attention to Herbert A. Simon's decision-making theory. Since the analytic unit of decision-making was individuals, Simon tried to analyse individuals' decision-making process in organizations from the perspective of social psychology. Nonaka cherished researching Simon's theory with the question of why Simon's theoretical approach was social psychology.[7] Nonaka never accepted Simon's theory without critique. He had his own opinion. For example, Nonaka criticized that "Simon cut away the value system of human beings."[8] or that "Simon almost ignored tacit knowledge and experiences; he attached more importance to explicit knowledge and information and data contained in knowledge."[9] Nonaka agreed with Henry Mintzberg's opinion that "management is art" and embraced the view that management was not only science but also art.[10] After his investigation on product development at Japanese companies in preparation for his paper presentation at an academic conference on management innovation held at Harvard Business School in 1984, Nonaka came to realize that the actual situations were quite different from Simon's theory. Thus, Nonaka's attention shifted from information processing to information creation. In other words, he parted ways with Simon.

Nonaka admits that, Simon's information processing model and contingency theory were what exerted the major influence on the creation of knowledge creation theory.[11] Contingency theory was advanced by T. Burns & G. M. Stalker, J. Woodward, P. Lawrence & J. Lorsch and others, and was developed on a large scale from the 1960s to the latter half of the 1970s. In contrast to Simon's information processing model that regards individuals as an analytic unit, contingency theory takes up organizations as analytic unit.

Centred on Simon's information processing model, Nonaka addressed (1) relationships between environment and organization; (2) organization decision-making; and (3) information processing in organization in his Ph.D. dissertation entitled *Organization and Market*.

As shown by the subtitle of *Contingence Theory of Organization* showed, Nonaka tried to construct early on his own theoretic model. His Japanese version of the Ph.D. dissertation was published by Chikura Publishing in 1974 and won a Nikkei Award of Economy and Culture the following year. Tadao Kagono enumerated in his book eight main researches of contingency theory in the world, one of which was Nonaka's research. Kagono commented: "Nonaka's research (1972, 1974) focused on specific conditions of the general proposition comprised by contingence theory on organization-environment, and tried to deduce propositions from the perspective of fit between the information processing load required by the environment and the structure of information processing in organization. He contributed to the development of a measuring method that facilitates the description of the environmental characteristics from the perspective of information load on the organization."[12]

Approach to organizational information-creating theory

Being aware of the limitations in information processing theory, Nonaka switched his attention to information-creating as previously mentioned. He contended that, in an environment in which inexplicable and unpredictable changes take place, enterprise had to proactively create information and make propositions to the environment, for its purpose it requires a managerial environment that to believe in the abilities of human and can exert creativity at all levels of the organization.[13]

Nonaka created a new concept of self-organization, that is, an organization capable of creating order (information) from the chaos. In response to the question under what conditions such an organization works, Nonaka developed a theory on the management of information creation. In1985, his research results were incorporated in his book *Enterprise Evolution: Management of Information creation,* published by Nihon Keizai Shinbun-sha.

Information creation referred to the preceding concerns, the creation of "meaningful information" or a concept that would provoke a drastic change in the way of thinking or viewpoints in an organization. Regarding the so-called enterprise evolution Nonaka held: "Pieces of information generated at all echelons of the organization (competing among them. Often times complementing each other, and sometimes undergoing "sublation" are integrated to become higher-order information, and will lead to the transformation of organizational mind-set. In the process organizational set-up and system in its support as well as its new behavioural patterns will be given shape to. Enterprise evolution comprises all this process. Among the constituents of the process outstands "information creation" as its relevant driving force."[14] In other words, information creation is the starting point of corporate evolution.

In *Enterprise Evolution,* Nonaka discussed the principle of self-organization, and identified seven conditions at a self-innovative organization in continual evolution. They were as follows.[15]

(1) Variation in the external environment. A constantly evolving organization is faced with an environment full of change and choice. An organization in a competitive environment enjoys more accelerated evolution than others in a less competitive environment.
(2) Creation of a fluctuation (*yuragi*) in the organization. What we call fluctuation refers to a generic term that comprises a variety of choice in the structural units of the organization such as hesitation, ambiguity, play (space for movement), irregular changes and instability. In an organization that incorporates fluctuation into the day-to-day organizational activities, the activity of information creation is more active than the organization that does not do so. If fluctuation is constantly accumulated, the organization is likely to evolve.
(3) Autonomy. This refers to the state in which the organizational members are not subject to such rule and restrictions as dictated by others and may act in accordance with the norms of their own.
(4) Self-transcendence. Evolution is a phenomenon of "self-transcendence." In other words, evolutionary organization constantly tries to reach the place beyond the limits of the system itself.
(5) Resonance of individual members and the whole. Many of the innovations are dependent on how to deal with a chance. Therefore, in order to tackle consciously complement of chance and necessity within the organization, along with ensuring the autonomy of micro, the organization has to ensure that the conditions of the micro and macro components can be resonance.
(6) Conversion of information into knowledge. An organization that is constantly evolving has to organize information into knowledge. In other words, it has to stock up on information. That is, it converts novelty into confirmation and holds the balance of both.
(7) Teleonomy[16]. The most important trend in theory of evolution contends that it is the capability to provoke behaviour changes, either internal controlled or purpose-oriented, that plays the important role to determine the overall course of evolution. Teleonomy signifies the value of the orientation.

Of these seven conditions, two merit special attention. 1. The first appearance of "knowledge" concept which is the keyword of Nonaka Theory. At the time, he used "confirmation" instead of "knowledge." Because confirmation means check, verify or approval, I suspect that Nonaka tried to stress the organization of new information into something valuable (knowledge). This clearly showed Nonaka's thinking process was directed to "knowledge." 2. The use of "fluctuation" and "autonomy." These words later became important concepts in Nonaka Theory.

Until the middle of the 1980s, Nonaka studied the process of enterprise evolution and proposed a theory of enterprise evolution. But when he became aware that the word evolution might signify natural or spontaneous occurrences, he stopped using it. He adopted a wider view of the field and began to strive to build a higher level of theory, namely, the knowledge creation theory.

Sublimation of the theory of organizational knowledge creation

The year of 1986 was meaningful for Nonaka's life of research because both a paper and book published that became a turning point for his academic research.

Early that year, good news arrived from the United States. Nonaka's English paper, "The new new product development game" (co-authored with Hirotaka Takeuchi) was published in the famous *Harvard Business Review*. This was the beginning of Nonaka's name spreading throughout the world; until then, Nonaka self-deprecatingly had called himself a "domestic human being." Although his main concepts still comprised both "information processing" and "information creation," through his research on the new product development process his attention shifted from "information creation" to "knowledge creation."

Second, Nonaka and his colleagues published *Self-innovation of Enterprise: Chaos and Creative Management* (in Japanese) from Chuokoron-sha May that year[17]. This book was a revised collection of research on the ten companies chosen from the original case studies of eighteen Japanese companies, published in the journal *Will* (Chuokoron-sha) from January 1984 until June 1985. Nonaka reminisced: "For me, this book meant the turning-point from the concepts of information processing and information creation to knowledge creation."[18]

In researching the process of new product development, Nonaka discovered, unlike Simon's idea, situations in which human figures challenged almost insanely the "limits" of their abilities and overcame their individual limited information processing capability by means of teamwork. It led him to cherish the following idea: "by mere information processing human wishes could not be realized. Information creation neither was able to buy people in. The key role to justify own beliefs and thoughts might be played by knowledge creation process, neither by information processing nor by information creation."[19] Thus, Nonaka undertook to build the theory of "knowledge creation" from "information processing" and "information creation."

In December 1990, Nonaka's book *Management of Knowledge Creation: a Theory of Organizational Knowledge Creation* that summarized his research was published by Nihon Keizai Shinbunsha. It was the first book that established and saved a systematic treatment of the concept and theory of "knowledge creation."

Lying at the base of Nonaka Theory on creation of knowledge is a hypothesis that the dynamic interaction of tacit knowledge and explicit knowledge is the foundation of knowledge-creating. In order to verity it, Nonaka visited about twenty leading Japanese companies including Fuji Xerox, Honda, NEC, Epson, Canon, Matsuda and Matsushita, and conducted research with energy. His research on City (Honda), the Mini-copier (Canon) and the Home Bakery bread-making machine (Matsushita) – all of which were hit products – included minute fieldwork with interviews with the people in charge, the study of design drawings, and built up a theory on the process of organizational knowledge-creating, the outcome of which might be considered to be a masterpiece of case studies.

The 1990 book consisted of five chapters, which, except for Chapter 1, discussed the theory of organizational knowledge-creating, the management of organizational knowledge-creating, knowledge creation at enterprises as case study subject and overcoming organizational knowledge-creating. Many concepts that were mentioned in the book became the important components of Nonaka Theory – for example, "the interaction of tacit knowledge and explicit knowledge," "intellectual creation process," "middle-up-down management" that were mentioned in the book became the important components of Nonaka Theory. Therefore, anybody wishing to understand Nonaka Theory very well should read it.

In the following year, thanks to being awarded the Management Science Literature Award from the Japan Management Association, the book was recognized immediately by the academic circle in Japan.

In 1995, Nonaka's book, *The Knowledge-Creating Company*, co-authored with Hirotaka Takeuchi, was published by Oxford University Press. It was based fundamentally on *Management of Knowledge Creation,* and, while capturing the global views, proposed a new concept of "knowledge-creating company." The thrust was that, instead of the information processing paradigm of Herbert Simon's tradition, it reconsidered and rebuilt the entire areas of the organization's management (planning, product development, human resources, production, marketing, accounting and so on) from the perspective of the "knowledge creation" concept, and proposed a new management paradigm.[20] In particular, as expressed in the subtitle, *"How Japanese Companies Create the Dynamics of Innovation,"* Nonaka showed the importance of tacit knowledge even for Western people who had so far been considering Japanese management style as a mystery; and Nonaka clearly brought to Westerners' notice that the most important source of international competitiveness of Japanese companies was organizational knowledge creation. Mass media in America and Europe such as *The Economist* magazine, *the Wall Street Journal* and *Slone Management Review* all published articles or book reviews one after another.[21] As a result, the book won the Best Book of the Year from Association of American Publishers.

Several important concepts are contained in Nonaka Theory.

Tacit knowledge

The term tacit knowledge is not an invention of Nonaka. In Europe and America, it was known from *The Tacit Dimension* which was written by Michel Polanyi (1891–1976), a Hungarian-born philosopher.[22] In this book, Polanyi considers tacit knowledge, that is, "we can know more than we can tell" as a starting point when he rethinks human knowledge.[23] But since Polanyi's argument was limited only to the discussion on tacit knowledge itself, his contributions to Nonaka Theory were limited. The essence of Nonaka Theory involves the interaction of both tacit knowledge and explicit knowledge, and their process of conversion.

Ba

The first time that Nonaka used the word Ba was in his book *Organization and Market* in 1974.[24] The source of the word was the "field theory" proposed by Kurt Lewin (1890–1947), a Gestalt psychologist and the founder of group dynamics. But it was used for groups in the beginning.

According to the Dai Ji Sen Japanese Dictionary, Ba has multiple meanings, namely:

> (1) Place to put things or person. location; (2) Place that will be held; (3) Situation where that has been done. And its atmosphere; (4) Opportunity; (5) Such as theatre and film scene; (6) In Gestalt psychology, the environment and conditions that directly affect and related to the way of action and reaction and (7) In physics, space is considered that extends around the power of itself. Electromagnetic field. Gravitational field, and so on[25].

Nonaka's awareness of "place" went in-depth as knowledge-creating theory was developed.

1996: "It is here that they share experiences and synchronize their bodily and mental rhythms."[26]

1998: "For those unfamiliar with the concept, *ba* can be thought of as a shared space for emerging relationships."[27]

2002: "Such a composition of knowledge creation unit is '*ba*'."[28]

2003: "Status of the issues that the 'users' of knowledge are facing."[29]

2008: "We define *ba* as a shared context in motion, in which knowledge is shared, created, and utilized. *Ba* is the foundation for knowledge-creating activity."[30]

2010: "In order to create continuously knowledge by human interaction with dialogue and practice, it is necessary that a psychological, physical or virtual space which raises such interaction. We called such space as *ba* in Knowledge Creation Theory, and argued the importance in the process of organizational knowledge creation."[31]

In other words, it is possible that all relationship between human and human or human and nature may offer a ba of knowledge creation. In particular, with the progress of internet society, the virtual ba is more than real ba. Therefore, if we convey this concept to foreign countries, it is obviously impossible to equate "ba" with the word of "field" in English. For fear of misunderstanding about Nonaka Theory, Nonaka started using the Japanese word "ba" in his papers and books that were published after 1998 in the United States. Not surprisingly, Western society was unable to understand and did not accept the term at first, but with the diffusion of Nonaka Theory, many scholars came to accept the term and are presently using it.

Middle-up-down management

This is a Japanese-English word that was coined by Nonaka. We were able to find the source of the term from *The Adventures of Interpretation* (edited by Hiroshi Shimizu). In Chapter 5, Nonaka first used the term as a theme of a paper, namely, "The Methodology of Organizational Creation of Information: A Propose of Middle-up-down management."[32]

For the understanding of the term middle-up-down management, I will first briefly explain the traditional top-down management and bottom-up management. The former, emphasized the top management's decision-making, transmitted downward along the organizational hierarchy, which would be implemented and enriched as to its contents in lower management. The assumption of top-down management is the presence of a strong top executive.

The latter is a management style that emphasized that the information conveyed upward from the lower side of the organization would reversely influence the decision-making at the top echelon. The assumption of the bottom-up management was organizational democracy.

In contrast, "Middle-up-down management is an infinite regression of management. It aims to break off the essential contradiction between (a) the grand and abstract concept which was created by top on the one hand and (b) the concrete concept which was created on the other by the people in the field, who propose parametric ideas mediating the gap between (a) and (b)."[33] Nonaka stressed, "The fact that middle-up-down management emphasizes the dynamic role of the middle managers sharply distinguishes our theory from the conventional managerial wisdom."[34]

SECI model

SECI model is the most important tool for understanding the Nonaka Theory. Nonaka explains how tacit knowledge and explicit knowledge undergo conversions and related to organizational knowledge creation with the SECI model, which ultimately became the core part of Nonaka Theory. SECI is an acronym of socialization (from tacit knowledge to tacit knowledge), externalization (from tacit knowledge to explicit knowledge), combination (from explicit knowledge to explicit knowledge) and internalization (from explicit knowledge to tacit knowledge). It shows clearly the process of knowledge creation. Of these, externalization is the most confusing but important stage.

Needless to say, the SECI Model was not created suddenly, but was a product of continuous improvement that took many years. We can find its embryonic concept in *Management of Knowledge Creation* (1990) and its almost complete form in *The Knowledge-Creating Company* (1995).[35] And it took up the form in 2000,[36] but Nonaka has been improving on it, which shows his never-ending zest to better himself and his work.

Conclusion

In this chapter, I reviewed a vast corpus of the literature comprising Nonaka's huge publications list, and discussed the making and development of Nonaka Theory. It pointed to a developmental process from information processing to information creation, knowledge creation and organizational knowledge creation.

I conjecture that there are two reasons why Nonaka Theory was born in Japan yet his work has been widely studied outside Japan. First, the 1980s was the heyday of Japanese companies. In many countries, especially in the United States, both the public and private sector organizations had been researching the sources of the excellence of Japanese companies and published many books and reports. But because of the shortcomings due to the unfamiliarity with the language, culture, institutions and emotion, the authors were unconvincing. Apart from foreign researchers, Japanese researchers' publications almost remained at the level of general argument. In fact, there were few that dealt with the sources of the excellence of Japanese companies.

This circumstance may explain why Nonaka has been receiving attention in the world. He had been investigating leading Japanese companies for many years and developed a theory of his own.

The second reason relates to Nonaka's career and personality. He graduated from the School of Political Science and Economy, had worked for a large company, majored in marketing, organization theory and sociology at Berkeley and had been engaging in teaching and research at different universities (National Defence University, National universities and private university). Thus, his academic attainment is deep and his insights are broad. In addition, he had strong a creative desire to create an original theory or research method from a younger age, lead by the interaction of external factors and internal factors. As a synergy effect, Nonaka's original theory was born.

Overall, Nonaka Theory may not be perfect. Nonaka is aware of this, and is trying hard to complete and develop his theory even more. Nevertheless,

Nonaka Theory will stand the proof of time in the academic world. Indeed, as David J. Teece, a distinguished professor of Hass School of Business, University of California, Berkeley proposed: "Ikujiro Nonaka has become, for many of us, the new Peter Drucker-offering a deep intuitive understanding of management and the ability to see gaps and deficiencies in existing theories, as well as emerging trends which will impact on the nature of business enterprise and its management."[37]

Acknowledgements

I would like to thank Susan Moger who is the Senior Fellow in Leadership at Manchester Business School for her valuable comments.

Notes

1. Shigemitsu Ashizawa & Sadaaki Hidaka. (2007). *The Foundation of Modern Management.* Tokyo, Gakubunsha. p. 68 (in Japanese).
2. Ikujiro Nonaka. (2008). I and Management (1): Herbert A. Simon. Tokyo: Mitsubishi Research Institute *MRI CLUB*, January 2008. p. 22.
3. Ikujiro Nonaka and Hirotaka Takeuchi. (1995). *The Knowledge-Creating Company.* New York: Oxford University Press. p. x.
4. Ikujiro Nonaka. (1974). *Organization and Market.* Tokyo: Chikura Publishing. p. 1 (in Japanese).
5. Ibid., p. 1.
6. Ibid., p. 5.
7. Ibid., p. 102.
8. Ikujiro Nonaka. (2008). I and Management (1): Herbert A. Simon. Tokyo: Mitsubishi Research Insitute *MRI CLUB*. January 2008. p. 22 (in Japanese).
9. Ibid., p. 23.
10. Ibid., p. 25.
11. Ikujiro Nonaka. (2008). I and Management (2): Contingency Theory. Tokyo: Mitsubishi Research Institute *MRI CLUB*. February 2008. p. 20 (in Japanese).
12. I. Nonaka, T. Kagono, Y. Komatsu, A. Okumura & A. Sakashita. (1978). *Theory and Measurement of Organizational Phenomenon.* Tokyo, Chikura Publishing. p. 35 (in Japanese).
13. Ikujiro Nonaka. (1985). *Enterprise Evolution: Management of Information-Creating.* Tokyo: Nihon Keizai Shinbun-sha. p. ii (in Japanese).
14. Ibid., p. ii.
15. Ibid., pp. 132–157.
16. The property of living systems of being organized towards the attainment of ends without true purposiveness (*Shorter Oxford Dictionary*, 6th Edition).
17. Takeuchi, H., Sakakibara, K., Kagono, T., Okumura, A. & Nonaka, I. (1986). *Self-innovation of Enterprise: Chaos and Creative Management.* Tokyo: Chuokoron-sha (in Japanese).
18. Ikujiro Nonaka. (2008). I and Management (6): From Information Processing and Information-Creating to Knowledge-Creating. Tokyo: Mitsubishi Research Institute *MRI CLUB*. June 2008. p. 18 (in Japanese).
19. Ibid., p. 20.

20. Ikujiro Nonaka & Hirotaka Takeuchi (translated by Katsuhiro Umemoto). (1996). *The Knowledge-Creating Company*. Tokyo: Toyo Keizai Shinpo-sha. p. 369 (in Japanese).
21. Ibid. p. 371.
22. Michel Polanyi (translated by Keizo Sato). (1980). *The Tacit Dimension*. Tokyo: Kinokuniya (in Japanese).
23. Ibid., p. 15.
24. Ikujiro Nonaka. (1974). *Organization and Market*. Tokyo: Chikura Publishing. p. 40 (in Japanese).
25. Akira Matsumura. (1995). *Dai Ji Sen*. Tokyo: Shogakukan. p. 2087 (in Japanese).
26. Ikujiro Nonaka & Hirotaka Takeuchi. (1995). *The Knowledge-Creating Company*. New York: Oxford University Press. p. 85.
27. Ikujiro Nonaka & Noboru Konno. (1998). The concept of "*Ba*": building a foundation for knowledge creation. *California Management Review*. 40 (3), 40.
28. Ikujiro Nonaka. (2002). Concept of knowledge-based theory of enterprise. *Organization Science*. 36 (1), 6. (in Japanese).
29. Ikujiro Nonaka & Noboru Konno. (2003). *Methodology of Knowledge Creation*. Tokyo: Toyo Keizai Shinpo-sha. p. 198 (in Japanese).
30. Ikujiro Nonaka, Ryoko Toyama & Toru Hirata. (2008). *Managing Flow: A Process Theory of the Knowledge-Based Firm*. Hampshire: Palgrave Macmillan. p. 34.
31. Ikujiro Nonaka, Ryoko Toyama & Toru Hirata. (2010). *Managing Flow: A Process Theory of the Knowledge-Based Firm*. Tokyo: Toyo Keizai Shinpo-sha. p. 59 (in Japanese).
32. Hiroshi Shimizu (ed.) (1986) *The Adventures ofInterpretation*. Tokyo: NTT Publishing. pp. 456–485. (in Japanese).
33. Ikujiro Nonaka. (1990). *Management of Knowledge Creation*. Tokyo: Nihon Keizai Shinbun-sha. p. 123 (in Japanese).
34. Ikujiro Nonaka & Hirotaka Takeuchi. (1995). *The Knowledge-Creating Company*. New York: Oxford University Press. p. 127.
35. Ikujiro Nonaka. (1990). *Management of Knowledge Creation*. Tokyo: Nihon Keizai Shinbun-sha. p. 61. (in Japanese); Ikujiro Nonaka & Hirotaka Takeuchi. (1995). *The Knowledge-Creating Company*. New York: Oxford University Press. pp. 71–72.
36. Ikujiro Nonaka, Ryoko Toyama & Noboru Konno (2000) "SECI, *Ba* and leadership: a unified model of dynamic knowledge creation" *Long Range Planning*, 33, 5–34.
37. David J. Teece. (2008). Foreword: from the management of R&D to knowledge management *in* Ikujiro Nonaka, Ryoko Toyama & Toru Hirata (2008) *Managing Flow*. Hampshire: Palgrave Macmillan. p. ix.

References

Ashizawa, S. & Hidaka, S. (2007). *The Foundation of Modern Management*. Tokyo: Gakubunsha (in Japanese).

Konno, N. & Nonaka, I. (1995). *Intellectualizing Capability*. Tokyo: Nihon Keizai Shinbun-sha (in Japanese).

Mitsubishi Research Institute. (2008–2009). *MRI CLUB*, January 2008–March 2009 (in Japanese).

Nonaka, I. (1974). *Organization and Market*. Tokyo: Chikura Publishing (in Japanese).

Nonaka, I., Kagono, T., Komatsu, Y., Okumura, A. & Sakashita, A. (1978). *Theory and Measurement of Organizational Phenomenon*. Tokyo: Chikura Publishing (in Japanese).

Nonaka, I. (1985). *Enterprise Evolution: Management of Information-Creating*. Tokyo: Nihon Keizai Shinbun-sha (in Japanese).

Nonaka, I. (1990). *Management of Knowledge Creation*. Tokyo: Nihon Keizai Shinbun-sha (in Japanese).

Nonaka, I. & Takeuchi, H. (1995). *The Knowledge-Creating Company*. New York: Oxford University Press.

Nonaka, I. & Takeuchi, H. (translated by Umemoto, K.). (1996). *The Knowledge-Creating Company*. Tokyo: Toyo Keizai Shinpo-sha (in Japanese).

Nonaka, I. & Konno, N. (1998). The concept of '*Ba*': building a foundation for knowledge creation. *California Management Review*. 40, 40–54.

Nonaka, I., Toyama, R. & Konno, N. (2000). SECI, *Ba* and leadership: a Unified model of dynamic knowledge creation. *Long Range Planning*. 33, 5–34.

Nonaka, I. (2002). Concept of knowledge-based theory of enterprise. *Organization Science*. 36, 4–13 (in Japanese).

Nonaka, I. & Konno, N. (2003). *Methodology of Knowledge Creation*. Tokyo: Toyo Keizai Shinpo-sha (in Japanese).

Nonaka, I., Toyama, R. & Hirata, T. (2008). *Managing Flow: A Process Theory of the Knowledge-Based Firm*. Hampshire: Palgrave Macmillan.

Nonaka, I., Toyama, R. & Hirata, T. (2010). *Managing Flow: The Dynamic Theory of Knowledge -Based Firm*. Tokyo: Toyo Keizai Shinpo-sha (in Japanese).

Polanyi, Michael. (translated by Sato, K.) (1980). *The Tacit Dimension*. Tokyo: Kinokuniya (in Japanese).

Shimizu, H. (ed.) (1986). *The Adventures of Interpretation*. Tokyo: NTT Publishing (in Japanese).

Takeuchi, H. & Nonaka, I. (1986). The new new product development game. *Harvard Business Review*. Jan–Feb, 137–146.

Takeuchi, H., Sakakibara, K., Kagono, T., Okumura, A. & Nonaka, I. (1986). *Self-innovation of Enterprise: Chaos and Creative Management*. Tokyo: Chuokoron-sha (in Japanese).

Part II

4

Nonaka's 'Dynamic Theory of Knowledge Creation' (1994): Reflections and an Exploration of the 'Ontological Dimension'

Robert M. Grant

The impact of Nonaka (1994)

The first thing to note about Nonaka's theory of organizational knowledge creation is how radical it was. Prior to 1994, a great deal had been written about knowledge creation by firms, however, for the most part it emphasized two processes: first, discovery through search, as in the case of scientific discovery, technological research and market research (Jewkes et al., 1961; Von Hippel, 1988; McFadden, 1986); second, learning – especially learning-by-doing (Argyris & Schon 1978; Argote & Epple, 1990). Nonaka's theory of knowledge creation says little about the discovery of knowledge that is new to the world, rather its focus is on the processes through which knowledge develops and expands within organizations. Nonaka's 'knowledge spiral' comprises a number of organizationally-embedded processes through which knowledge is shared, transformed, integrated, reinterpreted and activated. In doing so, Nonaka (1994) constitutes a major advance in the emerging 'knowledge-based view of the firm'. For example, while Kogut and Zander (1992) had referred in general terms to the firm as an knowledge processing institution, Nonaka is much more explicit about the 'higher order organizing principles' through which 'individual and social expertise is transformed into economically useful products and services'; and about the operation of the firm as a 'social community of voluntaristic action' (Kogut & Zander, 1992, p. 384). As such, Nonaka also offers a conception of the firm that is distinctively different from either the shareholder or stakeholder views. In Nonaka's conceptualization, the firm does not exist to serve the interests of its constituents, whether shareholders or stakeholders; the firm is an institution for fostering the creativity that permits the transformation of silicon and copper into microprocessors, oil into plastic toys, and human imagination into computer games. In his subsequent writings, Nonaka has been more explicit about his view of the firm as an agent of value creation where 'profit is a result of such value creation, not a purpose in itself' (Nonaka et al., 2008).

A second characteristic of the paper is its richness in terms of the density of ideas and insights it embraces. At the core of the paper is Nonaka's 'knowledge spiral' through which knowledge is transformed and developed along the 'epistemological' and 'ontological' dimensions (more on this later). However, around this core are a wealth of observations and propositions. In several instances, Nonaka (1994) either anticipates or stimulates subsequent development in management thought or in management practice. For example:

- Nonaka's emphasis on the role of intentionality – and, more broadly, on consciousness, anticipated subsequent interest in the role of management attention – notably Ocasio's 'attention-based view of the firm' (Ocasio, 1997).
- Nonaka's concept of the hypertext organization envisages an organizational with the flexibility to 'switch between the various contexts of organizational knowledge creation to accommodate changing requirements from situations both inside and outside the organization' (Nonaka, 1994, p. 32). This capacity to reconfigure in order to adapt to the different 'contexts of knowledge creation such as the acquisition, generation, exploitation, and accumulation of knowledge'.This notion of an organization [that] is able to encompass both the 'heterarchical self-organizing activities of teams that are indispensable to generate new knowledge' and the 'hierarchical division of labour [that] is more efficient and effective for implementation, exploitation, and accumulation of new knowledge' parallels closely the concept of the 'ambidextrous organization' (O'Reilly & Tushman, 2004; Raisch et al., 2009).
- Nonaka's 'middle-up-down' of dynamic interaction within organizations has provided a key input into the recent reassessment of the role of middle management (see for example, Huy, 2002; Taylor & Helfat, 2009). When Nonaka's (1994) article appeared, the dominant perception of middle managers was as relics of hierarchical bureaucracies that were barriers to organizational change, inhibited organizational responsiveness, and could be dis-intermediated through information technology thereby permitting 'de-layering'. In Nonaka's model of the organization, middle managers are at the interface of top-down and bottom-up knowledge flows and mediate between top management and lower levels of the organization:

  > In the middle-up-down model, top management provides 'visions for direction' and also the deadline by which the visions should be realized. Middle management translates these visions into middle-range visions, which are to be realized in the fields – the groups. Middle

managers create their visions out of those from top and lower managers and materialize them vis-à-vis the two levels (Nonaka, 1994, p. 30).

- In terms of management practice, some of the most important contributions of Nonaka (1994) relate to the management of new product development. Much of the empirical foundation of his theory of knowledge creation was Nonaka's meticulous studies of product development processes in Japanese companies. In addition to Nonaka's emphasis on the dynamic interaction that nourishes creativity and problem solving in product development teams, Nonaka outlined his 'rugby-style' approach to product development the centrepiece of which was his 'scrum' methodology. This agile approach has had a transformational impact on software development over the past decade and a half (Schwaber & Beedle, 2002).

More generally, Ikujiro Nonaka is one of a small group of scholars – others include J-C Spender and Haridimos Tsoukas – that have created a bridge between epistemology and management introducing management scholars to the ideas of Plato, Descartes, Locke, Kant, Michael Polanyi and other prominent contributors to the philosophy of knowledge.

In drawing upon the three millennia of both Western and Eastern philosophy, Nonaka plays a major role in expanding our ideas of what constitutes knowledge and what management is about. At the outset, Nonaka defines knowledge as 'justified true belief' and takes pains to distinguish knowledge from information. (In doing so he clearly differentiates his knowledge creating view of the firm from the more established information-processing view of the firm, e.g., Galbraith, 1974.) However, as Nonaka develops his knowledge spiral, Nonaka moves from a Platonic view of knowledge towards recognition of knowledge as subjective realization, knowledge as social process, and knowledge as intention. In emphasizing the 'embodiment of knowledge' Nonaka challenges the tradition in Western epistemology that views a separation of mind and body. Nonaka rejection of Descartes' views on the independence of the human mind is consistent with the neurologically-based studies of Antonio Damasio (1994) and Maurice Merleau-Ponty's phenomenological approach to perception and consciousness (Merleau-Ponty, 1962). Nonaka's notion of 'knowledge of experience' which embraces 'personal bodily experience rather than "objective" scientific conceptualization' offers an approach to the development of intuition and the role of management wisdom whose impact on Western thinking about leadership has been mainly limited to expanding our ideas of intelligence to include social and emotional intelligence (Goleman & Boyatzis, 2008).

A key feature of Nonaka's bridging of management science and epistemology is that Nonaka's theory of organizational knowledge creation is not only an intellectual breakthrough. Although Nonaka's theory does not purport to be based upon inductive analysis, it is clearly grounded in his careful observation of product development processes within Japanese companies. This empirical grounding contributes to the realism of Nonaka's theory and, as I discuss later, may limit the scope of his theory.

In addition, there are themes within Nonaka (1994) that have yet to be developed and explored by management scholars. Some of the most interesting insights the article offers concern the dynamics of organizational evolution. Since the late 1990s, our understanding of organizational evolution has been transformed by concepts and principles drawn from complexity theory. However, a dominant influence on this literature has been Kauffman's NK framework and methodology (see for example, Levinthal, 1997). Within NK models, management activity is reduced to the fairly mundane task of searching its surrounding landscape. Nonaka, drawing upon different streams of literature (notably von Foerster, 1984; Jantsch, 1980), provides a very different analysis of organizational adaptation in which 'creative chaos' triggered by environmental fluctuation (or internal crisis) focuses attention on forming and solving new problems. The determinant of whether the resulting chaos is destructive or creative is reflection. The challenge for organizations is to 'institutionalize this reflection-in-action in its process as well as in its structure to make the chaos truly "creative"' (Nonaka, 1994, p. 28).

The Nonaka knowledge spiral: the epistemological dimension

Nonaka's spiral of knowledge creation within organizations involves the movement of knowledge within two dimensions: movement between different types of knowledge (the 'epistemological dimension') and the movement of knowledge between different levels – in particular between the individual level and the organizational level (the 'ontological dimension').

The first of these dimensions – between types of knowledge – has been the primary focus of subsequent commentary on and extensions of Nonaka's theory of knowledge creation, and is widely known as the 'SECI' framework. SECI comprises four modes of knowledge 'conversion':

- *Socialization* is the transfer of tacit knowledge among individuals through creating shared experiences.
- *Combination* involves the exchange and combination of individuals' explicit knowledge held by ndividuals through communicating information and 'reconfiguring existing information through the sorting, adding, re-categorizing, and re-contextualizing of explicit knowledge' (Nonaka, 1994, p. 19).
- *Externalization* involves the conversion of tacit into explicit knowledge – a process that involves dialogue among organizational members and the use of metaphors to articulate hidden tacit knowledge.

- *Internalization* involves the conversion of explicit into tacit knowledge – a process which is closely analogous to organizational learning and which typically involves experimentation.

Although Nonaka (1994) gives attention to each of these processes of 'knowledge conversion' (with a particular focus on externalization and combination), the emphasis is on the dynamic interaction between them:

> While each of the four modes of knowledge conversion can create new knowledge independently, the central theme of the model of organizational knowledge creation proposed here hinges on a dynamic interaction between the different modes of knowledge conversion. That is to say, knowledge creation centres on the building of both tacit and explicit knowledge and, more importantly, on the interchange between these two aspects of knowledge through internalization and externalization (Nonaka, 1994, p. 20).
>
> All of these conversion modes interact in a dynamic and continuous 'entanglement' to drive the knowledge creation process (Nonaka, 1994, p. 34).

Nonaka's 'ontological dimension' – the interaction between different organizational levels, comprising the individual, group, organizational, and inter-organizational domains – has received less attention. This provides the focus for the remainder of the paper.

The ontological dimension of Nonaka's knowledge spiral

The role of organizations in the creation, processing and application of knowledge remains a contentious issue in the knowledge based view. As Spender (1996) discusses, knowledge-based theorizing about the firm and the role of management has been bedevilled by confusion over the nature and extent to which organizations 'know'. Nonaka's approach concentrates upon the role of individuals and views organizations as producing a context and platform for knowledge creation by individuals:

> The organization supports creative individuals or provides a context for such individuals to create knowledge. Organizational knowledge creation, therefore, should be understood in terms of a process that 'organizationally' amplifies the knowledge created by individuals, and crystallizes it as a part of the knowledge network of organization.
>
> In this line, it is possible to distinguish several levels of social interaction at which the knowledge created by an individual is transformed and legitimized. In the first instance, an informal community of social interaction provides an immediate forum for nurturing the emergent

> property of knowledge at each level and developing new ideas (Nonaka, 1994, p. 17).

Social interaction is at the core of Nonaka's conception of the processes through which organizations promote knowledge creation. 'The interaction between knowledge of experience and rationality enables individuals to build their own perspectives on the world. Yet these perspectives remain personal unless they are articulated and amplified through social interaction' (Nonaka, 1994, p. 22). This social interaction creates a 'field' within which individual knowledge is shared and the interaction produces new, shared conceptualizations. Nonaka relates this notion of field to the concept of 'organizational mind' – which likens communication, knowledge sharing and cognitive interactions within an organization to the operation of the human brain. Key components of these interactions include:

- *Conceptualization* – the emergence and articulation of a common perspective through continuous dialogue between organizational member.
- *Crystallization* – the embodiment of the knowledge created within an organizational field into 'into some concrete form such as a product or a system' (Nonaka, 1994, p. 25).
- *Justification* – 'the process of final convergence and screening, which determines the extent to which the knowledge created within the organization is truly worthwhile' (Nonaka, 1994, p. 26).
- *Knowledge networking* – involves the integration of 'the concept that has been created, crystallized and justified... into the organizational knowledge-base' (Nonaka, 1994, p. 27).

Nonaka' explanation of the role of organizations in the processes through which knowledge is developed and deployed combines abstraction and specificity. The abstraction is the result of an analysis of knowledge processes which draws heavily upon epistemology and lacks a firm grounding within the economic tasks of organizations. Implicit in Nonaka's theory of knowledge creation is the normative idea that the goal of organizations is to maximize the creation of knowledge. Yet for most organizations, the primary goal is to produce goods and/or services and economic viability requires that revenues for such activities are at least equal to their costs. Nonaka's theory of knowledge creation takes little account of the costs of knowledge creation. Introducing costs into Nonaka's theory has important implications. If knowledge is costly to create, transfer and store, then specialization by organizational members is essential to efficiency.

Yet, Nonaka's analysis also includes implications that are notably specific in their predictions and recommendations. For example, Nonaka's discussion of the fairly abstract notions of field and organizational mind are closely linked to a specific organizational form – the self-organizing team.

Here Nonaka makes recommendations with regard to optimal team sizes (10 to 30 members), team structure (four to five core members who...form focal points in the team) and team dynamics (including the role of information redundancy). What is apparent here is that Nonaka's theory of knowledge creation draws heavily upon his deep empirical knowledge of product development among Japanese companies. Indeed, to the extent that Nonaka's theory of knowledge creation relies upon the insights derived from the context of product development practices, the scope of the theory may well be restricted.

In order to extend our understanding of the role of organizations – business enterprises in particular – knowledge processes we need to address these limitations of Nonaka's theory. In particular, we need to recognize:

- The role of knowledge within organizations.
- The economic context of organizations – notably the costs of knowledge creation and transfer and the need for efficiency among organizations.
- Subsequent developments in knowledge-based approaches to management, in particular, the nature and role of organizational capability.

The role of knowledge within organizations

Nonaka's theory of knowledge creation approach inevitably raises questions about what it means to create knowledge. Nonaka's views knowledge creation broadly – it relates less to the idea of novel discoveries as to the notion of expanding the organization's stock of knowledge. Nonaka's subjective concept of knowledge where knowledge is justified within the organization rather than externally implies that transferring knowledge among organizational members, combining separate items of knowledge, and reconceptualizing knowledge are all aspects of knowledge creation.

Exploration of the concepts of knowledge and knowledge creation give rise to a further insight. What constitutes 'knowledge creation' is exceedingly difficult to define. Is it the creation of new knowledge? If so, then new to whom: new to the world, new to the individual, or new to the organization? Alternatively, if knowledge creation simply the expansion in the amount of knowledge within an individual or an organization? Nonaka suggests the latter – thus much of what Nonaka describes as knowledge creation is the dissemination of knowledge within the organization. Yet, even here we encounter difficulty: if knowledge cannot be measured in any quantitative sense, what do we mean by an expansion in the stock of knowledge possessed by an individual or organization? Once we acknowledge the subjective character of knowledge and knowledge extends beyond data to action and meaning, then concepts of knowledge being created or expanding become problematic (Gourlay, 2006).

A distinction that has arisen in the literature on knowledge management and the knowledge-based view of the firm is between the creation/production/generation of knowledge and its application/utilization/exploitation. In my earlier work (Grant, 1996), I have relied heavily on this distinction as a means of distinguishing between the activities of individuals and organizations: while individuals are the primary agents for creating knowledge, organizations are engaged in applying this knowledge. However, one of the implications of the knowledge dynamics described by Nonaka's 'knowledge spiral' is that is impossible to distinguish knowledge creation from other knowledge processes. Yet, if we are unclear what it means to 'create knowledge' and if we are uncertain as to our ability to identify knowledge that has been created, what then is Nonaka's 'dynamic theory of organizational knowledge creation' a theory of?

The economic context

The answer to this problem is found in providing a more realistic context to knowledge processes of firms. Although Nonaka (1994) is a positive theory of how organizations create knowledge, its motivation is normative:

> This paper proposes a paradigm for managing the dynamic aspects of organizational knowledge creating processes ... A theoretical framework is developed which provides an analytical perspective on the constituent dimensions of knowledge creation. This framework is then applied in two operational models for facilitating the dynamic creation of appropriate organizational knowledge (Nonaka, 1994, p. 14).

Yet, the primary goal of firms is not to create knowledge. The goal of the firm is to create goods and services. Knowledge is an essential input, but before extolling the merits of knowledge creation by firms we need to introduce two qualifications. First, not all knowledge contributes to the firm's productive activities. My personal observations suggest that much of the knowledge sharing that occurs in organizations I am familiar with are devoted to gossip and complaint. Both of these knowledge-based activities are the sources of considerable pleasure to organizational members, but are dysfunctional in terms of organizational performance. Second, given the requirement that, in converting inputs into outputs, customers willingness to pay for these outputs must exceed the costs of the inputs, so too the value added by knowledge creation needs to exceed the costs of knowledge production.

Introducing the costs of creating and acquiring knowledge, offers a different perspective on the relationships between individuals and organizations than that offered by Nonaka. In Nonaka's knowledge spiral, the relationship between individual and organizational knowledge is wholly complementary. Yet, recognition of the costs involved in acquiring knowledge from individuals reveals the potential for organizational knowledge to substitute for individual knowledge (Figure 4.1).

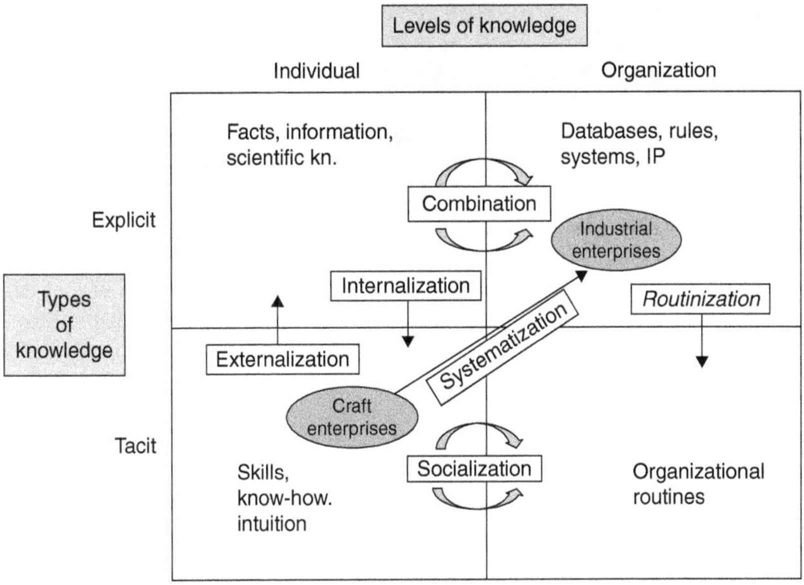

Figure 4.1 Reframing of Nonaka's epistemological and ontological dimensions to consider the two primary types of knowledge (explicit and tacit) and two levels of knowledge (individual and organization)

Source. The author.

Figure 4.1 shows Nonaka's four knowledge conversion processes (socialization, externalization, combination and internalization). However, once we distinguish different levels of knowledge, we can extend and refine these knowledge conversion processes. For example while Nonaka's concept of internalization refers primarily to individual's internalizing explicit knowledge, the internalization of systems, protocols and procedures by organizations involves *routinization*. Similarly, the externalization of individuals' tacit skills into the creation of industrial hardware and systems is a process we can refer to as *systematization*.

Systematization is the source of a fundamental economic and social transformation known as *industrialization* in which craft enterprises based upon individual, tacit knowledge, are replaced by industrial enterprises based upon explicit, organizational knowledge. The classic example is Ford Motor Company. Henry Ford's Model T was initially produced on a small scale by skilled workers, one car at a time. Ford's assembly line mass-production technology systematized that tacit knowledge and built it into machines and processes. The Ford industrial system was no longer dependent upon skilled craftsmen – the assembly lines could be operated by former farm workers and immigrants straight off the boat.

Systematization has also transformed service industries. When Ray Kroc discovered the McDonald brothers' hamburger stand in San Bernardino, California, he quickly recognized the potential for systematizing and replicating their process. The result was a global fast-food empire in which the McDonald's business model was replicated through operating manuals and training programs and now 400,000 employees serve 50 million customers. Most employees' culinary skills are rudimentary; the knowledge is embedded in McDonald's systems.

This systematization of knowledge offers massive potential for value creation. The craft enterprise is typically small scale and skilled employees appropriate a major share of the value that is created. Systematization allows replication and deskilling. Ford and McDonalds were able to expand worldwide. Other service transformed by systematization and now led by a few multinational corporations in hotels (Accor, Marriott, Hilton), car rental (Hertz, Avis), IT consulting (Accenture, IBM, HP/EDS) and in coffee shops (Starbucks).

This replication of knowledge is a powerful and lucrative source of scale economy. Its power is well recognized by venture capitalists: a key criterion for evaluating a new business proposal is: 'Is it scalable?' Low cost replication requires systematization: the translation of a business concept and operating system into a set of rules and procedures that provide programmed instructions for the creation of new business units.

In some cases, the substitution of individual knowledge by organizational knowledge embedded in a business system may be such that there are no individuals in the organization that can access and comprehend this embedded knowledge. In such instances, replication can still occur but it must be based upon imitation. In the case of Intel's microprocessors, fabrication processes are so complex and the know-how involved so deeply embedded within fine-tuned production systems that the only way that Intel can replicate its production capabilities is by replicating its lead plant in every detail – a process called 'Copy Exactly'.

Capability as organizational knowledge

The tendency for the 'ontological dimension' of Nonaka's knowledge spiral to receive much less attention than has been accorded to the 'epistemological dimension' is partly a reflection of the surge of interest in organizational knowledge that has emerged from a different research tradition. Within strategic management, research into the sources, structure, characteristics and application of organizational knowledge has been concentrated under the broad heading of 'organizational capability'. Since the early 1990s, organizational capability has emerged as one of the most active and vibrant topics of theoretical and empirical research within the field of strategic management (see Figure 4.2).

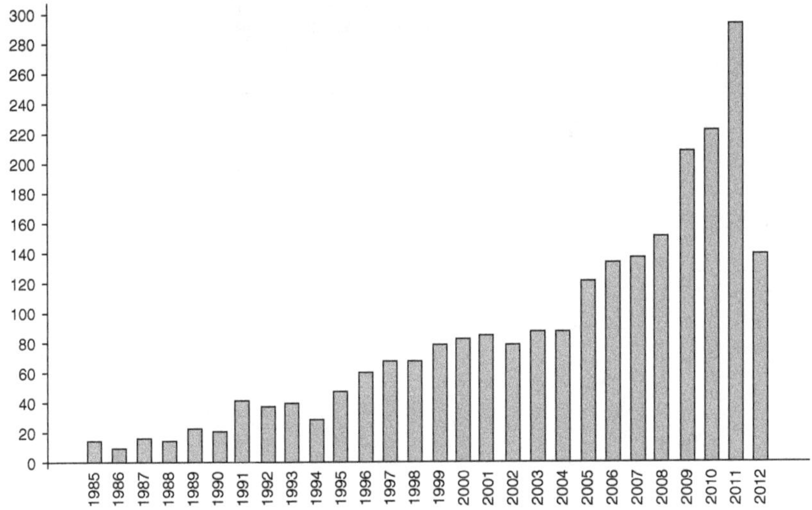

Figure 4.2 Number of articles appearing in management journals featuring 'capabilit' or 'competenc' in the title, January 1992–May 2012

Source: Web of Science.

Organizational capability is an organization's ability to perform a particular function or activity. Helfat and Lieberman (2002, p. 725) define organizational capability as a 'firm's capacity to deploy resources for a desired end result'. McKinsey & Co. are even simpler: 'We defined a capability as anything an organization does well that drives meaningful business results' (McKinsey & Company, 2010). However despite the practicality and simplicity of the concept, research into organizational capability has been bedevilled by terminological confusion: organizational capabilities have been defined in different ways and different terms have been used to describe the same construct. Thus, 'competency' and 'competence' (e.g., Selznick's (1957) 'distinctive competence' and Prahalad & Hamel's (1990) 'core competence') are synonymous with capability.

Identifying organizational knowledge with organizational capability offers two major gateways into comprehending knowledge processes within the firm. First, it allows us to describe, classify, even measure organizational knowledge since the organization's vast and complex mass of knowledge can be classified in terms of functions, value chain activities, or even as a hierarchy (Grant, 1996). The term 'capability architecture' has been used to describe the structuring of capabilities within firms (Jacobides, 2006; Bakhru & Grant, 2012). Second, it can help us unravel the relationships between individuals and organizations in creation and application of organizational knowledge.

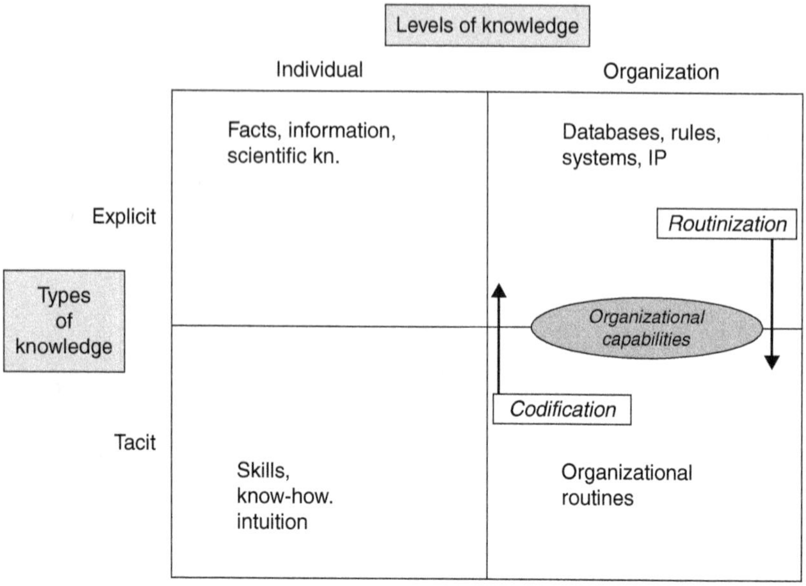

Figure 4.3 Organizational capability as the combination of both explicit and tacit organizational knowledge
Source: The author.

In terms of the knowledge classification shown in Figure 4.1, we may view organizational capability as the combination of both explicit and tacit organizational knowledge (see Figure 4.3). What does the vast and rapidly expanding capability literature tell us about the sources of organizational capability and the mechanisms through which they are created? Case-based research into the development of organizational capabilities points to four major organizational conditions that are conducive to high performing capabilities: processes, structure, motivation and organizational alignment.

Processes. Our understanding of organizational capabilities has been strongly influenced by the evolutionary economics tradition has provided the primary intellectual source of our thinking about organizational capability. Nelson and Winter (1982) view the capabilities of an organizational as the analogue of the skills of an individual and identify their foundation as routinized behaviour within organizations. While Nelson and Winter (1982) emphasized the emergent processes through which routines develop, more recent research shows that intention and conscious decision making gives organizational routines their potential to become sources of flexibility and change (Feldman & Pentland, 2003). Research into capability development in individual companies also recognizes the role of intentional decision and purposeful action – especially the leadership exercised by managers in establishing direction, allocating resources, conferring legitimacy and designing organizational processes (Kim, 1998; Raff, 2000; Rosenbloom, 2000; Montealegre, 2002).

It appears, therefore, that organizational capabilities develop through a combination of emergence and intentionality. Winter (2000) shows how learning occurs through the automatic accumulation of experiential knowledge ('covert learning') and deliberate experimentation and problem solving ('overt learning'). This combination of intentionality and automatic, routinized behaviour is modelled by Gavetti who shows how 'managers' cognitive representations of their strategic decision problem fundamentally drive organizational search, and therefore the accumulation of capabilities' (Gavetti, 2005, p. 599). Given this role of managerial leadership in building the coordinated activity that permits knowledge integration among individuals, I believe there is a strong case for following the operations management literature and adopting *process* rather than *routine* to refer to the mechanisms of coordinated activity within organizations. Whereas *routine* emphasizes spontaneous coordination and automaticity, process has the advantages of being readily recognized by practicing managers and avoiding the intellectual baggage that have become attached to routines. Our understanding of the micro-foundations of organizational capabilities have been extended greatly by the detailed empirical studies of operation and development of organizational processes by Pentland (1992), Pentland and Reuter (1994), Crowston (1997) and Narduzzo et al. (2000) and systematic approaches to the analysis and design of processes (Malone et al., 1999).

Structure. At the most basic level of analysis, there are two simple truisms that result from a knowledge based approach to the design of organizational structures. First, if the people involved in a process are to achieve the level of coordination necessary for high performance, then they need to be located within the same organizational unit. Second, decision-making authority needs to be located with those people who possess or have access to the knowledge relevant to those decisions.

Beyond these simplistic principles, the knowledge-based approach to designing effective structures rests primarily upon the principle of modularity. Modular systems are characterized, first, by near-decomposability (strong relationships within modules; weak relationships between modules) and second, by an organizational hierarchy bases upon integration needs. Activities and processes where coordination needs are most intense are organized into modules. This idea of hierarchies organized around intensity of interaction is a feature of Simon's analysis of the 'architecture of complexity' (Simon, 1969) and developed further by Thompson (1967) in his analysis of organizing on the basis of intensity of interdependence (from 'pooled interdependence, through 'sequential' interdependence, to the most intense – "reciprocal" interdependence').

In the development and exercise of organizational knowledge, modularity offers three key benefits:

- It takes account of 'bounded rationality' and, more generally, the constraints on the knowledge acquisition and retention capacities of individuals, which provide the rationale for knowledge specialization ('division of labour') among individuals and groups.
- It recognizes the innovation and learning advantages of decentralization (Sanchez & Mahoney, 1996).
- It is robust to external disruption (as outlined in Herbert Simon's example of the two watchmakers, Tempus and Hora (Simon, 1969, pp. 188–189).

Motivation. A common theme in the practitioner literature on organizational capability has been the notion of 'extraordinary performance from ordinary people' (Ward et al., 2007). Collins and Porras (1996) emphasize the role of an 'envisioned future' articulated as 'big, audacious, hairy goals' as essential to building outstanding firm capabilities. The academic literature also emphasizes the role of leadership in building the commitment which creates focus and subjugates individual interests to organizational goals. At the initial stage of the capability lifecycle, Helfat and Peteraf emphasize the need for a team organized around a central objective 'the achievement of which entails the creation of a new capability' (Helfat & Peteraf, 2003, p. 1000). Achieving directed purpose requires a combination of strategic focus and performance aspirations. Hamel and Prahalad use the concept of 'strategic intent' to refer to the combination of vision and target which 'envisions a desired leadership position and establishes the criterion the organization will use to chart its progress, (Hamel & Prahalad, 1989, p. 64). The implications for capability development are that: '...strategic intent creates an extreme misfit between resources and ambitions. Top management then challenges the organization to close the gap by building new competitive advantages' (Hamel & Prahalad, 1989, p. 66). The same principle drives Winter's (2000) satisficing model of capability development: when aspirations exceed actual performance, overt learning is reignited. Again we come back to the fundamental driver of performance in organizations: without motivation not only will individuals give less than their best but, equally important, they will not set aside their personal preferences and prejudices to integrate as a team. The role of strategic aspirations in driving capability building is apparent in almost all case studies of capability development among individual firms. Kim (1998) describes how Hyundai Motors built automotive capabilities through a sequence of projects each characterized by ambitious goals, tight time schedules, and a perception within each team of looming crisis deliberately engineered by top management.

Organizational alignment. Finally, there is the issue of *fit*. In the same way that different activities within the firm are complementary with one another (Milgrom & Roberts, 1990; Porter & Siggelkow, 2008), so too are the capabilities through allow these activities to be performed. The notion of fit between capabilities and other characteristics of the firm goes even wider – as the literature on organizational alignment (Powell, 1992) and corporate coherence (Teece et al., 1994; Tell, 2002) suggests – capabilities need to fit with the culture of the organization, with the skills and aptitudes of organizational members, with the heritage of the organization, and with the strategy. Imperfect alignment can stunt capability development: the failure of established airlines' low-cost subsidiaries (BA's Go, United's Ted, Continental's Continental Lite) reflects a misfit between the capabilities needed by a budget airline and traditions, behavioural norms and management systems of the legacy carriers. Corporate culture is a critical ingredient in this fit: in the privatized, competitive, deregulated telecom markets of the 21st century, former national monopolies such as British Telecom (BT), Deutsche Telecom and Verizon have had difficulty developing the capabilities needed to compete successfully outside their home markets.

Conclusion

There is no doubt as to the scale and scope of the impact of Nonaka's dynamic theory of organizational knowledge creation. But is it really a theory of knowledge creation? To the extent that we do not know what knowledge is (Nonaka (1994) certainly does not define knowledge with either precision or consistency), we cannot know what knowledge creation is or when it has occurred – hence a theory of knowledge creation seems impossible. If Nonaka's theory is something less than 'a dynamic theory of organizational knowledge creation," what then is it, how can we best utilize the penetrating insights that it offers, and how can we link it to subsequent research into knowledge management and the knowledge-based view of the firm? Let me offer a few thoughts.

First, the analysis of organizational knowledge creation set out in Nonaka (1994), from a scientific point of view, represents pre-theory rather than theory. It is a *model*: a simplified representation of a highly complex process that captures and categorizes the processes involved (Baden-Fuller & Morgan, 2010). As I have suggested, the model is neither comprehensive as to the mechanisms through which knowledge is created by social and cognitive interactions within organizations, nor is it explicit about many aspects of these mechanisms. The Nonaka 'knowledge spiral' and, in particular, the SECI model of knowledge conversion thereby offers enormous scope for development, verification, contradiction and adaptation that has only partially been taken up by subsequent researchers.

Second, it is clear from the examples and illustrations that Nonaka uses that his theory is heavily grounded within his empirical research into new product development among Japanese companies. This raises questions concerning the domain ('boundary conditions') of Nonaka's theory of knowledge creation. Does the knowledge spiral through which knowledge is concerted through social interaction apply to all forms of organizational knowledge, or to just certain forms? As the earlier discussion of the nature and pre-conditions of organizational capability indicate, many forms of organizational knowledge are developed without obvious reliance on the types of interaction that Nonaka describes. I conclude that processes of knowledge conversion and the roles that Nonaka attributes to conceptualization, crystallization, justification and networking are suitable primarily to team-based creative activities such as new product development rather than to the entire range of productive activities within organizations.

And what about the range of organizations to which Nonaka's theory applies? Clearly, large companies with their product development teams can profit greatly from the insights that Nonaka's SECI model offers. But what about small firms? Their dependence on inter-firm rather than intra-firm knowledge transfers may mean that managing explicit knowledge through externalization and combination may play a particularly important role.

Third, in terms of understanding more fully, the relationship between individuals and organizations in the production and application of knowledge, the concept of organizational capability offers huge potential which has been only partially revealed. Whereas the concept of organizational capability encounters difficulties of definition, identification and measurement which have made the field; these difficulties pale into insignificance compared to those of knowledge.

In linking Nonaka's theory of organizational knowledge creation to the capability literature, the concept of dynamic capability offers a potentially useful bridge. Despite the terminological confusion – Danneels (2008, p. 536) describes the field as 'a semantic morass," whereas Zahra et al. (2006, p. 917) observe that the literature 'is riddled with inconsistencies, overlapping definitions, and outright contradictions' – the huge interest in the topic points to our lack of understanding into how organizations can develop the capacity for change. The dynamics of organizational knowledge creation described by Nonaka have the potential to provide the much needed 'microfoundations' for dynamic capabilities which may be applicable, not just to new product development, but to other capabilities where the key to effectiveness is creativity and reconceptualization rather than routinization. Such dynamic capabilities might including new business development, strategic planning, novel approaches to product differentiation, and business model innovation.

References

Argote, L., & Epple, D. (1990). Learning curves in manufacturing. *Science*. 247 (4945), 920–924.

Argyris, C., & Schon, D. A. (1978). *Organizational Learning.* Reading, MA: Addison-Wesley.

Damasio, A. (1994). *Descartes' Error: Emotion, Reason and the Human Brain.* New York: Putnam.

Baden-Fuller, C., & Morgan, M. (2010). Business models as models. *Long Range Planning.* 43, 156–171.

Bakhru, A., & Grant, R.M. (2012). *Beyond Core Competence: Building Capability Systems in New Businesses.* Working Paper, Dept. of Management, Bocconi University.

Collins, J. C., & Porras, J. I. (1996). Building your company's vision. *Harvard Business Review.* 74 (4), 65–77.

Crowston, K. (1997). A coordination theory approach to process design. *Organization Science.* 8, 157–175.

Danneels, E. (2008). Organizational antecedents of second order competences. *Strategic Management Journal.* 29, 519–543.

Feldman, M. S., & Pentland, B. T. (2003). Reconceptualizing organizational routines as a source of flexibility and change. *Administrative Science Quarterly* 48, 94–118.

Galbraith, J. R. (1974). Organization design: an information processing view. *Interfaces.* 4, 28–36.

Gavetti G. (2005). Cognition and hierarchy: rethinking the microfoundations of capabilities' development. *Organization Science.* 16 (6), 599–617.

Goleman, D., & R. Boyatzis. (2008). Social intelligence and the biology of leadership. *Harvard Business Review.* 86 (9), 74–81.

Gourlay, S. (2006). Conceptualizing knowledge creation: a critique of Nonaka's theory. *Journal of Management Studies.* 43 (7), 1415–1436.

Grant, R. M. (1996). Prospering in dynamically-competitive environments: organizational capability as knowledge integration. *Organization Science.* 7 (4), 375–399.

Hamel, G., & Prahalad, C. K. (1989). Strategic intent. *Harvard Business Review.* 67 (3), 63–76.

Helfat, C. E., & Lieberman, M. B. (2002). The birth of capabilities: market entry and the importance of pre-history. *Industrial and Corporate Change.* 11 (4), 725–760.

Helfat, C. E., & Peteraf, M. A. (2003). The dynamic resource-based view: capability lifecycles. *Strategic Management Journal.* 24 (10), 997–1010.

Huy, Q. N. (2002) Emotional balancing of organizational continuity and radical change: the contribution of middle managers. *Administrative Science Quarterly.* 47, 31–69.

Jantsch, E. (1980). *The Self-Organizing Universe.* Oxford: Pergamon Press.

Jewkes, J., Sawers, D., & Stillerman, R. (1961). *The Sources of Invention.* London: Macmillan.

Jacobides, M. G. (2006). The architecture and design of organizational capabilities. *Industrial and Corporate Change.* 15, 151–171.

Kim, L. (1998). Crisis construction and organizational learning: capability building in catching-up at Hyundai Motor. *Organization Science.* 9 (4), 506–521.

Kogut, B., & Zander, U. (1992). Knowledge of the firm, combinative capabilities and the replication of technology. *Organization Science.* 3, 383–397.

Levinthal, D. A. (1997). Adaptation on rugged landscapes. *Management Science.* 43, 934–950.

Malone, T. W., Crowston, K. G., Lee, J., Pentland, B., Dellarocas, C., Wyner, G., Quimby, J., Osborn, C. S., Bernstein, A., Herman, G., Klein, M., & O'Donnell, E. (1999). Tools for inventing organizations: toward a handbook of organizational processes. *Management Science.* 45, 425–443.

McFadden, D. (1986). The choice theory appoach to market research. *Marketing Science*. 5 (4), 275–297

McKinsey & Company. (2010). McKinsey Global Survey results: building organizational capabilities. *McKinsey Quarterly*, March.

Merleau-Ponty, M. (1962). *The Phenomenology of Perception*. London: Routledge.

Milgrom, P. R., & Roberts, J. (1990). The economics of modern manufacturing: technology, strategy, and organization. *American Economic Review*. 80 (3), 511–528.

Montealegre, R. (2002). A process model of capability development: lessons from the electronic 6)e strategy at Bolsa de Valores de Guayaquil. *Organization Science*. 13 (5), 514–531.

Narduzzo, A., Rocco, E., & Warglien, M. 2000. Talking about routines in the field. In Dosi G., Nelson R. R., & Winter S. G., (eds) *The Nature and Dynamics of Organizational Capabilities*. Oxford: Oxford University Press (pp. 27–50).

Nelson, R. R., & Winter, S. (1982). *An Evolutionary Theory of Economic Change*. Cambridge, MA: Harvard University Press.

Nonaka, I. (1994). A dynamic theory of organizational knowledge creation. *Organization Science*. 5, 14–37.

Nonaka, I., Toyama, R., & Hirata, T. (2008). *Managing Flow: A Process Theory of the Knowledge-Based Firm*. London: Palgrave Macmillan.

Ocasio, W. (1997). Towards an attention-based view of the firm. *Strategic Management Journal*. 18 (Summer Special Issue), 187–206.

O'Reilly, C. A., & Tushman, M. L. (2004). The ambidextrous organization. *Harvard Business Review*. 82 (4), 74–81.

Pentland, B. T. (1992). Organizing moves in software support hot lines. *Administrative Science Quarterly*. 37, 527–548.

Pentland, B. T. & Rueter, H. H. (1994). Organizational routines as grammars of action. *Administrative Science Quarterly* 39, 484–510.

Porter, M. E., & Siggelkow, N. (2008). Contextual interactions within activity systems and sustainability of competitive advantage. *Academy of Management Perspectives*. 22 (2), 34–56.

Powell, T. C. (1992). Organizational alignment as competitive advantage. *Strategic Management Journal*. 13, 119–134.

Prahalad, C. K., and Hamel, G. (1990). The core competence of the corporation. *Harvard Business Review*. 68(3), 79–91.

Raisch, S., Birkinshaw, J., Probst, G., & Tushman, M. L. (2009). Organizational ambidexterity: balancing exploitation and exploration for sustained performance. *Organization Science*. 20, 685–695.

Raff, D. M. (2000). Superstores and the evolution of firm capabilities in American bookselling. *Strategic Management Journal*. 21, 1043–1059.

Rosenbloom, R. S. (2000). Leadership, capabilities and technological change: the transformation of NCR in the electronic era. *Strategic Management Journal*. 21, 1083–1103.

Sanchez, R., & Mahoney, J. T. (1996). Modularity, flexibility, and knowledge management in product and organizational design. *Strategic Management Journal*. 17 (Winter special issue), 63–76.

Schwaber, K., & Beedle, M. (2002). *Agile Software Development with Scrum*. Upper Saddle River, NJ: Prentice Hall.

Selznick, P. (1957). *Leadership in Administration*. New York: Harper and Row.

Simon, H. A. (1969). The architecture of complexity. In H.A. Simon, *The Sciences of the Artificial*, Cambridge, MA: MIT Press, pp. 192–229.

Spender, J.-C. (1996). Making knowledge the basis of a dynamic theory of the firm. *Strategic Management Journal*. 17 (winter special issue), 46–62.
Taylor, A., & Helfat, C. E. (2009). Organizational linkages for surviving technological change: complementary assets, middle management, and ambidexterity. *Organization Science*. 20, 718–739.
Teece, D., Rumelt, R., Dosi, G., & Winter, S. (1994). Understanding corporate coherence: theory and evidence. *Journal of Economic Behavior and Organization*. 23, 1–30.
Tell, F. (2002). *Strategy, Capabilities and Corporate Coherence: Exploring Some Dynamics of Learning*. Department of Management and Economics, Linköping University, Sweden.
Thompson, J. D. (1967). *Organizations in Action*. New York: McGraw Hill.
Von Foerster, H. (1984). Principles of self-organization in a socio-managerial context. In H. Ulrich, & G. J. B. Probst (eds), *Self-organization and Management of Social Systems*, Berlin: Springer-Verlag.
Von Hippel, E. (1988)., *The Sources of Innovation.*, New Yorkel: Oxford University Press.
Ward, K., Bowman, C., & Kakabadse, A. (2007). *Extraordinary Performance from Ordinary People*. Amsterdam: Elsevier.
Winter, S. G. (2000). The satisficing principle in capability learning. *Strategic Management Journal*. 21, 981–996.
Zahra, S. A., Sapienza, H. J., & Davidsson, P. (2006). Entrepreneurship and dynamic capabilities: a review, model and research agenda. *Journal of Management Studies*, 43 (4), 917–955.

5

The Purpose of the Firm As Proposed by Nonaka: A Review Based on the Aristotelian–Thomistic Tradition

Guillermo Fariñas Contreras

Introduction

In the introduction to one of his most recent books, Ikujiro Nonaka, referring to a knowledge-creating firm purpose, asserts: 'In our view, the essence of business is not about bettering the competence to maximize profit. It is about the relentless pursuit of the firm´s own standard of excellence' (Nonaka, Toyama, & Hirata, 2008, p. 3). And further: 'Excellence emerges only with an unyielding commitment and practice to serve the common good of the company, its employees, its customers and other stakeholders, and the larger society, based on the company´s own vision and values' (*Idem*, p. 3). And after studying successful cases of Japanese companies which exemplify the creation of knowledge, he adds: 'what these firms pursue ultimately is the happiness of the community and themselves (...) communities of individuals driven by their own beliefs, shared dreams, and a vision relentlessly pursued to create unique value leading to happiness in the community' (*Idem*, p. 243).

Focusing on some key terms that are present in his writings may help better assess Nonaka's understanding on the purpose of the firm. In his seminal work, *The Knowledge-Creating Firm*, he proposes the need to create a *knowledge vision* (Nonaka & Takeuchi, 1995, pp. 227–228). This concept becomes a key element in his theory of the *knowledge-creating organization* (Nonaka, Toyama, & Hirata, 2008, pp. 26–29). When the author addresses knowledge, he relates it to *truth* (*Idem*, p. 11).[1] Then, when he adopts the Aristotelian *Phronesis,* he associates *(common) good* with *purpose* (*Idem*, pp. 55–57).[2] From the classical tradition, he takes the ideas of *excellence* and *happiness* present, respectively, in the purpose of firms and in the aspirations of its members (*Idem*, p. 57).[3]

Aristotle was possibly the first author to relate truth, good, purpose, perfection and happiness.[4] The Medieval thinker Thomas Aquinas complemented these ideas.[5] Based on the writings of these authors, this chapter proposes identifying the ways in which these topics converge in organizational human action. Thus, it attempts to find a conceptual basis in the classical tradition for Nonaka's proposal on the purpose of the firm.

This chapter is divided into four sections. The first one summarizes Aristotelian-Thomistic tradition regarding these key ideas. The second one reviews Nonaka's theory on the purpose of the firm. The third one delves into the notion of the common good. Finally, the fourth one integrates personal and organizational excellence with the purpose of the firm.

The classical proposition

'Although the end may be last in the order of execution, it is first in the order of the agent's intention' (Aquinas, 1947, I–II, q. 1, art. 1). This statement made by the medieval philosopher falls within the framework of Aristotle's teleological proposal: for man, as well as for all reality, there is a perfective order which is achieved in time, an order which, in man, is attained through action. It is a teleological order, an order aimed toward purposes that are viewed as goods to be attained. This is because, according to the Stagirite, 'the good has rightly been declared to be that at which all things aim' (Aristotle, 1985, 1094a 3). Thus, the good has reason of purpose for the one who desires it (Aristotle, 1985, 1097a 15–25). One may conclude that, in human action, good and purpose are interchangeable in both their apprehension and fulfilment.

Aristotle also asserted that the human faculty that best adapts to good is the will. But for the good to be the object of will, that is, for it to be desired, it must first be known, because what does not fall within one's intellect cannot be the object of will (Aristotle, 1907, 433b). Thomas Aquinas (1947, I–II, q. 9, art. 1, co.) states that '(...) the intellect moves the will; since the good itself is apprehended under a special aspect as contained in the universal true'.[6]

The Aristotelian assertion that truth is in the mind while good is in reality (1953, 1027b) does not contradict Aquinas aforementioned statement. The fact that the truth is in the intellect and the good is in things does not necessarily mean that the good is not also in the intellect. It is in things as something real, whereas it is also in the intellect once it is known, but known as the good. Certainly, as far as we know, reality precedes the good according to reason (Aquinas, 1947, I, q. 5, art. 2, co.) but, there is no actual precedence, given that it is the same to be of the thing and to be of the good: the thing *is* and, at the same time, the thing *is good.*

Aquinas continues to argue that being, truth and good identify themselves in reality (*sunt ídem in re*), but differ in reason (Aquinas, 1947, I, q. 5, art. 1, co; I, q. 16, art. 3, co.). Rational differences consist in new knowledge of the same reality. Thus, necessary reality, or that which cannot be otherwise, does not change; it is our knowledge of that reality that improves (or deteriorates). In contrast, contingent reality may be transformed by human action. On the basis of this concept, one may assert that knowledge does not only change because known reality mutates, but that knowledge gives rise to the transformation of reality in human affairs, such as organizational reality. For example, the productive process will change if we conceive it better (theoretical knowledge) and execute it masterfully (practical knowledge and virtuosity in action.)

The goods – and, therefore, the ends – are multiple and varied. In his *Nicomachean Ethics*, Aristotle affirms that 'as there are many actions, arts, and sciences, their ends are also many; the end of the medical art is health, that of shipbuilding is a vessel, that of strategy is victory, that of economics is wealth' (1985, 1094a 5–9). Now then, this multiplicity possesses a hierarchy. This is so because, in reality, not everything is in the same plane or has the same value. And since reality and good are interchangeable, it follows that there exist several levels of good.

The hierarchy of goods and ends demands a gradation of the corresponding levels of knowledge. If the knowledge of the good follows the being of things, and if the greater the entity or the complexity of reality, the greater the knowledge that is required, then a greater good needs greater knowledge and a greater effort to apprehend it.

Similarly, if the good is apprehended by different acts of knowledge, then it is not the same good for each case, although they are all goods. If at one moment we apprehend an aspect of reality and then another aspect, both are different goods belonging to the same reality. Again, the *hierarchy* of goods is manifest.[7]

In addition, because the moral good is especially present in living beings with free will (Aristotle, 1953, 1020b 20–24), we must distinguish three degrees of goods: those that are external, those that belong to the body and those that belong to the soul (Aristotle, 1985, 1098b 10–18). Hence, some goods are more perfect than others, demonstrating that the good indicates *perfection* (Aristotle, 1933–1935, 246a 13–14).

As I claimed before, one thing is the knowledge of the truth and another is the knowledge of the good. This is the basis for the classical distinction between *theoretical reason* and *practical reason*. Presenting the good as good belongs, in general terms, to *practical reason* and, in this regard, one alludes to the fact that the good is the first thing that falls within practical apprehension (Aquinas, 1947, I–II, q. 4, art. 2, ra, *and* I–II, q. 13, art. 5, ra).[8] Thus, the good is the truth of the practical intellect because it is the end apprehended from the operation.

Aristotle insists that the good is the *final cause* of the activity (1953, 983a 31–35; and 1985, 1097a 15–25). He also argues that the notion of an *end* implies *perfection*, the finishing point, completion, so if the good is the final cause, the good is perfect for each reality (Aristotle, 1953, 1021b 23–24).

Another view of the good as being perfectible as an end is that the good is perfectible as another mode of completion, in the sense that it is that which is desired or craved by the one who still does not possess it, and loved or enjoyed by the one who has already attained it.

The allusion to the *final cause* in the knowledge of *practical judgment* is essential in order to understand the good because it is the final cause to be discovered and the most important one from the ontological point of view.[9] The final cause consists in the *order of the universe* because, since it is the highest cause, it has to be the most universal, effective and profound of all. The good of the universe consists in a twofold order, to wit, the order of its parts among themselves and the order of the whole universe. This is because, 'according to the Philosopher, in Book XII of his *Metaphysics,* the excellence of order in the universe appears in two ways, first, inasmuch as the whole universe is referred to something beyond the universe, as an army to its leader: secondly, inasmuch as the parts of the universe are referred to one another, like the parts of an army; and the second order is for the sake of the first' (Aquinas, 1905, b. I, ch. 78, n. 4).[10]

The ultimate good of man is *happiness* (Aristotle, 1985, 1095a 14–21). Happiness is characterized as the attainment of the ultimate end and the perfect good (Aristotle, 1985, 1096a and 1099b). The will cannot stop desiring it.[11] Identifying the good that fulfils the will and constitutes the happiness of the human person is the fruit of a superior knowledge, the *inborn disposition of knowledge* or *synderesis* (Aquinas, 1947, II–II, q. 47, art. 6).[12] Identifying and choosing the means to attain proper happiness is the task of the habit of prudence or *phronesis.*

For Aristotle, 'it is thought to be the mark of a man of practical wisdom to be able to deliberate well about what is good and expedient for himself' (Aristotle, 1985, 1140a 24–26). This is not regarding what is produced – which is outside of man and would correspond to the *habit of art or technique* (Aristotle, 1985, 1140a 1–23)[13] –but regarding the good and the evil of the man who actually generates such production, which is that of *ethics.*

Determining the goodness of certain ethical actions and behaviours is no trivial matter. In human activities the superiority of a good to be attained over another, or of an action to be carried out over another, is not so clear-cut. This is when *practical advice* or *eubolia* must be used in order to deliberate on the potential goods or the potential actions (Aristotle, 1985, 1142a 32–b 33). Additionally, there is uncertainty regarding these potential goods because they are yet to be a reality, given that they are in the future; they are to be the product of human action.

This chapter proposes that, based on the previous assertions, it has been possible to examine the relationship between end, truth, good, excellence and happiness according to Aristotle and Aquinas. These topics are present in Professor Nonaka's proposal, which is analyzed in the next sections. The points that connect it with the classical tradition are mentioned as his thesis is explained, or his works are cited to find their relations with Aristotelian-Thomistic philosophy.

Nonaka's proposition

As everyone knows, knowledge plays a leading role in the publications of Professor Nonaka. For example, he has adopted the concept of vision from corporate strategy. He qualifies vision as a cognitive concept and calls it 'knowledge vision'. He frequently uses this term in his writings, especially when he describes his theory of the knowledge-creating firm (Nonaka, Toyama, & Hirata, 2008).[14] The author describes this component of his model with broad expressions, such as this 'is an ideal picture of how we want to be' (Nonaka, Toyama, & Hirata, 2008, p. 28), and 'a mental image of a possible and desirable future state of the organization' (Nonaka & Toyama, 2005, p. 432).[15] A vision can be both a corporate mission, such as a set of values, a set of ideas or a plan (von Krogh, Kazuo, & Nonaka, 2000, p. 104). In fact, the examples that follow to illustrate this point are both missions – as in the case of Honda, which is 'to provide good quality cars for their clients' – and values – as in the case of Eisai, which is 'human health care'.

Regarding corporate fields of action, a cognitive vision must provide a mental map of (1) the world in which the members of the organization live, (2) the world in which they would like to live and (3) the organizational knowledge required to attain and create such a world, in order to go from one world to the other (von Krogh, Kazuo, & Nonaka, 2000, p. 103). In other words, 'the current and future organizational state and the broad contours of knowledge that the organization should seek and create in order to move from the current to the future state' (Nonaka, von Krogh, & Voelpel, 2006, p. 1188). The strong cognitive emphasis of this term is obvious in Nonaka's writings. It would resemble the Aristotelian notion of the term 'purpose' not as the final cause, but as formal, efficient and material causes, because it describes the actions required to attain it.[16] A 'knowledge vision gives the firm direction and focus concerning the knowledge to be created' (Nonaka, Toyama, & Hirata, 2008, p. 27).

In his seminal work of 1995, Nonaka states that the knowledge vision is similar to the organizational intention, 'which is defined as an organization's aspiration to its goals' (Nonaka & Takeuchi, 1995, p. 74). Now then, aspiration refers to the effort needed to attain the desired objective, the good present in each goal. This would correspond to that which Aristotle proposed, which is that the good is the end of all activity (1953, 983a 31–34).

In his early writings, in which he develops the concept of knowledge vision, Nonaka does not propose the final cause, that is, the good present and desired in the knowledge vision, the reason for attaining it. It is in his more recent works that he explains about the future aspired by the corporation, stating that, 'the knowledge vision arises from confronting the fundamental questions: "Why do we do exist?" By going beyond profits and asking "Why do we do what we do?" the mission and domain of the firm becomes defined"' (Nonaka & Toyama, 2005, p. 424).

The knowledge vision does not demand a single purpose for the firm. Each firm should discover it based on its own condition and context. This could be explained by the cognitive focus exclusively adopted by Nonaka in his early writings on this topic. Up until the time when he takes into consideration the virtue of prudence – *phronesis,* which requires the consideration of the good – he stays within the realm of *truth,* which is really *verisimilitude,* that is, practical, contingent and non-definitive knowledge.[17] In order to be consistent with his proposals, the truth put forward in the knowledge vision was not predetermined; it was yet to be discovered or realized and could be changed.

However, when he addresses the good, goodness, what is good, as in *phronesis,* he proposes a firm foothold, which must be objective, not dependent on subjectivity and context. On the contrary, it should be a guideline to be more dynamic, to aim at new things. He seems aware of the nefarious consequences that could result from the moral relativism of corporate leaders. It is then that his proposal on the purpose of the firm is linked to both the individual and collective good. In his own words, 'It is this kind of value of the *common good* that gives a firm an absolute value to pursue that is a goal in itself' (Nonaka & Toyama, 2007, p. 381).[18] The following paragraph allows us a better view of the importance of the common good regarding the purpose that is traditionally assigned to the firm. According to Nonaka, the common good is,

> not simply a means to maximize profits, which is the end that is implicitly assigned to management academics in their theories of the firm. In his introduction to his *Metaphysics,* Aristotle asserts that, 'All men have by nature the desire to know', and, in his *Nicomachean Ethics,* he states that, 'All art and all research and, similarly, all action and free will seem to tend toward some good'. In conclusion, man must search for the good in himself, not because that good provides benefits or advantages over others. They are not simply means, but intrinsic goods, such as happiness, or more specifically for the firm, for its own fulfillment. Money is not a good in itself, but a means to an end, which is the good. Profits are something that is always obtained as a result of the exercise of *Phronesis* instead of the final goal of the firm (Nonaka, Toyama, & Hirata, 2008, pp. 56–57).

In a recent article, he elaborates on this idea, saying that, 'Don't get us wrong – maximizing shareholder wealth can lead to goodness, as can making a profit. But these leaders [who practice *phronesis*] set their sights higher: They believe that their actions should have a moral purpose' (Nonaka & Takeuchi, 2011,

p. 61). Later on, in the same text, he quotes a Toyota´s former president, who said that, 'Doing the right things, when required, is a calling from on high'.[19] Moral purpose and doing the right thing are linked to Aristotelian ethics, to doing the right thing for the one who acts.

From this point of view, this chapter puts forth that one can say that Nonaka believes that the ultimate end of the firm is about the common good, which is closely related to goodness, with the good. The following are some considerations of these notions.

The common good

As previously quoted, Aristotle stated that, 'the good is that to which all things tend' (1985, BK1094a 1–3). And things tend toward their own perfection; therefore, the greater the perfection achieved, the greater the good. Good is that which makes the entity more perfect (Aristotle, 1946, 1252b).[20] For man, his perfection is to increasingly become a man, which requires his developing his cognitive and volitional faculties. It is growing in the intellect of his different acts and habits; of the will in his different acts and virtues. Hence, when seeking excellence in his intellectual habits and in his moral virtues, man becomes better. For man, the good will then become that which makes him a better man, which perfects him.

Nonaka pursues this idea when he indicates that, 'at the end, the ultimate goal, both for individuals and for organizations, must be the relentless pursuit of excellence. Indeed, MacIntyre sees the ultimate goal of practice as achieving "standards of excellence," an idea that can also be found in Aristotle' (Nonaka, Toyama, & Hirata, 2008, p. 57).[21] That is, the Japanese author would be proposing that the purpose sought by the firm is related to the quest for excellence, for its own perfection. And that this purpose is intrinsically related to the excellence of the people that make up the firm. One way in which this happens is when the members of the firm cultivate *phronesis* so the firm may be resilient – because growth in the virtue of prudence make them better professionals and better people. 'According to Aristotle, *phronesis* is the character embodied in a good man' (Nonaka, Toyama, & Hirata, 2008, p. 57). And 'is acquired through the pursuit of excellence, the effort to perfect one´s craft, which makes one a virtuous artisan' (Nonaka, Toyama, & Hirata, 2008, p. 14).[22]

This relationship between the perfection of the organization and that of its members is found in Aristotle. In his political writings, he puts forth that, 'there is one thing clear about the best constitution: it must be a political organization which will enable all sorts of men to be their best and live happily' (Aristotle, 1946, 1324a 5). That is, the more perfect its citizens, the more perfect the State, and both purposes coincide: that of individuals and that of the group; the individual good and the common good. As the Stagirite concluded: 'The most perfect State is, at the same time, the happiest and the most prosperous one. Happiness can never accompany vice; thus the State, as well as man, does not prosper unless both are virtuous and prudent' (Aristotle, 1946, 1323b 11). It is therefore clear that Nonaka borrows from this classical idea, at least partially. As I previously wrote, when he refers to Japanese companies that create knowledge, he states: 'What these firms pursue ultimately is the happiness of the community and themselves' (Nonaka, Toyama, & Hirata, 2008, p. 243).

The concept of the common good is more complex. It can be used in two senses: one is metaphysical and the other political. From the metaphysical point of view, it is that in which a plurality of beings can partake. This happens only with intangible goods, the use of which does not cause their degradation and which can be possessed or shared by many, notwithstanding the fact that some may access it. Knowledge, therefore, is clearly a common good.

The political notion of the common good bears a close relationship with the metaphysical notion. Today this notion belongs, almost exclusively, to the terminology used by the Magisterium of the Roman Catholic Church and Christian political thought (Saralegui, 2010, p. 139). For Catholic Social Teaching the common good is 'the sum total of social conditions which allow people, either as groups or as individuals, to reach their fulfilment more fully and more easily' (Pontifical Council for Justice and Peace, 2004, n. 164). Certainly this definition looks more at the means – conditions – than at the end, and it highlights the idea that human flourishing or happiness is not independent of the social conditions under which human beings live. Actually, another complementary definition of the common good looks primarily at the end of human fulfilment and it defines the common good as 'the good of all people and of the whole person' (Pontifical Council for Justice and Peace, 2004, n. 165). Therefore, a common good is not a simple amalgam of private and individual goods, or a good of the community, which ignores the good of its members. In fact, 'a common good is considered to be a human perfection or fulfilment achievable by a community, such when the community members all share it, both as a community, and individually, as persons' (Alford & Naughton, 2001, p. 41)[23] The notion that the common good is the good of each individual expresses the communitarian dimension of human good. 'Just as the moral actions of an individual are accomplished in doing what is good, so too the actions of a society attain their full stature when they bring about the common good. The common good, in fact, can be understood as the social and community dimension of the moral good' (Pontifical Council for Justice and Peace, 2004, n. 164). Indeed, the common good is what gives purpose to the political order of each community.[24] Nonaka is in agreement with this, as he affirms that in the knowledge-creating organization, *phronetic* leadership 'is the ability to judge goodness for the *common* good. This kind of judgment requires a higher point of view to be able to see what is good for the whole, even though that view stem from one individual´s values and desires' (Nonaka, Toyama, & Hirata, 2008, p. 56). He later adds: 'it is this kind of value of the common good, that gives a firm an absolute value to pursue, that is a goal in itself' (Nonaka, Toyama, & Hirata, 2008, p. 56). Another ability that Nonaka attributes to *phronesis* in leaders is that of exercising political power in favour of the common good (Nonaka, Toyama, & Hirata, 2008, pp. 62–33).

Taking the Aristotelian-Thomistic division of reality in material and formal as the starting point[25], the common good in the firm could also be built on a formal dimension and a material dimension. The formal aspect would be the work of its members, which gives form to the inputs, such as goods and services. Thus, capital, raw materials and products would make up the material dimension of the common good, in some cases as the means and in others as the ends. An important part of the material common good is the benefits. Without them there is no formal common good. But capital requires good work from the firm's members in order for it to render results. So, profits are neither the only element of the common good nor the most important one (Sison & Fontrodona, 2011, p. 104). As Benedict XVI affirms in his most recent social encyclical, 'Profit is useful if it serves as a means towards an end that provides a sense both of how to produce it and how to make good use of it. Once profit becomes the exclusive goal, if it is produced by improper means and without the common good as its ultimate end, it risks destroying wealth and creating poverty' (Benedict XVI, 2009, n. 21).[26] Nonaka has expressed similar ideas: 'Of course, firms cannot continue to exist without profit' but 'profit is a *result* of the firm´s pursue of excellence and ideals, not a *purpose*' (Nonaka, Toyama, & Hirata, 2008, p. 243). 'When a company pursues the common good, good business results follow and are sustainable' (Nonaka, Toyama, & Hirata, 2008, p. 104).[27]

Given that the political concept of the common good is the one that interests us in order to understand Nonaka's proposal, we review it according to Aristotelian-Thomistic thought. We are then be able to relate the purpose of the firm with the excellence of the organization and with the personal human development of its members.

The purpose of the firm, organizational and personal excellence

Aristotle admits three levels of practical rationality (Sellés Dauder, 2000, p. 14), namely, (a) that of *art or technique*, which applies productive work to the transformation of external reality; (b) that of *politics*, which relates to the activities carried out inter-subjectively among free men; and (c) that of *ethics*, which is the highest level and which implements the actions resulting in the benefit of the one who acts, making him better because of the growth of his virtues. This chapter argues that, based on the idea of *phronesis*, Nonaka's thought moves within these three levels. This deduction comes from the fact that Nonaka allocates the following abilities to practical wisdom: attaining particulars from universal ideas; exercising political power to realize the common good; and fostering *phronesis* in others to build a resilient organization (Nonaka, Toyama, & Hirata, 2008, pp. 55–65).

According to Aristotle, technique, politics and ethics are hierarchical at the conceptual level and are relative at the practical level. They are hierarchical in the subordination of the ends they seek. Indeed, in the most elementary sense, the first one must be subordinate to the second and the second must be subordinate to the third. This means that the end of productive work is social organization, which he calls politics, and its purpose is the improvement of virtue in citizens, the ethical plane. The three levels are relative in their dependence for their fulfilment, given that the highest level is a necessary condition for the intermediate level, as the latter is for the lowest one, that is, that we know how to organize ourselves when we are increasingly virtuous, and that the work of transformation is more productive as (the) political organization becomes more orderly.[28] Often, the right measure or solution to problems in one level is to be found in the superior ones, for there is a feedback loop among them. From the corporate point of view, Mary Parker Follet, a pioneer in the area of management theory, also saw the relationship among these planes when she stated that, 'A large organization is a collection of local communities. Individuals and institutional growth are maximized when these communities are self-governing to the maximum degree possible' (Hamel, 2007, p. 186). According to this reasoning, Peter Drucker stated many times that, without good management, there can be no human or material progress, meaning that bad management hampers – and may even stifles – the progress of mankind.

As we can see, the classical proposal moves in three inter-related planes, but each one is attained through its own means and logic. To expect a human community – and the firm is such a community – to move in only one plane – such as the economic or the political plane – is myopic, but to ignore the fact that each one has its own aspiration is no less than foolish. We have to provide the means to tend toward all of them simultaneously, aware of the fact that, on occasions, we have to make compromises or – according to Nonaka – synthesize apparent contradictions in order to arrive at innovative solutions that reconcile seemingly conflicting ends. Obviously, the means are scarce and, sometimes, the ends compete for them – especially for time and money. Therefore, one must value, not ignore, the goods that are present in each situation; one must analyze them, decide which are more expedient in order to accomplish the ends, and then insist in their attainment. That is, being both prudent and virtuous – the classical Aristotelian-Thomistic proposal previously described. In his more recent work, Nonaka assumes the inter-relationship of planes, when he stresses the function of the Aristotelian *phronesis*: 'While it includes a general awareness of the highest human good, it also involves the appreciation of particular facts; its function is to put into practice the values that the moral virtues provide'. In other words, 'practical wisdom involves knowing the right values and being able to put them into practice in concrete situations' (Nonaka & Zhu, 2012, p. 391).[29]

Nonaka affirms, 'Profit is something gained as a result of pursuing *phronesis*' (Nonaka, Toyama, & Hirata, 2008, p. 57). For this to happen, the three planes and their respective means must be well related. A causal link is obtained when workers attain prudence in the good execution of their work. 'Man cannot be separated from his actions. To further the success of a firm does not only mean to implement some sort of productive rationality, but also allowing all its members to find in it a way toward personal improvement, to become better than what they are' (Martínez-Echevarría, 2011, p. 147). This is also Nonaka's thinking when he says that practical wisdom 'must be both effective and ethical, and "cannot be dissociated from the normativity of action"' (Nonaka & Zhu, 2012, p. 392).[30]

Back to human work as constitutive of the formal dimension of the common good, it is important to emphasize that work itself could be a source of human flourishing, because men at work could develop their technical, artistic and moral virtues. Therefore, the common good of the firm is the work in common that allows human beings not only to produce goods and services with profits (the material dimension), but more importantly, to develop workers (the formal dimension) (Sison & Fontrodona, 2011, p. 105).

Now then, personal growth by means of prudence is a necessary, although not sufficient, condition for the achievement of economic results. This is so because, in the reality of contingent means, practical knowledge is not infallible. For example, knowing about a decision or action does not imply that one always unequivocally knows their consequences. One must take into consideration that there is a deficit of rationality in human and contingent realities and that, therefore, there exists the possibility of making a mistake. 'But a *mistake* can be *rectified*. Practical reason goes well when it progresses under a regime of *right reason,* but the right reason is a *correct* reason' (Sellés Dauder, 2000, p. 63). The possibility of making this correction demands a prudent reordering of the means according to the end. First, regarding the concrete end being pursued, but, finally, with reference to the purpose of human life (Aquinas, 2000, b I, l. VI). Hence, practical reason is *right* when the *means,* on which practical reason sheds its light, are properly subordinated to the *right end:* 'right reason requires that things aimed at an end should be used in a measure proportionate to that end' (Aquinas, 1947, II–II ps., q. 152, a. 2, co.). The means are means because they are ordered based on the end. The medial character is derived from the end. The end governs the means because it is an end. The means are right if they are related to the right end, if they adapt to the end.

It is possible to see the levels of *art, politics and ethics* in corporate reality. This is because the *raison d'être* of the firm is to provide goods and services that are useful to society through productive transformation; because a firm can be understood as a community of people, which requires direction in order to comply with its end; and because those who work in that firm can become good, grow in virtues – especially in prudence or *phronesis* – while complying with the corporate end. As Nonaka reminds us: 'Aristotle defines *phronesis* as the virtuous habit of taking actions that serve the common good' (Nonaka & Zhu, 2012, p. 391); with the understanding that the common good is 'what is good for the whole' (Nonaka, Toyama, & Hirata, 2008, p. 56).[31] In words of a contemporary author: 'The purpose of the firm has to be open to the attainment of the good of the people who are part of it, who come together to carry out an activity that may be good for society' (Martínez-Echevarría, 2011, p. 147).

According to the preceding, the contribution of the firm toward the common good must be provided on the basis of its condition of productive community. Jordi Canals, currently Dean of the *IESE Business School,* elaborates on this topic by saying,

> As a group within society, the firm must contribute to the common good of the society to which it belongs. Naturally, it achieves this in its own specific way by producing goods and services efficiently and generating economic value in the process. The purpose of the firm is not just to make a profit but to serve its customers, and grow and develop as a human group pursuing a specific mission in society (2010, p. 200).[32]

These ends, as previously explained, should be sought simultaneously because they are complementary. Practical reason – arbitrating the necessary means – should aspire to implement all of them simultaneously, aware of the fact that they are exemplary causes which demand minimum levels, but have no maximum levels. At the end, the objective of the firm is to provide a service. First, to the persons who work in that firm and, secondly, to the rest of society. Nonaka coincides with this when he states, 'excellence emerges only with an unyielding commitment and practice to serve the common good of the company, its employees, its customers and other stakeholders, and the larger society, based on the company's own vision and values' (Nonaka, Toyama, & Hirata, 2008, p. 3). This is something that does not work in distinct and separate timeframes because it is impossible to improve oneself without the others improving themselves too. A service cannot be judged just on the basis of the outputs, with a limited capacity to improve, but on the basis of the persons who are ultimately the inexhaustible source of improvement. This underlies Nonaka's thinking, as he assumes Aristotle's distinction between *techne* and *phronesis,* and their relation to production and action: 'while making (production) have and end other than itself, action cannot; for good action itself is the end' (Nonaka & Zhu, 2012, p. 391).[33]

Conclusion

I have quoted texts from Nonaka that refer to the final end of the firm. It seems to be a multipurpose end, involving at the same time the common good, excellence, and happiness. But it is really unitary, because the three coincide or are essentially related. It was pointed out that the common good, more than a specific purpose, represents the joint conditions allowing the perfection both of the community as of each individual member, the good of all people and of the whole person. In Nonaka's words: 'Excellence emerges only with an unyielding commitment and practice to serve the common good of the company' (Nonaka, Toyama, & Hirata, 2008, p. 3).

We also arrived at the Aristotelian conclusion, with Nonaka, that perfection and happiness coincide, and that these should be the end of the (political) community. Profits will come as additional, that is, they are the logical result of the firm's excellence, which in turn demands an improvement of its members in their efficient performance and their ethical behaviour, through the growth in *phronesis*. The effort does not conclude in happiness, but may be happiness itself. Nonaka has undertaken this challenge in his closing remarks of *Managing Flow*, asserting that the effort of a knowledge-creating firm by means of the 'continuous self-creation in pursuit of excellence and ideals is ultimately a pursuit of human happiness' (Nonaka, Toyama, & Hirata, 2008, p. 245).

Notes

An adaptation of the section 'The purpose of the firm in Nonaka' (original: *El fin de la empresa según Nonaka*), from the doctoral dissertation of the author of this chapter, called *Ikujiro Nonaka and the theory of the knowledge-based firm. A cognitive approach (original: Ikujiro Nonaka y la teoría de la empresa basada en el conocimiento. Una aproximación cognitiva).*

1. Knowledge 'is a dynamic human/social process of justifying personal belief in search of the truth' (Nonaka, Toyama, & Hirata, 2008, p. 11).
2. They wrote about one of the abilities of phronesis: 'Judging goodness refers to the ability to practice one's moral discernment on what is "good" and act on that judgment on a practical level according to the particular situation. It is the ability both to conceive an ideal and to pursue its realization' (Nonaka, Toyama, & Hirata, 2008, p. 55).
3. '(...) the knowledge creating firm, whose continuous self-creation in pursuit of excellence and ideal is ultimately a pursuit of human happiness' (Nonaka, Toyama, & Hirata, 2008, p. 245).
4. The idea of finality is a *leit motiv* in the written works of the Stagirite, gathered in his model of the four causes, in which he includes the final cause (Aristotle, 1953, b. V, ch. 2, BK 1031a 24–34). The topics of the good, perfection and happiness are the basis for his *Nicomachean Ethics*, as mentioned by some of his most recent commentators, namely, Rus Rufino, S. (Aristotles, 2009, LVI–LVIII) and Ayllón (2011, p. 9).

5. Aquinas thoroughly develops the topics of the truth and the good in his *De Veritate*, which can be considered as a treatise on the theory of knowledge and the theory of affectivity (Aquinas, 1999, Introduction *by J. F. Sellés*). He bases his writings on the end, perfection and happiness contained in his *In Ethicorum* regarding the work of the Stagirite. He integrates these topics in his *Summa Theologica*, which is the main text used in this chapter as a reference for his ideas on these concepts.
6. If what is pursued is understood as the end, it is because reason apprehends it, knows it as real; whereas, if it is seen as a good, it is the will that desires it, that likes it. In the first case, we are in the cognitive faculty of man; in the second case, we are in the volitional faculty. Both planes are related: the intellect wants the will to desire to know the end and, once it is known, to set out to attain it; and the will requires prior knowledge of the good at which it aims. If nothing is desired unless it is previously known as a good, one can infer that one will want something more intensely, if it is freely desired, if one knows more about it.
7. A gradation of goods and ends also exists in the corporate world. Some are goals, others are objectives, and some are ends, one of which should be the organizational purpose or mission. This gradation derives from its potential for instrumentation: goals allow us to reach objectives. These are related to the ends that tend toward the mission, either partially or totally. Usually, the corporate mission is put forth as an aspiration, not a concrete objective, always tensing toward action, but never resolving it in practice.
8. In the knowledge of the good, there can be a theoretical consideration of that good, that is, the good could be considered according to a speculative knowledge if only its truth is considered. (Aquinas, 1947, I, q. 16, art. 4). Thus there are two types of knowledge of the good, a theoretical knowledge and a practical knowledge. One can relate them with Nonaka's differentiation of knowledge in explicit and tacit.
9. The model of the four causes, among which we find the final cause, is essential in the Aristotelian metaphysics and cosmology. According to the Philosopher, all reality is explained by the material, formal, efficient and final causes (Aristotle, 1953, 983a 24–34). His example of the statue is paradigmatic. The material cause is the raw material from which the statue is made. The formal cause is the model used by the sculptor. The efficient cause is the sculptor in his modeling action. The final cause in the sculptor is the reason why he does his work –earning money, embellishing a place or worshiping a deity, among others.
10. Aquinas refer to a classical Aristotle´s text: "We must consider also in which of two ways the nature of the universe contains the good, and the highest good, whether as something separate and by itself, or as the order of the parts. Probably in both ways, as an army does; for its good is found both in its order and in its leader, and more in the latter; for he does not depend on the order but it depends on him" (Aristotle, 1953, 1075a 7–8). This text was used by Chester Barnard as epigraph in *The Functions of the Executive.*
11. No one wants to be sorrowful. This is why the classical tradition has argued that this inclination toward happiness is not the result of free will in man, but that it is inherent to his nature. And the perception of what happiness is for each may vary. There is freedom in the selection of the means to attain happiness.
12. "Natural reason imposes the end to moral virtues, which we call *synderesis*." (Aquinas, 1947, II–II, q. 47, art. 6, ad. 1)
13. Another Aristotelian distinction that is useful to differentiate prudence from art is between that which is *agible* and that which is *feasible*, which correspond,

respectively, to action and production. In the *Metaphysics* (Aristotle, 1953, 1050a 23–24) both operations are differentiated. The act always remains in the subject who operates, while production is external to that subject. Seeing, knowing and wanting are acts, while the constructive process would be production. The scope of this article does not allow us to delve into Nonaka's definition of knowing as a process on the basis of these concepts (2008, 11), but it is analyzed in Fariñas (2011, p. 251).

14. See also Nonaka & Takeuchi (1995), von Krogh, Kazuo, & Nonaka (2000), Nonaka & Toyama (2005), among others.
15. The same words are found in Bennis, W. and Nanus, B. (1985, p. 89). The American authors continue by saying: "This image, which we call *vision,* can be as vague as a dream or as precise as a goal or a mission."
16. See note 9 in this chapter.
17. The truth relates to the reality that is known. There is a necessary or theoretical reality, and there is a contingent or practical reality. A large part of the physical world is necessary. In contrast, the universe of human actions is full of events and situations which could be different or stop being so at a certain point, mostly because of the freedom of men. Regarding the reality which cannot be otherwise, some authors argue that there is *truth,* while, regarding the reality of contingent beings, they speak of *verisimilitude* or possibility (Sellés Dauder, 1997, pp. 95–96) For further explanation of the metaphysical statute of the truth and how it is different from verisimilitude, see Fariñas, (2011, pp. 236–241, section: "Nonaka entre la verdad y la verosimilitud").
18. Their own italics. Thomas Aquinas asserts that there can be only one ultimate end. "It is impossible for one man to have several ultimate ends, which are not subordinate among themselves" (Aquinas, 1947, I–II, q. 1, a. 5, c; a. 6, c y ad 3).
19. With this quote, Nonaka seems to argue that the absolute good is an end that transcends man, a call from the highest. It would be a way to admit that practical knowledge demands a wise knowledge (wisdom), which is not exhausted in man as a term of reference, but which transcends him.
20. "The nature of a thing is precisely its end, and what each being is, once it has reached it full development, is considered to be its own nature" (Aristotle, 1946, 1252b).
21. Reference is to MacIntyre's book *After Virtue: A Study on Moral Theory,* from 1984.
22. I do not think Nonaka intends the firm to have as its end the improvement of its members, but perhaps the establishment of the conditions that make it possible, encouraging the cultivation of *phronesis.*
23. In order to distinguish between the common good and individual 'goods' that are not common, we believe that its appropriate to refer to a play called *A Visit from the Old Lady* (*Der Besuch der alten Dame,* 1956) by Dürrenmatt. One day, an old lady returns to the town she left forty years earlier. In those four decades, everything has changed. While the town and its inhabitants are impoverished, in ruins, the old lady is now a widow, whose husband was an oil magnate, and who has inherited one of the largest fortunes in the world. The hopes of the town become a potential reality when its illustrious daughter promises to donate one billion dollars, five hundred million for the municipality and five hundred million to be distributed among the families living there. However, the old lady had left her home town in disgrace when she was still a young girl because she was pregnant with the child of the man she had loved, but who had abandoned her to her fate. Now, she suddenly imposed one condition for her largesse, which

was that this man should be killed. The mayor angrily reminded the lady that 'we are in Europe, not in the jungle,' and, on behalf of the town, rejected the offer, saying, 'we would rather be poor and not stain our hands with blood.' Alfred, the man who abandoned the old lady when they were both under twenty, now has a grocery store and is very popular with the neighbours. His customers now visit him to offer their unconditional support. Meanwhile, they start buying groceries beyond their means and do not pay in cash, saying 'put it on my bill'. They ask for the best beef, the most expensive tobacco and the priciest whisky. They also start to buy electrical appliances and cars on credit, new clothes...The town is happy, unrecognizable, and Alfred starts to realize that people are 'getting ready to celebrate my murder.' He isn't far from the truth. The mayor visits him one night to give him a loaded rifle, saying, 'It is your duty to put an end to your life now, to face the consequences like a man of honour, don't you think? Even if it is only for the sake of solidarity, for the love of your hometown. You know how poor we are, our bitter penury, our deprivation, children going hungry...' The end of the story will remain untold here because, actually, everything ends when the town succumbs to the temptation of wealth and plans Alfred's murder. Letting him live would not change anything, while killing him would be an excellent deal. Money has always had a powerful attraction and one can always find reasons to justify the unjustifiable. *A Visit from the Old Lady* is a useful parable to explain that benefiting many does not necessarily mean that the decision is a good one. The common good must never go against the individual good. In fact, killing Alfred was neither good nor common. It was not even the lesser evil. It was the result of a simple miserly calculation driven by the people's own interest, in this case, the interest of many people.

24. "The common good is the reason that the political authority exists" (Pontifical Council for Justice and Peace, 2004, n. 168).
25. Aristotle proposed a *hylomorphic* synthesis, which argues that all corporeal entities are essentially made up of substantial form and raw material (1933–35: b. I; 1953: b. VIII; and the related comments by Thomas Aquinas, 1963: b. I; 1961: b. VIII). Form and matter constitute two principles or realities that determine the being of the corporeal entity. Since they are complementary and inseparable, they can be called co-principles because each exerts its function together with the other. A corporeal substance is such (gold, silver, iron) by virtue of the form, and it is individual (this gold, this silver, that iron) by virtue of the matter.
26. "Surely, profit in itself is not to be rejected nor excluded from the scope of legitimate business objectives. We are simply warned against seeking it as an end in itself, instead of as a means to achieve human and social ends. Furthermore, we are cautioned about falling into the trap of engaging in financial speculation for short-term profit and into believing that profit maximization is the sole rationale for business" (Sison & Fontrodona, 2011, p. 105). John Paul II wrote on this: "Profit is a regulator of the life of a business, but it is not the only one; other human and moral factors must also be considered which, in the long term, are at least equally important for the life of a business" (1991, n. 35).
27. Also: "Money is not goodness in itself, but a means to achieve a goal that is goodness. Profit is something gained as result of pursuing *phronesis* rather than being the ultimate goal" (Nonaka, Toyama, & Hirata, 2008, p. 57).
28. These levels of human action, of practical rationality, are clearly related to the practical intellectual habits described by Aristotle in *Nicomachean Ethics*. The first level – knowing how to work – corresponds to the habit of art or technique. The

second level – knowing how to politically organize society – has to do with the habit of politics. The third level – knowing how to improve as a man, which includes knowing how to do and prudential knowledge – belongs to the habit of prudence.

29. This work cites Tsoukas, H. and Cummings, S. (1997).
30. This work cites Statler, M. and Roos, J. (2005).
31. Nonaka, I. et al. (2008), p. 56.
32. The IESE director deducts this purpose from his notion of the firm, saying: "A firm is a group of people, led by an entrepreneur, who work together to offer goods and services to customers. In this process, the firm creates economic and customer value, provides a context for people's professional and personal development, and creates social value by making other contributions to society." (Canals, 2010: 200).
33. See note 13: distinction between action and production.

References

Alford, H. J., & Naughton, M. J. (2001). *Managing as if Faith Mattered: Christian Social Principles in the Modern Organization.* Notre Dame: University of Notre Dame Press.

Aquinas, T. (1905). *Summa contra Gentiles (Of God and His Creatures)* (An Annotated Translation (With some Abridgement) ed.). (J. Rickab, Trad.) London: Burns and Oates.

Aquinas, T. (1947). *Summa Theologica.* (F. o. Province, Trad.) Cincinnati, Ohio: Benziger Bros. Edition.

Aquinas, T. (1961). *In Metaphysics or Commentary on the Metaphysics.* (J. P. Rowan, Trad.) http://www.josephkenny.joyeurs.com/CDtexts/Metaphysics.htm.

Aquinas, T. (1963). *In Physics or Commentary on Aristotle's Physics.* (R. J. Blackwell, R. J. Spath, & W. E. Thirlkel, Trads.) New Haven: Yale University Press.

Aquinas, T. (1999). *De veritate. Cuestión 21, Sobre el bien* (Introduction, translation and notes ed.). (J. F. Sellés, Trad.) Pamplona, España: EUNSA.

Aquinas, T. (2000). *Comentario a la Ética a Nicómaco de Aristóteles.* (A. Mallea, Trad.) Pamplona, España: EUNSA.

Aristotle. (1907). *De Anima.* (R. D. Hicks, Trad.) Cambridge, MA: Harvard University Press.

Aristotle. (1933–35). *Physics* (Loeb Classical Library ed.). (H. Tredennick, Trad.) Cambridge, MA: Harvard University Press.

Aristotle. (1946). *The Politics.* (E. Barker, Trad.) London: Oxford University Press.

Aristotle. (1953). *Metaphysics.* (W. Ross, Trad.) Oxford: Clarendon Press.

Aristotle. (1985). *Nicomachean Ethics.* (T. Irwin, Trad.) Indianapolis: Hackett Publishing.

Aristotle. (2009). *Ética a Nicómaco.* (S. R. Meabe, Trad.) Madrid: Tecnos.

Ayllón, J. R. (2011). *Ética de Aristóteles.* Madrid: Palabra.

Benedict XVI. (2009). *Encyclical Letter Caritas in veritate.* Vatican city: Libreria Editrice Vaticana.

Bennis, W. G. & Nanus, B. (1985). *Leaders: Strategies for Taking Charge.* New York: Harper Business.

Canals, J. (2010). Rethinking the firm's mission and purpose. *European Management Review. 7*, 195–204.

Dürrenmatt, F. (1958). *The Visit* (M. Valency, Adapt.) New York: Random House.

Fariñas Contreras, G. (2011). *Ikujiro Nonaka y la teoría procesal de la empresa basada en el conocimiento. Una aproximación cognitiva.* Universidad de Navarra, Instituto Empresa y Humanismo. Pamplona: http://hdl.handle.net/10171/20870.

Hamel, G. (2007). *The Future of Management.* Boston: Harvard Business School Publishing.

John Paul II. (1991). *Encyclical Letter Centessimus annus.* Vatican city: Libreria Editrice Vaticana.

Martínez-Echevarría, M. A. (2011). La empresa, un camino hacia el humanismo. *Cuadernos Empresa y Humanismo.* (116), 109–150.

Nonaka, I., & Takeuchi, H. (1995). *The Knowledge-Creating Company.* New York: Oxford University Press.

Nonaka, I., & Takeuchi, H. (2011). The Wise Leader. How CEOs can learn Practical Wisdom to Help them do What's Right for their Companies – and Society. *Harvard Business Review.* 89 (5), 58–67.

Nonaka, I., & Toyama, R. (2005). Theory of the knowledge creating firm: subjectivity, objectivity and synthesis. *Industrial and Corporate Change.* 14, 419–436.

Nonaka, I., & Toyama, R. (2007). Strategic management as distributed practical wisdom (Phronesis). *Industrial and Corporate Change.* 16 (3), 371–394.

Nonaka, I., & Zhu, Z. (2012). *Pragmatic Strategy: Eastern Wisdom, Global Success.* Cambridge, UK: Cambridge University Press.

Nonaka, I., Toyama, R., & Hirata, T. (2008). *Managing Flow: A Process Theory of the Knowledge-based Firm.* Basingstoke, UK: Palgrave Macmillan.

Nonaka, I., von Krogh, G., & Voelpel, S. (2006). Organizational knowledge creation theory: evolutionary paths and future advances. *Organization Studies.* 27 (8), 1179–1208.

Pontifical Council for Justice and Peace. (2004). *Compendium of the Social Doctrine of the Church.* Vatican city: Libreria Editrice Vaticana.

Saralegui, M. (2010). Bien común. En Á. L. González, *Diccionario de filosofía.* Pamplona, España: EUNSA.

Sellés Dauder, J. F. (1997). *Curso breve de teoría del conocimiento.* Bogotá: Ediciones Universidad de la Sabana.

Sellés Dauder, J. F. (2000). *Razón teórica y razón práctica según Tomás de Aquino.* Pamplona, España: Servicio de Publicaciones Universidad de Navarra.

Sison, A., & Fontrodona, J. (2011). The Common Good of Business: Addressing a Challenge Posed by «Caritas in Veritate». *Journal of Business Ethics.* 100, 99–107.

Statler, M., & Roos, J. (2005). *Reframing Strategy Preparedness: an Essay on Practical Wisdom. Working Paper n. 63.* From imagilab.org: www.imagilab.org

Tsoukas, H., & Cummings, S. (1997). Marginalization and recovery: the Emergence of Aristotelian Themes in Organization Studies. *Organization Studies.* 18 (18), 655–683.

von Krogh, G., Kazuo, I., & Nonaka, I. (2000). *Enabling Knowledge Creation: How to Unlock the Mystery of Tacit Knowledge and Release the Power of Innovation.* London: Oxford University Press.

6

Out of the Garbage Can? How Continuous Improvement Facilitators Match Solutions to Problems

Florian Rittiner and Stefano Brusoni

Introduction

This chapter builds upon and extends the discussion about knowledge management processes in New Product Development (NPD). We refine Nonaka's (1994) SECI model by focusing on what and – more specifically – who triggers the transition across the different learning modes, i.e., socialization, externalization, combination and internalization. To do so, this study integrates Nonaka's distinction between different forms of knowledge – tacit vs. explicit – with Davenport's (1993) distinction in terms of knowledge content – *process knowledge* (the knowledge of how to develop products) vs. *improvement knowledge* (the knowledge of how to improve business processes).

To oversimplify a bit, we look at process knowledge as the stock of 'problems' waiting for a 'solution', stored in improvement knowledge. Process knowledge provides the specific issues, imbalances or errors, which enable engineers to focus their attention on specific problems and start looking for a possible solution that fits their needs. Improvement knowledge provides a stock of possible solutions to such problems. Both process and the improvement knowledge exist in different forms at different places within the organization, or outside. Both can be partly stored and made available in explicit forms through manuals and checklists, and partly mastered in tacit form by the employees or memorized in organizational routines (Nonaka & Toyama, 2003). While the explicit forms of knowledge are typically available to most organizational members, tacit knowledge is managed by heterogeneous and often distant actors. Improvement knowledge is very often available in codified forms through external sources of knowledge: consultants, academics, or professional associations. On the other hand, process knowledge is held by those who actually work with the processes. The task of process management actors is then to match the solutions to these problems. Such a matching process, as we discuss, is a complex process of learning, negotiation and adaptation, which can be, to a large extent, explained and interpreted on the basis of Nonaka's approach.

Also, this is a classic case of a garbage can model of decision making (Cohen, March, & Olsen, 1972). As we speculate later in the chapter, process management fits in surprisingly well with the discussion of 'organized anarchies' that rely on the garbage can logic, with random allocations of solutions to problems. However, as opposed to such a random process, we propose to look at *continuous improvement facilitators* (hereafter CI facilitators) as those agents that manage the matching process of solution to problems.

This chapter delivers a threefold contribution to the literature on organizational learning. First, we argue that the starting point of Nonaka's learning spiral varies with the knowledge content. That is to say, learning about improvement knowledge starts with explicit knowledge being combined and internalized, while learning about process knowledge starts with tacit knowledge being socialized and externalized. Second, we show that the learning spirals of improvement knowledge and process knowledge are connected. Finally, we show that this link is mediated by specific organizational roles, namely CI facilitators, who deploy different knowledge brokering strategies to acquire improvement knowledge and subsequently apply it to facilitate the creation of process knowledge.

The remainder of this chapter is organized as follows. After introducing the empirical context of our study, we briefly review the literature on process management and organizational learning. Then we use Nonaka's SECI model to describe the co-creation of improvement and process knowledge. To illustrate this process, we provide examples from our research project on lean product development. We then discuss how this framework enhances our understanding of process management activities and highlight the important role of CI facilitators in driving the spiral of knowledge creation. Finally, we suggest further avenues for the research on process management from an organizational learning point of view. We hope that our study does not only advance research, but also supports process management actors in better understanding their attempts towards the introduction of improvement initiatives.

The context: Process management in the automotive industry

Understanding the interplay of the process knowledge and of the improvement knowledge spirals matters not only for the organizational learning literature, but also for practice. We have long known that adhering to proven process templates makes operations more stable and predictable, generating efficiency gains (Adler et al., 2009). We also know that an efficiency focus may lead to undesired side effects. Adler et al. (2009) built upon the productivity dilemma identified by Abernathy (1978), to argue that short-term efficiency gains will eventually lead to long-term ineffectiveness in terms of the ability to innovate and adapt to changing environments. This tension between efficiency and effectiveness is a central dilemma in the NPD literature and practice.

In production and manufacturing settings, considerable efficiency gains were achieved by systematically working on processes and thereby striving for continuous improvements (Benner & Tushman, 2003; Womack, Jones, & Roos, 1990). Firms are striving to increase efficiency not only in manufacturing and operations, but also in white collar work, as for example new product development (Anand & Kodali, 2008; Bartezzaghi, Corso, & Verganti, 1997) or business development (Hammer, 2002; Schroeder, Linderman, Liedtke, & Choo, 2008). Karlsson and Åhlström (1996) introduced the idea that lean practices can also be applied in NPD, in order to eliminate waste (Anand & Kodali, 2008). The application of such strictly rule-based strategies to knowledge-intensive processes to achieve continuous improvement seems to be more complex and extremely challenging (Martínez León & Farris, 2011; Morgan & Liker, 2006). Indeed, process management actors still struggle to replicate these successful practices, imported from the operations domain, in research and development. This chapter intends to focus on such complexity, developing a framework which explains why the application of lean principles to NPD is difficult, and how firms are getting organized to overcome these difficulties.

To do so, we adopt an organizational learning framework that builds upon the distinction between tacit and explicit knowledge (Nonaka, 1994). To this model, we add a second analytical building block: the distinction between process knowledge and improvement knowledge. In fact, the improvement of business processes requires different types of knowledge (Davenport, 1993). The first type of knowledge is what we refer to as improvement knowledge, which is the knowledge of *how to* improve processes. Under this label, we summarize both the knowledge about suitable improvement methodologies like lean management (Womack & Jones, 1996; Womack et al., 1990), as well as the competence to apply specific process improvement tools as for instance value stream mapping (Rother & Shook, 2003; Schulze et al., 2011). Improvement knowledge, in a way, is a stock of existing 'solutions' to a certain class of managerial problems, often – yet not always – framed in relatively general and abstract categories, waiting to be deployed to solve the specific problems of a specific organization. The second type is the knowledge of *what to* improve. We refer to this knowledge as process knowledge. This is the knowledge of the process that is to be improved. One has to know the actual process fairly well in order to understand what impedes a better process performance and to propose meaningful improvements (Rother, 2010).

Successful process improvement activities require both types of knowledge. This implies that the spiral of improvement knowledge creation and the spiral of process knowledge creation are to be connected. However, we argue that the two spirals would not necessarily and automatically follow each other as they rely on very different types of learning modes. The creation of process knowledge follows Nonaka's conceptualization. However, the creation of improvement knowledge, although following the same sequence, begins at the combination mode. This is because the sources for improvement knowledge are typically quite explicit and located outside the firm. Hence, the CI facilitators need to span organizational boundaries to learn about them. For example, they participate in conferences and workshops to learn about possible solutions to their internal problem. In doing so, process managers collect explicit improvement knowledge that is embodied in manuals, brochures and presentations. Yet, these solutions are often unrelated to the specific context in which the knowledge is to be applied. Hence, CI facilitators must customize this explicit improvement knowledge so that it matches the needs of their firms. Company-specific tacit knowledge serves as guideline and yardstick at this stage. The next step refers to the application of the improvement knowledge to create new process knowledge, i.e., which is the main goal of improvement initiatives. During this process, new improvement and process knowledge is co-created. The final step in our model represents the articulation and diffusion of the knowledge, which leads to separate, but interacting spirals of improvement and process knowledge creation.

As Von Krogh et al. (2012) argue, this depends on the extent to which a group can create new knowledge and on the degree to which knowledge assets can be mobilized. Hence firms need somebody who is creating the field in which the different actors meet to generate organizational level learning (Nonaka, 1994). Many organizations have a special process management unit that are in charge of such a coordinating function. At other companies, in particular smaller ones, there are single employees in charge for those process management activities, which is then often a part time job.

To illustrate these process management activities, we show examples from four automotive supplier companies that are about to implement lean management in their product development departments. All of them are located in the German-speaking area and participate on a larger research project on lean product development (LPD). The firms have dedicated personnel who is responsible for the management and improvement of NPD processes. We refer to these employees as CI facilitators, as their main task is to ensure the continuous adaptation of the companies' NPD processes to meet ever increasing requirements. Two companies, hereafter named Company A and Company B, have process managers organized in a staff function. At another company, Company C, the process manager works part-time on process management activities and is reporting directly to the head of R&D. The last company, Company D, employs an hybrid organization where the process manager is reporting directly to the division head, but also part of a company-wide process management organization that is setting standards together. We have been able to study the companies for one and a half years at various occasion. We visited the companies to do interviews and observations, we organized a number of workshops in which the companies discussed different topics related to the introduction of lean principles to NPD. In doing so, we were able to observe how these companies go about the tedious introduction of managerial innovations (Birkinshaw, Hamel, & Mol, 2008), i.e. the attempt to implement lean management to new product development. We identify the key actors in the introduction process and characterize their role in the knowledge creation process.

Process management and knowledge requirements

Benner and Tushman view process management as 'concentrated efforts to map, improve, and adhere to organizational processes (2003, p. 238)'. Over the decades, a number of concepts have been developed to support these process management attempts. Total Quality Management (TQM) became prominent in the 1980s (Hackman & Wageman, 1995; Repenning & Sterman, 2001; Westphal, Gulati, & Shortell, 1997), Six Sigma in the 1990s (Pande & Holpp, 2001) and more recently Lean Management (Womack & Jones, 1996; Womack et al., 1990). The elimination of waste and the root cause of process variability is thereby one of the key elements (Ittner & Larcker, 1997; Rother, 2010). The benefits from those process improvement activities are numerous, including increased yields, less rework and waste, tighter organizational linkages and thereby faster product development along with shorter delivery times (e.g. Armistead, 1999; Karlsson & Åhlström, 1996). Nevertheless, critical voices are saying that those initiatives have hardly any impact on organizational and financial performance (Benner & Tushman, 2003; Ittner & Larcker, 1997; Powell, 1995). Furthermore, process improvement activities are still seen as additional work that prevents engineers from doing their 'real' work (Repenning & Sterman, 2002). Engineers are mainly interested in developing technically superior products and perceive the advancement of the organization as a management task (Nilsson-Witell, Antoni, & Dahlgaard, 2005).

Improvement knowledge

Knowledge about improvement methodologies and tools is an important ingredient of process improvement activities (Davenport, 1993). From a process management perspective, this knowledge describes how to best improve business processes. We label this type of knowledge 'improvement knowledge'. Improvement knowledge is hierarchically structured. We observe both general principles, e.g., eliminate waste, and batteries of tools to implement those principles, e.g., value stream mapping (Rother & Shook, 2003; Schulze et al., 2011). For example, Karlsson and Åhlström (1996) and Anand

and Kodali (2008) list a number of such tools and techniques that support lean management efforts. Many of them support problem-solving activities. In garbage logic terms, they represent concrete solutions to specific problems. These tools and techniques are well described in books, cases, examples and manuals.

Process knowledge

The knowledge of NPD processes and their current condition is what we name 'process knowledge'. This is the knowledge of what to improve, which is hold by process owners and process users. The former are typically middle or top managers. Process users are the engineers who actually develop the products. Process knowledge tells us what problems matter to specific people within different functions. Feldman (2000) identifies 'the potential for change in the internal dynamics or the routine itself, and in the thoughts and reactions of the people who participate in the routines' (2000, p. 626). This implies that the need for improvement is best sensed by those who actually work with the processes. Similarly, Nelson and Winter (1982) argue that problem solving is activated by puzzles or anomalies that arise during routine operations. Sometimes, these anomalies can be retrieved in explicit form through process performance data. However, the measurement and documentation of development process performance is cumbersome and the effort put into collecting such data varies greatly among firms. Hence, directly involving the engineers who are working with the processes is an important and efficient way for process management actors to learn about actual practices and gather first hand performance information.

Process management as garbage can process

Cohen and March (1972) introduce the garbage can model to explain decision making in what they called organized anarchies. These organizations are characterized by three general properties. First, these organizations are guided by problematic preferences, which means that they have inconsistent or ill-defined preferences. The second property is unclear technology, which means that the company operates according to simple trial-and-error procedures. Finally, these organizations are characterized by fluid participation, which implies that the amount of time and effort that participants devote to different domains varies. Cohen and March describe the organization as 'a collection of choices looking for problems, issues and feelings looking for decision situations in which they might be aired, solutions looking for issues to which they might be the answer, and decision makers looking for work' (1972, p. 2).

Our case study companies share the characteristics of organized anarchies. Conflicting preferences exist on a number of scales. Furthermore, when we refer to improvement knowledge as the 'technology' that is to be mastered by the process management organization, we may well speak of an 'unclear technology'. Indeed, the knowledge that is required to successfully improve NPD process is often not available within the boundaries of the firm. Therefore, improvement activities resemble trial-and-error procedures with uncertain outcomes. Even if CI facilitators reach outside the organization and learn about different improvement methodologies and the corresponding tools, it remains unclear whether their efforts lead to the expected results. Last, with respect to the third property of organized anarchies, CI facilitators involve engineers and designers in their improvement initiatives only when deemed necessary. Hence, the participants in process management activities vary from case to case. Process management entails a number of decisions to be taken by a variety of organizational actors. The efficiency and effectiveness by which these decision are taken depends on how successful the organization can activate its members and direct their attention to the problems at hand (Cohen et al., 1972).

Organizational learning and knowledge characteristics

According to Polanyi (1966), we know more than we can tell. This observation gave rise to the development of various characterizations of knowledge (e.g., Gourlay, 2006). For example, Nonaka and Takeuchi (1995, pp. 58–59) describe knowledge as 'a meaningful set of information', Myers (1996, p. 2) calls organizational knowledge 'processed information', and Davenport et al. (1998, p. 43) describe knowledge as 'information combined with experience'. These definitions indicate that knowledge is somehow richer than information and propose a hierarchy in which knowledge is seen as the more advanced construct (Alavi & Leidner, 2001). The discourse about information and knowledge, and in particular how they are set apart from each other, is inherently related to the discussion about how easily knowledge can be articulated. Knowledge that can be easily articulated and transferred is referred to as explicit knowledge (Nonaka, 1994; Polanyi, 1966). Tacit knowledge, on the contrary, stands for knowledge that is difficult to articulate and that can be shared only with great difficulty (Nonaka, 1994; Polanyi, 1966).

Many have argued that organizational learning is the most important factor to achieve competitive advantage in product development. The most widely used model for organizational knowledge creation is probably the SECI framework, for which Vaccaro et al. (2009) report references to a variety of research fields such as management information systems, organization studies, strategic management and technology management and policy. Gourlay (2006) notes 543 citations for Nonaka's 1994 paper in management journals until 2004. This number increased to 2263 until early 2012[1], showing the sustained attractiveness of the model. In this chapter, we apply the model to further examine and visualize the process of knowledge creation that is underlying process management in new product development.

Nonaka and Toyama (2003) provide the link to process management activities as they use the framework to analyse Toyota's continuous process innovation in manufacturing. One of their key findings is that workers have to share their knowledge in order to be able to make improvements to the process. Dyck et al. (2005) confirmed Nonaka's four-phase knowledge creation process empirically by using data from the examination of product development activities of an automotive company. Unlike in this chapter, Nonaka and Toyama (2003) and Dyck et al. (2005) focused on technical product and production knowledge, rather than development process knowledge.

Given the distinction between improvement and process knowledge on the one hand, and explicit and tacit forms of knowledge on the other hand, process management organizations have to master four distinct types of knowledge. In Table 6.1, we link the four types of knowledge we consider to their main repositories. Explicit forms of improvement and process knowledge are easily accessible, for example through process databases or manuals on the intranet. Tacit knowledge is more difficult to access, as it is held by a variety of organizational actors. In this chapter, we refine Nonaka's model of knowledge creation to describe the interactions among those four knowledge types, which are in one way or another required to successfully improve organizational processes.

Nonaka and Toyama (2003) argue that despite the ever growing body of research on organizational knowledge creation, 'we are still far from understanding the process in which organizations create and utilize knowledge' (Nonaka & Toyama, 2003, p. 2). Much of the literature on organizational knowledge creation is mainly concerned with the particularities stemming from the distinction between explicit and tacit forms (Nonaka, 1994; Nonaka, Toyama, & Konno, 2000), and between individuals and organizations as the main unit of knowledge creation (Grant, 1996; Nonaka, 1994). This literature is focusing on different knowledge forms rather than varying knowledge content. We argue that the influence of knowledge content has been underappreciated in the knowledge creation literature so far.

Table 6.1 Distinct types and repositories of improvement and process knowledge

	Improvement knowledge	**Process knowledge**
Explicit knowledge	Manuals Guidelines etc.	Process descriptions Development manuals etc.
Tacit knowledge	CI facilitators (Process managers)	Process owners(middle and top management) Process users(engineers)

Source: The authors.

The co-creation of improvement and process knowledge

We argue that the creation of improvement and process knowledge follows a four stage process that leads to two separate, but interacting spirals of organizational knowledge creation. The first stage relates to the acquisition of improvement knowledge, which typically originates outside the firm. The second stage describes the integration of the newly acquired improvement knowledge into the organizational context. The third stage corresponds to the actual co-creation of improvement and process knowledge, through the interaction of improvement and process knowledge holders. The final step refers to the subsequent externalization of the knowledge. In the following paragraphs we develop the four-stage model step-by-step and illustrate it with examples from our research project on lean product development.

Stage 1: Acquisition of improvement knowledge (combination)

The first stage of our model describes the acquisition of improvement knowledge (I_E). At the very beginning of introducing lean management into product development, there is typically very little knowledge available inside the organization. CI facilitators have to reach over the boundaries of the firm to gather adequate improvement knowledge. The CI facilitators act as brokers, who enable the flow of improvement knowledge into the organization. Fernandez and Gould define brokerage as 'a relation in which one actor mediates the flow of resources or information between two other actors who are not directly linked' (1994, p. 1457). This particular type of brokering relation is known as boundary spanning (e.g., Fleming & Waguespack, 2007; Tushman, 1977) or gate keeping (e.g., Fernandez & Gould, 1994). The concept of brokerage has been thoroughly examined by a number of scholars (among others Burt, 1992, 2005; Granovetter, 1973; Lingo & O'Mahony, 2010; Obstfeld, 2005; Simmel, 1950). Innovation performance is positively influenced by the extent to which organizations, teams and individuals can access knowledge across boundaries (Tortoriello & Krackhardt, 2010), as it was shown in a number of studies on product innovation (Allen & Cohen, 1969; Katz & Tushman, 1979; Tushman & Scanlan, 1981).

The four sample companies started their journey in the top-left quadrant of Figure 6.1 when they joined a purpose-designed workshop on lean product development. Process management actors at all companies, mainly CI facilitators, got an identical reading list and started working with the very same material on lean thinking. CI facilitators read books (in particular, Morgan & Liker, 2006; Reinertsen, 2009; Rother, 2010) and a number of selected articles (among them Haque & James-Moore, 2004; Reinertsen & Shaeffer, 2005; Sobek, Liker, & Ward, 1998). On this basis, a number of workshops were organized to discuss issues and problems. Moreover, CI facilitators as well as managers from the participating companies attended a conference on lean management, where they learned about the experience of other companies that work with the lean management approach.

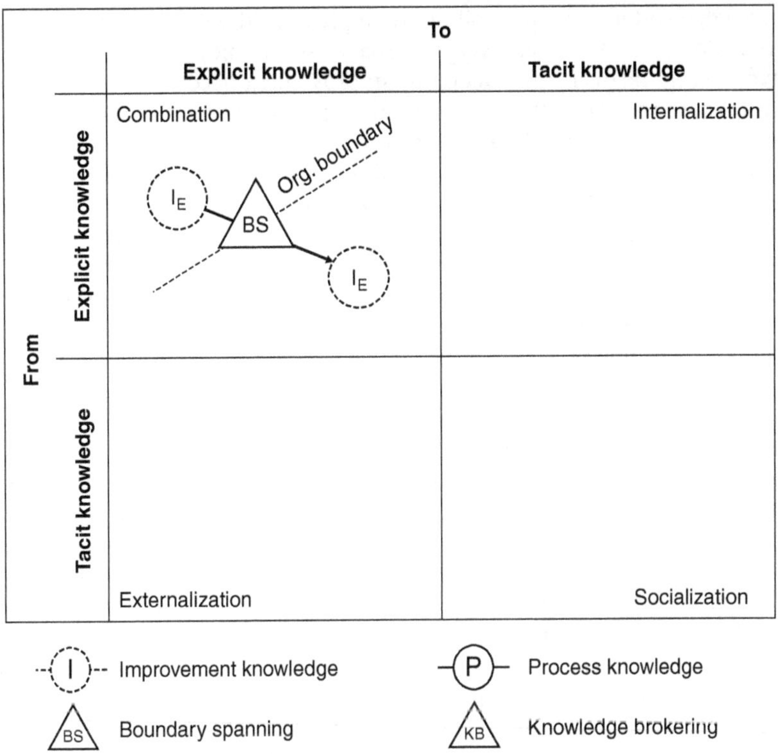

Figure 6.1 Stage 1 of the model of knowledge co-creation
Source: The authors.

These activities exposed them to the explicit improvement knowledge, as articulated in books, articles, examples, case studies and conference proceedings. Although the material had been discussed in detail, the discourse remained on a rather general and abstract level. These initial activities thus represent the transfer, combination and diffusion of explicit knowledge and correspond to the activities that take place at the combination mode of Nonaka's model (Nonaka, 1994). At this stage, the acquisition of improvement knowledge in explicit form represents the main activity of the CI facilitators.

Stage 2: Contextualization of improvement knowledge (Internalization)

At the first stage, CI facilitators introduce new improvement knowledge in the organization through their boundary-spanning activities. Yet, such knowledge is kept within the process management organization. CI facilitators have to make the R&D organization aware of this newly acquired improvement knowledge and identify possibilities to apply it. In the words of a CI facilitators at Company A: 'I would say that I have several roles. On the one hand, I have to keep the overview [to identify improvement needs] and on the other hand, I have to try to sell the [process management] function to the different R&D units, in order to gain a certain acceptance'. Lean management, similar to TQM or Six Sigma, presents a comprehensive improvement methodology that is difficult to implement as a whole (Westphal et al., 1997). CI facilitators need to identify those elements that are likely to deliver the 'quick wins' necessary to obtain support and acceptance. This is the stage when the range of possible solutions embodied in the newly acquired improvement knowledge, is broken down in simpler tools, which are matched to specific engineering problems.

To do this, CI facilitators involve further organizational actors. They have to convince those people who might benefit from their initiatives to support and sponsor them. They engage process owners who are responsible for the optimization of organizational processes (Trkman, 2010). Through a long and often time consuming process of meetings, seminars, and informal discussions, CI facilitators learn how engineers in their organizations perceive lean management, which aspects they favour, which they dislike, and why. The interactions with those who hold process knowledge (P_T), facilitate the internalization of improvement knowledge (I_E) by the CI facilitators as they represents a reality check in the light of the organizational characteristics. Part of the newly formed tacit improvement knowledge (I_T) is, for instance, the knowledge about which problems to prioritize in order to solve them with the tools made available by the lean management toolbox. Similar to Dyck et al. (2005) and Vaccaro et al. (2009), we observed that the internalization mode is triggered by 'learning-by-doing': explicit and external improvement knowledge needs to be applied to be really made relevant to organizational members.

The adaptation and implementation of the Obeya concept (for more information see: Morgan & Liker, 2006; Oppenheim, 2004) at Company C is an excellent example to illustrate the internalization of explicit improvement knowledge (see top-right quadrant in Figure 6.2).

The CI facilitator learned about the Obeya at a workshop with other CI facilitators. She was convinced that having all relevant development data available at one place would help them to fasten their development process. At different occasions, she presented the idea to the company's middle and top management. She learned that transforming one of their meeting rooms into an Obeya is not feasible. The reason was simple; there was not enough office space available. Through the many discussions, however, she learned that there is indeed a need for visualizing critical project information. Thus she adapted the concept of the Obeya to match the company's requirements. Together with one middle manager, she initiated the creation of a so-called 'LEAN-corner', to display information about ongoing improvement

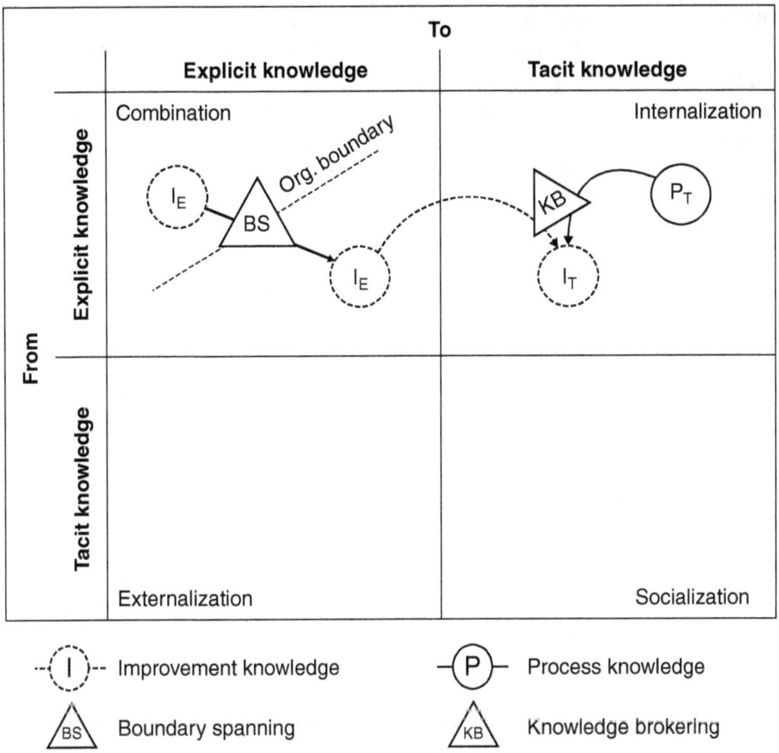

Figure 6.2 Stage 2 of the model of knowledge co-creation
Source: The authors.

initiatives, preliminary results and general development information. This corner was perceived very well by the employees and not much later all departments in R&D installed such a board.

The internalization of improvement knowledge by the CI facilitators goes hand in hand with its diffusion into the R&D organization and the familiarization of relevant process management actors. Through the education of the process owners and other management representatives, the CI facilitators gain credibility for their initiatives and further support for the use of the methodology.

Also, at this stage, CI facilitators act as knowledge brokers. However, their role is slightly different. At stage 1, they acted as boundary spanners to activate the flow of explicit improvement knowledge into the organization. At this stage, they contextualize this knowledge (I_E) considering tacit process knowledge (P_T), which is held by process owners and users, into tacit improvement knowledge (I_T). Burt (2004) distinguishes between four levels of brokerage through which an organizational actor can create value. The first level is making people on either side of a structural hole aware of each other's interests. The second level refers to the transfer of best practices between two groups. Brokers at the third level draw analogies between groups that are at first sight irrelevant to one another. The fourth level refers to the synthesis of knowledge from different groups. The boundary spanning activities at the first stage of our model refer to the second of Burt's (2004) levels. CI facilitators collect knowledge about lean management, which we can refer to as codified best practice from other companies such as Toyota (Morgan & Liker, 2006; Womack & Jones, 1996), and transfer it into the own organization. The activities at the second stage are more complex. The contextualization of improvement knowledge requires the synthesis from both improvement and process knowledge, in order to determine which elements of the lean management methodology might as well work for the own company. This brokering activity thus matches the fourth level of Burt's (2004) typology.

Stage 3: Co-creation of improvement and process knowledge (Socialization)

The third stage of our model describes the actual application of improvement knowledge (I_T), in order to enhance process knowledge (P_T). This is the central step through which simultaneously new improvement knowledge and process knowledge (I_T+ and P_T+) are created. CI facilitators apply their improvement knowledge and learn how to advance their tools and methods. Process owners and users benefit from optimized processes through the application of improvement methods introduced by the CI facilitators. Most of the knowledge that is involved at this stage is tacit, although the companies have descriptions for most of their processes. Nevertheless, these explicit descriptions rarely account for the complexity of process knowledge. Furthermore, engineers who are developing products for years do no longer refer to these process descriptions as they know the process by heart. One engineer at Company C put it this way: 'That is my experience and I know more or less how the processes look like. However, I cannot tell whether they correspond to the process that we find somewhere on the intranet'. The notion of *more-or-less* is what often makes the difference. The growing variation in the way of working is not uncommon, as organizational routines naturally evolve over time (Nelson & Winter, 1982). Hence, actual routines often deviate from the standards that have been set earlier on (Nelson & Winter, 1982). Process management activities, in particular the mapping and subsequent improvement of processes (Benner & Tushman, 2003), capture those deviations and, if necessary, provide the tools to optimize the corresponding processes. However, this is only possible, if those people who know about the current routines and their inadequacy are involved in the improvement activity. Hargadon and Bechky (2006), for example, state that 'when participants come together in collective problem-solving efforts, one person often has a good understanding of the problematic situation, while others have potentially relevant ideas and experiences to contribute' (2006, p. 492). CI facilitator offer methods and tools to facilitate this dialogue. As mainly tacit knowledge is shared, the main part of knowledge creation at this stage correspondingly happens through socialization (Nonaka, 1994).

Value stream mapping (VSM) provides an excellent example to describe the complex activities at this stage. We provide a short illustrative episode from a value stream mapping workshop at Company A and the subsequent improvement of the prototyping process.

There was the general perception that processes at the prototyping workshop are not as smooth as they could be. The CI facilitator identified the need for a thorough analysis of the working processes. He invited relevant stakeholders and organized a value stream mapping workshop to visualize the current processes. Eight employees from all relevant functions in prototyping and two employee from the development organization, representing the internal customer, participated. As this was the first VSM workshop for them, the CI facilitator invited two external experts from the university to assist him in conducting the workshop. During the workshop, the participants identified 22 weaknesses of the current process. Of these 22, one issue seemed to be particularly pressing to the participants.

Prototypes are shipped weakly to the OEM (Original Equipment Manufacturer) for testing and there was the perception that all of them are brought to quality inspection and subsequent shipping on Friday afternoon, which leads to an accumulation of work and eventually to delayed shipment. There was a lot of discussion about this issue, but the actual root-cause could not be identified during the workshop. Thus the CI facilitator and the employee who is responsible for testing, performed a more thorough processes analysis and collected data about when the prototypes actually arrive. They found that delays are not caused because too many prototypes arrive on Friday, but because of the many set-up procedures that were necessary as prototypes of different dimensions arrived randomly.

Eventually, the solution was that the testing worker ask on Monday morning which prototypes that are to be tested and shipped in that week. By doing so, he can schedule the upcoming testing activities well in advance and thereby avoid congestion towards the end of the week. The improvement of the process, which is only a minor one, saves them up to 4 hours in set up time. Without the VSM workshop, however, they would have continued as before.

In this example, optimizing the process for prototype testing refers to creating enhanced process knowledge (P_T+). The successful application of the VSM tool and the subsequent analysis of the process through the collection of additional data, as proposed by Rother (2010) for instance, can be seen as enhanced or justified improvement knowledge (I_T+). The success of the workshop is a strong signal to the R&D organization that the methods

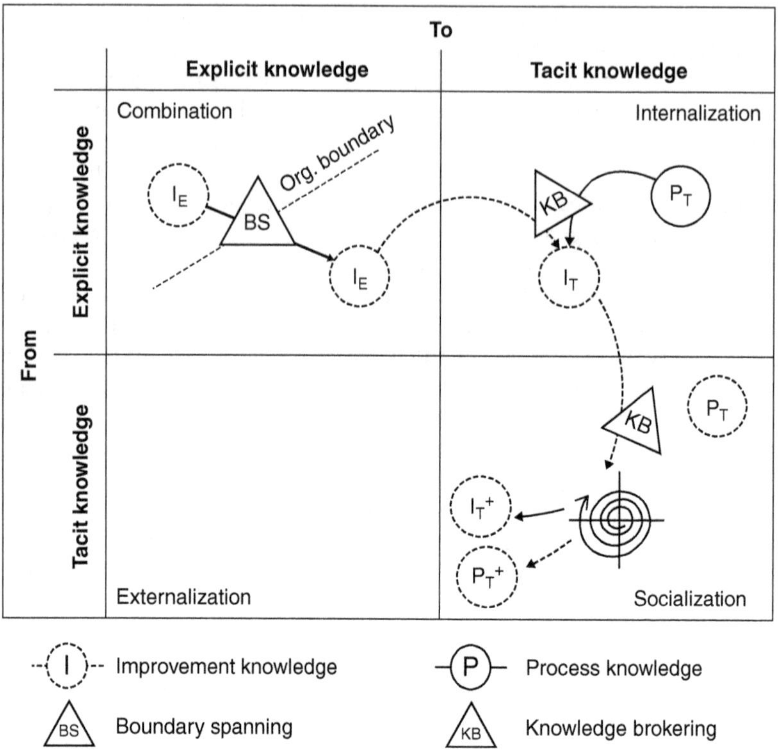

Figure 6.3 Stage 3 of the model of knowledge co-creation
Source: The authors.

and tools employed by the process management organization have a positive influence on product development performance.

In this short episode, we can see how versatile the role of CI facilitators is and how they facilitate the co-creation of improvement and process knowledge, which is driven by different types of brokering activity. First, the CI facilitator identified the need for a more thorough process analysis through the monitoring of the activities within the R&D department. On this basis, he proposed and organized the VSM workshop and invited all relevant stakeholders (he acted as a coordinator). Then, he brought the knowledge about VSM as an improvement tool into the organization (stages 1 and 2) and identified a promising opportunity to apply it (stage 3). In doing so he acted as boundary spanner during stage 1, as a broker who synthesizes different types of knowledge during stage 2, and as coordinator during stage 3 (represented in the bottom-right quadrant of Figure 6.3). Also, the CI facilitator brought external experts into the firm to support the first VSM workshop in order to benefit from a much broader set of experiences with the VSM method (he was a gate keeper again). Thus, the CI facilitator promoted the sharing of experience between two distant organizational functions, namely the prototyping organization and the development organization (he acted as coordinator). Crucially for the internalization phase, the CI facilitator acted as itinerary broker (Fernandez & Gould, 1994) between the different workers from the prototyping workshop, getting involved directly in solving a specific problem. As the battle lines were drawn within the shop floor, the VSM workshop and in particular the subsequent process analysis by the CI facilitator allowed for a constructive dialogue on the prototyping process.

The conversion from tacit to tacit knowledge happens through the interaction between individuals (Nonaka, 1994). Nonaka et al (2000) argue that 'tacit knowledge can be acquired only through shared experience, such as spending time together or living in the same environment' (2000, p. 9). Close physical interaction through the sharing of time and space is important to share the context and form a common language among participants (Nonaka et al., 2000). It is the task of the CI facilitator to create this kind of environment that allows the participants to share their tacit knowledge and improve their understanding of their development work that will eventually lead to better processes and increased performance. The knowledge about how to create such an environment is exactly what we refer to as improvement knowledge.

Stage 4: Externalization of improvement and process knowledge (Externalization)

The fourth stage in our model (see bottom-left quadrant of Figure 6.4) represents the externalization of the enhanced improvement and process knowledge that has been created in the previous stage. Externalization refers to the articulation of tacit knowledge into explicit forms that can easily be shared and diffused (Nonaka, 1994; Nonaka et al., 2000). Visualization methods such as value stream mapping eases the articulation of tacit knowledge. The visual map represents an abstract version of the newly created tacit knowledge (P_T+) and helps to convey it to other workshop participants. Nevertheless, such a map is of limited use to people who did not participated in the workshop. The tacit knowledge that comes out of the socialization mode has to be externalized and combined with explicit knowledge accounts, such as the visual map from the workshop and other existing process documentation. These explicit accounts of the tacit knowledge (P_E+) can then be used to communicate and educate the wider R&D organization about the workshop results and subsequent improvements of the NPD process.

CI facilitators learn a lot when they apply one of the improvement tools. During the workshop (at stage 3), CI facilitators thus acquire new improvement knowledge (I_T+). After the workshop this knowledge is as well externalized and stored in explicit forms (I_E+), for example as best practices, for future applications.

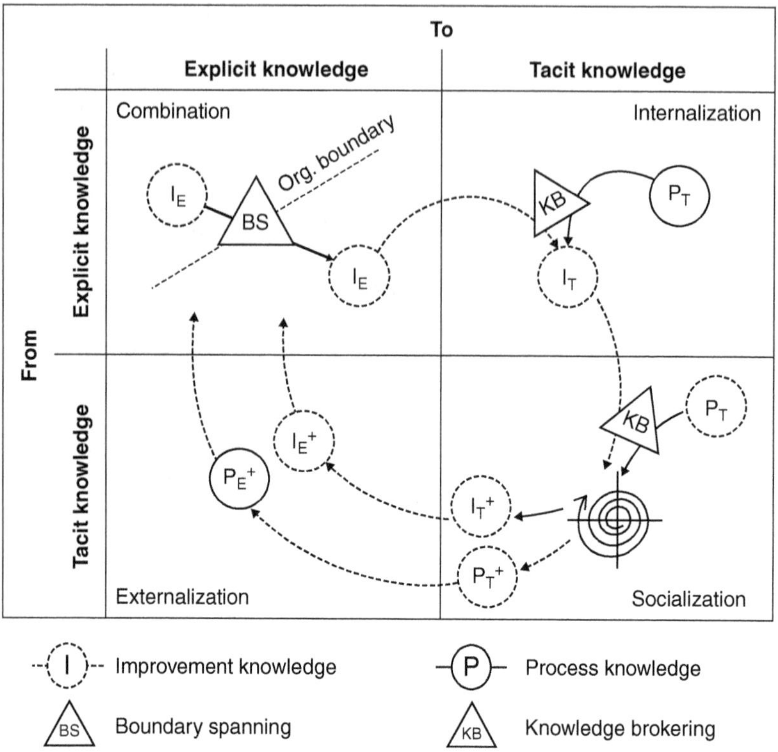

Figure 6.4 Stage 4 of the model of knowledge co-creation

Source: The authors.

At the fourth stage, the CI facilitators play again a critical role. They are in charge of reformulating both the newly acquired improvement and process knowledge and making available to those who will work according to those instructions. Also, in the fourth step the process of improvement and process knowledge flows into two separate spirals of knowledge creation, following Nonaka's model (Nonaka, 1994).

Discussion

This chapter contributes to the existing literature on process management and organizational learning in three distinct ways. First, we show that process management depends on two distinct types of knowledge – improvement and process knowledge. Second, we disentangle and examine the process through which these two types of knowledge are simultaneously created. Third, we show the significant role that dedicated process management actors, in particular the CI facilitators, play in driving the knowledge creation process.

We have argued that successful process management activities depend on two distinct types of knowledge: the knowledge of how to effectively improve business processes, i.e., improvement knowledge, and knowledge of what to improve, i.e. process knowledge. We are able to show that the creation of either type is dependent on the other one, but also exhibit important differences in terms of their starting point and the type (explicit vs. tacit) of knowledge they chiefly rely on.

We believe that this line of reasoning is important to understand how firms escape the classic garbage can model. The key function played by our facilitators is indeed one of matching 'solutions' (as embedded in management methods) to 'problems', as revealed to engineers as they go about their everyday design activities. To understand which solutions match to which problems, CI facilitators act as brokers. And they do so in various ways (e.g., they connect, they span, they synthesize) according to the specific phase of the Nonaka's spiral in which they operate.

Implications for management

We disentangle and illustrate the process of co-creation of improvement and process knowledge. R&D managers benefit from a better understanding of this complex process in a number of ways. Knowing that there are two types of knowledge that have to be considered allows them to organize their process management activities accordingly. They know which organizational actors are to be involved in the process. Nonaka and Toyama (2003) argue that in order to understand knowledge creation it is important to understand the interactions among the individuals and work groups involved in the process. Recently, von Krogh et al. (2012, p. 254) stressed that the 'collaboration between individuals is an essential part of organizational knowledge creation'. However, these individuals and work-groups may well have different interests and goals, which is a central property of anarchistic organizations as which process management can be framed (Cohen et al., 1972). For CI facilitators, process improvements are the main part of their work and what they are evaluated for. In order to successfully improve processes, however, they depend on the support of the NPD organization whose main target is the development of products. These contradicting goals might lead to tension in the process management process, which requires the top management to clearly signal that the activities of the CI facilitators are necessary and valuable to the organization. Leadership is thus an integral part of organizational knowledge creation and depending on the perspective, leadership can either be something that is attributed to a central authority or something that is distributed among different individuals (von Krogh et al., 2012). The shift towards distributed leadership can be attributed to an increased division of labour, new interdependences and coordination between task, and multiple team practices that shape knowledge-intensive work (Gronn, 2002; von Krogh et al., 2012). In the model that we propose, leadership is clearly distributed among different roles and tasks are distributed among different actors. Process management actors, before all CI facilitators, play unquestionably a significant role in the improvement of a firms NPD process landscape. As boundary spanners they reach over the boundaries of their firms to facilitate the flow of improvement knowledge into the organization. Subsequently, they orchestrate its application and diffusion within the organization. Nevertheless, they need the approval of the upper management to engage in these boundary spanning activities. We hope that our findings support process management actors in finding the necessary backing for their initiatives, and gaining recognition for their efforts.

Limitation and future research

This chapter clearly raises more questions than it is able to answer. Further research is needed to clarify the micro-level activities of organizational learning, and the interplay of organizational vs. individual level factors. One crucial step that we have not given adequate attention too, is the initial selection of the specific tool to implement to gain credibility internally, what we referred to as the 'quick win'. In choosing it, the CI facilitator plays a tremendously important role: they 'simplify' a whole management philosophy to help their colleagues visualize and perceive its advantages. Further research is needed to understand how do they actually choose the specific tool to first implement? Moreover, how do they transfer what they learns from its implementation to the next stage? Why so often, despite the initial success, they fail to give continuity to the process (witness the wealth of studies highlighting the lack of diffusion of lean management as an overall philosophy, and its only partial success as a set of tools and techniques). Why is it so hard to learn how to match existing solutions to actual problems? Why is it so hard, in other words, to escape from the garbage can? In this chapter, we have analysed the very first step of this process, the introduction of first specific tool, that sets the stage for the subsequent introduction of further tools and eventually the whole improvement philosophy.

Conclusion

Successful process management activities depend on two distinct types of knowledge, namely improvement and process knowledge. The creation of either type depends on the other one, which means that the two spirals of improvement and process knowledge creation are inherently connected. Hence, process management is a complex task. CI facilitators, a specific and vastly understudied organizational role, play a very important function as they facilitate the flow of improvement knowledge into the firm and orchestrate its application to the benefit of the wider R&D organization. The quest for more efficiency and effectiveness in the fuzzy front end of NPD goes through a deeper understanding of what facilitators do, and how they do it. Professor Nonaka's work provides robust and relevant foundations to such an endeavour.

Note

1. According to the ISI Web of Science citation report in May 2012.

References

Abernathy, W. J. (1978). *The Productivity Dilemma: Roadblock to Innovation in the Automobile Industry*. Baltimore, MD: Johns Hopkins University Press.

Adler, P. S., Benner, M., Brunner, D. J., MacDuffie, J. P., Osono, E., Staats, B. R., Takeuchi, H., Tushman, M., & Winter, S. G. (2009). Perspectives on the productivity dilemma. *Journal of Operations Management*. 27 (2), 99–113.

Alavi, M., & Leidner, D. E. (2001). Review: knowledge management and knowledge management systems: conceptual foundations and research issues. *MIS quarterly*. 107–136.

Allen, T. J., & Cohen, S. I. (1969). Information flow in research and development laboratories. *Administrative Science Quarterly*. 14 (1), 12–19.

Anand, G., & Kodali, R. (2008). Development of a conceptual framework for lean new product development process. *International Journal of Product Development*. 6 (2), 190–224.

Armistead, C. (1999). Knowledge management and process performance. *Journal of Knowledge Management*. 3 (2), 143–157.

Bartezzaghi, E., Corso, M., & Verganti, R. (1997). Continuous improvement and inter-project learning in new product development. *International Journal of Technology Management*. 14 (1), 116–138.

Benner, M. J., & Tushman, M. L (2003). Exploitation, exploration, and process management: the productivity dilemma revisited. *Academy of Management Review*, 28 (2), 238–256.

Birkinshaw, J., Hamel, G., & Mol, M. J. (2008). Management innovation. *Academy of Management Review*. 33(4), 825–845.

Burt, R. S. (1992). *Structural Holes: The Social Structure of Competition*. Cambridge, Massachusetts: Harvard University Press.

Burt, R. S. (2004). Structural holes and good ideas. *American Journal of Sociology*. 110 (2), 349–399.

Burt, R. S. (2005). *Brokerage and Closure: An Introduction to Social Capital*: Oxford University Press, USA.

Cohen, M. D., March, J. G., & Olsen, J. P. (1972). A garbage can model of organizational choice. *Administrative Science Quarterly*. 17 (1), 1–25.

Davenport, T. H. 1993. *Process Innovation: Reengineering Work Through Information Technology*. Cambridge, MA: Harvard Business Press.

Davenport, T. H., De Long, D. W., & Beers, M. C. (1998). Successful knowledge management projects. *Sloan management review*. 39 (2), 43–57.

Dyck, B., Starke, F. A., Mischke, G. A., & Mauws, M. (2005). Learning to build a car: an empirical investigation of organizational learning. *Journal of Management Studies*. 42 (2), 387–416.

Feldman, M. S. (2000). Organizational routines as a source of continuous change. *Organization Science*. 11 (6), 611–629.

Fernandez, R. M., & Gould, R. V. (1994). A dilemma of state power: brokerage and influence in the national health policy domain. *American journal of Sociology*. 99 (6), 1455–1491.

Fleming, L., & Waguespack, D. M. (2007). Brokerage, boundary spanning, and leadership in open innovation communities. *Organization Science*. 18 (2), 165–180.

Gourlay, S. (2006). Conceptualizing knowledge creation: a critique of Nonaka's theory*. *Journal of Management Studies*. 43 (7), 1415–1436.

Granovetter, M. S. (1973). The strength of weak ties. *American Journal of Sociology*. 78 (6),1360–1380.

Grant, R. M. (1996). Toward a knowledge-based theory of the firm. *Strategic Management Journal*. 17, 109–122.

Gronn, P. (2002). Distributed leadership as a unit of analysis. *The Leadership Quarterly*. 13(4), 423–451.

Hackman, J. R., & Wageman, R. (1995). Total quality management: empirical, conceptual, and practical issues. *Administrative Science Quarterly*, 309–342.

Hammer, M. (2002). Process management and the future of Six Sigma. *MIT Sloan Management Review*. 43 (2), 26–32.

Haque, B., and James-Moore, M. (2004). Applying lean thinking to new product introduction. *Journal of Engineering Design*. 15 (1), 1–31.

Hargadon, A. B., & Bechky, B. A. (2006). When collections of creatives become creative collectives: a field study of problem solving at work. *Organization Science*. 17 (4), 484.

Ittner, C. D., & Larcker, D. F. (1997). The performance effects of process management techniques. *Management Science*. 43 (4), 522–534.

Karlsson, C., & Åhlström, P. (1996). The difficult path to lean product development. *Journal of Product Innovation Management*. 13 (4), 283–295.

Katz, R., & Tushman, M. (1979). Communication patterns, project performance, and task characteristics: an empirical evaluation and integration in an R&D setting. *Organizational Behavior and Human Performance*. 23 (2), 139–162.

Lingo, E. L., & O'Mahony, S. (2010). Nexus work: brokerage on creative projects. *Administrative Science Quarterly*. 55 (1), 47.

Martínez León, H. C., & Farris, J. A. (2011). Lean product development research: current state and future directions. *Engineering Management Journal*. 23 (1), 29–51.

Morgan, J. M., & Liker, J. K. (2006). *The Toyota Product Development System: Integrating People, Process, and Technology*. New York: Productivity Press.

Myers, P. S. (1996). *Knowledge Management and Organizational Design*. Newton, MA: Butterworth-Heinemann.

Nelson, R. R., & Winter, S. G. (1982). *An Evolutionary Theory of Economic Change*. Cambridge: Belknap press.

Nilsson-Witell, L., Antoni, M., & Dahlgaard, J. (2005). Continuous improvement in product development. *International Journal of Quality & Reliability Management*. 22 (8), 753–768.

Nonaka, I. (1994). A dynamic theory of organizational knowledge creation. *Organization Science*. 5 (1), 14–37.

Nonaka, I., & Takeuchi, H. (1995). *The Knowledge-Creating Company: How Japanese Companies Create the Dynamics of Innovation*. New York: Oxford University Press.

Nonaka, I., & Toyama, R. (2003). The knowledge-creating theory revisited: knowledge creation as a synthesizing process. *Knowledge Management Research; Practice*. 1 (1), 2–10.

Nonaka, I., Toyama, R., & Konno, N. (2000). SECI, Ba and leadership: a unified model of dynamic knowledge creation. *Long range planning*. 33 (1), 5–34.

Obstfeld, D. (2005). Social networks, the Tertius Iungens orientation, and involvement in innovation. *Administrative Science Quarterly*. 50 (1), 100–130.

Oppenheim, B. W. (2004). Lean product development flow. *Systems engineering*. 7 (4), 352–376.

Pande, P. S., & Holpp, L. (2001). *What is Six Sigma?* New York: McGraw-Hill Professional.

Polanyi, M. (1966). *The Tacit Dimension*. London: Routledge & Kegan Paul.

Powell, T. C. (1995). Total quality management as competitive advantage: a review and empirical study. *Strategic Management Journal*. 16 (1), 15–37.

Reinertsen, D., & Shaeffer, L. (2005). Making R&D lean. *Research-Technology Management*. 48 (4), 51–57.

Reinertsen, D. G. (2009). *The Principles of Product Development Flow: Second Generation Lean Product Development*. Redondo Beach: Celeritas Publishing.

Repenning, N. P., & Sterman, J. D. (2001). Nobody ever gets credit for fixing problems that never happened. *California Management Review*. 43 (4), 64–88.

Repenning, N. P., & Sterman, J. D. (2002). Capability traps and self-confirming attribution errors in the dynamics of process improvement. *Administrative Science Quarterly*. 47 (2), 265–295.

Rother, M. (2010). *Toyota Kata : Managing People for Continuous Improvement and Superior Results*: New York: McGraw-Hill.

Rother, M., & Shook, J. (2003). *Learning to See: Value Stream Mapping to Create Value and Eliminate Muda*: Productivity Press.

Schroeder, R. G., Linderman, K., Liedtke, C., & Choo, A. S. (2008). Six Sigma: definition and underlying theory. *Journal of Operations Management*. 26 (4), 536–554.

Schulze, A., Schmitt, P., Heinzen, M., Mayrl, P., Heller, D., & Boutellier, R. (2011). Exploring the 4I framework of organisational learning in product development: value stream mapping as a facilitator. *International Journal of Computer Integrated Manufacturing*. 1 (15), 1–15.

Simmel, G. (1950). The Sociology of Georg Simmel (K. H. Wolff, Trans.). Glencoe, IL: The Free Press.

Sobek, D., Liker, J., & Ward, A. (1998). Another look at how Toyota integrates product development. *Harvard Business Review* July–August, 36–49.

Tortoriello, M., & Krackhardt, D. (2010). Activating cross-boundary knowledge: the role of Simmelian ties in the generation of innovations. *The Academy of Management Journal (AMJ)*. 53 (1), 167–181.

Trkman, P. (2010). The critical success factors of business process management. *International Journal of Information Management*. 30 (2), 125–134.

Tushman, M. L. (1977). Special boundary roles in the innovation process. *Administrative Science Quarterly*. 22 (4), 587–605.

Tushman, M. L., & Scanlan, T. J. (1981). Boundary spanning individuals: their role in information transfer and their antecedents. *Academy of Management Journal*. 24 (2), 289–305.

Vaccaro, A., Veloso, F., & Brusoni, S. (2009). The impact of virtual technologies on knowledge-based processes: an empirical study. *Research Policy*. 38 (8), 1278–1287.

von Krogh, G., Nonaka, I., & Rechsteiner, L. (2012). Leadership in organizational knowledge creation: a review and framework. *Journal of Management Studies*. 49 (1), 240–277.

Westphal, J. D., Gulati, R., & Shortell, S. M. (1997). Customization or conformity? An institutional and network perspective on the content and consequences of TQM adoption. *Administrative Science Quarterly*. 42 (2), 366–394.
Womack, J., & Jones, D. (1996). *Lean Thinking*. New York: Simon & Schuster.
Womack, J., Jones, D., & Roos, D. (1990). *The Machine that Changed the World*. New York: Rawson Associates.

7

The Knowledge-Based Theory of the Firm and the Question of Firm Boundaries

Pedro López Sáez, José Emilio Navas López, Gregorio Martín de Castro and Jorge Cruz González

Introduction

Corporate strategy and firm growth is probably one of the most relevant topics for management practice. This kind of decision has been addressed by theories of the firm as the question of firm boundaries. Economic theories of the firm have mainly used a cost-related perspective to answer this question. Nevertheless, from the mid-1990s, the strategy field has claimed a richer perspective in order to explain the existence, boundaries and internal organization of the firm, according to the requirements of a knowledge-based economy (Grant, 1996; Kogut & Zander, 1996; Conner & Prahalad, 1996; Foss, 1996). The Knowledge-Based Theory of the Firm (KBT) steps ahead of this claim. It has been considered as the largest subset of the growing literature on strategic theories of the firm, although with some weaknesses in explaining the existence of the firm yet with strengths for understanding value creation and the location of firm boundaries (Phelan & Lewin, 2000).

This chapter describes the main arguments of the KBT for answering the question of firm boundaries. We focus on this question because it is the field in which the KBT has proved to be most useful, and also because it becomes critical for a full development of this theory of the firm. Our purpose is to deliver a comprehensive guide for using the KBT as a theoretical framework for corporate strategy decisions and research.

We briefly revisit the key questions to be explained by a theory of the firm, and the foundations of the KBT, coming from the Resource-Based View of competitive advantage and Evolutionary Economics. Then, from a theoretical perspective we address how and why knowledge determines the boundaries of the firm, and finally we provide some examples of successful Spanish firms that illustrate these arguments on corporate strategy decisions.

Some key elements in theories of the firm

The theory of the firm is a theoretical and empirical challenge because it is difficult to obtain a complete picture of such a multifaceted phenomenon from a single theory. Thus, several theoretical perspectives complement or substitute each other, depending on the questions they seek to answer (Garrouste & Saussier, 2005).

A theoretical perspective claiming to become a theory of the firm has the difficult task of answering three questions (Grant, 1996):

- The nature of the firm. This is to explain the existence of the firm as an institution for the organization of economic activities (transactions/production processes), in contrast or substitution to other economic institutions as markets or complex contracts as alliances. Why do firms exist?
- The boundaries of the firm. This question is usually simplified as the 'make or buy decision'. In fact, from the original Coase seminal article, a theory of the firm should explain why some activities (transactions/production processes) are internalized whereas others are externalized. Which forces drive and limit firm growth?
- The internal organization of the firm. This means to explore the nature of coordination within the firm, analyzing organizational structure, hierarchy, incentives and control mechanisms. How are firms organized? How are activities (transactions/production processes) organized?

In order to answer these questions, each theory of the firm takes a different unit of analysis. In the case of transaction cost theory, transactions are the basic element for determining if the firm or alternative governance forms (mainly markets) will be selected for conducting economic activities. Thus, when a transaction becomes organized inside the firm, this is created (showing the nature of the firm according to the transaction that it embodies). As long as new transactions become internalized, the firm grows until it becomes less efficient, in terms of transaction cost, than the market. Due to its economic roots, transaction cost theory is not really capable of addressing the issue of internal organization, leaving this question with the not fully determined answer as 'firms should choose those organizational forms that minimize internal transaction costs'.

In the case of agency theory, the unit of analysis is the contract, whatever will be its specific kind: market, employment, collaboration and so on. From this perspective, firms do not really exist, because they are just 'collections' of contracts signed by a legal entity. This simplified way to see the firm considers the contracts signed by the firm (as a representation of its owners or principal), and its employees as the counterpart. Once these contracts replace market contracts among the owners of different production factors, the firm rises. As employees and other contributing agents must be rewarded and controlled for respecting their contracts, as firms internalize more and more contracts substituting the market, agency costs increase, posing a limit for firm growth. The answer for the problem of firm internal organization becomes directly solved through the flexibility and cost that internalized contracts provide through 'knowledge substitution'(Conner & Prahalad, 1996).

Although some controversy and even confrontation can be found between the KBT and this alternative approaches to the theory of the firm, we believe that it is necessary to consider this perspective as a complement for enriching alternative visions. Thus, as the unit of analysis of the KBT is a certain knowledge piece, we must highlight that most kinds of knowledge can be the object for transaction and contracts. For example, from a transaction cost perspective, decisions about vertical integration need to calculate the cost of transacting through markets, for its comparison with those of internalizing the production processes of suppliers or customers. Nevertheless, the knowledge required for conducting those processes is the ultimate determinant of internal organization costs, so the costs of acquiring the required productive knowledge lie at the heart of the transaction cost decisions.

In the same vein, every agent tied to the firm through employment (or any other kind) of contract, provides a certain and specialized piece of knowledge as he/she earns a salary as compensation. Agency costs come from supervising those agents that provide all the compromised knowledge. Thus, analyzing knowledge becomes critical for assessing the relative performance of those contracts signed in order to get access to the knowledge required for firm economic activities.

As we have already mentioned, we focus on the question about firm boundaries, adopting a knowledge-based view perspective for its explanation. Before doing so, we need to describe the foundations and assumptions that shape the KBT, in order to argue their implications for corporate strategy decisions.

Foundations of the KBT

In the previous section, we roughly depicted the starting point for the KBT, which is the recognition of knowledge as the central element of all economic activity. As Grant (1996) points out '...all human productivity is knowledge dependent, and all machines are simply embodiments of knowledge' (p. 112). This argument is present in different strategic and economic theoretical bodies which, conveniently melted and extended, give rise to the KBT, from a rich definition of knowledge (Nonaka & von Krogh, 2009). We can highlight two main origins for the development of the KBT: the Resource-Based View (KBV) of competitive advantage (Penrose, 1959; Wernerfelt, 1984; Barney, 1991; Grant, 1991; Peteraf, 1993), and Evolutionary Economics (Schumpeter, 1934; Nelson & Winter, 1982; Teece, Pisano, & Shuen, 1997; Zollo and Winter, 2002).

The KBT and the RBV

In the present, the RBV is probably the dominant approach for explaining competitive advantage in the field of firm strategy. Their two basic axioms (Barney, 1991) are shared with the KBT. First, firms are heterogeneous because of the resources/knowledge they control. Second, due to market imperfections, resources/knowledge are imperfectly mobile across firms, so differences in resources/knowledge endowments may persists over time. This way, firm competitive advantage comes from better resources/knowledge, and its related markets provide the basis for sustaining that advantage.

Although the KBT is sometimes considered an evolution or extension of the RBV, the economic roots of the former, building upon the innovation, entrepreneurship, and evolutionary perspectives go far beyond RBV arguments, and can be even considered as confronted in some aspects. Thus, one of the main criticisms to the RBV is its static nature, because it does not explain how environmental dynamism erodes or enhances resources'/knowledge value (Priem & Butler, 2001).

Following Lewin and Phelan (2000), the value attributed to a certain resource or piece of knowledge must be considered as part of the market process underlying the formation and mutation of the resource/knowledge structure. The RBV provides a diagnostic for competitive advantage positions according to the value of the resources/knowledge base that companies own or control at a specific point in time. Nevertheless, as resource/knowledge value is claimed to include the discounted total of the (estimated) income stream attributable to it, estimations about future incomes would change over time.

As we can see, the RBV shares a common flaw with the Structure-Conduct-Performance (SCP) paradigm that it replaces/complements. According to this, firms should detect structurally appealing industries and penetrate and seize them against competition in order to gain rents. In turn, the RBV propose to detect appealing resources (according to the VRIN criteria for example), and get and protect them in the quickest and most effective way in order to obtain and sustain rents. Both approaches do not address the point that any firm action, whenever that means acting in an industry or factor market, start dynamics within their competitive contexts, changing the status quo of the analyzed industry or resource market.

The equilibrium orientation of the RBV approach limits its usefulness for explaining how organizations learn in the face of novelty, which is a key element of real world economics, and usually not in 'perfect' competition models (Horwitz, 2011). Thus, although both the evolutionary theory and the RBV are knowledge-based explanations of the firm (Garrouste & Saussier, 2005), they are also distinct approaches, with different purposes, and its evolutionary economics which allow to address the static limitations of the RBV and to move towards the explanations required for a theory of the firm.

The KBT and Evolutionary Economics

Bounded rationality (Simon, 1982) can be considered as the cornerstone of the evolutionary twist of the KBT. Although transaction cost theory mainly takes this concept for explaining opportunistic behaviour and its prevention, a wider use of it provides an outstanding explanation of the restrictions found on learning or knowledge creation processes (Simon, 1991; Dossi & Marengo, 2000). Limited cognitive abilities explain why individuals and firms differ in their knowledge endowments, so even in the absence of opportunism, bounded rationality remains (Conner & Prahalad, 1996).

Bounded rationality is especially worthwhile for the 'fundamental asymmetry in the economics of knowledge' (Grant, 1996): knowledge acquisition requires more specialization, time and efforts than those needed for its utilization.

As a consequence of bounded rationality, economic agents, whatever it will be firms or individuals contracting in the market possess different types of knowledge, and their knowledge base determines their absorptive capacity (Cohen & Levinthal, 1990) for new knowledge domains. Thus, even in the presence of the same knowledge inputs, different agents can create alternative knowledge outputs, or as Winter argues: 'knowing how to bake a cake' is clearly not the same thing as 'knowing how to bring together in one place all of the ingredients for a cake' (2006, p. 131). The same recipe can taste very different according to the chef that prepares it. Besides, the best chefs can manage to change ingredients for creating new recipes when, for example, facing ingredient shortage or satisfying different diners.

The link between evolutionary economics and knowledge is that knowledge is not only an input and output of the production process embodied in firm resources and products. Knowledge is also the essence of the production function, and an important divergence with neo-classical economics is that the production function of any firm is not generally adopted in the industry nor optimal in the mathematical sense, but firm learning and ongoing change rules, and is not just an exception for general modelling.

In this sense, from their different knowledge bases, each firm will design their own production function. Besides, through learning, each production function will be changing over time in a trial and error fashion, seeking to improve its own operation so as to enhance the productivity of its elements, resources or knowledge pieces (Horwitz, 2011). In this alternative to the production function view, firms are seen as institutions that are created to solve knowledge problems and are engaged in an ongoing process of learning. They face an uncertain future where they must entrepreneurially anticipate what their customers want, gathering knowledge about product markets, obtain different kinds of capital resources (including intellectual capital) necessary to meet those wants, and then develop linkages between those capital resources and activities through evolving routines.

Innovation and entrepreneurial judgment (Casson, 2005) relies on a certain knowledge base that shapes the perception of opportunities to create new economic value from competitive imperfections in factor or product markets (Alvarez & Barney, 2007), where knowledge acts both as an input and as an output of economic activities. Innovation and entrepreneurship represent the essence of the classic evolutionary paradigm of variation-selection-retention (Zollo y Winter, 2002). Thus, every firm in an industry tries to create new knowledge (or a better judgement about extant knowledge pieces) generating variations within the industry context. Those productive combinations of knowledge which become more strategically or financially successful within the competitive arena provide higher Schumpeterian rents for entrepreneurial firms. Rent seeking behaviours and knowledge spillover lead to imitation and the erosion of these rents, so that knowledge that once is considered as the 'best practice' becomes more or less quickly a well known and diffused 'industry recipe' (Coff et al., 2006), and those firms unable for learning and adaptation will fade away according to the competition rates of each industry.

Firms that operate in highly competitive environments are more likely to learn and respond well to the unexpected. In such environments, economic survival is tightly linked to finding a more effective production function that bridge resources/input knowledge and firm activities. In a similar way, only monopoly protections (externally or internally built) or the absence of competitive environments will allow an organization to survive with a lower and slower learning (Horwitz, 2011).

When competition demands adaptation for survival and innovation for Schumpeterian value creation, environmental scanning becomes critical. Entrepreneurs create firms in order to monitor environmental volatility for detecting opportunities to be exploited. Organizations take advantage of the division of labour in the search and use of new knowledge, but they face increasing costs of communication and coordination due to specialization. Thus, firms can be understood as social communities specializing in the speed and efficiency in the creation and transfer of knowledge (Kogut & Zander, 1996).

As social learning procedures and identity arise, they shape complex collective knowledge which, in turn, is path dependent (Barney, 1991; Foss, 1994). Inertia (Tripsas & Gavetti, 2000) and repeated behaviours for knowledge acquisition and usage (Nelson & Winter, 2002) can lead both to dynamic capabilities (Teece, Pisano, & Shuen, 1997) or learning myopia (Levinthal & March, 1993). This way, in a constant disequilibrium or evolutionary framework, knowledge and learning are not only the source of competitive advantages, but also of its decline when routines become 'core rigidities'. These hinder the detection of new opportunities from the environment as they limit the deep and wide of new knowledge search and internal variation.

The mixed arguments extracted form the RBV and evolutionary economics that we have already explained represent a heterogeneous body of research aimed to solving very different problems as inter-firm competition (Barney, 1991), firm adaptation (Teece, Pisano, & Shuen, 1997) or knowledge acquisition strategies (Levinthal & March, 1993). Nevertheless, our purpose is to use them for addressing the problem of firm boundaries, that is, the question about which phenomena drive and limit firm growth along different industries and countries. In the following two sections, we explain the theory underlying this issue, and we provide some examples from it.

Delimitation of firm boundaries

According to the KBT, corporate strategy decisions about firm boundaries are driven by to counteracting forces, which embody a value creation perspective and a cost perspective. The former represents the rent seeking behaviour that lies in the benefits of developing or acquiring new knowledge for the already extant knowledge base.

Following Lewin and Phelan (2000), a rent is just the value of the services that a certain resource or knowledge piece can provide, so all resource/knowledge-based strategies come down to the creation, enhancement and protection of such value.

If every kind of knowledge can be considered a type of 'capital' (Foss et al., 2007), value is created by entrepreneurial decision makers who form new capital combinations, and strategic rents come from discovering discrepancies about the expected future rents yield by these combinations (Lewin & Phelan, 2000). This way, new knowledge can be a source of Schumpeterian rents when: (a) it allows to introduce the firm into a new business; and (b) complementarities among the present knowledge base, and the product, activities and businesses portfolio allow to seizure value creating opportunities from already available knowledge. Thus, the value of current knowledge is enhanced through new combinations, and a firm knowledge base is extended and recombined in order to exploit its rent-earning potential (Madhok, 1996).

The later force that explain the limits for firm growth is closer to more traditional theories of the firm as transaction cost economics or agency theory, because it deals with the costs of creating new knowledge or with increasing communication and coordination costs for realizing synergies. Division of labour makes people increasingly more competent in their specialization, but the process by which specialization drives increasing performance implies the problem of coordination, so costs of communication, coordination and new combinations are the main limitation when considering boundary decisions for firms (Kogut & Zander, 1996).

In this vein, decisions about internalizing new knowledge pieces embodied into employees, activities or businesses can require investments and risks hardly to assess ex ante, which can lead to sunk costs. In conditions of environmental uncertainty, the value of any piece of knowledge is assumed to take into account the discounted value of its expected future rental stream. Nonetheless, different firms will have different estimates of these rental streams (Lewin & Phelan, 2000) according to their available knowledge base and the coordination mechanisms needed to appraise the value of knowledge pieces. Estimations need to cope both with uncertainty about increased productivity for complementing knowledge, and also about the cost for linking different kinds of knowledge.

The search for synergies and complementarities among the knowledge pieces already available in the firm knowledge base can also be depicted as a problem of internal organization (with coordination and communication costs) or firm government (with incentive and control costs). The cognitive limits of working out better knowledge combinations can demand new rules and procedures of coordination and a feasible redistribution of power and authority (Kogut & Zander, 1996).

Traditional explanations for the theory of the firm have taken market transaction costs or those tied to different kinds of contracts as determinants of firm boundaries. The KBT does not neglect these costs, because they are often a consequence of knowledge characteristics (as tacitness, collective or even public good character), but it broadens the focus from minimizing the costs of running economic activities under a particular governance arrangement to the managing of value inherent in a knowledge base, in terms of both erosion and enhancement (Madhok, 1996). The main difference of this focus is taking knowledge creation or combination as a source of benefits that guides and also limits firm growth in order to address the question of firm boundaries. Efficient production is a result not of having better knowledge resources, but of knowing more accurately the relative productive performances of those knowledge resources, because on the contrary to the given production function of basic neoclassical economics, such knowledge is not given, but has to be created or discovered (Foss et al., 2007).

Corporate decisions about extending firm operations in the vertical, horizontal and geographical dimensions deal with the previously mentioned problems. When the required knowledge base for new activities is very close to the one already available within the firm, entering these activities may have a value enhancing potential. This potential comes from the fact that the investment for acquiring or developing that knowledge have been already made for conducting the traditional activities of the firm. Besides, the value of the already available knowledge increases because it becomes more adaptable and gains more uses or 'multiple specificity' (Lewin & Phelan, 2000).

Nevertheless, before the final decision about firm growth is made, the expectations about gathering all the rest of required knowledge for the new venture, and developing the integration mechanisms (which are in turn a form of knowledge) for connecting it with the extant knowledge base, must be made. The newly projected knowledge combinations can only demonstrate its value creating potential once they are put into test. Then, only after investing in obtaining the necessary but not available knowledge for the new activities, and connecting it to the previous knowledge base, ex-post value of the designed knowledge combination can be known.

When the proposed knowledge combination does not lead to the expected profits, value and cost expectations will be modified, but even more important is the fact that the trial provides useful feedback for improving the learning process for discovering the value of the knowledge base of the firm. Thus, the external environment acts as an evolutionary mechanism that provides the firm with signals for ascertain which applications of knowledge become more valuable, and which proposed knowledge combinations and firm behaviours should be discarded (Zollo & Winter, 2002). In this sense, the market process is a disequilibrium process driven by the ongoing arrival of new knowledge that falsifies old expectations, as time and learning belong together (Lewin & Phelan, 2000).

Choosing an alternative for entering new businesses, firms should assess the benefits of speed, complementarity, and protection desired for the required new knowledge, as well as their corresponding costs. Natural growth, mergers and acquisitions, and alliances are usually alternative solutions for addressing firm growth. Nevertheless, when they are analyzed as methods for acquiring knowledge in order to enter new business, they show different advantages and strengths that can not lead to a prescriptive and optimal decision rule. A contingency approach should be developed for the firm in order to decide which of these modes represents the best option for a specific situation.

The knowledge based theory of the firm on corporate strategy decisions: some cases of Spanish firms

The field in which the KBT has been most fruitfully applied is international business. Since the seminal works by Kogut and Zander (1992, 1993, 1996), we can say that the knowledge based theory of the multinational corporation (MNC) has evolved towards an explanation of the existence, boundaries and internal organization of any kind of firm. Knowledge based arguments have transformed the international business research (Fransson et al., 2011), proposing that the MNC advantage over local firms lies in its superior capabilities to internally transfer knowledge among subsidiaries located in different countries, managing a complex network of distributed and shared knowledge (Gupta & Govindarajan, 2000).

Knowledge can easily be taken as the reason for internationalization, but also for selecting entry modes for entering foreign markets. Reusing knowledge in multiple locations is one of the keys for obtaining competitive advantage over local firms (Jensen & Szulanski, 2004). As we have argued before, although new knowledge will also be necessary to penetrate targeted locations, a proven successful knowledge base represents a powerful tool in this kind of situations. Some examples of successful internationalization by Spanish firms can show how this works in the real world.

Santander and BBVA, the biggest Spanish banks, were born from a national industry consolidation process played through mergers and acquisitions. From the 1990s, both banks, with a strong position in their original market, shaped by a deep knowledge base about commercial banking, began their internationalization throughout Latin-America. Trying to replicate the success of their business models in the targeted markets, they only needed direct market knowledge and infrastructures. This is the reason why the chose mainly mergers and acquisitions as the entry mode. M&A granted a quick access to the new customers, and protected their knowledge base from competitor appropriation or learning. The success of the proposed combination of knowledge gathered form the Spanish market and industry with those acquired in the new markets increased the knowledge of BBVA and Santander about entering new countries and conducting M&A. Thus, the next step was entering also into other European countries and even taking a step ahead into China.

The same principles that rule the exploitation of the current knowledge base can also be found when analyzing horizontal boundaries of the firm. When a company decides to extend its product range or even enter new industries with new products, decision makers face the dilemma of how much of the already available knowledge can be reused in those products or industries, and which pieces should be internally or externally obtained for complementarities to be worthwhile enough to start diversification. Although product or industrial domains could seem disperse or unconnected, when considering a firm knowledge base as the main determinant of firm boundaries, we must look into knowledge complementarity instead. Our illustrative example for this case is Indra, a Spanish firm that defines itself as a global technology, innovation and talent company.

Indra was born in 1993 as the merger of four Government companies or agencies mainly related to the R&D and project development for the military: ERITEL (consultancy and IT services), DISEL (automation and control), CESELSA (electronics for defence) and INISEL ESPACIO (space industry). In 1999, Indra went public, and it started to define its business portfolio with clear criteria of enhancing the value of its knowledge base and seeking complementarities between it and new knowledge domains. Thus, Indra undertakes its internationalization in order to reuse the knowledge gathered from certain projects, with some adaptation or deepen for covering the new needs of the new customers. For example, in 2003, Indra became the only non-American provider of the US Navy, and it startsed the development of cutting-edge technology for the Single European Sky Initiative. In 2006, it entered the Chinese Security market with a contract for developing Hong Kong's border surveillance system.

The main purpose of any entry mode selected and all mergers and acquisitions carried out by Indra has been reinforcing its knowledge base with complementary or deeper knowledge that could improve its performance. This way, in the last decade Indra has acquired firms specialized in IT consulting and development, strategic consultancy and BPO services for the financial sector. After those steps, Indra gets a strong knowledge base within its business, defined as 'solutions' and 'services', that makes the company ranking second in Europe by R&D spend, investing about €500m during the last three years. The knowledge base of the company is focused on a combination of electronics, communications, and information technology that is tailored to the needs of customers in order to develop turnkey and proprietary solutions. Services are a complementary business area devoted to managing outsourcing and application maintenance services, that has lead Indra into the development of a network of production services centres in Spain, Latin America and Eastern Europe. All of the knowledge gathered for developing solutions and applications also becomes very useful for understanding how to improve its management for customers.

The main argument about the case of Indra is that their knowledge base is continuously deployed and redeployed for developing and managing specialized services and applications that shape the product base of the company. Nevertheless, if we take a look at the industries and clients for which Indra is working, this firm would seem and incredible diversified company, acting in so different industries as transport and traffic, energy, consumer goods and services, public administration, healthcare, finance, insurance, security and defence, and telecom and media. This illustrates that knowledge and business portfolios are two related dimensions, and the task of managers is to create and enhance value form the former through the later (Grant, 1996).

Vertical integration decisions are the most commented upon corporate strategy from the transaction cost perspective. From this viewpoint, upstream and downstream vertical integration are just a decision about controlling opportunism related and operation costs. Nevertheless, some useful complementary insights may be obtained from the KBT also for vertical boundaries. When strong complementarities exist between the knowledge required in the different supply chain stages, in a similar vein than horizontal and geographical boundaries, appraisal of those value creation opportunities can make these decisions interesting. In addition, there are some cases in which vertical integrated firms can enhance protection of knowledge, and even increase the value of critical knowledge. One of the most studied cases of highly integrated operations worldwide is Inditex (see for example Ferdows et al., 2004 or Lopez & Fan, 2009).

The main difference between Inditex and its competitors is its vertical integration degree, aimed to achieve a faster turnaround time, improving adaptation to local markets and fashion trends. Its 'fast fashion' business model is based upon knowledge flows throughout all the supply chain. Design, production and logistics are centralized, and must be always fine-tuned coordinated. The proposed and extended production function is precisely based on knowledge management. Its advantage versus less integrated competitors lies in knowledge combination. Stores capture knowledge about demands, whereas the design departments has to fulfil these requirements, adding new couture trends as they appear. New knowledge is quickly embodied into new designs, which are fastly send into the production lines and stores. But the most important part is learning to be quick and effective, the learner must receive quick and effective feedback from the external environment and must also bear fully the costs and benefits that the feedback provides (Horwitz, 2011), and this happens through IT tools that connect each retail store with the company headquarters at La Coruña.

Inditex can be also an example of geographical and industry growth according to its knowledge base. Its vertically integrated system has increased its value making possibilities, with the access to 78 countries. Besides, its knowledge management system has been applied into eight store formats (Zara, Pull, & Bear, Massimo Dutti, Bershka, Oysho, Zara Home and Uterqüe). Nevertheless, the value of the already available knowledge poses serious concerns about moving outside the fast fashion industry, due to the fact that an important rate of additional knowledge will be required for that kind of corporate decision and the value of the current knowledge could diminish in very different applications. Thus, the knowledge base of Inditex can be seen both as the driving and constraining force for its vertical, international and industrial boundaries.

References

Alvarez, S. A., & Barney, J. B. (2007). The entrepreneurial theory of the firm – guest editors' introduction. *Journal of Management Studies*. 44 (7), 1057–1063.

Barney, J. B. (1991). Firm resources and sustained competitive advantage. *Journal of Management*. 17 (1), 99–120.

Casson, M. (2005). Entrepreneurship and the theory of the firm. *Journal of Economic Behavior and Organization*. 58 (2), 327–348.

Coff, R. W., Coff, D. C., & Eastvold, R. (2006). The knowledge-leveraging paradox: how to achieve scale without making knowledge imitable. *Academy of Management Review*. 31(2), 452–465.

Cohen, W. M., & Levinthal, D. A. (1990). Absorptive capacity: a new perspective on learning and innovation. *Administrative Science Quarterly*. 35 (1), 128–153.

Conner, K. R., & Prahalad, C. K. (1996). A resource-based theory of the firm: knowledge versus opportunism. *Organization Science*. 7 (5), 477–501.

Dossi, G., & Marengo, L. (2000). On the tangled discourse between transaction cost economics and competence-based views of the firm: some comments. In N. J. Foss, & V. Mahnke (eds), *Competence, Governance, and Entrepreneurship* (pp. 80–92). New York: Oxford University Press.

Ferdows, K., Lewis, M. A., & Machuca, J. A. D. (2004). Rapid-fire fulfillment. *Harvard Business Review*. 82 (11), 104–110.

Foss, N. J. (1994). The biological analogy and the theory of the firm: Marshall and monopolistic competition. *Journal of Economic Issues*. 28 (4), 1115–1136.
Foss, N. J. (1996). Knowledge-based approaches to the theory of the firm: some critical comments. *Organization Science*. 7 (5), 470–476.
Foss, K., Foss, N. J., Klein, P. G., & Klein, S. K. (2007). The entrepreneurial organization of heterogeneous capital. *Journal of Management Studies*. 44(7), 1166–1186.
Fransson, A., Håkanson, L., & Liesch, P. W. (2011). The undetermined knowledge-based theory of the MNC. *Journal of International Business Studies*. 42 (3), 427–435.
Garrouste, P., & Saussier, S. (2005). Looking for a theory of the firm: future challenges. *Journal of Economic Behavior and Organization*. 58 (2), 178–199.
Grant, R. M. (1991). The resource-based theory of competitive advantage: implications for strategy formulation. *California Management Review*. 33 (3), 114–135.
Grant, R. M. (1996). Toward a knowledge-based theory of the firm. *Strategic Management Journal*. 17 (1), 109–122.
Gupta, A. K., & Govindarajan, V. (2000). Knowledge flows within multinational corporations. *Strategic Management Journal*. 21, 473–496.
Horwitz, S. (2011). The sensory order and organizational learning. In B. Butos (ed.), *The Social Science of Hayek's Sensory Order* (pp. 263–284). Bingley, UK: Emerald Publishing.
Jensen, R, & Szulanski, G. (2004). Stickiness and the adaptation of organizational practices in cross-border knowledge transfers. *Journal of International Business Studies*. 35 (6), 508–523.
Kogut, B., & Zander, U. (1992). Knowledge of the firm, combinative capabilities, and the replication of technology. *Organization Science*. 3 (3), 383–397.
Kogut, B., & Zander, U. (1993). Knowledge of the firm and the evolutionary theory of the multinational corporation. *Journal of International Business Studies*. 24 (4), 625–645.
Kogut, B., & Zander, U. (1996). What firms do? Coordination, identity, and learning. *Organization Science*. 7 (5), 502–518.
Levinthal, D. A., & March, J. G. (1993). The myopia of learning. *Strategic Management Journal*. 14 (1), 95–112.
Lewin, P., & Phelan, S. E. (2000). An Austrian theory of the firm. *Review of Austrian Economics*. 13 (1), 59–79.
Lopez, C., & Fan, Y. (2009). Internationalisation of the Spanish fashion brand Zara. *Journal of Fashion Marketing and Management*. 13 (2), 279–296.
Madhok, A. (1996). The organization of economic activity: transaction costs, firm apabilities, and the nature of governance. *Organization Science*. 7 (5), 577–590.
Nelson, R. & Winter, S. G. (1982). *An Evolutionary Theory of Economic Change*. Cambridge, MA: Belknap Press.
Nelson, R., & Winter, S. G. (2002). Evolutionary theorizing in economics. *Journal of Economic Perspectives*. 16 (2), 23–46.
Nonaka, I., & von Krogh, G. (2009). Tacit knowledge and knowledge conversion: controversy and advancement in organizational knowledge creation theory. *Organization Science*. 20 (3), 635–652.
Penrose, E. (1959). *The Theory of the Growth of the Firm*. New York: Wiley.
Peteraf, M. (1993). The cornerstones of competitive advantage: a resource-based view. *Strategic Management Journal*. 14(3), 179–191.
Phelan, S. E., & Lewin, P. (2000). Arriving at a strategic theory of the firm. *International Journal of Management Reviews*. 2 (4), 305–323.
Priem, R. L., & Butler, J. E. (2001). Is the resource-based view a useful perspective for strategic management research? *The Academy of Management Review*. 26 (1), 22–40.

Schumpeter, J. A. (1934). *The Theory of Economic Development: An Inquiry into Profits, Capital, Credit, Interest, and the Business Cycle*. Cambridge, MA: Harvard University Press.

Simon, H. A. (1982). *Models of Bounded Rationality*. Cambridge, MA: The MIT Press.

Simon, H. A. (1991). Bounded rationality and organizational learning. *Organization Science*. 2 (1), 125–134.

Teece, D. J., Pisano, G., & Shuen, A. (1997). Dynamic capabilities and strategic management. *Strategic Management Journal*. 18 (7), 509–533.

Tripsas, M., & Gavetti, G. (2000). Capabilities, cognition, and inertia: evidence from digital imaging. *Strategic Management Journal*. 21 (10/11), 1147–1161.

Wernerfelt, B. (1984). A resource-based view of the firm. *Strategic Management Journal*. 5 (2), 171–180.

Winter, S. G. (2006). Toward a neo-schumpeterian theory of the firm. *Industrial and Corporate Change*. 15 (1), 125–141.

Zollo, M., & Winter, S. G. (2002). Deliberate learning and the evolution of dynamic capabilities. *Organization Science*. 13(3), 339–351.

8

Russia's First Handbook of Knowledge Management As a Reflector of a KM Landscape Sui Generis

Nigel J. Holden

Introduction: Russia needs KM

The 'new' Russia is a country, whose lurch towards the market economy has been described 'painful and contradictory' (Shkuta, 2008); a country which has been graphically described as 'an Old Testament land, a place of plagues and floods, of locusts and blizzards and power outrages without end' Meier (2004: 50); and a country where the business environment is 'merciless' *The Economist* (2011a), and where 'entrenched bossdom' (Holden, 2012 variously discourages initiative, empowerment and creativity. Beyond that Puffer and McCarthy (2011) have contended that:

> One of the defining characteristics of Russian business is the weak legitimacy of Russian institutions, which fosters dependency on informal institutions such as culture and ethics. This combination of environmental influences limits the range of viable options on bridging mechanisms such as corporate governance and business strategy.

Proceeding from there, these authors argue that the engrained Russian 'distrust of formal organisations' (Puffer & McCarthy, 2011) is not only holding back the country's economic progress, but is also *a serious constraint on knowledge management,* whereby the very global competitiveness of Russian firms is seriously constrained.[1] Against this perturbing background, the relatively recent publication of Russia's first major reference work on KM, *The Handbook of Knowledge Management* (Andreyeva & Gutnikova, 2009) is an event of no passing significance: not only as a new stage in Russia's fraught attempts to embrace the market-economy system, on the one hand, and its struggle to absorb Western management concepts, on the other, but also (implausible as this may sound) as a notable landmark in KM as an international practice.

The purpose of this chapter is to build a narrative around those propositions about *The Handbook* by a process of recontextualisation, this being 'the process of extracting knowledge from one context to be converted and adapted to another context' (Thompson, Warhurst, & Callaghan, 2001). By dint of this exegesis, *The Handbook* becomes a medium for revealing aspects of Russia's KM landscape,[2] as a context-specific confection of possibly unthinkable features and of equally unthinkable 'philosophical stances and practical orientations' (Michailova, 2011). There is no landscape like it on this planet.

Language and KM: largely unchartered territory

Recontextualization in this case will mean, among other things, delving into the complexities of translating English-language KM terms into Russian.[3] At first glance this may seem like a dry, obscure task. Yet, as we shall see, the glimpses into the processes of cross-cultural transformation undertaken by *The Handbook*'s editors not only directly challenge our own often uncontested assumptions about KM, but also reveal the sloppiness in the creation and use of the discipline's terminology in English. The relationship between language – that is to say, 'the great human fact of Language' (Entwistle, 1974; original emphasis) and KM is poorly charted, though the process has in fact already been initiated by Nonaka and Takeuchi in *The knowledge-creating company*. These distinguished authors make explicit reference to 'the structure [and] the ambiguous nature of the Japanese language', arguing that the verb in Japanese has precious – and unmistakably unWestern – attributes for facilitating the transfer and sharing tacit knowledge (for further discussion, see Holden & Glisby, 2010).

But Nonaka and Takeuchi do not dwell long on the intricacies of the Japanese verbal system, being more concerned with the Japanese language as facilitator of mood than as a bearer of KM terminology. For the record, we should note Nonaka and co-authors in *Managing Flow* (2008) devote some eight pages to a discussion of the (almost sacred) term *ba*. That aside, neither KM terminology nor its translation into other language appears to be of any interest whatsoever to the KM community (but see Holden & Glisby (2010) for a discussion of language and tacit knowledge). Yet there is probably not one member of it who, if he or she were to care to think about it, would deny that the KM terminology is the very guarantor of the discipline as a distinct academic and practical domain.

So what KM terminology 'looks like' in other languages should be of relevance to all KM specialists who in theory and practice are challenged by issues to do with the cross-cultural transfer of knowledge. Who after all would have imagined that in Russian you cannot, literally speaking, *share* knowledge or that everyday terms like knowledge worker or community of practice test translators' resourcefulness to the limit? But our recontextualization of *The Handbook* will go beyond 'mere' translation (and not, by the way, require any discussion of the behaviour of the Russian verb). The technique nevertheless allows us to generate from the deep structures of the Russian text insights into nature of knowledge and organisational knowledge in Russian enterprises. In passing, we supply some cautionary words for foreign firms engaged in knowledge sharing with Russian business partners.

The Handbook: provenance and purpose

The Handbook of Knowledge Management belongs to a series produced by the Graduate School of Management of University of St. Petersburg under the general title *Contemporary management classics*. Other volumes address topics of significance under such titles as 'resources, dynamic capabilities, and corporate strategy', 'management of change', 'business ethics', 'strategic human resource management', 'marketing – classical and new concepts'.

The *Handbook* consists of 23 contributions in Russian, all of which first appeared in English (see Appendix 7.1 for a list of references). Of these contributions 20 have been selected from academic journals ranging from *Harvard Business Review, Sloan Management Review, Academy of Management Executive* and *Knowledge and Process Management*. One contribution is a chapter from an edited book. All the items were originally published in the period from 1991 to 2004. Translation was undertaken by the two editors in collaboration with 15 other translators. The contributions were selected on the grounds of their significant conceptual importance, their authorship by world authorities, their perceived central impact on KM as a management discipline and – this is important – relevance to Russian practitioners.

In his introduction to the *Handbook*, the dean of the Graduate School of Management of St Petersburg University notes that in the last 50 years there has been 'tremendous development', which has seen a shift from vocational establishments to university level business schools. These business schools recognize that the modern manager needs 'analytical competence and a new mind-set which is in tune with the processes of globalization and emergence of the knowledge economy'. But the dean also notes that Russian business schools have been lagging behind in these processes, and for a major reason: Russian professors are not familiar with the leading management journals which represent 'the main world's platform for the development of management thinking, formulating hypotheses and testing them with quantitative methods'. His message to Russian managers is forthright and uncompromising:

> Today Russian business education is developing energetically, trying to keep up with leaders in their various sectors and their standards. But there is no way whereby the world standard can be attained through education except by means of studying the output of the leading academic journals.

In common with the companion volumes, the dean declares that the *Handbook* on KM will 'correct' this unsatisfactory state of affairs. He adds that it is an aspiration of all the handbooks in the series that they are 'especially useful to those who are becoming acquainted with a given discipline for the first time'.

Noting that Russian management educators focus on teaching and consultancy and tend to concentrate on marketing, strategy, finance and organizational management, the editors are, like the dean, aware of Russian managers' unfamiliarity with the latest ideas in management. With this in mind and according to editors Andreyeva and Gutnikova (2009), the stated aim of the handbook is to:

- 'Introduce and elucidate for Russian students the basic concepts of knowledge management and explain the relevance of these issues for contemporary organizations'.
- 'Present key concepts of knowledge management, in the first place describing the fundamental organizational processes connected with knowledge'.
- 'Show how these concepts are reflected and applied in various aspects of organizational management (strategy, structure, culture, personnel management, evaluation of results of activities)'.

Translating the often untranslatable

In their introduction, the two editors begin by posing a serious question: Why is KM suddenly so important, if knowledge 'has accompanied mankind – and correspondingly organizations – throughout human history?' The answer, they suggest, has to do with the fact that in the modern world, under the pressure of globalization and the march of new technologies, organizations avail themselves of a wide range of resources, and knowledge is needed for making best use of these resources. This, according to them, is the essence of knowledge management: 'an interdisciplinary approach to the attainment of organizational goals by way of more effective use of knowledge'. While this sounds straightforward elsewhere, in Russia this approach entails many challenges.

To begin with, the editors note that in the Russian context it is very difficult to explain how knowledge (a resource) differs from information (a commodity). They are aware that many readers would be able to see no clear-cut distinction between knowledge society and information society, even though information systems were already well established management tools in the late Soviet era.[4] Hence knowledge management itself is 'a rather complicated concept', as it is not 'a concrete function in an organization, but an ideology penetrating all spheres of operation'. By ideology they emphatically do not mean 'an abstraction far from organizational realities, but rather a new way of looking at familiar things, including a new conception of completion of tasks of functional subdivisions'.

Editors Andreyeva and Gutnikova (2009) suggest that KM should be viewed from three general perspectives: knowledge engineering, strategic management and organizational and human aspects. The focus of the *Handbook* is on the latter theme. Beyond that they are aware is the KM field in the English-speaking world that is characterized by having 'no unitary terminology or unitary understanding of the scope of the topic'. Accordingly the editors, and by an unexpected route, have found common ground with the many commentators, who are also struggling to specify the epistemological and practical status of KM.

This issue confronted the editors and translators with the severe problems of (a) dealing with terminological imprecision in English and (b) finding Russian equivalents. The two editors, who also served as translators, were aware that many readers would not be clear about the difference between and knowledge assets and intellectual assets. This attributive (i.e., adjectival) use of knowledge was particularly tricky. For example, the editors cite no fewer than seven attested translations of the term knowledge worker. They also created a new term for knowledge as an adjective [*znanieviy*], but this word, they admit, has 'not established itself in the Russian language'. This improvization has been widely used in the translation of knowledge as an attributive in several of the translations of the titles. We now turn to a selection of the troublesome terms which the translators had to come to grips with.

You cannot share knowledge in Russian

For the benefit of their readers, the editors compiled a glossary of 107 KM terms. However, by no means all of them form what one might the terminological core of KM; a clear majority are explanations of expressions used by the authors whose works have been translated into Russian. Admirably the editors even consulted authors to clarify their use of particular terms to help with the translations into Russian. Core KM terms include: absorptive capacity, community of practice (see the following), declarative knowledge, explicit knowledge and implicit knowledge. Terms that are peculiar to authors include words and expressions such as appropriability, exploiter, failure to capture, folk knowledge, infinitely flat organization, knowledge friction, learning-before-doing, organizational forgetting and so on. We should mention that the four key terms of the influential Nonaka and Takeuchi (1995) model of knowledge conversion, namely socialization, externalization, combination and internalization, are explained in the glossary. One core term is surprisingly absent: stickiness.

Of the 107 terms in the glossary, many have presented the translators with real challenges, as is evident when we perform a back-translation. For example, 'intangible' unsatisfactorily becomes in literal translation 'immaterial, whereas 'capture' as in 'knowledge capture' is rendered as 'assimilation of knowledge' (which is definitely not the same thing). The term 'gate-keeper' is defined in terms of an individual who acts as 'communicating mechanism', interacting with external organizations, reducing 'communication disruptions and cognitive mismatches', while enhancing organizational absorptive capacity. There is no suggestion in the Russian translation that gatekeepers are strongly influential in prioritizing information which they see ahead of decision-makers and determining who has access to them and when.[5]

Of considerable interest are the renditions into Russian of 'core knowledge' and 'knowledge sharing'. In back translation core knowledge becomes basic knowledge, but this is not quite the same thing. The word 'core' refers to 'the part of something that is central to its existence or character' (*Oxford*, 2006), whereas basic connotes 'forming an essential foundation or starting point' (*Oxford*, 2006). We do not include this observation simply to split hairs, but to emphasise that such near-miss translations reveal how casual is the working vocabulary of KM in English. In other words, KM joins the ranks of other management disciplines that do not take care of their specialist terms as do other professionals such as lawyers, engineers or medical practitioners. The discipline tolerates what Watson (2004) calls 'managerial pseudo-jargon', and this poses significant problems to translators into the world's languages, and not just Russian.

As for knowledge sharing, this most frequent of KM terms, is seemingly untranslatable into Russian. The literal Russian translation of knowledge sharing is, according to *The Handbook,* knowledge distribution (or dissemination), which does not convey an aspect of the intimate interchange of knowledge under concepts such as 'socialization' (Nonaka & Takeuchi, 1995, pp. 62–64) or not to mention 'dialoguing' (Christensen & Bukh, 2005, p. 27) and 'languaging' (McKenzie & van Winkelen, 2004, pp. 112–114). It may or may not be a coincidence that a country with management systems that allegedly prize knowledge hoarding and secrecy (see the following) no concept of knowledge sharing, hence the striking lexical void.

Community of practice in translation and back-translation

The term community of practice is widely discussed in the mainstream KM literature (Baumard, 2001, pp. 134–135, 209–212; Kohlbacher, 2007, pp. 28–30; McKenzie & van Winklelen, 2004, p. 38, pp. 120–126, 254–255; Nonaka et al., 2008, pp. 36–37; von Krogh et al., 2000, pp. 179–180; Wenger, 1998; Wenger & Snyder, 2000). There is broad agreement among these authors as to the role, purpose and general characteristics of roles of practice, yet not one author suggests that the effectiveness and durability of a CoP, a terrain of learning and knowledge sharing *par excellence,* depends on a shared set of terms intelligible to all parties. Baumard (2000, p. 134), however, makes the significant point that each and every CoP has its own language which is both an institutionalizing influence and sustainer of 'distinct symbolic universe'. No author suggests that the description of CoPs, many of which are in today's world not just global in reach but multi-cultural in their memberships, requires *consistent* KM terminology.

Taking our cue from Baumard, we may suggest that a CoP is a situation-specific creation, using a 'unique' language which, to paraphrase McKenzie and van Winklelen, links participants intellectually, emotionally and instrumentally (2004, p. 121). Such a concept of CoP might be thought to be universally applicable. Not so in the case of Russia, where the concept of CoP is not only problematic because of translation difficulties, but also because in Russia one of the legacies of the Soviet system is an entrenched 'hostility to knowledge sharing' (Michailova & Husted, 2003), which militates against the creation and maintenance of CoPs.

Dealing with the translation issue first, the editors found that the literal translation of the term community of practice into Russian did not convey the kind of assumptions embedded in the Western concept. They opted, in awkward back-translation, for 'community of practical people'. But the problem with this translation is that the word for practical people in Russian is not synonymous with the word practitioner in English, which implies attainment not through practice alone, but in combination with formal qualifications.

The other problem is of a more pragmatic nature. According to Michailova and Husted (2003), KM in Russia is characterized by three countervailing factors. First, Russian KM is marked by strong tendencies to hoard knowledge at the top by a conviction that knowledge sharing must compromise power and by suspicions of foreign knowledge which might expose Russian weaknesses and even mistakes. The mistrustful behaviour has been noted by Blom (2008) who notes a 'scarcity of trust in business-to-business relationships' among Russian companies. We conclude that the concept of community of practice is for the present at least 'socially untranslatable' into Russia.

Insights from the deep structures

The preceding commentary has not limited itself to listing of translational confusables between English and Russian. As we have seen, to understand why a particular English term is translated in this way into Russian requires an appreciation of Russia's socio-cultural environment for a discussion of Russia as a KM environment, involving aspects of (a) the intellectual legacy of communism and (b) Russian organizational behaviour. By means of recontextualization, which has converted deep structures of the Russian original into surface structures in English, it has been possible to give to Russia's KM environment what Holden and Glisby (2010) term 'mood and tone', which constitute an enhancement to the original in order to reveal aspects of the latent or tacit.

Beyond that, recontextualization enables us to make four important observations that might otherwise elude us about the characteristics of KM in Russia.

These four factors have relevance not only for the general KM community, but for other branches of professionals (and not least management educators) who are engaged in – or contemplating – activities in or with Russia. They concern: (a) the understanding of the term 'knowledge' in the management context; (b) knowledge, organizational power and Soviet mental software; (c) the current status of KM terminology in Russian; and (d) the nature of KM terminology in English as a source language for translation into Russian.

Knowledge, organizational power and Soviet mental software

Knowledge in the way that KM experts use the term in 'the West' appears not to coincide with Russian usage, which still prefers to see knowledge not as an organizational resource, but (as it were) as the contents of dense, wordy encyclopaedias (not mention contents of lectures delivered by professors at universities). The *Handbook* alerted us to this state of affairs, but did not add that with Russian managers it is not knowledge that counts so much as experience. One reason why Western management education initiatives failed in Russia time after time is that the Westerners delivered knowledge that had little connection to Russian realities. This represents a form of institutional stickiness that Westerners were only dimly aware of, if at all.[6]

The implicit assumption about knowledge in the Western KM theory and practice, in principle, is that it is a resource to be shared. But as we have noted, there is no satisfactory term for knowledge sharing, the closest expression being 'knowledge distribution'. But behind this lies something complex. In Russian organisations', knowledge (*pace* information) is an element of power of the privileged few at the top of an organization; it is in the gift of bosses who decide what is appropriate to filter down to underlings (even though, incidentally, it has been recognized that the new business conditions in Russia with an emphasis on 'partnership between enterprises and employees' presuppose 'a weakening of management *diktat*' (Gerchikova, 2005)).

Whereas the view of KM in Western countries would be that the sharing of knowledge is a necessity for effective teamwork and even motivation of employees in order to improve organizational processes ranging from quality management to after-sales service, in Russia knowledge is form of power (as absolute as possible, please!) for keeping people in place. Hence, as pointed out by Michailova and Husted (2003) in so many words, the premise of Russian-style KM is that knowledge is a resource to be hoarded, even kept secret.

A flavour of the nature of state power is given by the perceptive and well-informed American journalist, Andrew Meier:

> Beyond lust and fear, Moscow breeds power. You cannot help feeling that you are trespassing in its path. Every effort is mad to impress upon the populace its privileged proximity to the unlimited power of the state. This is not just state power as in other countries. This is not merely officialdom,

> but the deliberate demonstration of the state's power over the people, an ever-present slap in their face (Meier, 2003).

These environmental features explains why KM is hard to take root in Russia with its 'free-market pieties with quasi-Soviet practicalities' (Hanson, 2011), whereby Russian firms are daily exposed to officially approved menacem both at the national and local level.

Nor do foreign firms enjoy any exemption. Consider the following case in July 2011, in which *The Times* Moscow correspondent was reporting how 'BP's bruising battle with its billionaire Russian partners over control of TNK-BP showed that even the most powerful foreign companies find it hard to defend their interests here'. He added starkly: 'Capitalism in Russia remains red in tooth and claw, with force rather than best practice winning the day far too often'. Thus foreign firms involved in major knowledge-based transfer projects such as joint ventures or M&A operations should therefore proceed on the assumption that Russia does not have a KM-friendly business environment.

There is, as it happens, much discussion among management scholars as to the degree to which Soviet attitudes permeate Russian society today (Hanson, 2011; Holden, Kuznetsov, & Whitelock, 2008; Holden & Vaiman, 2013; Kuznetsov et al., 2009; Solomon, 2008). The consensus seems to be that the Soviet experience remains influential even if one cannot accurately quantify it. For its part, the British magazine *The Economist* has no doubts. Its Moscow correspondent filed a story under the telling title 'The long life of homo Sovieticus', in which it was reported that in the Russia of Vladimir Putin 'the Soviet mental software has proved more durable than the [defunct communist] ideology itself' (*The Economist*, 2011b).

The point to grasp about this putative Soviet mental software is that it does not necessarily represent any deep yearning for the good old days of central planning and Marxist-Leninism, but is a manifestation, to paraphrase Moynahan (1994, p. 3), of the persistence of the coercion and brutishness that came with Soviet totalitarianism. In other words, it is a projection of 'the mailed fist' (Hingley, 1977, p. 169) into post-communist times.

We may additionally surmise that their Russian partners may see something suspicious about the (high-quality) knowledge the foreign party wishes transfer and share, seeing that the very act may undermine Russian bosses' authority. At the same time the Russian partners might attribute suspicious motives to the foreign party for wishing to acquiring their knowledge, which could be interpreted as an insidious bid for a major facet of bosses' power. If this depiction of Russian attitudes in cross-cultural contexts is correct, it is a warning to foreign firms to proceed with caution.

The current status of KM terminology in Russian

The creation of a unitary and unambiguous vocabulary of KM in Russian is decidedly work under construction, as is the case with respect to the language of marketing (Holden et al., 2008; Jacob, 2001). First of all Russian has to draw on the English language for its KM concepts which entails translation of specialist terms into Russian. We have seen that some terms such as 'knowledge sharing' and 'community of practice' are virtually untranslatable owing to the lack of shared assumptions and the lexical voids in Russian. Hence, Russian finds it difficult to translate the term 'knowledge worker' in such a way that the translation avoids designating such a person as an intellectual. It is of course one thing for the specialist translators to supply KM's core vocabulary in Russian, but it is quite another for their terms to be accepted by the business community. Given the arduous, even haphazard way in which the Russian language is adapting itself to the demands of the market economy system, it may be several years before KM and its specialist terms obtain acceptance; and for that to happen, KM practices need to have taken root.

English as a source language of KM terms

For various reasons, as we have noted, KM's working vocabulary in English is itself a source of challenge to translators. As with other branches of management as a practice and domain of study, the terminology of KM is a confection of four elements: (a) sociological discourse ('structured knowledge', 'hypertext organisation', 'organizational unlearning', 'appropriability'); (b) the management-functional, focusing on tasks and performers ('technology transfer', 'socialisation', 'chief knowledge officer', 'knowledge worker', (c) the folksy ('explorer', 'itinerant', 'gatekeeper'); and (d) words or expression that (for the time being) have a catchy, modish ring ('infinitely flat organization', 'starburst organisation', 'transactive memory').

Furthermore, the word knowledge is qualified by various adjectives and nouns that operate adjectively ('advanced', 'common', 'core', 'declarative', 'explicit', 'human', 'implicit', 'innovative', 'organizational', personal', 'prepositional', 'procedural', 'social', 'specialized', 'structured'). Then the word knowledge can function adjectively in combination with various nouns ('absorption', 'acquisition', 'asset', 'economy', etc.). All the terms in italics have been taken from the 107 words and expressions that form the *Handbook's* glossary, which obviously does not cover many would consider to be the domain's key terms, seeing that the selected entries derive from the translated articles.

You do not need to be a professional translator to realize that the haphazard growth of KM terminology acts as major constraint on attaining intermappability of domain's terms between English and Russian. The editors of *The Handbook* have done not just the KM community but even the wider world of management education and research a favour by reminding them that their core terms are upon examination often imprecise, inconsistent and therefore hard to translate into other languages – and not just Russian.

The editors of the *Handbook* were professional enough to seek clarification of problematical terms to ensure the highest possible accuracy in their renditions. However great their frustrations with the English terms, they have no alternative but to work with them; their task as translators is to achieve the highest possible level of professional interanimation across a language divide of exceptional complexity. Finally, it must be emphasised that the haphazard and inconsistent nature of KM terminology in English is an impediment to smooth translation not just into Russian, but into any other language of countries where KM is alien as a set of concept and body of practices.

Conclusion: a weakness in the living heart of KM

The process of recontextualization of the *Handbook of Knowledge Management* has unearthed insights into the not so straightforward nature of Russia's KM landscape. The process has plainly supported the conviction that 'there is a clear understanding, essential to any communication within and between languages, of the ways in which a text may conceal more than it conveys' (Steiner, 1975). It has demonstrated that the Russian language does not merely 'hold forth historically developed dimensions of interests – attributes of concern or the lines along which things of the world will be distinguished' (Deetz, 2003), but that the dimensions of interests are strongly shaped by the Russian context.

It has been suggested that the insights are not just of broad general interest, but contain implications for academic practice and as well as for foreign executives engaged in activities in or with Russia. In 1993, *The Financial Times* described Russia as 'a cross-cultural minefield'. Our recontextualization of *The Handbook of Knowledge Management* has plainly revealed that this assessment remains valid today, even though it was obviously not the intention of the editors to supply an explicit let alone an implicit cross-cultural commentary beyond the discussion of troublesome terms in English. Furthermore our recontextualization endorses a key observation of Puffer and McCarthy (2011), according to whom 'knowledge is an important mechanism through which Russian companies could move beyond the ties of traditional cultural-cognitive institutions'. It is a noble sentiment, but anyone acquainted with Russian history will know how stubbornly resistant these ties actually are.

But the recontextualization technique has not merely shed light on aspects of KM in Russia. It has also revealed a particular weakness in the living heart of KM both as a practice and intellectual domain: the vague and casual nature of its basic working terminology in the English language. Were it not for the publication of *The Handbook* in a 'strange' language, we simply might not realize that without clarity and relative cross-cultural transparency KM's core terms simply cannot support the wider use of language to 'construct and communicate knowledge' (McKenzie & van Winkelen, 2004). This is why the appearance of *The Handbook* is indeed a landmark event in KM as an international practice. Yet, if there is one branch of management that should be concerned about its professional vocabulary for enhancing international communication and cooperation, it must surely be KM.

Coda

In a letter to the cybernetician Norbert Wiener in 1947, Warren Weaver, the pioneer of machine translation famously wrote: 'When I look at an article in Russian, I say 'This is really in English, but it has been coded in some strange symbols. I will proceed to decode' (cited in Hutchings, 1977). Here is the statement modified for putative Russian translators today: 'When I look at an article in English, I say "This is really in Russian, but it has been coded in some strange symbols. How on earth can I proceed to decode?"'

Notes

1. For the purposes of this article we may regard knowledge management to refer to all the procedures for converting knowledge as an organisational resource into forms of advantage (see Bukh et al., 2005; Glisby & Holden, 2010; McKenzie & van Winkelen, 2004).
2. The landscapes of Oliver and Roos (2000), using the metaphor of 'small mounds, hillocks and varing sized peaks' (McKenzie & van Winkelen, 2004) are not best suited to the vastness of Russia. Russia has to be understood in terms of a winter landscape that 'overpowers, oppresses, stuns'...where...' man is not created for such measurelessness' (Kapuściński, 1994, p. 30).
3. All translations from Russian have been made by N. J. Holden.
4. For a discussion of the development of informatics in the USSR, see the entry of Longdon in the *Cambridge Encyclopedia of Russia* (1994). For a brilliant reconstruction of the Soviet dream in the 1960s, see *Red Plenty* by Spufford (2010). Readers of Russian will find useful a fairly recent assessment of information systems Gerchikova (2005) ('Technology management', pp. 135–172).
5. Russian history has produced at least two gatekeepers of exceptional notoriety in the twentieth century. The mysterious priest, Grigorii Rasputin (1869–1916), who exercised an influence that was 'pernicious and deadly' (Utechin, 1961) over the Tsar Nicholas II and more especially his Tsarina to the extent that during the First World War 'developed a lucrative system of placements in the government, the Church and the Civil Service, all of which he boasted were under his control' (Figes, 1996, p. 31). Alexander Poskrëbyshev (1891–1965) had a long-standing 'crucial...master-and-dog relationship' with Joseph Stalin as his chief aide and secretary until the dictator's death in 1953. In the latter's last days, Poskrëbyshev decided which telegrams needed his master's attention (Service, 2004, p. 574).
6. The UK's foremost historian on Eastern Europe, Norman Davies (2007, p. 15), has argued that 'the nefarious concept of Western civilisation' has been a major impediment to 'a proper understanding of Europe *in toto*'. Also see Jankowicz (1994).

References

T. E. Andreyeva & T. Yu. Gutnikova. (eds) (2009). *Upravleniye znaniyami: Chrestomatiya/Handbook of knowledge management.* St Petersburg: Graduate School of Management.

P. Baumard. (2001). *Tacit Knowledge in Organizations.* London: Sage Publications.

R. Blom. (2008). 'Conclusion: structural change and managerial strategies in Russia'. In R. Blom (ed.) *Managers in Russia: Still so Different* (pp. 209–215), Aleksanteri Series 3. Helsinki: Gummerus Printing.

P. N. Bukh, K. S. Christensen & J. Mouritsen. (eds) *Knowledge Management and Intellectual Capital: Establishing a Field of Practice* (pp. 15–34), London: Palgrave Macmillan.

K. S. Christensen & P. N. Bukh. (2005). 'Knowledge management: two perspectives'. In P. N. Bukh, K. S. Christensen & J. Mouritsen. (eds) *Knowledge Management and Intellectual Capital: Establishing a Field of Practice* (pp. 15–34), London: Palgrave Macmillan.

N. Davies. (2007). *Europe East and West.* London: Pimlico.

S. Deetz. (2003). 'Disciplinary power, conflict suppression and human resources management'. In M. Alvesson & H. Willmott. (eds) *Studying Management Critically* (pp. 23–45) London: Sage Publications.

The Economist. (2011a). 'BP's Russian Troubles', 2 April, p. 68.

The Economist. (2011b). 'The Long Life of Homo Sovieticus', 10 November, pp. 29–31.

W. J. Entwistle. (1974). *The Spanish Language.* London: Faber & Faber.

O. Figes (1996). *A People's Tragedy: The Russian Revolution 1891–1924.* London: Pimlico.

I. Gerchikova. (2005). *Menedzhment (Management).* Moscow: Izdatelstvo Yuniti-Dana.

M. Glisby & N. J. Holden (2010). *Creating Knowledge Advantage: The Tacit Dimensions of International Competition and Cooperation.* Copenhagen: Copenhagen Business School Press.

P. Hanson. (2011). *The Economic Dimension of Russia's Modernization,* Research Project on Modernizing Russia: Internal and External Implications and Challenges. Milan: Instituto per gli Studi di Politica Internazionale.

R. Hingley. (1977). *The Russian Mind.* The Bodley Head, London.

N. J. Holden. (2011). Not with the Mind alone: A Critique of "Knowledge Transfer between Russian and Western Firms: Whose Absorptive Capacity is in Question?" by Snejina Michailova and Irina Jormanainen. *Critical Perspectives on International Business.* 7 (4), 350–356.

N. J. Holden & M. Glisby. (2010). *Creating Knowledge Advantage: The Tacit Dimensions of International Competition and Cooperation.* Copenhagen: Copenhagen Business School Press.

N. J. Holden, A. Kuznetsov, & J. Whitelock. (2008). Russia's struggle with the language of marketing in the communist and post-communist eras. *Business History.* 50 (4), 474–488.

N. J. Holden & V. Vaiman. (2013, forthcoming). 'Talent management in Russia: not so much war for talent as wariness of talent', accepted for publication in the special issue on Russian business and management in *Critical Perspectives on International Business.*

J. Hutchings. (1997). From first concepts to first demonstration: the Nascent years of machine translation. *Machine Translation.* 12 (3),195–252.

E. Jacob. (2001). The influence of western concepts on Russian marketing theory. *British Journal of Management.* 12 (2), 149–157.

A. D. Jankowicz. (1994). The new journey to Jerusalem: mission and meaning in the managerial crusade to Eastern Europe. *Organization Studies*. 15 (4), 479–507.
R. Kapuściński. (1994). *Imperium*. London: Granta Books.
F. Kohlbacher. (2007). *International Marketing in the Network Economy: A Knowledge-based Approach*. London: Palgrave Macmillan.
A. Kuznetsov, O. Kuznetsova, & R. Warren. (2009). CSR and the legitimacy of business in transition economies: the case of Russia. *Scandinavian Journal of Management*. 24 (2), 10–22.
L. W. Longdon. (1994). 'Automation'. In A. Brown, M. Kaser and G. S. Smith (eds) *Cambridge Encyclopedia of Russia* (pp. 315–316) Cambridge: Cambridge University Press.
J. McKenzie & C. van Winkelen. (2004). *Understanding the Knowledgeable Organization: Nurturing Knowledge Competence*. London: Thomson Learning.
A. Meier. (2003). *Black Earth: Russia after the Fall*. London: HarperCollins.
S. Michailova. (2011). Contextualizing in international business research: why do we need more of it and how can we be better at it? *Scandinavian Journal of Management*. 27, 129–139.
S. Michailova & K. Husted. (2003). Knowledge-sharing hostility in Russian firms. *California Management Review*. 45 (3), 59–77.
B. Moynahan. (1994). *The Russian century: A History of the Last Hundred Years*. London, Pimlico.
I. Nonaka & H. Takeuchi. (1995). *The Knowledge-creating Company*. New York: Oxford University Press.
D. Oliver & J. Roos. (2000). *Striking a Balance: Complexity and Knowledge Landscapes*. Maidenhead: McGraw-Hill.
Oxford Dictionary of English. (2006). J. Pearsall & J. Hanks (eds) Oxford: Oxford University Press.
S. M. Puffer and D. J. McCarthy. (2011). Two decades of Russian business and management research: an institutional theory perspective. *Academy of Management Perspectives*. 25 (2), 21–36.
A. Shkuta. (2008). *Evropeiskii Vector Gazovoi Strategii Rossii* [European Vector of Russia's Gas Strategy] (Moscow: EKOM-Pablishers).
R. Service. (2004). *Stalin: A Biography*. London: Palgrave Macmillan.
P. Solomon (2008). 'Administrative styles in Soviet history'. In T. Lahuse and P. Solomon (eds) *What is Soviet now?* Berlin: Literatur Verlag, 78–89.
F. Spufford. (2010). *Red Plenty*. London: Faber and Faber.
G. Steiner. (1975). *After Babel: Aspects of Language and Translation*. Oxford: Oxford University Press.
P. Thompson, C. Warhurst, & G. Callaghan. (2001). Ignorant theory and knowledgeable workers: interrogating the connections between knowledge, skills and services. *Journal of Management Studies*. 38 (7), 923–942.
S. V. Utechin. (1961). *Everyman's Concise Encyclopedia of Russia*. London: J. M. Dent & Sons.
G. Von Krogh, K. Ichijo, & I. Nonaka. (2000). *Enabling Knowledge Creation: How to Unlock the Mystery of Tacit Knowledge and Release the Power of Innovation*. Oxford: Oxford University Press.
T. J. Watson. (2004). Managers, managism, and the tower of Babble: making sense of managerial Pseudo-jargon. *International Journal of the Sociology of Language*, (166), 67–82.
W. Weaver. (1947). Letter to N. Wiener, cited in Hutchings op. cit.

E. Wenger. (1998). *Communities of Practice: Learning, Meaning and Identity.* Cambridge: Cambridge University Press.

Wenger, E. & W. Snyder. (2000). Communities of practice: the organizational frontier. *Harvard Business Review.* 78 (1), 139–145.

Appendix 8.1

List of 23 articles translated and included in the *Handbook of Knowledge Management.*

M. Alvesson & D. Karreman. (2001). Odd couple: making sense of the curious concept of knowledge management. *Journal of Management Studies.* 38 (7), 995–1018.

L. Argote & P. Ingram. (2000). Knowledge transfer: a basis for competitive advantage. *Organizational Behavior & Human Decision Processes.* 82, 150–169.

C. Argyris. (1991). Teaching smart people how to learn. *Harvard Business Review.* May–June, 99–110.

N. Bontis. (2001). Assessing knowledge assets: a review of models used to measure intellectual capital. *International Journal of Management Reviews.* 3 (1), 41–60.

A. Daghfous. (2004). Absorptive capacity and the implementation of knowledge-intensive best practices. *SAM Advanced Management Journal.* 69 (2), 21–27.

P.M. de Holan, N. Phillips, & T.B. Lawrence. (2004). Managing organizational forgetting. *Sloan Management Review.* 45 (3), 45–51.

D. W. Delong & T. Davenport. (2003). Better practices for retaining organizational knowledge: lessons from the leading edge. *Employment Relations Today.* 30 (3), 51–63.

D. W. Delong & L. Fahey. (2000). Diagnosing cultural barriers to knowledge management. *Academy of Management Executive.* 14 (4), 437–457.

P. F. Drucker. (1992). The new society of organizations. *Harvard Business Review.* September–October, 70 (5), 95–104.

C. Garavelli, M. Gorgoglione, & B. Scozzi. (2004). Knowledge management strategy and organization: a perspective of analysis. *Knowledge and Process Management.* 11 (4), 273–282.

D. Garvin. (1993). Building a learning organization. *Harvard Business Review.* 71 (4), July–August, 78–93.

M. Glisby & N. J. Holden. (2003). Contextual constraints in knowledge-management theory: the cultural embeddedness of Nonaka's knowledge-creating company. *Knowledge and Process Management.* 24 (10), 29–36.

M. G. Grant. (1993). Towards a knowledge-based theory of the firm. *Strategic Management Review.* 17, 109–122.

K. Husted & S. Michailova. (2002). Diagnosing and fighting knowledge-sharing hostility. *Organizational Dynamics.* 31 (1), 60–73.

E. Kelloway & J. Barling. (2000). Knowledge work as organizational behavior. *International Journal of Management Reviews.* 2 (3), 287–304.

T. Mason. (2004). Why KM's work is never done. *Inside Knowledge.* 7 (6), http://www.ikmagazine.com/xq/asp/sid.FE1B1456-DFD9-422D-B217-0FD2406A5D32/volume.7/issue.6/qx/displayissue.htm, on 25 June 2013.

I. Nonaka (1991). The knowledge-creating company. *Harvard Business Review.* 69 (6), November–December, 96–105.

I. Nonaka, I. R. Toyama, & T. Hirata. (2008). *Managing Flow: A Process Theory of the Firm.* London: Palgrave Macmillan.

J. B. Quinn, P. Anderson, & S. Finkelstein. (1996). Managing professional intellect: making the most of the best. *Harvard Business Review.* 74 (2), March–April, 71–81.

P. M. Romer. (2001). Interview by J. Kurtzman in *strategy + business,* 20 November.
E. Wenger & W. M. Snyder. (2000). Communities of practice: the organizational frontier. *Harvard Business Review.* January–February, 139–147.
M. H. Zack. (1999). Developing a knowledge strategy. *California Management Review.* 41 (3), 125–145.
M. H. Zack. (2002). Developing a knowledge strategy: epilogue'. In N. Bontis & C. W. Choo (eds) *The Strategic Management of Intellectual Capital and Organizational Knowledge: A Collection of Readings.* Oxford: Oxford University Press.

9

A Humanistic Approach to Knowledge-Creation: People-Centric Innovation

Yingying Zhang, Yu Zhou and Jane McKenzie

Introduction

Greatly differentiated from the perspective of information processing for decision making of Herbert A. Simon, an earlier mentor who influenced Ikujiro Nonaka's thought at Berkeley, Nonaka shifted from information processing to information creation, and then advanced the management theory with knowledge creation (Xu, 2013). While *The Knowledge-Creating Company* gained its influence in the management world, and paved foundation for knowledge management field, one of the basic premises of Nonaka Theory is the humanistic approach (Nonaka, 2011a). This approach essentially distinguishes Nonaka's thought from other Schools in the field, especially from these concerning technological aspect of knowledge sharing and learning process.

This humanistic approach has been reflected in Nonaka's work since the very beginning of Knowledge Creation publications, stressing people-centric knowledge creation processes that rely on so-called knowledge workers as the essential vehicle for embedding knowledge within the organizational offering. Knowledge creation is a continuously ongoing process that occurs through 'human interaction with dialogue and practice' (Nonaka, Toyama, & Hirata, 2010). More specifically, Nonaka (2011a) states, 'my view of the firm is *human-centric*' and 'we do not dissociate the individuals and the knowledge, and individuals and their firms on the one hand from their environment on the other' (p. xix).

In line with his human-centric thought, Nonaka (2011b) calls for a move forward to innovation theory from the knowledge creation community. Yet, in parallel, the research field of innovation has developed independently from other disciplines. Some scholars in the field focus on technological innovation such as Shane (2008) and others on the micro-behavioural aspects (Baer & Frese, 2003). In spite of high academic interest and investigation into innovation, there are gaps between what Nonaka calls for, i.e., a human-centric innovation theory and the current state of the art in innovation theory development. In this chapter, we attempt to review literatures on human factors that drive innovation and innovative outputs, to put forward a people-centric innovation perspective for knowledge creation within organizations.

Knowledge, people and innovation

As knowledge may be the 'the only meaningful resource' (Drucker, 1993), knowledge creation has become a principal strategic issue for firm prosperity. Nonaka and his followers have consistently insisted on the concept of firm as a knowledge-creating entity (Nonaka, 1994; Nonaka & Konno, 1998; Nonaka et al., 2000; Nonaka & Toyama, 2003; Nonaka & von Krogh, 2009), others argue that the economic role of the firm is to integrate knowledge to create societal value (Grant, 2002, 2013; Spender, 2002).

Two core dimensions of Nonaka's 'knowledge spiral' of knowledge transformation are 'epistemological' (i.e., SECI framework for knowledge conversion) and 'ontological' (i.e., social interaction and the interplay of knowledge creation between individual and organizational level), though the latter has received much less attention (Grant, 2013). Thus, the essence of Nonaka's theory of knowledge management has been very much grounded in the SECI knowledge model and the concept of 'Ba'. The SECI model outlines the phases of knowledge conversion between tacit and explicit knowledge at different stages in the spread of innovation through the organization, from individual, to group, intergroup and the organization, after which it creates a context and legacy for further knowledge creation and learning. It offers something of a taxonomy of types of knowledge creation and transfer mechanism – Socialization, Externalization, Combination and Internalization. However, that is its most basic contribution. Based on this foundation, the logic is that organizational leaders and knowledge workers can consider how to adjust organizational structures, information flows, corporate culture, relationships and future strategic considerations in order to facilitate the key types of knowledge creation, transfer mechanisms and foster mutual understanding. The complementary concept of 'Ba' focuses on the place where knowledge creation occurs, because context constitutes the core conditions for knowledge creation. As a shared space, *ba, which may be physical, virtual or mental,* describes an ideal environment where knowledge can be 'acquired through one's own experience or reflection on the experiences of others' (Nonaka & Kono, 1998, p. 41). Each facet of knowledge transfer in the SECI model requires a different Ba. But whether it is direct experience and practice or reflection on the experience of others, a people orientation is the underlying assumption in the innovative knowledge creation process.

Innovation, as the process for knowledge creation, has been developed as an independent research field since 1950s with strong growth recently (Fagerberg, Fosaas, & Sapprasert, 2012). Considered as the internal sources and key to achieving the purpose of firms in knowledge economy (Grant, 2010; Spender & Grant, 1996), innovation studies emerged and evolved in response to different challenges, which organizations confronted. In the cluster analysis carried out by Fagerberg et al. (2012), three phases of the evolution of innovation field were identified. The early phase until around 1970 is when the field was in its infancy with most work confined to two established disciplines within social sciences: economics and sociology. Little interaction across the disciplines took place and different trajectories were developed with only rare consideration of the other. The growth phase continued until the late 1980s, when it quickly developed into a global phenomenon attracting large number of researchers into the field; also, more emphasis on multi- and inter-disciplinary thinking rather than narrow disciplinary focus characterized this phase. Links were made with other scientific worlds such as engineering science. By the end of 1980s, the field showed signs of maturity with the creation of specialized professional associations devoted to advancing innovation and specialized journals focusing on the field's development.

According to Fagerberg et al. (2012), innovation studies can be classified into three clusters: Economics of R&D, Organizing Innovation, and Innovation Systems. In the cluster of Economics of R&D, not only is 'Economic' the dominant thematic focus, but the largest citing field is also 'Economics', followed by 'Social Sciences & Humanities'. Organizing Innovation strongly focuses on innovation, organization, sector/industry and firms, with the largest citing field of 'Business' followed by 'Management'. Innovation Systems focuses on the interaction between 'Innovation' and 'Systems', with relatively small size and predominant European contributions in contrast of the American-base in the previous two clusters (p. 1141).

As a result of their analysis, a cluster of work on Organizing Innovation grew rapidly in the second phase of field evolution from 1990 onward. Now it exceeds the Economics of R&D cluster representing the largest part of the field, as evidenced and reflected by citations in scholarly journals. The cluster called Innovation Systems, focusing on the role of innovation and regional development, emerged by the end of 1980s. This added to the diversity of innovation studies in terms of geographical broadness, thematically and methodological variation. As March (2004) states, diversity in a research community such as knowledge creation is natural and even beneficial. Nonetheless, it also represents new challenges for the field development (Fagerberg et al., 2012, p. 1147).

Martin (2012, p. 1232) recognizes a basic distinction between organizational innovation and technological innovation. He draws on earlier works such as Kimberly and Evanisko's (1981) influence of individual, organizational and contextual factors on technological and administrative innovations; Barley's (1986) technological stimulation of organizational structure; Ettlie et al.'s (1984) model of organizational innovation process; Dewar and Dutton's (1986) predictors for radical and incremental innovations; Markus and Robey's (1988) analysis of IT's role in organizational change; Damanpour's (1991) meta-analysis of the relationships between organizational innovation and its determinants; and Woodman, Sawyer, and Griffin (1993) theoretical framework for understanding organizational creativity.

Despite the upswing in interest around organizational innovation and even though the field could now be considered as reaching a relatively mature position (Fagerberg et al., 2012), there is no agreed integrating framework (Mayer, 1999). Perhaps, following an alternative path and taking a humanistic approach to the study of knowledge-based innovation may be a pivotal step in taking the field forward. How knowledge is created and managed amongst individual knowledge workers are key issues for knowledge creation (Nonaka, 2011a) within the organizational setting and essential for the sustainable competitive advantage of the firm.

Although the works of Nonaka (1991, 1994) and Nonaka & Takeuchi (1995) have been considered as part of the core literature in the innovation field (Fagerberg et al., 2012; Martin, 2012), a humanistic approach to innovation has been less appreciated in the general literature review of innovation studies, even in their review of organizational innovation. In an effort to increase the momentum behind Nonaka's humanistic vision of knowledge creation, we attempt to explore Organizational Innovation and the area of human resources in relation to innovation within organizations in the following section, to engage further scholarly discussion on this line of thought.

Human creativity and innovation

Nonaka (1994) views organizations as a platform and context for individuals to create knowledge and disseminate it through social interaction across different organizational levels. If considering innovation as knowledge creation, individual innovation is much based on human creativity whereas organizational innovation as high performing capabilities is much pending on processes, structure, motivation and organizational alignment (Grant, 2013).

Schumpeter (1934) defined innovation as a new integration of production elements and conditions based on an enterprise's function; meanwhile, it also involves organizational issues of system design. At organizational level, management of people and related policies has become a focus of attention with respect to firm competitive advantage (Pfeffer, 1998; Huselid, 1995; Wright & Boswell, 2002). Nonetheless, most of the studies have concentrated on discussing and testing the effects of human resources practices on firm performance and innovation. The research on the relationship between human resource systems and organizational innovation is sparse almost to the point of being non-existent (Shipton et al., 2005).

In line with the humanistic approach to knowledge and innovation, the capacity of a firm's knowledge workers to generate new knowledge and valuable ideas becomes fundamental to gain and sustain competitive advantage, perhaps more so nowadays than traditional material assets (Amabile, Conti, Lazenby, & Herron, 1996; Massetti, 1996). Human creativity and individuals' participation and contribution to innovation activity are of strategic importance for a firm's sustainable development.

Amabile (1998) argues that human creativity is the principal factor in organizational innovation. It is both the spark and the fuel in innovation processes, which requires learning both at individual and organizational level. Individual creativity and organizational innovation, mutually interfere and influence each other at many levels – economic, industry, structural, procedural and relational. But as a necessary element for organizations to develop and innovate, recognizing and encouraging individual creativity has many starting points. Only when individual creativity is determined, can innovation be better managed at organizational level.

Despite their crucial contribution, innovative individuals have not received much attention in the focal literature of innovation studies. No cluster of relevance in this area was highlighted in Fagerberg's cluster analysis. While the discipline of economics and sociology contributed essentially to innovation studies at the early phase of the field (Fagerberg et al., 2012), most psychologists and organizational behaviourists paid little attention to innovation until 1950, when Guilford, in his speech at American Psychology Association, highlighted that only 0.2 per cent of publication at Psychological Abstract was related to innovation and creativity, calling for more research to better understand the characteristics of innovation and creativity.

Over the next sixty years, studies on innovation and creativity from a psychological perspective increased, produced a so called 'creativity behaviour theory'. Simultaneously, journals specialized in the field appeared, the *Journal of Creative Behavior* founded in 1967 and *The Creativity Research Journal* in 1988. However, despite these efforts, the studies of creativity in relation with innovation have neither become mainstream in psychology (Sternberg & Lubart, 1996), nor in the field of innovation studies. A reflection of this fact is the multiple angles of viewpoint in psychology have not even been acknowledged as adding a contribution to the development of innovation studies by any mention in Fagerberg et al. (2012).

The literature also shows a lack of agreement in the psychological school of creativity and innovation. Magyari Beck (1991) uses the metaphor of the blind men and elephant to describe the state of the art in creativity studies. Mayer (1999) notes the existence of debates about conceptualization in his literature review. That is, for example: Is creativity a property of human, or a process? Is creativity possessed by few talents, or anybody? Is creativity a universal capability or related to specific needs and contexts? The definition of creativity and innovation appears to be challenging for future studies. The following summarizes nine perspectives that illustrate different people related foci which have emerged in the study of creativity and innovation.

A thinking perspective: Guilford (1950) and Torrance (1974) consider that 'divergent thinking' is the basic essence of creativity. It is an abnormal thinking mode that explores solutions from alternative aspects, paths, and angles. Thus, the inductive management thinking mode prevalent in Asia compared to the predominant emphasis on deductive thinking in the Western (Kase, Slocum, & Zhang, 2011) may explain the emerging innovative capacity of Asian enterprises.

A cognitive perspective: Smith, Ward, and Finke (1995) propose a Genexplore Model for the exploration of creativity formation. That is, the psychological process of creativity is an integration process: in the generative phase individuals construct mental representations; and in the exploratory phase these structures are used to generate creative ideas.

A personality perspective: This view considers that creativity relies on certain personal characteristics. Personality traits often include independence of judgment, self-confidence, attraction to complexity, aesthetic orientation and risk-taking as measures for the creativity of individuals (e.g., Amabile, 1988; Oldham & Cummings, 1996).

A motivation perspective: Strong desire for self-realization and individual intrinsic motivation has been considered as important source for driving innovative behaviour. Amabile (1983) proposed a two-pronged hypothesis in relation to the motivational mechanism to innovative behaviour. Namely, intrinsic motivation positively affects innovative behaviour while extrinsic motivation negatively influences innovative behaviour.

A knowledge perspective: Many researchers consider that knowledge creation is independent from the actual accumulated knowledge or experience of individuals (e.g., Amabile, 1989). The study of Simonton (1984) further points out that the relation between creativity and knowledge (measured by education level) turned to be an inverse 'U' curve. Hayes (1989) discovers a 'ten-year rule' that innovative talents often go through hard studies and practices. Weisberg (1999) therefore concludes in terms of the relation between creativity and knowledge that knowledge is only a necessary but not sufficient condition for innovation.

An intelligence perspective: Generally it is agreed that the relation between innovation and intelligence is non-linear (Sternberg & O'Hara, 1998). Innovative talents often possess IQ level higher than average; for these who have IQ value higher than 120, the effect of IQ on creativity is not as clear as for these who have IQ value lower than 120; and extremely high IQ probable has negative effect on creativity. Hence there is a difference in the relationship between IQ and creativity in accordance with the level. Goleman and

Boyatzis (2008) thus extend the intelligence conceptualization by including social and emotional intelligence.

A capability perspective: it also considers creativity and innovation as a capacity to propose or generate novel (that is unique) and adequate (that is useful and suitable for determined needs) work outcome (Sternberg, 1988; Sternberg & Lubart, 1996).

A performance perspective: similar to the definition of Sternberg and colleagues, Amabile (1983) indirectly describes the particularity of innovation and creativity through performance to outcome. That is, newly generated products or solutions are adequate for human being's activities, with emphasis on the result of innovation.

An environment perspective: this debate focuses on the possibility to learn creativity. That is, external environmental factors such as culture, resource investment and learning and education mode will influence the generation and release of human creativity (e.g., Simonton, 1994).

Despite the debates, there is some generally accepted conceptualization about what constitutes the principal characteristics of creativity. That is, creativity is a capacity to propose and generate novel and useful work outcomes (Lubart, 1994; Ochse, 1990; Sternberg, 1998; Sternberg & Lubart, 1991, 1995, 1996). This conceptualization emphasises the uniqueness and utility of creativity based on the capability perspective. Or saying in another way, creativity is a capacity that is able to generate highly unique and practical possibilities to feed into the innovation activities.

One widely recognized conceptual model in the field is componential conceptualization (Amabile, 1983) suggest creativity is composed of three aspects: expertise, creativity related skills and task motivation. A systems perspective on creativity (Csikszentmihalyi, 1988, 1996) proposes that creativity is a process observable only at the intersection where individuals, domains (cultural or symbolic aspect), and fields (social aspect) interact; investment theory (Sternberg & Lubart, 1991, 1992, 1995, 1996) uses a confluence approach to set creativity requirement with six distinct but interrelated resources: intellectual abilities, knowledge, styles of thinking, personality, motivation and environment. This sort of integrative vision of creativity studies not only provides a much broader space for the field, but also calls scholars' attention to the issue of how to generate, develop and release it.

The interactionist model of Woodman and Schoenfeldt (1989) considers creativity as a complex outcome of individual behaviour in a determined context. Based on this model, Woodman et al. (1993) propose organizational creativity theory, extending the interactionist model to levels of individual, group and organization. The model provides a system theoretical framework, integrating personality, cognitive characteristics and social psychology to explain the principal elements of creativity. As a consequence, organizational creativity is understood as to build upon the interactional effects of each element with others: innovation process, product, people and environment.

The creative capability of individuals and collectives fuel innovation in the firm. Different angles of view and perspectives can be integrated to comprehensively understand human creativity and innovation, with special focus on six aspects: personality, motivation, knowledge and skills, cognitive ideation, environment and performance. Human creativity at individual level offers a foundation for organizational innovation. Among the studied factors, personality seems to be one of the principal determinants that influence mental cognitive model, motivation and learning capacity to acquire knowledge; an intrinsic and result-oriented motivational system could promote individuals actively use their ideation to produce innovative thinking and encourage an explorative cognitive model, hence to actively learn and accumulate specialized knowledge, skills, experience and competency to carry out their tasks; these elements interact and jointly prompt employees to behave innovatively and produce innovation for the final performance. Since investment theory (Sternberg & Lubart, 1991) emphasizes the external environment, environmental factors (including aspects like education, macro social factors and organizational conditions) have a distinct influence on the various human factors previously noted.

While creativity as a concept is focused at the individual level, the term innovation is applied normally to the organizational level. If the definition of creativity emphasises its uniqueness and practicability, then innovation could be understood as the process that generates unique outcomes and values. This process is carried out by managerial instruments. But most current management studies on innovation simply approach the scope of innovation management, technological innovation management and knowledge management, by looking at the organization as a whole rather than focusing on the benefits of different levers at different levels. There are two principal angles directly related to human resources which may be fruitful in deconstructing the study of creativity and innovation at different levels of the organization. One is organizational behaviour, which explores certain psychological characteristics or behavioural variables' which could influence creativity and performance; the other angle is from human resource management, which focuses on the effects of certain practices or systems designed to manage individuals and create a link between human creativity and organizational innovation performance.

Human resource management practices and innovation

The Knowledge School of Management is distinguished from other theories of the firm by a fundamental assumption that humans and organizations are dynamic beings, and by a focus on the processes inside the firm (Nonaka, Toyama, & Nagata, 2000, p. 2). The interaction between human creativity

Table 9.1 Human resource mechanisms and innovation approach

Innovation approach	Individual property	Organizational property	Human resource mechanism
Thinking perspective	X		2,5,8
Cognitive perspective	X		1,5
Personality perspective	X		2,5
Motivation perspective	X		1,3,6,7,8
Knowledge perspective	X	X	1,2,4,8,9
Intelligence perspective	X		4,8
Capability perspective	X	X	1,2,4,5,8,9
Performance perspective	X	X	1,4,5,6,8
Environment perspective		X	1,3,4,8,9

and innovation at individual and organizational level is the key issue for the humanistic approach to knowledge creation. As there is a common orientation of encouraging coherent behaviour between organization behaviour theorists and human resource management experts, we have selected the ten most popular managerial practices associated with orienting human resources toward innovation from the combined fields. Nine elements on human resources mechanisms are presented in the following paragraphs with their relation to innovation approaches (see Table 9.1).

Strategic orientation: innovation oriented humanistic vision and culture

Humans and organizations are both dynamic systems with an independent life of their own (Nonaka et al., 2000). It is through their interactions that knowledge is mobilized, know how flows to a point of need and creates new potential for innovative outcomes. To manage this flow of human creativity and translate it into organizational innovation, takes systematic effort combined with a concern for managing people and the influences on innovation performance as well as the status of the firm, its legacy and position in the industry. From the viewpoint of innovation strategy, it is important to align human resource management with a firm's strategic choices (Schuler, 1992) in order to realize the value of human potential. However, this alignment is not simply a matter of static fit to fulfil a pre-determined strategy implementation; it requires vision of interaction between different strategic elements to creatively reformulate strategy either in response to market needs (Zhang, Dolan, Lingham, & Altman, 2009) or to deliberately shape market opportunities (Vandermerwe, 1997, Arthur, 1996). This leads to the development of ideas like organizational dynamic capabilities, which depend heavily on the willingness of individual's to learn and unlearn, combine and recombine their individual knowledge and creativity to produce different firm level responses to market situations (Eisenhardt & Martin, 2000; Easterby-Smith & Prieto, 2008).

Individual humans are appreciated as leading actors who develop and play their role as environmental change agents, in dynamic theories of knowledge management (Nonaka, 2011a, p. xix). To fulfil the aspirations of arguments about the knowledge-based view of the firm human resource management would need to adopt a similarly dynamic perspective in order to contribute to firm performance. Zhang et al. (2009) identify leadership, learning, structure and human resource systems as strategic elements to manage people dynamically, support their interactions and constantly renew their knowledge. Corporate culture and market orientation have also been highlighted as organizational and external environments that affect these dynamics. DeGraff and Lawrence (2002) classify the innovation strategy of the firm into four types: incubate, imagine, improve and invest. In terms of culture, the common held belief, values and norms could promote or impede the generation of innovation (Martins & Terblanche, 2003). The recognition and encouragement toward innovation from organization and management team, job support from the team, possession of certain levels of autonomy and freedom, providing enough resource support, work challenge and suitable pressure are six elements that facilitate innovation (Amabile, 1996, 1997).

An organizational climate which considers employees' engagement, interests and interrelationships as a means of facilitating communication, increasing trust and willingness to take risk is more conducive to generating innovation (Ruppel & Harrington, 2000). Also, organizations with more initiatives are more likely to generate innovation and firm performance (Baer & Frese, 2003).

From this brief overview of the literature, a common pattern associated with an innovative organizational culture contains the following: an emphasis on employees' agreement and responsibility toward organizational objectives; ways to release employees' initiative and autonomy in the workplace; encouragement for risk taking and transformation while being tolerant of mistakes; promoting open communication and participation; welcoming employees' creative suggestions; reinforcing organizational and individual learning; building team spirit and co-operative working relations based on trust; timely awarding changes and employees' innovative behaviours.

Recruitment: diversified competency oriented

Empirical studies have demonstrated that the complementarities between diverse personalities and areas of expertise could promote interaction between individuals, which would promote a potential for innovation. For example, GE, Microsoft and Apple not only seek recognition of their strategy and value system in the recruitment, but also actively choose and respect individuality and distinctive competence to encourage diversity in their talent pool. This promotion of diversity encourages people to generate 'chemical' reactions within organizations because of the different viewpoints with different forms. However, the challenges of surmounting the epistemic cultures which separate different areas of expertise are very real and must be actively addressed for the value of diversity to be realized (van Winkelen & Mckenzie, 2012) and for innovation to emerge from sustained interactive dynamics.

The paradoxical tension between the policies which encourage value standardization and those that seek diversity needs careful management. On the one hand, talent recruitment and selection might emphasize fit with organizational values so employees come to have particular pattern of values, beliefs and behavioural characteristics. On the other hand, the diverse composition of human nature is needed to stimulate chemical reactions between different talents, to drive innovation through interaction and recombination. These two apparently opposite policies – one encouraging convergence, and another divergence – have to be simultaneously managed and merged within the organization for better performance both generally and in the specific context of innovation.

Job design: empowerment focused

In terms of job design, researchers consider that diversified, challenging and complex job content, as well as certain autonomy in job position are likely to stimulate employee innovation (Amabile, 1997; Hackman & Oldham, 1980. The traditional example is 3M where research and development (R&D) employees are given 15 per cent of work time to carry out research work according to their personal interests, regardless of whether their activity will bring direct profit to the company. Some argue that this freedom stimulates human creativity which drives to a better innovation performance. However, others argue that a more purposeful investment of organizational time brings greater rewards. von Krogh and Ichijo (2000) make a strong argument on balance, that the introduction of some slack in the system retains flexibility and dynamism in the system. Ambiguity in terms of job description content also provides space for more flexibility and organic humanistic development of individuals. Although high work pressure from an excessive work load negatively affects employees' creativity, a certain level of pressure from the task challenge is necessary to positively influence human creativity (Amabile et al., 1996).

Empowerment has also been viewed as an important factor in stimulating employees' innovative behaviours. In the leadership literature, researchers note that a controlling type of leaders' behaviour has negative relation with innovative output of R&D employees and employee creativity (George & Zhou, 2001). Generally, transformational leadership demonstrates a positive relationship with employees' innovation. So it is possible to argue that, empowerment to a certain extent is likely to encourage innovation because employees have enough space and power to manage in their workplace.

Communication: cross-functional and employee suggestion systems

Organizational learning plays a part in the necessary strategic human resource development for organizational innovation (Zhang et al., 2009). However, it is often the knowledge managers who focus on the organizational learning processes, whilst the HRD experts focus on individual learning. The underlying objective of flat organizational structures and boundaryless, networked information flows is to strengthen communication and interaction between internal functions and external environments, to speed up transfer and sharing of knowledge and information. From the organizational learning to learning organization, multiple studies have demonstrated that there is a positive relation between firm innovation performance and organizational learning process such as market-oriented knowledge learning and internal information sharing.

Strengthening internal communication and employee participation is an important part of organizational learning and innovation support. However, there is also a need to provide appropriate learning support for individuals in line with strategic capability needs, or the whole process becomes random and opportunistic. In some ways, this addresses the diversity/unity paradox mentioned earlier, because it encourages a focus to activities, alongside open communication, opportunistic exploration and flexible combinations of thinking and expertise. Most studies on communication and innovation point out that the openness of organizational communication is positively related to organizational innovation performance. Generally, when employees receive more innovation related information, they have more chances to integrate innovative ideas and get to know more about innovation output and its implementation meaning. This in turn increases the chance of further innovation, through the process of increasing returns (Arthur, 1996). Internal knowledge sharing is also very positive for team and organizational innovation. The study of Lovelace, Shapiro, and Weingart (2001) from the angle of communication style also found that collaborative and self-critique communications positively influences team innovation results. Several studies also note that employees' participation in decision making, as a managerial instrument, is positively related to individual creativity and organizational innovation performance.

As a way to provide individual knowledge to organization, employees' participation and suggestion system is a practice that plays relevant role in organizational innovation. The popularized system of Kaizen Teian (continuous improvement suggestion system) in Japanese companies has been important for innovation performance and operational efficiency advantage.

Training: holistic development oriented

Psychologists question formal and specialized training on innovation. Some consider that innovation is an autonomous behaviour, and an overemphasis on shaping people's mind may ignore the self-efficacy of a creative individual (Bell & Staw, 1989). Some others consider that innovation could be learnt and trained (Drucker, 1985). De Bono designs many interesting creativity development games and training courses, which have been popularly applied in management practices. The initiative of GE and other hundreds of firms in 1970s to create a Centre for Creative Leadership (CCL) has become a research and training platform for leadership and innovation development.

Nonetheless, a training system for innovation is not only about providing specialized creativity development training course for employees in the specific area, but also oriented to holistically develop the capability of employees with integrated training plan and content. Holistic training is a way for organization to invest in human capital that encourages the overall practice of organizational learning; consequently, it is expected to positively influence individual and organization innovation. It could also include some development of professional skills which help employees to continuously improve in specific task areas (Amabile, 1983); exploration and cultivation of in-depth personality, potential and motivation could be included to improve general competency of employees for high performance and innovation.

Performance appraisal: formative to improve performance management

Shalley (1995) finds that setting a creativity objective for employees can help increase innovation performance; yet setting a *measurable quantitative* objective such as quota of innovative products may reduce innovation performance. Whereas employees with a set innovation objective demonstrate higher innovation performance than these without this type of objective, most studies of performance appraisal consider that when people expect their work performance will be precisely measured, their creativity and innovative levels reduce.

In contrast to summative means of assessing performance, formative mechanisms for improvement centres on defining performance objectives together with employees, providing support for employees to improve performance, focusing on performance results rather than strictly controlling work process, and giving feedback and advices for improvement after performance appraisal. For knowledge workers, especially in R&D or integrative management positions, task boundaries may be implicit and fuzzy, job content is likely to be ambiguous and diverse, work format relatively flexible. In this context, innovative behaviour is hard to evidence from individual employee concrete tasks. Encouraging employees to participate in defining innovation objectives from their own perspective helps stimulate their motivation for innovation. Meanwhile, performance feedback is also observed to contribute to improving innovative behaviour and increasing performance, perhaps even more than the performance appraisal process itself.

Reward system: comprehensive intrinsic and extrinsic system

The research on the relation between reward system and innovation performance is complex. Despite the complexity, the main theme to follow is the effectiveness of intrinsic and extrinsic reward systems. Some classical studies point out that intrinsic motivation (i.e., whether the job is interesting, attractive and supports self-actualization and so on) is more positively related to human creativity and innovation performance than extrinsic motivation. Over explicitly defined extrinsic motivation could diminish or deflect employees' intrinsic motivation, and consequently reduce innovation capability (Zhou, Zhang & Montoro, 2011). Comprehensive reward systems integrate intrinsic motivation and extrinsic economic reward, to offset the problems of overemphasizing extrinsic economic rewards through compensatory spiritual/emotional rewards that satisfy deeper psychological needs and personal development for example awards, recognition of intellectual property, or fulfilment through the benefits of the innovative outcomes in terms of their contribution to wider society.

Long-term commitment: diverse opportunity in career development and job stability

Allen and Katz's (1986) case studies on companies such as 3M and HP demonstrate that double-channel career development systems are helpful for innovation and performance. Leavitt (1996) also finds that, firms with well-designed career development plans for knowledge workers have relatively high level of job satisfaction and innovation performance without the need for high remuneration. Diversity in career development plans not only provide a possibly suitable research career model but also apply practices such as job rotation to integrate horizontal organizational knowledge. Cross-functional or cross-field job rotation systems are becoming popular as a managerial practice to stimulate employees to understand better diverse areas of expertise, which facilitates innovation.

In parallel to provide diverse career development opportunities, long-term employment is considered to improve organizational commitment. And because employees acquire firm-specific knowledge over time, it should eventually facilitate innovation (Pfeffer, 1998). Innovation often is a process of long-term accumulation, thus commitment-oriented job security could improve employees' innovation capacity. However, criticism also points to the possibility of stable employment reducing individuals' competitiveness dulling the leading edge of initiatives, consequently reducing performance level. Stable employment potentially induces complacency and group think, as well as a resistance to change. Therefore, the benefit of stable employment needs complementary human resource management systems to maintain organizational competitiveness.

External collaboration: collaboration with external intelligent resources

From the perspective of regional innovation systems, the collaboration and interaction between enterprises, universities, research institutes and professional consultancies, positively increases innovation outcomes (Doloreux, 2002). External collaboration not only with these specialized research institutions but also with other agents and stakeholders in the industrial value chain such as customers and suppliers could interactively promote continuous learning process and stimulate creative ideas. Christiansen (2000) empirically finds that these collaborations with external individuals or institutions could improve innovation process. In this sense, organization is created as an organic configuration of ba to foster knowledge creation (Nonaka & Toyama, 2003). Applying social network and stakeholder approach to innovation could consequently put one step forward for a people-centric model for a humanistic approach of innovation.

Discussion and conclusion

In Fagerberg, Fosaas, & Sapprasert's (2012) comprehensive review of the knowledge base of innovation over five decades, they point out that 'new scientific fields or specialties, within or across disciplines, emerge from time to time in response to challenging problems and the resulting need for new knowledge' (p. 1146). Innovation is a relatively new field in organizational studies, in comparison with other established disciplines, so could be considered as still evolving in terms of the knowledge base.

Individuals as knowledge workers are the embedded vehicle for knowledge creation, transfer, learning and unlearning. When Nonaka and Takeuchi (2011) argue for wise leadership in managing knowledge, they also promote distributed practical wisdom through the organization, considering that 'fostering distributed leadership is ... one of the wise leader's biggest responsibilities' (p. 66). Distributed *phronesis* (i.e., distributed practical wisdom) is also claimed to be a requirement of effective strategic management (Nonaka & Toyama, 2007). In this essay, we attempt to approach organizational innovation through the lenses of humanistic vision on which Ikujiro Nonaka found the Knowledge School of Management.

At the organizational level, five organizational factors have been generally considered to enhance creativity and innovation in the workplace: organizational climate, leadership style, organizational culture, resources and skills and structure and systems. In parallel, Grant (2013) suggests the relevance of processes, structure, motivation and organizational alignment for an economic perspective of organizational knowledge creation. With the review of human creativity, innovation, as well as human resource management practices in relation to both, several interconnections could be highlighted. Taking knowledge creation as a dynamic theory (Nonaka, 1994), innovation is strategically important for a firm to gain and sustain competitive advantage, thus a dynamic perspective on managing human resources as a strategic instrument is appropriate to the formation of a people-centric vision of innovation. Taking the proposed dynamic model of strategic human resources

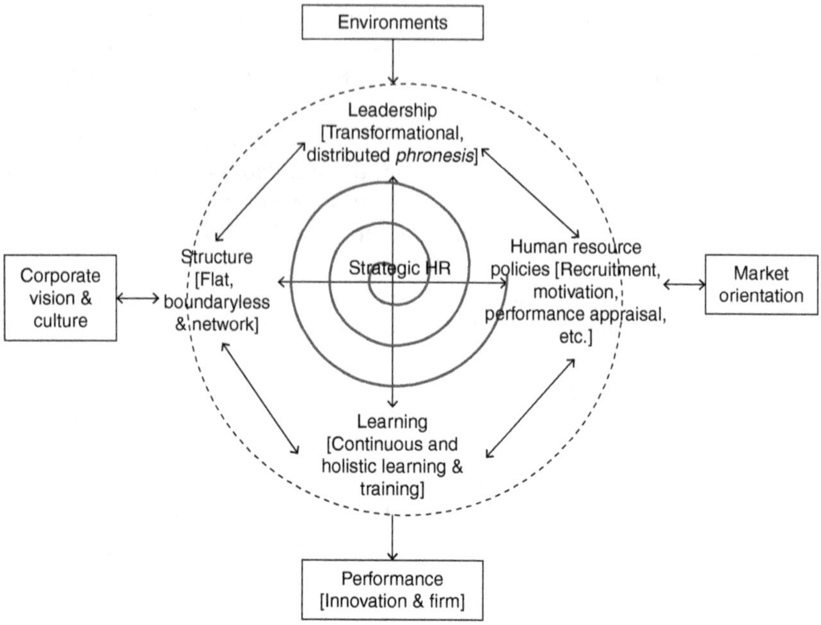

Figure 9.1 A people-centric innovation process through strategic human resources
Source: Adapted from Zhang et al. (2009, p. 216).

(Zhang et al., 2009, p. 216), we adapt it for a people-centric innovation process through strategic human resources (see Figure 9.1).

Firms attempt to achieve innovation and firm performance within the changing and diversified environments that they operate in. We argue that continuous self-renewal (through knowledge exploration and learning) is vital if humans are to really act as strategic assets for the firm. The model contains four essential strategic human resources elements (i.e., leadership, structure, learning and human resource policies), two organizational alignment factors (i.e., corporate vision and culture, and market orientation) and two external factors out of the organizational black box: one as input – environment, and another as output – performance (i.e., innovation performance and general firm performance).

Within the dynamic process of strategic human resource management, corporate culture and vision determine the type of structure, leadership and other strategic human resource factors that the organization has. Market orientation continues to fuel demands and interact with the intent of strategic human resources activities, policies and consequently the relevance of individual and organizational learning.

Four strategic human resource elements also interact to dynamically achieve knowledge management and creation. Transformational leadership supports the formative personnel policies to improve employees' capability, while distributed leadership fosters people at various organizational levels able to exercise *phronesis* in their own situation (Nonaka & Toyama, 2007, p. 380). Continuous learning and training provides employees opportunities to constantly self-improve, and holistic development offers ampler experience to foster divergent thinking as well as cross functional knowledge. These two dynamic elements self-organize at the individual level, whereas structure and human resource policies are organizationally based to provide platform for knowledge creation to be possible. On one hand, flat, boundary-less and networked types of structure increase collaborative innovation opportunities for both internal, cross-functional and external learning; on the other hand, different human resource policies including recruitment, reward (motivation), performance appraisal and others endow with facilities to manage innovation flow.

In virtue of taking Nonaka's knowledge management from the perspective of managing people at organizational level, we attempt to look at knowledge conversion from organization's perspective (see Figure 9.2). That is, how knowledge is created and transferred across levels between individual and organization, then how organization scan manage their innovative people to better perform with their corresponding strategic human resource mechanisms. We adopt SECI model (Nonaka, 1994; Nonaka & Toyama, 2003, p. 5) with organizational foci, turning the focus on organizational capability to

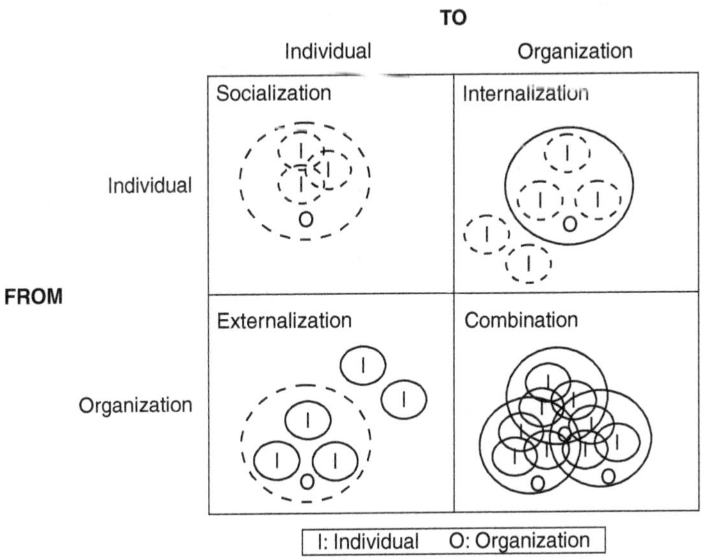

Figure 9.2 Knowledge conversion across levels

Source: Modified based on Nonaka and Toyama (2003, p. 5).

transfer individual's knowledge creation ability and innovative behaviour to organizational ones. Thus 'internalization' refers to convering the explicit knowledge of an individual member to the organizational shared knowledge; 'externalization' is to convey organizational common shared knowledge to individuals; the social interaction between individuals ('socialization') is individual based but with organization providing an appropriate environment; and 'combination' is principally inter-organizational innovative activity with boundary-less network and flat structured individuals' participating and sustaining the underlying human dynamics.

Different from Grant's (2013) proposal on reformulating Nonaka's knowledge conversation framework, Figure 9.2 focuses on exploring the underlying human dynamics across individual and organizational level in knowledge creation and innovation. This is from an earlier proposed model on strategically managing people from a dynamic approach that constitutes human mechanism and fosters innovation and knowledge creation in an organization, specifically dynamizing human interaction across individual and organizational levels. Innovation-oriented corporate vision and culture offers a flexible ambience for knowledge workers to release their potentials and ideas into reality to be tested and effectively implemented. This allows 'socialization' among individuals and loosely contributing to the general knowledge base of the organization. Transformational and distributed leadership cherishes and encourages individuals to employ their judgment and practical wisdom to reflect and decide at ambiguous points that emerge often in the innovative processes. Other human resource policies such as flexible, autonomous and challenging job design empower knowledge workers to interconnect with others according to the needs and self-organize to suit the situation.

External collaboration with other institutions such as universities and laboratories as well as organizations such as consultancies facilitates inter-organizational knowledge 'combination', with the support of underlying human dynamics. In this sense, continuous learning from different stakeholders such as customers and suppliers also determinates effective knowledge acquisition and combine them for new knowledge creation. An orientation to market ensures an efficient usage of firm resources to guarantee economic value maximization. Hence, organizational structure tends to be boudaryless and flat in order to be responsive to different external changes. In such a way, the system self-organizes to manage the paradox between innovation outcomes and firm performance such as financial ones.

In order to 'internalize' knowledge of an individual to the organization, one of the effective manners to attract and retain them, and empower the release of their creativity to apply to organizational strategic needs. Both diversified recruitment and long term commitment are useful human resource mechanisms to align with this strategic need of talents in an innovative firm. To free knowledge workers' potential to innovate for the firm, motivation mechanism is also critical as argued earlier. In concrete, intrinsic reward systems has been deemed to more effective while extrinsic rewards could be necessary but not determinant, especially it could cause negative effect when intrinsic motivation of employees is high (Zhou, Zhang, & Montoro, 2011).

The 'externalization' of knowledge from organization to individuals in turn could facilitate individuals being more innovative. For instance, as suggested earlier, the communication of new organizational innovative results could stimulate the assimilation of new knowledge for further knowledge creation, as well as serve positive competitive motivation. Holistic training, diverse career development and formative performance appraisal renders similar purpose, to share the existing organizational knowledge in order to promote potential future innovation or simply its effective application.

Highlighting the humanistic vision of Nonaka's knowledge theory, we endeavour to develop a dynamic approach to human resource management which would contribute strategically to firm performance, through sustained knowledge creation and innovation. This people-centric innovation's viewpoint could be a step forward in strategic human capital's theoretical development, as well as contributing to the understanding of knowledge management.

Equal contribution from the first and second author.

References

Allen, T. J., & Katz, R. (1986). 'The dual ladder: motivational solution or managerial delusion?' *R&D Management*. 16 (2), 185–197.

Amabile, T. M. (1983). 'The social psychology of creativity: a componential conceptualization'. *Journal of Personality and Social Psychology*. 43, 357–377.

Amabile, T. M. (1988). 'A model of creativity and innovation in organizations'. In B. M. Staw, & L. L. Cummings (eds), *Research in Organizational Behavior*. 10, 123–167. Greenwich, CT: JAI Press.

Amabile, T. M. (1989). *Growing up Creative: Nurturing a Lifetime of Creativity*. Buffalo, NY: Creative Education Foundation.

Amabile, T. M. (1996). *Creativity in Context*. Boulder, CO.: Westview Press.

Amabile, T. M. (1997). 'Motivating creativity in organizations: on doing what you love and loving what you do'. *California Management Review*. 40 (1), 39–58.

Amabile, T. M. (1998). 'How to kill creativity'. *Harvard Business Review*, September, 77–87.

Amabile, T. M., Conti, R., Lazenby, J., & Herron, M. (1996). 'Assessing the work environment for creativity'. *Academy of Management Journal*. 39 (5), 1154–1184.

Arthur. (1996). 'Increasing returns and the new world of business'. *Harvard Business Review*. 74 (4), 100–109.

Baer, M., & Frese, M. (2003). 'Innovation is not enough: climates for initiative and psychological safety, process innovations, and firm performance'. *Journal of Organizational Behavior*. 14, 569–586.

Barley, S. R. (1986). 'Technology as an occasion for structuring: Evidence from observations of CT scanners and the social order of radiology departments'. *Administrative Science Quarterly*. 31 (1), 78–108.

Bell, N. E., & Staw, B. M. (1989). 'People as sculptors versus sculpture: the role of personality and personal control in organization'. In M. B. Arthur, D. T. Hall, & B. S. Lawrence (eds), *Handbook of Career Theory* (pp. 232–251). New York: Cambridge University Press.

Christensen, J. F. (2002), 'Building innovative assets and dynamic coherence in multi-technology companies.' In Foss, N. J., & Robertson, P. L. (eds), *Resources, Technology and Strategy Explorations in the Resource-based Perspective.* London and New York: Routledge.

Csikszentmihalyi, M. (1988). 'Society, culture, and person: A systems view of creativity'. In R. J. Sternberg (ed.), *The Nature of Creativity: Contemporary Psychological Perspectives* (pp. 325–330), New York: Cambridge University Press.

Csikszentmihalyi, M. (1996). Creativity: *Flow and the Psychology of Discovery and Invention.* New York: Harper Perennial.

Damanpour, F. (1991). 'Organizational innovation: A meta-analysis of effects of determinants and moderators'. *Academy of Management Journal.* 34, 555–590.

De Bono, E. (1971). *Lateral Thinking for Management.* New York: McGraw-Hill.

De Bono, E. (1985). *Six Thinking Hats.* Boston: Little, Brown.

De Bono, E. (1992). *Serious Creativity: Using the Power of Lateral Thinking to Create New Ideas.* New York: HarperCollins.

DeGraff, J., & Lawrence, K. A. (2002). Creativity at Work: *Developing the Right Practices to Make Innovation Happen.* San Francisco (CA): Jossey-Bass.

Dewar, R. D., & Dutton, J. E. (1986). 'The adoption of radical and incremental innovations: An empirical analysis'. *Management Science.* 32 (11), 1422–1433.

Doloreux, D., (2002). 'What we should know about regional systems of innovation'. *Technology in Society.* 24 (3), 243–263.

Drucker, P. F. (1985). *Innovation and Entrepreneurship-practice and Principles.* New York: Harper & Row.

Drucker, P. (1993). *Post-Capitalist Society.* London: Butterworth Heinemann.

Eisenhardt, K. M. & J. A. Martin (2000). 'Dynamic capabilities: what are they?' *Strategic Management Journal.* 21 (10/11), 1105.

Easterby-Smith, M., & I. M. Prieto (2008). 'Dynamic capabilities and knowledge management: an integrative role for learning?' *British Journal of Management.* 19 (3), 235–249.

Ettlie, I. F., Bridges, W. P., & O'Keefe. R. (1984). 'Organization strategy and structural differences for radical versus incremental innovation'. *Management Science.* 30 (6), 682–695.

Fagerberg, J., Fosaas, M., & Sapprasert, K. (2012). 'Innovation: exploring the knowledge base'. *Research Policy.* 41, 1132–1153.

George, J. M., & Zhou, J. (2001). 'When openness to experience and conscientiousness are related to creative behaviour: An interactional approach'. *Journal of Applied Psychology*, 86, 513–524.

Goleman, D., & R. Boyatzis (2008). 'Social intelligence and the biology of leadership'. *Harvard Business Review.* September, 8 (9), 74–81.

Grant, R. M. (2002). 'The knowledge based view of the firm'. In C. W. Choo & N. Bontis. (eds), *The Strategic Management of Intellectual Capital and Organizational Knowledge.* Oxford: Oxford University Press.

Grant, R. M. (2010). *Contemporary Strategy Analysis* (7th ed.). London: Blackwell.

Grant, R. M. (2013). 'Nonaka's "Dynamic Theory of Knowledge Creation" (1994): reflections and an exploration of the "Ontological Dimension"'. In Von Krogh,

G., Kase, K., & Canton, C. (eds), *Towards an Organizational Theory*. Hampshire (UK): Palgrave Macmillan.

Guilford, J. P. (1950). 'Creativity'. *American Psychologist*. 5, 444–454.

Gupta, A. K., & Singhal, A. (1993). 'Managing human resources for innovation and creativity'. *Research Technology Management*, 36 (3), 41–48.

Hackman, J. R., & Oldham, G. R. (1980). *Work redesign*. MA: Addison-Wesley.

Hayes, J. R. (1989). *The Complete Problem Solver* (2nd ed.). Hillsdale, NJ: Erlbaum.

Huselid, M. A. (1995). 'The impact of human resource management practices on turnover, productivity, and corporate financial performance'. *Academy of Management Journal*. 38, 635–672.

Kase, K., Slocum, A. & Zhang, Y. (2011). *Asian Versus Western Management Thinking: Its Culture-Bound Nature*. Hampshire (UK): Palgrave MacMillan.

Kimberly, J. R., & Evanisko, M. J. (1981). 'Organizational innovation: The influence of individual, organizational, and contextual factors on hospital adoption of technological and administrative innovations'. *Academy of Management Journal*. 24, 689–713.

Leavitt, W. M. (1996). 'High pay and low morale – can high pay, excellent benefits, job security, and low job satisfaction coexist in a public agency'. *Public Personnel Management*. 25 (3), 333–341.

Lepper, M. R., & Greence, D. (1978). 'Over justification research and beyond: towards a means-end analysis of intrinsic and extrinsic motivation'. In M. R. Lepper, & D.Greene(eds), *The hidden Costs of Reward: New Perspectives on the Psychology of Human Motivation*. (pp. 109–148). Hillsdale, NJ: Lawrence Erlbaum.

Lovelace, K., Shapiro, D., & Weingart, L. (2001). 'Maximizing crossfunctional new product teams' ability to innovate and adhere to budgets: A conflict communications perspective'. *Academy of Management Journal*. 44, 779–794.

Lubart, T. I. (1994). 'Creativity'. In R. J. Sternberg (ed.), *Thinking and Problem Solving*. New York: Academic Press, pp. 289–332.

Magyari-Beck, I. (1991). 'The dignity of creativity studies'. *International Creativity Network Newsletter*. 1 (3), 1–2.

March, J. G. (2004). 'Parochialism in the evolution of a research community: the case of organization studies'. *Management and Organization Review*. 11, 5–22.

Markus, L.M., & Robey, D. (1988). 'Information technology and organizational change: Causal structure in theory and research'. *Management Science*. 34 (5), 583–598.

Martins, E. C. & Terblanche, F. (2003). 'Building organizational culture that stimulates creativity and innovation'. *European Journal of Innovation Management*. 6 (1), 64–74.

Massetti, B. (1996). 'An empirical examination of the value of creativity support systems in idea generation'. *MIS Quarterly*. March, 20 (1), 83–97.

Martin, B. R. (2012). 'The evolution of science policy and innovation studies'. *Research Policy*. 41, 1219–1239.

Mayer, R. E. (1999). 'Fifty years of creativity research'. In R. J. Sternberg (ed.), *Handbook of Creativity*. London: Cambridge University Press, pp. 449–460.

Nonaka, I. (1991). 'The knowledge-creating company'. *Harvard Business Review*. November–December, 96–104.

Nonaka, I. (1994). 'A dynamic theory of organizational knowledge creation'. *Organization Science*. 5 (1), 14–37.

Nonaka, I. (2011a). 'Prologue'. In Kase, K., Slocum, A., & Zhang, Y., *Asian Versus Western Management Thinking: Its Culture-Bound Nature*. Hampshire (UK): Palgrave Macmillan.

Nonaka, I. (2011b). *Towards An Innovation Theory: Knowledge-creation Community, Presentation at Inaugural Symposium of Nonaka Centre for Knowledge and Innovation.* 15th November 2011, Madrid.

Nonaka, I., & Konno, N. (1998). 'The concept of "Ba": Building a foundation for knowledge creation'. *California Management Review.* 40 (3), 40–54.

Nonaka, I., & Takeuchi, H. (1995). *The Knowledge-creating Company: How Japanese Companies Create the Dynamics of Innovation.* New York-Oxford: Oxford University Press.

Nonaka, I., & Takeuchi, H. (2011). 'The wise leader'. *Harvard Business Review.* 89, 58–67.

Nonaka, I., & Toyama, R. (2003). 'The knowledge-creating theory revisited: knowledge creation as a synthesizing process'. *Knowledge Management Research & Practice.* 1, 2–10.

Nonaka, I., & Toyama, R. (2007). 'Strategic management as distributed practical wisdom (phronesis)'. *Industrial and Corporate Change.* 16 (3), 371–394.

Nonaka, I., Toyama, R., & Hirata, T. (2010). *Managing Flow: A Process Theory of the Knowledge-Based Firm.* Tokyo: Toyo Keizai Shinpo-sha, p.59. (in Japanese)

Nonaka, I., Toyama, R., & Nagata, A. (2000). 'A firm as a knowledge-creating entity: a new perspective on the theory of the firm'. *Industrial and Corporate Change.* 9 (1), 1–20.

Nonaka, I., & von Krogh, G. (2009). 'Tacit knowledge and knowledge conversion: controversy and advancement in organizational knowledge creation theory'. *Organization Science.* 20 (3), 635–652.

Ochse, R. (1990). Before the Gates of Excellence: *The Determinants of Creative Genius.* Cambridge: Cambridge University Press.

Oldham, G. R., & Cummings, A. (1996). 'Employee creativity: personal and contextual factors at work'. *Academy of Management Journal.* 39 (3), 607–634.

Pfeffer, J. (1998). 'Seven practices of successful organizations'. *California Management Review.* 40 (2), 96–124.

Ruppel, C. P., & Harrington, S. J. (2000). 'The relationship of communication, ethical work climate, and trust to commitment and innovation'. *Journal of Business Ethics.* 25, 313–328.

Schuler, R. S. (1992). 'Strategic human resource management: linking people with the needs of the business'. *Organizational Dynamics.* 21 (1), 18–32.

Schumpeter, J. A. (1934). *Theory of Economic Development.* New York: Oxford University Press.

Senge, P., Roberts, C., & Ross, R. B. et al. (1994). *The Fifth Discipline.* New York: Doubleday.

Shalley, C. E. (1995). 'Effects of coaction, expected evaluation, and goal setting on creativity and productivity'. *Academy of Management Journal.* 38(2), 483–503.

Shane, S. A. (2008). *Handbook of Technology and Innovation Management.* J.Wiley & Sons, Chichester.

Shipton, H., Fay, D., West, M., Patterson, M., & Birdi, K. (2005), 'Managing people to promote innovation'. *Creativity and Innovation Management.* 14 (2), 118–128.

Simonton, D. K. (1984). *Genius, Creativity, and Leadership: Historiometric Inquiries.* Cambridge, MA: Harvard University Press.

Simonton, D. K. (1994). 'Artistic creativity and interpersonal relationships across and within generations'. *Journal of Personality and Social Psychology.* 46 (6), 1273–1286.

Smith, S. M., Ward, T. B., & Finke, R. A. (1995). *The Creative Cognition Approach.* Cambridge, MA: MIT Press.

Spender, J. C., & Grant, R. M. (1996). 'Knowledge and the firm: overview'. *Strategic Management Journal.* 17, 5–9.

Spender, J. C. (2002). 'Knowledge management, uncertainty, and an emergent theory of the firm'. In C. W. Choo, & N. Bontis (eds), *The Strategic Management of Intellectual Capital and Organizational Knowledge*. Oxford: Oxford University Press.

Sternberg, R. J. (1988). 'Mental self-government: a theory of intellectual styles and their development'. *Human Development*. 31, 197–224.

Sternberg, R. J., & Lubart, T. I. (1991). 'An investment theory of creativity and its development'. *Human Development*. 34, 1–32.

Sternberg, R. J., & Lubart, T. I. (1996). 'Investing in creativity'. *American Psychologist*. 51 (7), 677–688.

Sternberg, R. J., & O'Hara, L. J. (1998). 'Creativity and intelligence'. In R. J. Sternberg (ed.), *Handbook of Creativity*, Cambridge University Press, pp. 251–272.

Strivers, B. P. & Joyce, T. (2000). Building a balanced performance management system. *SAM Advanced Management Journal*. Spring, 65 (2), 22–31.

Torrance, E. P. (1974). *Torrance Tests of Creative Thinking*. Lexington, MA: Personnel Press.

Vandermerwe, S. (1997). 'Increasing returns. competing for customers in a global market'. *Journal of World Business*. 32 (4), 333–351.

Van Winkelen, C., & Mckenzie, J. (2012). *An Exploration of Epistemic Culture as a Barrier to Knowledge Flows*. European Conference on Knowledge Management Cartagena Spain 6th and 7th September.

Van Winkelen, C. (2007). 'Integrating business learning strategies: bridging divides in KM and HR learning strategies at Orange, GSK and QinteQ. KM Review'. October, pp. 16–21

von Krogh, G., & K. Ichijo, et al. (2000). *Enabling Knowledge Creation: How to Unlock the Mystery of Tacit Knowledge and Release the Power of Innovation*. Oxford: Oxford University Press.

Weisberg, R. W. (1999). 'Creativity and knowledge: A challenge to theories'. In R. Sternberg (ed.), *Handbook of Creativity*, Cambridge: Cambridge University Press, pp. 226–250.

Woodman, R., & Schoenfeldt, L. (1990). 'An interactionist model of creative behaviour'. *Journal of Creative Behaviour*, 24, 10–10.

Woodman, R. W., Sawyer, J. E., & Griffin, R. W. (1993). 'Toward a theory of organizational creativity'. *Academy of Management Review*. 18, 293–321.

Wright, P. M., & Boswell, W. R. (2002). 'Desegregating HRM: A review and synthesis of micro and macro human resource management research'. *Journal of Management*, 28, 247–276.

Xu, F. (2013). 'The formation and development of Ikujiro Nonaka's knowledge creation theory'. In Von Krogh, G., Kase, K., & Canton, C. (eds), *Towards an Organizational Theory*, Hampshire (UK): Palgrave Macmillan.

Zhang, Y., Dolan, S., Lingham, T., & Altman, Y. (2009). 'International strategic human resource management: a comparative case analysis of Spanish firms in China'. *Management and Organization Review*. 5 (2), 195–222.

Zhou, J., & Oldham, G. R. (2001.) 'Enhancing creative performance: effects of expected developmental assessment strategies and creative personality'. *Journal of Creative Behavior*. 35, 151–167.

Zhou, Y., Zhang, Y., & Montoro, M.A. (2011). 'Utilitarianism or romanticism: the effect of rewards on employees' innovative behaviour'. *International Journal of Manpower*. 32 (1), 81–98.

10

Leaping to Optima? Knowledge Creation and Behavioral Theory

Patrick Reinmoeller

Thought leaders' influence

Since the 1990s, Knowledge Creation Theory has had much influence in different areas of management research including organization theory, strategic management, innovation management and related areas of scientific inquiry. Its central concepts have become a major influence to many theoretical and empirical studies focused on knowledge-based phenomena in organizations. Instead of reviewing the seminal concepts of SECI model and enabling conditions (Nonaka, 1994; Nonaka & Takeuchi, 1995), or later concepts such as 'ba' (Nonaka & Konno, 1998), enablers (von Krogh, Ichijo, & Nonaka, 2000), knowledge creating capabilities (Nonaka, Toyama, & Nagata, 2000) and creative routines (Nonaka & Reinmoeller, 2002). By documenting their impact, I choose to attend to the complementary relationship between Knowledge Creation Theory (Nonaka, 1994; Nonaka & Takeuchi, 1995, von Krogh, Ichijo, & Nonaka, 2000) and the Behavioral Theory of the Firm (Cyert & March, 1963), arguably one of the most influential theories that clearly is foundational for the Evolutionary Theory of the Firm (Nelson & Winter, 1982) the attention-based view of the firm (Ocasio, 1997) but also an inspiration for Ikujiro Nonaka's Knowledge Creation Theory.

Surprisingly the relationship between Knowledge Creation and the Behavioral Theory remains largely unexplored. Given that centrifugal forces in strategic management research, a field of plagued by 'parochialism and disjointedness' (Hambrick, 2004, p. 97), bandwagon effects, a 'habit of coining neologisms' (Brandenburger & Vinokurova, 2012, p. 287) that can lead to language games and reification (Giudici & Reinmoeller, 2012), it is indeed time to consolidate our gains. Cyert and March (1963) and Nonaka (1994) are separated by more than 30 years, by thousands of miles and a cognitive distance that could convincingly be measured by the distance between English and Japanese. While differences in time, geography and importantly language 'equip different firms with different cognitive tools' (Brandenburger & Vinokurova, 2012, p. 287), they also seem to bestow a range of cognitive capabilities and intellectual preferences. I can only attempt a rough outline of the relationships because bringing the 'best of both worlds' together in a single chapter like this is impossible. Fortunately, the key concepts and impact of the Behavioral Theory of the Firm have been recently reflected upon (e.g., Gavetti, Greve, Levinthal, & Ocasio, 2012; Argote & Greve, 2007; Mahoney, 2004). Building on their lucid work, I briefly highlight selected similarities and differences between the theories and interpret their relationship to advance an understanding of their complementarity.

Explaining decision making in organizations, Cyert and March (1963) 'eschewed normative implications, especially those that rested on forward looking rather than backward-looking behaviour, and those that rested on distant rather than incremental or local processes of search and change'. (Gavetti et al., 2012, p. 26). It follows that the 'Behavioral Theory of the Firm has given strategy and organization scholars a backward-looking, incremental sensibility that gives many useful insights on organizational change. For a fuller view, however, the field also needs to incorporate forward-looking decision making and actions made for distant and uncertain benefits' (Gavetti et al., 2012, p. 26). This insight that management theory may need complementary ways of representing not only the world of decision making but also the world of innovation and self-renewal, i.e., leaps, 'analogous to introducing new colour words, one might look for an effect of introducing a new [concept] into the conversation' (Brandenburger & Vinokurova, 2012, p. 287), serve as guidelines to mobilize languages of organizational knowledge.

Inspired by Gavetti et al.'s (2012) question 'can this influence [of The Behavioral Theory of the Firm] continue?', I reflect on how it may, together with Knowledge Creation Theory, form a basis for more comprehensive understanding of how continuity, change and innovation in organization occurs. Finally, as an appreciation of Knowledge Creation Theory is especially meaningful in the context of the Behavioral Theory of the Firm, and vice versa, I point to a 'joint' agenda of a shared quest and accentuated insights and to emergent complementaries. I conclude with implications for future research.

Behavioral Theory: opening the black box of organizational decision making

The foundational concepts of Behavioral Theory of the Firm go back to Simon's view that 'decision making is the heart of administration' (Simon, 1947, p. xlvi), making a choice between alternatives, which is characterized by limits of rationality. This led to the defining role of bounded rationality for the Carnegie School (Gavetti et al., 2012). 'Whereas neoclassical economic man maximizes – selects the best alternative from among all those available to him – organizational man satisfices – looks for a course of action that is satisfactory or good enough. Economic man deals with the real world in all of its complexity, whereas organization man perceives a drastically simplified model of the real world' (Mahoney, 2004, p. 8)

Compared to the conventional theory of the firm that had focused on outcomes of the market mechanism, i.e., price and quantities, Cyert and March (1963) directed attention to the importance of the process of decision making in firms. With 'more frontal assaults on the assumptions [of the standard economic theory of the firm]' (Cyert & March, 1963, p. 8; Gavetti et al., 2012), Cyert and March (1963) asked, at the time, new and thought-provoking questions mainly about the 'actual' process of decision making of the firm such as price, output, and resource allocation.

This 'was a call for answering a broader set of questions of firm behaviour' (Gavetti et al., 2012, p. 3) that set the agenda in 1963, extending the earlier work of the Carnegie School. This inspiring departure from neoclassical views aimed at understanding 'the internal workings' (Argote & Greve, 2007, p. 344) included 'a commitment to ... take a process view for the sake of predicting the reality of decisions (and their outcomes)' (Gavetti et al., 2012, p. 3). Cyert and March (1963) articulated these key ideas related to bounded rationality with 'cognitive' and 'relational' concepts. The cognitive concepts presented an especially 'irreverent attitude towards classical economics' (Gavetti et al., 2012, p. 4). In short, Cyert and March (1963) presented a radical departure from less realistic and restrictive assumptions of a dominant paradigm. Based on different assumptions, they developed a model that captured how 'decision makers lack perfect knowledge and must search for information, their actions are usually inconsistent with the maximization postulate of the rational agent model ... [following] different decision rules' (Gavetti et al., 2012, p. 4).

Satisficing, search and status quo

Three central keywords encapsulate Cyert and March's (1963) departure from the standard economic model – satisficing, search and status quo. Boundedly rational individuals achieve satisfactory outcomes by picking the first alternative that meets their aspirations. These aspirations are often based on experience, prior performance history or observation of competitors (Argote & Greve, 2004). These individuals search for information to make decisions that better meet their aspirations and they cease searching when they expect an alternative to satisfy. Automatic rules help when problems arise, e.g., performance falls below the aspiration level. Such rules or standard operating procedures limit efforts and areas of search by focusing on 'the neighbourhood of the current symptom ... and the neighbourhood of the current alternative', leading to 'a cause [that] will be found "near" its effect and a new solution will be found "near" an old one' (Cyert & March, 1963, p. 170). These automatic rules substitute intuition, planning or forecasting by relying mainly on experience. 'All in all, bounded rationality leads to a representation of choice as a semi-automatic process that is informed by the past and operates in the present,individuals (and firms) are rule-based actors who solve pressing problems, search their local environment, and adopt solutions that rarely violate the status quo' (Gavetti et al., 2012, p. 5).

Together with the more cognitive concepts, satisficing, search and status quo, four relational concepts, quasi-resolution of conflict, uncertainty avoidance, problemistic search, and organizational learning, i.e., 'encoding inferences from history into routines that guide behaviour' (Levitt & March, 1988, p. 320), all form 'a more behaviourally realistic approach to predict organizational action than the optimizing and equilibrium ideas of the traditional theory of the firm' (Gavetti et al., 2012, p. 6). Shifting coalitions in organizations negotiate temporary compromises between different goals and lead to the quasi-resolution of conflicts as outcomes of political processes in organizations. Importantly, uncertainty avoidance biases feedback seeking to a strong short-term orientation. Problemistic search 'is motivated by the goal of overcoming performance shortfalls, directed by simple models of causality, and biased by organizational experiences and individual goals' (Gavetti et al., 2012, p. 6) In the basic model performance discussed in the following paragraph, aspiration initiates search for solutions, in the vicinity of the problem and the existing actions, which leads to a bias against distant and large changes in behaviours. Performance shortfalls also lead to adaptation of the aspiration level towards the actually experienced performance (Cyert & March, 1963, pp. 120–123). Organizational aspiration levels are derived generally from comparisons to past performance and to competitors (Argote & Greve, 2007). Furthermore, so are quantitatively measureable goals that can be directly attributed to the actions of the organization trigger search. When organizations search by matching problems with preexisting solutions (Greve, 1998) and seek to overcome low performance by imitating the innovations of others (Massini, Lewin, & Greve, 2005), they limit organizational change by sticking, largely (cf. Baum & Dahlin, 2007), to what is known and close by, internally and externally. 'Organizational learning occurs when cycles of search and change lead to adaptations of goals, attention rules, and search rules through reinforcement of actions that organizational members interpret as having caused improvements' (Gavetti et al., 2012, p. 6), yet remain close to the status quo.

'Behavioral Theory's opposition against the rationality assumptions of standard economics, the anticipation of distant futures, or of the consequences of distant courses of action..., the role of organizational expectations or, more broadly, the role of an anticipatory logic has [influenced also] contemporary work in the Carnegie tradition' (Gavetti et al., 2012, p. 9). Explanations of organizational functioning, individual habits or collective routines, remain constrained to a limited consideration of possible choices, mostly to a narrow set (Gavetti et al., 2012) of knowns. Building on and extending the preceding, the Carnegie School and contributions close to it share 'a similar view of behaviour (both at the individual and organizational level) as driven by semi-automatic, habit-based decision processes and action patterns' (Gavetti et al., 2012, p. 8). The behavioural pattern 'striving more and expecting less' seems to summarize how the Behavioral Theory describes and explains how organizations make decisions.

Knowledge Creation Theory: attending to innovation and self-renewal

Since his doctoral work at University of California Berkley, Ikujiro Nonaka remains influenced by Simon, March and other authors associated with the Behavioral Theory of the Firm. Nonaka builds on behavioural concepts such as organizational learning (e.g., Nonaka & Johansson, 1985), corporate evolution (Nonaka, 1985), Simon's view that 'all learning takes place inside individual human heads' (Simon, 1991, p. 125), firm specific language and routines (e.g., Nonaka & Toyama, 2002), superstitious learning, overadaptation to a past success (Nonaka & Toyama, 2005), competence traps (e.g., Nonaka & Toyama, 2002) or exploration and exploitation (e.g., von Krogh, Nonaka, & Rechsteiner, 2012). However, at times, Nonaka et al. expresses clearly the distance from what has become the conventional view, i.e., in organizations boundedly rational cognition of individuals, devoid of subjectivity, select proximate solutions. For example, 'theories ... [that] are based on the assumption of bounded rationality and opportunism (Simon, 1945; Williamson, 1975, 1985) ... view a human as an isolated, static being' (Nonaka, Toyama, & Nagata, 2000, p. 4). Similarly, Simon 'insisted that factual premises have to be separated from value premises for management to become science' and this exclusion of subjectivity, value, and contexts misses an essential point of management research as a social science (Nonaka & Toyama, 2005, p. 420). For Nonaka (e.g., Nonaka & Toyama, 2005) bounded rationality and the view that individuals create knowledge, while firms exploit knowledge is conventional theory. Instead, organizational knowledge creation explains the process of amplifying knowledge created by individuals, justifying and renewing an organization's knowledge system (Nonaka, von Krogh, & Voelpel, 2006).

Sharing a quest for knowledge, attitude and 'open work'

The key ideas in the behavioural tradition and Knowledge Creation Theory endure, as shown by persistently high citation rates but also the key authors' continued involvement in the development of their theories as well as their application in practice. This may be explained with four characteristics (March 2007) these theories share..

The theories' continued ability to explain reality and instil passion with new generations of researchers for developing the concepts, is certainly important. March (2007, p. 541) reveals that Cyert and March (1963) were 'more aware of [their] dependence on [their] contemporary colleagues and on those who went before [them] for the ideas that [they] massaged'. Only later they recognized '[their] dependence on generations of later scholars trying to imagine what our words might be constructed to mean to make them interesting'. Similarly, one might say, the 'intergenerational, international pyramid' (March, 2007, p. 541) also supported Nonaka et al. during the first two decades of the Knowledge Creation Theory.

The Behavioral Theory of the Firm, as March concedes benefited from the language in which the book was written, 'English and published in North America at a time when English was rapidly becoming the most common language of scholarly discourse and North America the largest purveyor of scholarly writings. Had the book been written in Farsi and published in Tehran, it might not have fared as well' (March, 2007, p. 540). Similarly, having published with the subtitle 'How Japanese Companies Create the Dynamics of Innovation' (Nonaka & Takeuchi, 1995) may have helped initially because of Japanese Management's halo that had been built since the late 1970s. Yet, the success of The Knowledge Creation Company appears even more remarkable because in spite of its subtitle, the theory has continued to inspire researchers and practitioners while Japanese management lost two decades of attention.

Besides many other qualities of the theories as presented in the seminal books, both theories benefit from being 'open work' (Eco, 1989). Offering 'large sample size of speculations ... a fairly large number of ideas', unplanned 'evocative ambiguity', as March (2007, p. 540) suggests, seems advantageous for the ideas' lasting success, an impact 'noteworthy in terms of breadth rather than depth' (Argote & Greve, 2007, p. 337). The richness of both streams of research in terms of ideas, contributors and power to instil passion for truth owe much to their openness, multifaceted debates and international diversity of communities they inspire (cf. Argote & Greve, 2007; Gavetti, et al., 2012; Nonaka & von Krogh, 2009; Nonaka, von Krogh, & Voelpel, 2006).

A final characteristic seems to be the relationship to other theories, i.e., an irreverent attitude to conventional theories. Similar to the Cyert & March's 'frontal assault' (1963, p. 8), Nonaka uses conventional theories as background for their reasoning. 'Neoclassical economics ... [and] [o]ther theories of the firm, including transaction-cost theory, also view a firm as a static information-processing machine that takes and processes information from the environment to solve the problem and adapt to the environment based on a given goal. This is a static and passive view of organization, and fails to capture the dynamic process of knowledge creation. Instead of merely solving problems, an organization creates and defines problems, generates and applies new knowledge to solve the problems, and then further generates new knowledge through the action of problem solving (Cyert & March, 1963; March, 1991; Levinthal & Myatt, 1994). The organization actively interacts with its environment, and reshapes the environment and even itself through the process of knowledge creation. Instead of being given all the necessary information, as suggested in neoclassical economics or instead of processing information to overcome the information disequilibrium, as suggested by transaction-cost theory or principal agent theory' (Nonaka et al., 2000, pp. 2–3).

Reflective of Kuhn's (1962) views of paradigms, after 40 years, the behavioural tradition (Argote & Greve, 2007) may be viewed as part of the conventional tradition, as may lie in the future of Knowledge Creation Theory.

Accentuating cognitive steps and leaps of insight

Organizational practice is central to both perspectives. In what follows, I focus only on how they seek to explain and influence practice in their emphasis relative to innovation. The focus of behavioural researchers on how organizations make decisions to maintain the status quo certainly resonates with Nonaka's research and his emphasis on how knowledge is created, how organizations transform themselves and the ecologies in which they are embedded (Corno, Reinmoeller, & Nonaka, 1999). However, both theories illustrate a range of views on organizational change, less as aimless alteration but more as trajectory of maintenance or as a way to innovation. While accounts of slack and serendipity explain how organizations occasionally develop new products, technologies or practices even when they are not solving specific problems (Argote & Greve, 2007), the behavioural tradition mainly focuses on problemistic search and maintenance of the status quo.

Where the rational character of search in 'good' organizations suggests that 'among several alternatives involving the same expenditure the one should be selected that leads to the greatest accomplishment of organizational objectives, and, among several alternatives that lead to the same accomplishment, the one should be selected that involves the least expenditure' (Mahoney, 2004, pp. 10–11). With aspirations shaped by prior performance or that of competitors, 'choice takes place in an environment of givens – premises that are accepted by the individual as bases for choice – and behaviour is adaptive only within the limits set by these givens' (Mahoney, 2004, p. 12). The ability to imagine the best solutions to new problems distinguishes knowledge creation as process that changes organizations and their environments. Visions of organizational leaders shape the value system, i.e., what is taken for granted when in organizations the ideas are justified, evaluated to assess the quality of new knowledge. While rationality may be important, subjective elements, values and aesthetic or ethic views of knowledge are critical considerations that explain why firms differ in their ability to leap to distant optima. Although maintenance of the status quo and searching for innovation both matter, it is their accentuation and nuance that distinguishes both theories and makes them complementary. Searching for the 'first best solution' by making small steps, without taking too much risk (cf. Gavetti, 2012; Winter, 2012), is close but different from searching the 'best solution first'.

Viewing search as a cognitive approach to find existing solutions for existing problems as similar, yet different from employing mind and body to new solutions to hitherto unknown problems is important to understand how the behavioural tradition and knowledge creation complement each other. Organizations can innovate relying on capturing variety, selecting and retaining what works (cf. Winter, 2012) to meet their aspirations or to adapt to environmental requirements. Taking these steps to innovate seems less likely to help companies making strides, not to speak of leaping to new peaks of performance. Instead of decision making in organizations, knowledge creation focuses on organizations' desire to extend the boundaries of knowledge by exerting good judgment (Nonaka & Takeuchi, 2011), even at the risk of appearing selfless.

Important for taking steps and for making leaps is an organization's perspective, how far it needs to look ahead and survey a business landscape and how it imagines new business models. Characteristic of Nonaka's view on leadership (cf. Nonaka & Takeuchi, 1995; Nonaka & Takeuchi, 2011; von Krogh, Nonaka, & Rechsteiner, 2012) is the emphasis on the importance of tacit knowledge and a unique vision, and of what is 'insanely great' (cf. Takeuchi & Stone, 2012).

Emergent complementarities

In recent years, the complementarity between decision making and creating knowledge has become more nuanced. The Behavioral Theory of the Firm 'has not generated a behavioral theory of the firm... if we define theory as a consistent set of defined concepts and assumptions, and derived causal predictions. Instead, there are now many behavioral theories of the firm, each using different assumptions and deriving different predictions' (Argote & Greve, 2007, p. 337). The emerging consensus that '[f]or over a decade, researchers in strategic management have pointed to the *relative neglect of the attributes of human cognition* as a troublesome weakness in the intellectual foundations of the field. There has been a broad though somewhat hesitant movement toward doing something about this, accompanied by reaffirmations that, yes, it *is* a problem... [Gavetti & Tripsas (2000)] study provided evidence (shocking to some of us) that managerial commitment to a mere idea, a strategic heuristic of a very simple kind' (Winter, 2012, p. 288) can be pivotal for firms success or failure.

While scholars close to the Carnegie School have started to search for ways to accommodate ideas on superior opportunities being distant (Gavetti, 2012), forward-looking strategy analysis (Gavetti, Levinthal, & Rivkin, 2005), Nonaka et al. (2000, 2006), starting from their emphasis on how leading firms contribute knowledge that is 'new to the world', have put forth a theory of the firm that helps understanding how firms create knowledge that is new to them. These developments of Knowledge Creation Theory to broaden its scope include steps and conditions for organizations to amplify their knowledge in general and the views on power and politics in organizations. Knowledge creation's expansion resembles the behavioural traditions' search to overcome neglect and to explain leaps in strategic management. With the theories thus closing in, the nuanced complementarity becomes more intriguing.

Following Nonaka's Knowledge Creation, several contributions seek to make bounded rationality more realistic by articulating notions such as learning from external sources, boundedly rational foresight, heeding attention, beliefs and false negatives, analogical reasoning and dynamic capabilities.

With time the behavioural traditions' focus on learning internally, learning from external sources such as experiences of other organizations (Levitt & March, 1988) had come to be included to limit its 'emphasis on myopic search in Cyert and March (1963)' (Gavetti et al., 2012, p. 17). 'As Levinthal and March (1993) note, learning processes are often myopic in that feedback that is more proximate in time and space (location within the organization) tends to dominate adaptive processes' (Gavetti et al., 2012, pp. 18–19).

Only recently has research begun to consider decision makers who in simple ways anticipate long run implications of courses of actions. Gavetti and Levinthal (2000) and Gavetti, Levinthal, & Rivkin (2005) combined bounded rationality with simplified cognitive representation (analogy) of the environment and its possible future, i.e., boundedly rational foresight. Including 'a greater variety of goal variable[s] and lower level outcomes' (Gavetti et al., 2012, p. 13) and emphasizing organizational attention (Ocasio, 1997) and shifts therein which are influenced by top down and bottom up processes and structures, the stability, vividness and coherence (Rerup, 2009) of heeding weak signals are all steps to broaden the narrow patterns of explorative search towards making leaps in landscapes.

More scholars (e.g., Hodgkinson & Healey, 2011; Webb, Tihanyi, Ireland, & Sirmon, 2009) agree on bringing together cognition, beliefs and emotions, something that is foundational for the conversion of tacit and explicit knowledge, in the microfoundations of organizational capabilities (cf. Teece, 2007). 'The linkage between beliefs and sampling process is brought to the fore in a line of recent work (Denrell & March, 2001; Le Mens & Denrell, 2011). Since an adaptive organization is naturally going to sample alternatives for which it has more positive beliefs, than beliefs that are in some sense a "false positive," a not particularly promising alternative viewed favourably, will ultimately be corrected. However, a "false negative," a latently promising alternative that is viewed unfavourably, will be unlikely to be sampled and this inaccurate negative belief will persist, despite the organization being nominally adaptive' (Gavetti et al., 2012, p. 19).

In the behavioural tradition, a growing acknowledgement of the organizational need to also make wider steps is being articulated. 'The internal consistency of these inferior local peaks, incremental efforts at adaptation will not lead the organization to abandon this set of choices' (Gavetti et al., 2012, p. 20). The suggestions to make leaps include adopting 'the practices of other higher-performing organizations with the associated risks of imperfect imitation', relying on 'crude cognitive representation of the broader landscape and make a choice to move to a more distant location based on that representation (Gavetti & Levinthal, 2000)' or analogical reasoning (Gavetti, Levinthal, & Rivkin, 2005), remain however mostly cognitive. Based on the behavioural tradition (Argote & Greve, 2007; Mahoney, 2004), micro foundations related to cognition, learning and capabilities linked to routines and habitual decision rules that were mainly specific (Nelson & Winter, 1982) are now seen as more inclusive of general rules even pertaining to mindfulness (Levinthal & Rerup, 2006). While this may rejuvenate the behavioural tradition and resonate with Nonaka's view that knowledge creation is a *way*, a perspective on being, further developments may bring the theories even closer, if besides cognition also embodied and ecological experience of context in motion were to be included (cf. Whiteman & Cooper, 2011; Hargadon & Bechky 2006).

Conclusions and implications

With a focus on process-oriented models of the firm closely informed by empirical observations, the behavioural tradition and Nonaka's school develop theories y beyond the specific firms studied that have strongly shaped management research and practice.[1] Influenced by Cyert and March (1963), those who build on them and the way they attend to decision making steps since the early 1990s, Nonaka, Takeuchi, von Krogh and others are developing a comprehensive theory of the knowledge creating firm and of how leaders' judgment allows for leaping to optima.

Both theories show how researchers benefit from closeness to management practice, observation and experience, and how organizations struggle to make decisions and to create knowledge. A realistic reflexion of organizational action in the behavioural tradition explains how organizations search and select existing knowledge. Emphasizing how organizations create new knowledge by exploring a broader area of real and envisioned opportunities, may be the more realistic projection of organizational intentions that can inspire organizations.

Pointing forward, behavioural tradition in its 50s and Knowledge Creation Theory in its 20s offer largely unfilled opportunities for future generations of researchers as the focus of much of their traditions consider the strategic behaviour of *organizations* but has been less concerned with phenomena of important business practices that were unknown decades ago. Three questions for future research seem especially promising. How does the interplay among organizations, embedded in ecologies that span the boundaries of different institutions, influence decision making and knowledge creation capabilities? How does technology influence the routinization of work and knowledge creation that so strongly relies on subjectivity, beliefs and emotion? How can researchers build on the truly outstanding theories and work towards defragmenting and advancing our discipline?

Note

1. Nonaka and Takeuchi (1995) is referenced by 28,500 publications (Google Scholar, January 20, 2013).

References

Argote, L., & Greve, H. R. (2007). A behavioral theory of the firm – 40 years and counting: introduction and impact. *Organization Science*. 18 (3), 337–349.

Baum, J. A. C., & Dahlin, K. B. (2007). Aspiration performance and railroads' patterns of learning from train wrecks and crashes. *Organization Science*. 18 (3) 368–385.

Brandenburger, A., & Vinokurova, N. (2012). Comment on "Toward a Behavioral Theory of Strategy." *Organization Science*. 23 (1), 286–287.

Corno, F., Reinmoeller, P., & Nonaka, I. (1999). Knowledge creation in industrial sytems. *Journal of Management and Governance*. 3, 379–394.

Cyert, W. M., & March, J. G. (1963). *A Behavioral Theory of the Firm*. Englewood Cliffs, NJ: Prentice Hall.

Denrell, J. & March, J.G. (2001) Adaptation as information resricution: the hot stove effect, *Organization Science*. 12(5), 523–538.

Eco, U. (1989). *The Open Work*. Cambridge, MA: Harvard University Press.

Gavetti, G. (2012). Toward a behavioral theory of strategy. *Organization Science*. 23 (1), 267–285.

Gavetti, G., Levinthal, D.A. & Rivkin, J. (2005). Strategy making in novel and complex worlds: the power of analogy. *Strategic Management Journal*. 26: 691–712.

Gavetti, G., Greve, H. E., Levinthal, D. A., & Ocasio, W. (2012). The behavioral theory of the firm: assessment and prospects. *The Academy of Management Annals*. 6 (1), 1–40.

Giudici, A., & Reinmoeller, P. (2012). Dynamic capabilities in the dock: a case of reification? *Strategic Organization*. 10 (4), 436–449.

Greve, H. R. (1998). Performance, aspirations, and risky organizational change. *Administrative Science Quarterly*. 44, 58–86.

Hambrick, D. C. (2004). The disintegration of strategic management: it's time to consolidate our gains. *Strategic Organization*. 2 (1), 91–98.

Hargadon, A. B., & Bechky, B. A. (2006). When collections of creatives become creative collectives: a field study of problem solving at work. *Organization Science*. 17 (4), 484–500.

Hodgkinson, G. P., & Healey, M. P. (2011). Psychological foundations of dynamic capabilities: reflexion and reflection in strategic management. *Strategic Management Journal*. 32 (13), 1500–1516.

Kuhn, T. S. (1962). *The Structure of Scientific Revolutions*. Chicago: University of Chicago Press.

Le Mens, G. & Denrell, J. (2011) Rational learning and information sampling: on the "naivety" assumption in sampling explanations of judgment biases, *Psychological Review*. 118 (2). 379–392.

Levinthal, D. & March, J.G. (1993). The myopia of learning. *Strategic Management Journal*. 14 (Winter Special Issue), 95–112.

Levinthal, D., & Rerup, C. (2006). Crossing and apparent chasm: bridging mindful and less-mindful perspectives on organizational learning. *Organization Science*. 17 (4), 502–513.

Levitt, B., & J. G. March. (1988). Organizational learning. *Annual Review of Sociology*. 14, 319–340.

Mahoney, J. T. (2004). *The Economic Foundations of Strategy*. Thousand Oaks, CA: Sage Publications.

Massini, S., Lewin, A. Y., & Greve, H. R. (2005). Innovators and imitators: organizational reference groups and adoption of organizational routines. *Research Policy*. 34 (10) 1150–1569.

Nelson, R. R., & Winter, S. G. (1982). *An Evolutionary Theory of Economic Change*. Boston, MA: Belkamp.

Nonaka, I., & Konno, N. (1998). The concept of "ba": building a foundation for knowledge creation. *California Management Review*, 40 (3), 40–54.

Nonaka, I. (1994). A dynamic theory of organizational knowledge creation. *Organizational Science*. 5, 14–37.

Nonaka, I. (1985). *Kigyo Sinka Ron (The Theory of Corporate Evolution)*. Tokyo: Nikkei Shinbunsya.

Nonaka, I., & Takeuchi, H. (1995). *The Knowledge-creating Company: How Japanese Companies Create the Dynamics of Innovation*. New York: Oxford University Press.

Nonaka, I., & Johansson, J. K. (1985). Japanese management: what about the "Hard" skills? *The Academy of Management Review*. 10 (2), 181–191.

Nonaka, I., & Reinmoeller, P. (2002). Knowledge creation and utilization: promoting dynamic systems of creative routines. In M. A. Hitt, R. Amit, C. E. Lucier, & R. D. Nixon (eds), *Creating Value: Winners in the New Business Environment*. Oxford: Blackwell.

Nonaka, I., & Takeuchi. (2011). The wise leader. *Harvard Business Review*. 89 (5), 58–67.

Nonaka, I., & Toyama, R. (2002). A firm as a dialectical being: towards a dynamic theory of a firm. *Industry and Corporate Change*. 11 (5), 995–1009.

Nonaka, I., & Toyama, R. (2005). The theory of the knowledge-creating firm: subjectivity, objectivity and synthesis. *Industrial and Corporate Change*. 14 (3), 419–436.

Nonaka, I., & von Krogh, G. (2009). Tacit knowledge and knowledge conversion: controversy and advancement in organizational knowledge creation theory. *Organization Science*. 20 (3), 635–652.

Nonaka, I., von Krogh, G., & Voelpel, S. (2006). Organizational knowledge creation theory: evolutionary paths and future advances. *Organization Studies*. 27 (8), 1179–1208.

Nonaka, I., Toyama, R., & Nagata, A. (2000). A firm as a knowledge-creating entity: a new perspective on the theory of the firm. *Industrial and Corporate Change*. 9 (1), 1–20.

Ocasio, W. (1997). Towards an attention-based view of the firm. *Strategic Management Journal*. 18, 187–206.

Rerup, C. (2009). Attentional triangulation: learning from unexpected rare crises. *Organization Science*. 20 (5), 876–893.

Simon, H.A. (1945). Administrative behavior: a study of decision-making processes in administrative organizations. New York: Macmillan.

Simon, H. A. (1991). Bounded rationality and organizational learning. *Organization Science*. 2, 125–134.

Takeuchi, H., & Stone, V. (2012). Steve jobs as a wise leader. *Harvard Business School Compilation.* Compilation no.712–479, July 2012.

Teece, D. J. (2007). Explicating dynamic capabilities: the nature and microfoundations of (sustainable) enterprise performance. *Strategic Management Journal.* 28, 1319–1350.

von Krogh, G., Nonaka, I., & Rechsteiner, L. (2012). Leadership in organizational knowledge creation: a review and framework. *Journal of Management Studies.* 49 (1), 240–277.

Webb, J. W., Tihanyi, L., Ireland, R. D., & Sirmon, D. G. 2009. You say illegal, I say legitimate: entrepreneurship in the informal economy. *Academy of Management Review.* 34, 492–510.

Whiteman, G. & Cooper, W. H. (2011). Ecological sensemaking. *Academy of Management Journal.* 54 (5), 889–911.

Winter, S. G. (2012). Purpose and progress in the theory of strategy: comments on Gavetti. *Organization Science.* 23 (1), 288–297.

von Krogh, G., Ichijo, K., & Nonaka, I. (2000). *Enabling Knowledge Creation.* New York: Oxford University Press.

11

Revisiting the 'Knowledge Creating Firm' in the 'Post-Capitalist Society' Context

Noboru Konno

Introduction

This essay contributes to Dr. Ikujiro Nonaka's knowledge creation theory and in particular what Peter Ducker termed a theory for a post-capitalist society. The following four sections look back over thirty years from the beginning of the Japan miracle and current management theory as the development of the knowledge creation theory. It concludes with the author's proposal of 'purpose engineering'.

The first section deals with the history of knowledge creation as a theory of knowledge economy first proposed by Peter Drucker more than 40 years ago. Nonaka's 1991 study and theory highlighted the success of Japanese companies in the 1980s. After encountering the theory, the US became active in the knowledge management approach in the first major stage of the 1990s. The second major stage of development occurred in the first decade of the 21st century. Concepts dealing with intellectual capital, intangible assets and the value of innovation were developed and explored during this period. The third stage is now occurring in the second decade of this century. In particular, the whole organization and the fundamental management goal is the creation of knowledge for the society or social innovation.

The second section then introduces the current situation of knowledge creation theory. Discussion of the present day problems with the global economic system focuses on the necessity of a new management approach. We cite some of the problems that existed in Japan and some of the positive examples from the US. We then delineate our 'to do' list for 21st century management.

The third section focuses on the relationships with Hayek and others ideas, regarding the theories of innovation and the community. The significance of 'tacit knowledge' as well as innovation theory proposed by Schumpeter is explored. The four components of the 'SECI Model' are explained as a discovery process of new knowledge, and how they integrate the explicit and tacit knowledge of ecosystem in the knowledge process.

The final section on theory of 'ba' is quite extensive. Here we revisit the meaning of 'ba' and explain why it is necessary. We explore designs of 'boundary objects' which combine 'ba'. We discuss further the notion that knowledge creation must include the human component. The chapter ends with the concept of 'purpose engineering' or orchestration of purposes.

Drucker on capitalism and the necessity of knowledge theory

'In fact, knowledge is the only meaningful resource today.... We need an economic theory that puts knowledge into the centre of the wealth-producing process. Such a theory alone can explain the present economy, it alone can explain economic growth. It alone can explain innovation. It alone can explain how the Japanese economy works and, above all, why it works' (Peter F. Drucker, *Post-Capitalist Society,* 1993, italic by the author).

The paragraph is cited in Nonaka's new book (Nonaka & Konno, 2012). This essay discusses the past and the future of the knowledge creating theory, based on ideas presented in this new work.

Drucker questioned how economic value could be created in a knowledge-based capitalist society. He did not answer the question himself. Based on what he had observed about the 20th century modern world and industrial society, he predicted the evolution of an organizational society. Compared to the isolated and divided work style typical of early mass manufacturing, Drucker suggested that flexible networking and collaboration (socially organizing) among knowledge workers would be the key factors for creating value.

During his early years in Vienna, he foresaw the collapse of Soviet Union Russia and the rise of Nazism and totalitarian society. It could be that Drucker was sounding a warning to our society and that we should seek such an organizational evolution beyond the industrial society. Knowledge Creation theory is now becoming an answer to the question that Drucker posed.

Organizations that are founded upon the core principle of 'knowledge creation' require management that supports and fosters this organizational compass. Knowledge Creation Management (KCM) is a model whose foundation and core is the process of knowledge creation.

The idea of knowledge creation originally emerged from research into the process of new product development in Japanese firms. Japanese firms such as Honda, Canon, NEC and KAO were growing quickly in 1980s.

After its introduction in 1990s, the theory was refined by further research and examination into a holistic theory of management and organization. It resulted from an iterative struggle of weaning itself off the natural instinct to follow the successful ways of the past and trying to create new ways of thinking and doing. We can say that KCM is a relatively new concept in the field of management studies. As the interest of knowledge management (KM, not KCM) increased globally after 1990, it gradually started to spread on and off as an important concept impacting the fundamental notion of management.

In the 1990s, the idea of KM first gained traction in the US, especially in the field of information technology. Yet, it did not work well and virtually failed. Initially, American firms realized the importance of knowledge and that repeated restructuring and mergers often resulted in lost knowledge. They attempted to store and archive the organizational knowledge via information technology. The results were not always satisfactory because it was not knowledge sharing but simply information sharing. It was in the 1990s, after fully realizing the importance of human factors, that knowledge creation theory began to arouse people's interests as well as the new tide of management theories.

At that time, European and US companies' strategic views had been limited by their focus on environmental analysis and competitive strategies. Compared to the traditional analytical method of strategic planning, the new emerging models were concerned with intangible assets and an organization's internal resources such as organizational learning, core-competence and RBV (resource-based view). Among the new theories, the 'Nonaka group' was a pioneer in the concept of knowledge creation that focused on human knowledge; not tangible economic resources or systems thinking. What the Nonaka group eventually began to understand was that it was not just the process of knowledge creation; it needed a platform for innovation. Knowledge creation theory offered a new construct or pillar in many of the social disciplines including business and economics. The theory of 'ba' was published in 1998 (Nonaka & Konno, 1998).

In the 2000s, Theories and discussions on a 'New Economy' generated interest in how the hidden value of intangible knowledge assets IC (intellectual capital) could impact corporate performance. As the interest in innovation increased, the concern for knowledge creation, not just knowledge sharing increased. With the beginning of the new millennium, came the second period in knowledge creation theory. It became known as the basic theory of innovation and the concept of 'ba' (place or shared context) for knowledge creation was introduced.

Currently, it can be said that KCM has become a magnet or platform connecting social innovation, business model generation and a new paradigm software development method such as agile scrum. The use of scrum as an agile software framework is spreading globally in the software development field and is based on the knowledge creation approach.

In these practices and approaches, 'ba' works effectively in creating knowledge by the SECI process. Through the interactions, socialization, externalization, combination and internalization transpire rapidly among the development team members. As a result technical knowledge is transformed, coded and becomes accessible. In other words it becomes the capital of the whole development teams.

Scrum is a rugby term and it is similar to the word scrimmage in US football or skirmish in a battlefield. It describes the rough and disorderly struggle in which the football passes from different members on different teams. The goal is to share purpose for the struggle. The scrum, design thinking and all collaborative work styles have some process in common. They point to the fact that KCM has become the new order of work.

Now, the network of KCM researchers and business people continues to spread globally. We are at the point of re-examining the context of KCM from its inception, around 1980, to present. In other words, this is the era of great transformation of capitalism and society. It also reflects the turning point and true paradigm shift from the traditional theories of management. Fundamentally, companies need to move from the analytical to the creative model.

Revisiting the knowledge creation theory

As Drucker foresaw, the shift to the knowledge society is now a major global initiative. Management in such a society is founded upon and stems from the collective knowledge of the individuals. In this model of organizations, 'ba' offers the fundamental concept underpinning such a society. 'Ba' is the shared context among individuals, formed by their interaction for the creation of knowledge. An expanded definition of 'ba' is offered in the next section.

The knowledge society is a global phenomenon which includes some deep and common factors that can and will fundamentally change the existing social structure and system and impact individual networks and local life. Naturally, these are of critical importance in planning an organization's strategies and operations. Firms should consciously create 'ba' because it is the essential interface, the porous interface, between all levels of an organization, the inside and the outside.

Such management approaches largely differ from the 'traditional' style and methods. The context of organizational and managerial theories is transforming dramatically, and is approaching the integration phase. This transformation reflects the changes from 20th century industrial structure to the knowledge society economy as well as the reconsideration of market fundamentalism and the effects of diversification from globalization. How we treat knowledge is key for the synthesis. It must reach beyond the former techniques of analysis. For instance, social obligations and responsibilities are playing a greater role in management. This requires a balance of the needs of all stakeholders. And finally, the new leadership challenge is management that is virtuous and sagacious, i.e., a 'phronesis' or practical wisdom (Nonaka & Takeuchi, 2011).

However, then why is it that knowledge creation firms in Japan are not successful today? In the current global economy, Japanese firms should have quickly noticed and adopted the new management style suited to a knowledge-based economy. However, the law of inertia 'blinded' firms to a sense of crisis and responding to the challenge facing a fundamental transformation. For example, a number of manufacturing firms could not extricate themselves from the old industrial management model that focused mainly on manufacturing of things (mono-zukuri) and efficiency. As a result, their high manufacturing capabilities remained static and unexplored. Without the development of a new global markets and business models, survival will be difficult.

If Japan Inc. does not make up its mind now for fundamental change and transformation, there will be little hope for future growth and innovation. Japan needs both the ability to restructure itself and strong imagination, such as 'we will create the future society this way' and 'the new and better value for global society is this'.

Japan's 'lost two decades' did not simply happen because of comparative decreased capacity in the global market. It is not a matter of competitiveness. They continued producing high quality items but this was as a result an outdated idea. What they lacked was the imagination and innovation that could create a new society and change the world or its game. They needed to focus on customer value and creating a new ecosystem. Strong visions and ambitions such as 'we want this', 'we want to change this way' were not reflected in product or service designs.

Knowledge creation must be relearned by the Japanese themselves. In the US, on the other hand, there are some innovative firms such as Apple that promoted new visions and ideas. Currently, innovation does not mean simply supplying a new product, but creating a new relationship or generating a new business model.

In the last twenty years, the end of the cold war and the spread of the Internet has dramatically changed the global social system. These changes challenged and encouraged open relationships among organizations everywhere. The relationships between the society and the customers, firms and workers or partners all changed. There is no doubt that Japanese firms also need to develop the future relationships necessary to secure their organizational viability.

An ideal or at least the most suitable management approach must be seriously discussed in order to fill the gap between the new actualities of the society and an organization's existing system. Past management theories, especially studies in strategy and organization hinged on a model of the inner structure of the organization, which implied of course a model within closed boundaries. Based on this model, firms analysed the outside market and environment, learned the possibility of inner capital distribution and developed a reasonable logic; it then organized the best structure to achieve goals. Organizations persisting to use this model into the 21st century will likely reach a dead end and will cease to evolve in the new context. A global society whose economy is based upon knowledge demands and requires a management model devoted to knowledge creation, i.e., KCM.

We might ask, however, why the analytical paradigm no longer works? First, the idea behind this paradigm – a 'deterministic' way of thinking that we can always reach the right answer by narrowing down the question through analysis – has come to the end of its tether. In fact, it has become quite difficult for us to reach the right answer, in today's uncertain and complex business environment. This is not surprising, because we are unable to predict unexpected consequences of circumstances from the past data on which the analysis is based. Another consideration is that we cannot develop an effective strategy against volatile and unexpected rivals, with a one-solution-fits-all approach. For the same reasons, design thinking, thinking based on hypothesis, and the prototyping approach is now gaining attention (Konno, 2009).

KCM must supplant the existing industrial social model as the foundation of the new globally networked/holistic society and economy. It should be perceived as an ecosystem in which there are many players and therefore many relationships among customers, partners, workers and other competitive firms. The players and relationships must be treated fairly and equitably. KCM is now a model for such an era (see Figure 11.1.)

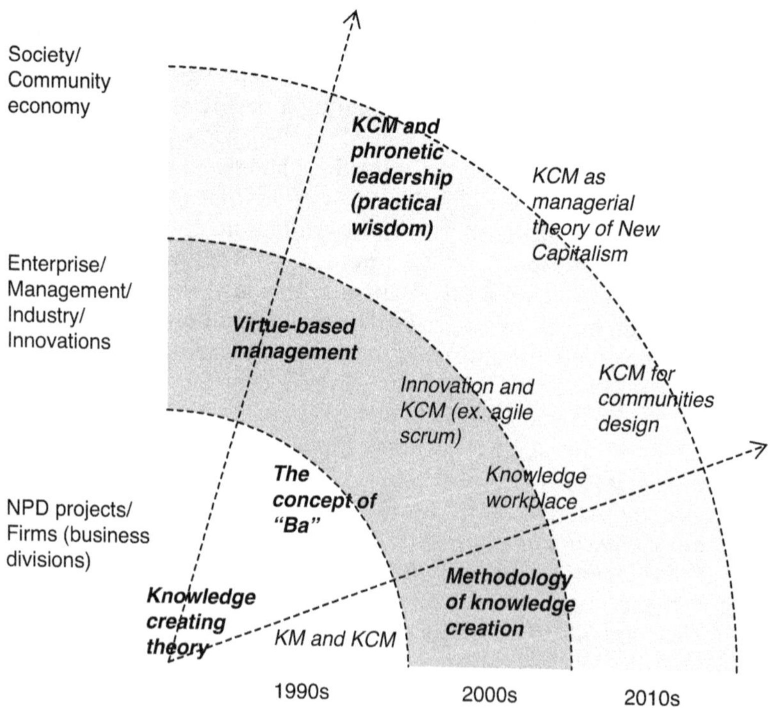

Figure 11.1 The 'Evolution' of KC theory and KCM

Source: The author.

Hayek: viewpoints on innovation and community

Hayek (Frederich A. Hayek) was one who introduced the notion of tacit knowledge to the study of economics. He used this concept, originally proposed by Michael Polanyi, to explain market characteristics. He also distinguished the two major types of knowledge as scientific/digital and subjective/analog. Hayek and M. Polanyi knew each other and although they eventually followed different paths, Polanyi influenced Hayek. Explicit knowledge is recognized by the brain and is logically based on general and scientific rules. Tacit knowledge is experienced through the body; it is emotional and subjectively associated with space, time and people. These two types of knowledge can be compared to digital and analogue; one recognized by the brain and the other by the body. True meaning occurs when these two forms of knowledge commingle and complement each other. The market should also be conceived as an ecosystem, an organic system, created by the complex interaction of tacit and explicit knowledge.

For Hayek, the market is comprised of individuals who discover the new knowledge. We can say it is based on 'ba' relationship. It means that people who throw themselves into the market, an ecosystem of knowledge, can develop the new economic values. Here people share, discover and create knowledge more actively and subjectively.

Hayek's theory is of course related to the innovation theory of Joseph A. Schumpeter. The group of scholars from the same Austrian institute, for instance, Israel M. Kirzner also believed the market process to be the discovery method of entrepreneurs. Entrepreneurs indeed discover the new knowledge, yet they face individual limits. Therefore, the systematic discovery process and the organized process of knowledge creation by firms, creating explicit knowledge from tacit knowledge, are important and necessary.

However, the process of knowledge discovery is divergent and indeterministic, too dynamic and not predictable. It is difficult to assume the goal since there are many uncertainties and possible outcomes. The effectiveness of market analysis based on past data (information) is also weak. It suffers additionally because the market is always influenced by subjective and non-rational motives. Economic experts cannot predict decisions, creations or choices of any individual player. The market is created by subjectivity and uncertainty. When we think of the market environment from this perspective, we cannot formulate a strategy. In the common discourse of economics, the well-planned competitive strategy is the driving idea, and it is based on the effective distribution of capital in a certain market brought about through free and open competition. If the economic authorities know and calculate all economic information, the market would be an effective system for creating wealth. Yet, it does not sound realistic. In the era in which we now find ourselves, matters based on data or facts (explicit knowledge) are not always realistic, valid or accessible to all. It is here that we can reposition knowledge creation theory and offer the SECI model for societal knowledge discovery and as an innovation process.

Creating knowledge transforms all the participants; the individuals, groups, customers and organizations, on both the tacit and explicit level. It is an inter-subjective experience. Through that process, the quality and the quantity of knowledge grow and develop. There is no meaning in debating which is more useful, explicit or tacit knowledge. The dynamic process is important; how we elicit tacit knowledge, transform it to explicit knowledge and use it efficiently. There are four mutual interactions between explicit and tacit knowledge that comprise the SECI model. They are:

- Socialization: the process learning new tacit knowledge from existing tacit knowledge. It is a beginning of the discovery process of knowledge from the 'unknown'.
- Externalization: the process learning explicit knowledge from tacit knowledge. Sharing and interacting experiences with customers, partners and colleagues. It is the process of the newly created knowledge.
- Combination: the process learning new explicit knowledge from existing explicit knowledge. It is to systemize ideas into concepts, prototypes or business models, etc.
- Internalization: the process learning explicit knowledge from tacit knowledge. It means to test prototypical ideas again with customers and partners.

It is possible to start from any point or process. However, we think that starting from socialization is the most effective.

The source of value lies in differences produced by knowledge creation or by innovation. A firm can survive only when it has the sensitivity to detect changes in an uncertain business environment, and to create and offer knowledge that achieves customer value based on an in-depth understanding (not just analysis) of the human and society.

To understand innovation as a discovery process from the perspective of the market and society it is best to think of the analogy of reverse engineering, in our case, reverse innovation. Grass roots innovation occurs from the demand side rather than the supply side. The SECI model outlines this process and the application or design complements the SECI model. Demand-side innovation ultimately seeks the common good.

The common good implies 'cooperation' and 'interdependency' not 'competition' among all players in the market and society. Therefore, KCM and management of ecological and green organizations share the common need for cooperation in order to survive, to be viable. This philosophical and operational approach stands in bold contrast to the prevailing business model based on competition and strategic management for advantage. During their long-term and in-depth research Nonaka and others realized and developed the concepts of virtue-based management. Not coincidentally, their work has produced an underlying business management precept known as phronesis, i.e., practical wisdom.

Management theory of 'ba'

It is unrealistic to conceive of the market as a structure solely created by competitors and rivals. The market consists of the whole environment in which the organization exists. What if we think this way? What if the market is conceived as an ecosystem created by groups of 'ba' where various knowledge is related. Firms also comprise part of the structure of that ecosystem. They create knowledge, a resource, while continually relating to other organizations, groups and individuals, and transform it, which adds to its economic value.

KCM differs from existing approaches of management style and strategy which believe that competitive strength and pursuing larger sales are the top priorities. Creating and nurturing knowledge needs 'ba'; the practical environment, where individuals from organizations can share their embodied knowledge, collect the various knowledge and transform it from the subjective to the objective. From such 'ba', co-emergence occurs while maintaining equilibrium among the social and economic factors.

The definition of 'ba' is a shared dynamic context and meaningful space. Originally, 'ba' was understood to be one of the important Japanese management parameters, but it was used mainly in the context of the working site of the organization, with the emphasis on positive points highlighting a tight and structured working place or the importance of the working field. 'Ba' in this paper, on the other hand, has a different point of view. 'Ba' offers a multi channel holistic approach to management. It is not a 'one way' linear model.

It is here where relationships and co-creation of knowledge exists and the I-and-you relationship of collaborative action and leadership emerges. 'Ba' comprises a couple of layers; physical stage (office space), social stage (care and trust), strategic stage (firm's strategy and organization), recognition stage (shared intelligent approach, thoughts) and the information system (environment stage).

'Ba' is place, not space. The concept of 'ba' is pretty old. In Japanese culture, it has been a bit abstract and relegated to specific places and situations. 'Place-ness' is about relationship with meanings, and contexts or inter-subjectivity. Physics and mathematics of the 19th and 20th century laid the foundation for the industrial production space. And Taylor's time studies supported the early mechanistic approach to western management. Hopefully, the incorporation or embodiment of the five dimensions of 'ba' will create the fundament for the structure and process of 21st century organizations.

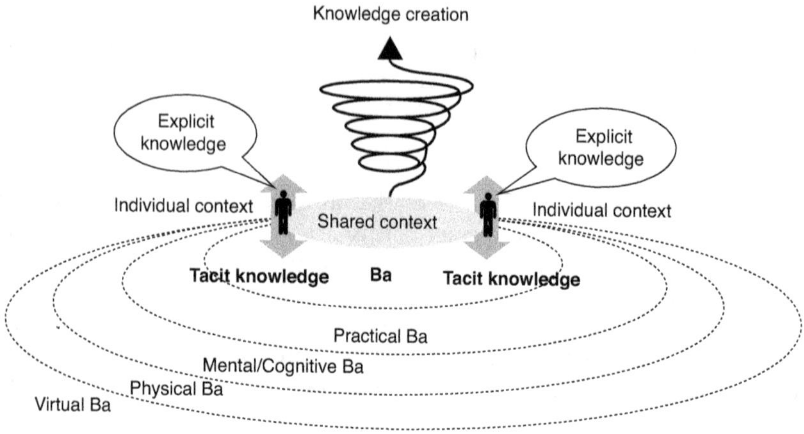

Figure 11.2 The concept of 'Ba'
Source: The author.

Sharing tacit knowledge and context is essential. The context is 'ba' itself. It is a dynamic context shared by knowledge workers, clients and all related persons. 'Ba' in the workplace constitutes more than just the physical space. It includes the whole system including office facility, atmosphere, IT network and shared culture in a designated space. Innovation, and therefore knowledge creation is integrally connected to the concept of 'ba'. Knowledge creation does not happen in a vacuum (see Figure 11.2).

As an intellectual construct, 'ba' has recently been cited in academic research discussing 'boundary object' (Star & Griesemer, 1989). Proponents claim that 'ba' exists in multiple situations and dimensions. 'Ba' is the interface between cultures, organizations, regions, communities and their general and local systems. 'Ba' facilitates open 'boundaries'.

A 'boundary object' refers to words and symbols (perhaps even items) existing in boundaries between different communities or systems. It functions as a bridge or interface between communities and can even create new communities. For example, two sections which have poor communication with each other, can connect and create a community by sharing boundary objects: the key words, concepts and symbols which both sides can commonly understand. 'Ba' can be understood as the place where boundary objects are created, inversely, 'ba' or a knowledge community, can be created by boundary objects. A Cartesian image might place Ba as the ordinate and boundary objects as the abscissa.

In order to change such limiting situations, it is essential that the borders be purposely crossed in order to allow for creative activity between actors on other sides of the borders. It is necessary to have some sort of media, which exists between the actual and the symbolic objects as well as arrangements which facilitate creative and mutual activities that will naturally open the boundaries between systems, organizations and different circumstances.

Commonly shared objects/concepts are created in 'ba'. The design then creates visual, physical and abstract boundary objects as an effective application. Creating knowledge by using the box design is now a fairly common practice. Currently there are innovative trial spaces in some urban environments such as 'future centre living', 'Labo' and so on. These offer excellent examples of 'ba' and boundary objects that surface and facilitate connections between organizations and firms. The new knowledge created in such situations makes the knowledge of all the organizations involved stronger.

'Future centre' is the place ('ba'), where organizations like firms, government and autonomies cooperate with each other. They broadly gather various types of people, discover new ideas and solutions through dialogue and create new knowledge by interactive collaboration. It is composed of lecture space, learning space, meeting space and so on. It is precisely the 'boundary object'. 'Ba' between firms and organizations are connected, and therefore the new knowledge is created to make organization knowledge firmer.

People who create boundary objects tend to be multidisciplinary type actors, who belong to several communities, and leaders with broad and diverse viewpoints. The natural tendency, for an individual, group, organization or institution, is to erect a border to protect its security and to foster, nurture and develop its own specialized knowledge. Boundary objects and their creators break these walls.

The interest in 'ba' inevitably leads to that of workplace. Connections between different 'ba's can be created among individuals, organizations, firms, local areas and societies. They are able to grow to national levels and even on a global scale. In the future, firms and organizations will have to consider their management in the broader network for creating new relationships. A simple example is when an organization decides to change from the traditional business model to one of innovation and knowledge creation. Sections, teams, corporate structure and strategy, essentially the whole organizational system, must also change. In such a management situation or approach requires social capital, and social resource support such as that embodied in the concept of Ba (see the following note). Consequently, the design of boundary objects that cross system borders are a very important factor (see Figure 11.3).

The Knowledge Leadership Institute at Tama University had a study group for 'Architecture of "ba"'. According to their research, interviewed executive officers of leading corporations imagine 'ba' as five aspects shown in the following discussion (the Study group interviewed current and former executive officers and analyzed by text mining). It indicates that no one believes

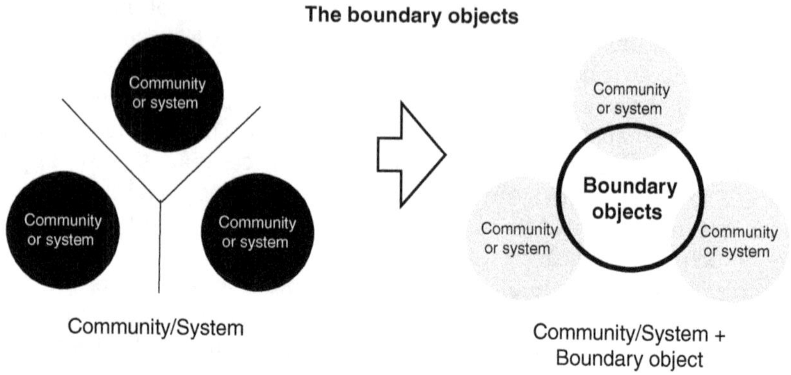

Figure 11.3 'Ba' as the boundary objects
Note: 'Ba' and the Concept of Organizations.
Source: The author.

that the office should be a conventional functional facility. They think that it should be a platform for stimulating and activating knowledge assets. The knowledge assets in an organization is invisible and waiting, as in 'Capital in Waiting' (Edvinsson, 2004).

(1) ['Ba' = organization] as an =open relationship:
  - It promotes diversity (combination of diversified knowledge) and nurtures people's relationships.
  - Ex) Office environment where workers transact and interact while pursuing different functions and tasks, and create dialogue. Core office unifying functions. Space where workers can gather.

(2) ['Ba' = organization] as the context for sharing values:
  - Communication with the outside is more developed. Individuals who share the firm's visions and social network connect with each other and create new values. Organizations act as the interface for the individual with corresponding societies or groups.
  - Ex) Organization or office as a part of the society, where clients and partners can communicate with workers.

(3) ['Ba' = organization] as the business model platform: Top managers realize the organization = 'ba' as the business platform to embody their business model.
  Ex) Office and IT environment reflecting the business model

(4) ['Ba' = organization] as the information space:
  - Organization includes the information space. It develops while expanding the information system and the knowledge worker's power for creating new knowledge.

- Ex) All workers are connected by IT networks and are always able to create knowledge. The organization is supported by system sharing and by utilizing information.

(5) ['Ba' = organization] as an organized system for knowledge:
- Conceptualizing organization as 'ba' underpins the navigation and operation of the firm. Developing an atmosphere and environment where knowledge workers can grow based on their companies' philosophy.
- Ex) Organizations advance through cultural and flexible strategies which can vary depending on sections and projects, not simply on the firm's fixed structure. The organization's philosophy encourages and empowers workers to work more flexibly in each of their projects. Project management system/Intellectual management system.

Capla (2002), the physicist, recently wrote in 'The Hidden Connections' that knowledge management should possess a human and dynamic component, while focusing both on group knowledge and social factors (not fixed tangible assets or capital). He also pointed out that the global interest in innovation and new desires are buried, hidden and ensconced in such knowledge. There certainly is a hidden connection. We have to realize that our society and economy have been changed by these hidden and diverse connections such as the Rhizome idea proposed by Deleuze and Guattari.

From these observations and discussions, it is clear that as organizations and corporations come to realize that knowledge and knowledge creation is the most valuable resource and asset, then it will follow that the management of knowledge will adopt 'ba' as the most essential and important core component to this process.

Conclusion

It is now time to seriously consider KCM for the knowledge ecosystem and to do extensive research on the social dynamics of what I call the knowledge ecology. In other words, it is time for research on the interacting variables of an ecosystem of knowledge creation and to utilize this knowledge asset in enterprises and the society.

Through the application of this knowledge asset the mutual interests of people will emerge in Ba as a nexus of subsystems and shared context, a matrix of relationships.

From this perspective or viewpoint, the business model and organization should be viewed as the medium or conduit for creating and supporting the knowledge ecosystem.

Apple has been an excellent example of an applied 'knowledge ecosystem'. After Steve Jobs returned to Apple they were able to create a multifaceted platform through their iOS, iTunes, Apple Store and so on. Their primary focus was not just the actual device but to create and prepare a common base so that users and partners could find and share common values, interests, experiences and business opportunities that were fun for the creators and the consumer. This type of vision was lacking in Japanese firms as well as companies like Nokia who suffered from Apple's approach.

In hindsight, we can see that many Japanese companies and organizations missed the opportunity to innovate. The most fundamental problem is to change and enrich human experience. Some companies, however, have noticed the need for innovation and are moving forward.

The most important point of the knowledge ecosystem is to recognize and acknowledge that the inner and outer changes of environments of organizations, which exists on the boundary, are always influencing each other, or the feedback loop. Now and then, a new variable will influence the system and have an impact yet the need for creating a richer and better natural and human world will be stronger. The competitive mentality of businesses has to change; the idea of management versus labour has to end. The revival and support of the communities and the knowledge ecosystem will benefit everyone.

In order to achieve this sort of knowledge ecosystem, we need one more effort to orchestrate 'purposes' reflecting the perspectives of the individual. 'Purpose' will be the key word, especially when people strive to create new value among societies, organizations and customers. This differs from the traditional industrial market model where the focus was to sell products through a hierarchical system; basically, a push down approach or supply-sided logic.

The most salient feature of 'purpose engineering' or orchestration of purposes proposed by the author is to focus on human-like subjective matters of organizational members and participants as opposed to the organizational structure itself or its system.

The author suggests that there are two different approaches to achieving an outcome or goal. The first is where a grand planner or group conceives and lists the steps or tasks that he/she or they believe will reach the goal; anonymous labour resources are aligned like cogs in a gear.

The other approach is to let all the participants, the actors, contribute their ideas to achieving the goal; their ideas reflect their motivations, that is, their purpose in achieving the goal. Labour and efficiency is maximized in this way. This orchestration of purposes is necessary when confronted by a large challenge or innovative problems.

Based on this theory, outputs are the consequence of linked actions emanating from the will of the individuals. This is in contrast to automated and systematic functions. Moreover, the theory of purpose engineering is to make people happy, not to protect organizations.

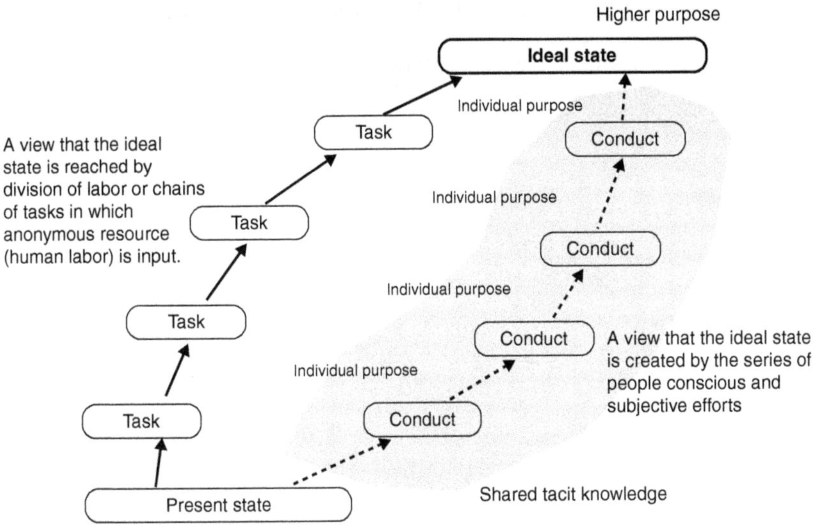

Figure 11.4 Purpose engineering: two paths toward the ideal state

Source: The author.

'Purpose Engineering' orchestrates the 'purpose clusters' for the common good of the society, the enterprise purposes and the individuals. It is to make purposes the 'engines' of change (see Figure 11.4). Because organizations are human creations they should resemble human beings and their nature. Organizations will be reconceived from the perspective of the knowledge ecosystem. This system will create things through a collective or aggregation of desires and actions of the individuals. The basic idea is closer in philosophy to the study of human science than it is to management.

References

Capla, F. (2002). *The Hidden Connections: Integrating The Biological, Cognitive, and Social Dimensions of Life into a Science of Sustainability*. New York: Doubleday.

Edvinsson, L. (2004). *Regional Intellectual Capital in Waiting – a strategic IC Quest*. Paper presented at the Italian Innovation week, November 22–26, 2004.

Konno, N. (2009). The age of knowledge design: a view from Japan. *Design Management Review*. 20 (2), Spring.

Nonaka, I., & N. Konno. (1998). The concept of 'Ba': building foundation for knowledge creation. *California Management Review*. 40 (3), Spring.

——. (2012). *Chishiki-sozo Keiei no Purinshipuru (The Principles of Knowledge Creation Management)-The Grammar of Knowledge Creating Management for Prudent Capitalism (in Japanese)*. Tokyo: Keizai Shinposha.

Nonaka, I. and Takeuchi, H. (2011). The Wise Leader, *Harvard Business Review,* 89 (5), 58–67.

Star, S. L., & Griesemer, J. R. (1989). Institutional ecology, 'Translations' and boundary objects: Amateurs and Professionals in Berkeley's museum of vertebrate zoology, 1907–39. *Social Studies of Science.* 19 (4), 387–420.

Part III

12

Building Core Capabilities: The Roles of Corporate Headquarters

Andrew Campbell

Nonaka's work helped rekindle an interest in organizational skills and knowledge that I had developed while working as a consultant at McKinsey & Co. It encouraged me to do my own research on knowledge and capability. As you will see from this chapter, I did not take up Nonaka's epistemology, but I was inspired by his fine-grained observations. My own interest lies in divisionalised companies, and in the roles of corporate headquarters. Hence my research used language and a unit of analysis appropriate to this perspective.

A capability is an ability to create a beneficial outcome that is at or near the efficiency frontier: either the outcome is superior given the resources consumed or fewer resources are consumed for a given outcome. For commercial organizations in a competitive environment, the efficiency frontier is defined by what competitors can do. In a non-competitive environment, the efficiency frontier is defined by past performance and what is known to be possible.

This chapter is about how corporate headquarters can help build capabilities across business divisions in a decentralized organization structure. Hamel and Prahalad's famous article, "The Core Competence of the Corporation" argued that one of the reasons for the multi-business firm is the existence of core competences or core capabilities.[1] Core capabilities are defined in this chapter as capabilities that are important to performance in more than one business division.

What follows draws on research in a number of large international companies, including 3M, BP, Electrolux, Mars, Philips, Shell and Unilever. All of these companies were attempting to build capabilities across business divisions, whether the divisions were defined by product or geography. The work combines two streams of research: research about decentralized organizations and the role of corporate headquarters and research on capabilities and knowledge. The main contribution is a language for describing capabilities in divisionalised organizations and a typology of different roles corporate headquarters can play in building core capabilities. Some practical guidance is also provided to help managers choose between roles.

Background

In the early days of the M-form organization, strong central functions were the norm. Business divisions had been set up to reduce the decision-making bottleneck at the top of the organization.[2] But, most companies retained large central functions, like technology, marketing, finance and human resources. These central functions existed in part as additional controls on the business divisions, but more importantly they were the holders of core capabilities. In Nonaka's terms, they were instrumental in 'knowledge conversion'.[3]

British Petroleum, for example, had a central engineering function of more than 1,500 people until the mid1980s. These central functions set policies and standards throughout the corporation. They also controlled most of the recruitment of functional experts, in particular the graduate intake, organized training and acted as skill reservoirs for their companies.

In the 1980s, many companies started to decentralize these central functions and reduce the size of corporate headquarters. Where functions were retained, their policy-making role was reduced and their service role emphasized.[4] At BP, for example, the IT function was set up as an internal consulting service, selling its expertise to the business divisions. Over a short period, the function shrank by more than half its former size because the divisions chose not to use its services.

The decentralization trend produced net benefits. Greater freedom and accountability promoted initiative at the division level. Also, it reduced overhead and bureaucracy which increased profit margins. But decentralization also had a cost. As companies decentralized and the control exerted by corporate headquarters reduced, they used 'lateral linkages', such as informal networking and corporate-wide projects, to replace the central functions.[5] For example, when Electrolux acquired businesses in the white goods industry, it did not centralize any functions. Instead, it pursued integration through coordination mechanisms in four product areas, networking mechanisms to encourage cross-fertilization, and five corporate-wide projects designed to improve operating performance.

These lateral linkages, however, proved harder to operate than expected. 'Horizontal planning', as Michael Porter called it, has frequently been crowded out by vertical, strategic business unit (SBU) planning.[6] Coordinating committees and networking mechanisms often proved time-consuming and delivered little value.[7] Business unit managers developed an aversion to corporate projects, which they saw as a distraction from their real priorities. And most HR functions did not take on the functional training or functional recruitment activities of the old central functions. The result of these changes was a loss of focus on core capabilities.[8]

Since 2000, many central functions have again been increasing in size. There are many reasons for this. New legislation, such as Sarbanes Oxley, has placed additional governance requirements on corporate headquarters. Improvements in digital technology have reduced the cost of moving information and knowledge around the organization making it easier to centralize some decisions without losing touch with markets or operating challenges. Finally, many companies have become less diverse so that there are more activities in common across business divisions and more value can be generated from building core capabilities.

Which core capabilities to build

The first problem facing managers in divisionalised companies is to decide which capabilities to try to build. At a high level, this may be a trivial question. If the businesses in the portfolio are all in consumer packaged goods, as at Unilever, then one of the important core capabilities to focus on is consumer goods marketing. If most of the businesses are connected by common technologies, such as precision coatings and polymers, as at 3M, then a core capability is the technology itself.

High-level descriptions, however, do not provide enough granularity for management action. For example, within marketing at Unilever, is consumer research a core capability that needs to be managed by headquarters? Is new product testing? Is advertising agency selection? Is product positioning? Is product packaging? And, outside marketing, is sales force management a core capability that Unilever's headquarters should focus on? Is industrial selling? Is the management of multi-country retailers? Headquarters managers need to develop a way of identifying those capabilities that will benefit the most from some central involvement both in developing the capability and in transferring good practice across business divisions.

To explore core capabilities, we start by examining the connection between capabilities and competitive advantage. We then examine the difference between the role of corporate headquarters in influencing the capabilities of a single business division and in managing core capabilities across business divisions.

Understanding capabilities and competitive advantage

To succeed against competitors, each business needs to have a strategy for gaining advantage in the market place. Without some kind of advantage in meeting market needs a business cannot expect to outperform its competitors.

Advantage comes from many different sources. Location can be a source of advantage, for example, due to lower labour costs in a particular area. Size can be a source of advantage due to economies of scale. But most sources of advantage are rooted in superior capabilities: the business makes better quality products, markets them better, has better salesmen or looks after the customers better, because of some superior capability.

Few businesses have superior capabilities in all areas. But successful businesses have an advantage in some activities that are important to the business's strategy. If the strategy is about quality, the business is likely to have an advantage in manufacturing processes such as total quality management. If the strategy is about service, the business is likely to have an advantage in service skills, through, for example, better systems, better training and recruitment processes or products designs that are easier to service.

To clarify the link between capabilities and strategy, it is helpful to draw a 'capability tree' that links the 'business capabilities' with the needs of the market place (Figure 12.1).[9] A business capability is an activity the business needs to do particularly well to succeed with its strategy. Most strategies involve a cluster of business capabilities. The confectionery business at Mars needs to have strong skills in volume manufacturing, quality management, product branding and new product development to succeed with the strategy of being the brand leader in the mass-market, snack-food sector of the confectionery market.

Because capabilities involve a combination of knowledge (both tacit and explicit) and other resources, such as assets, systems and people, each business capability can be analysed further into 'components' and 'sub-components'. Components are the factors needed to perform the capability to a high standard. Each component can then be broken down into sub-components and to even finer levels of detail. Figure 12.1 is an illustrative 'capability component analysis' of an important capability of a restaurant business – delivering delightful service.

Figure 12.2 illustrates the broad range of components that make up a business capability. Some components are inanimate, such as the quality of the parking facilities or the quality of the ambience. Others depend on the behaviour of individuals or teams such as the greeting of guests or the service provided by waiters. Each component, however, involves knowledge or know-how. If the component is a skill, such as being a good waiter, both tacit and explicit knowledge is required alongside personality characteristics, such as a friendly disposition. If the component is inanimate, like the size of the menu, the knowledge is more likely to be explicitly codified (e.g., a menu becomes daunting if it has more than 25 items on it). In any business capability, therefore, there are a large number of components each of which depends on knowledge. Even the friendly personality needed to be a good waiter has a knowledge sub-component: knowing that a friendly personality is important and knowing how to identify recruits with friendly personalities. It is, therefore, the management of knowledge that underpins the successful management of a business capability.

Some components are more important than others: they have a greater impact on the capability. We can call these 'key components': components where the quality of the knowledge can have a big impact on the overall

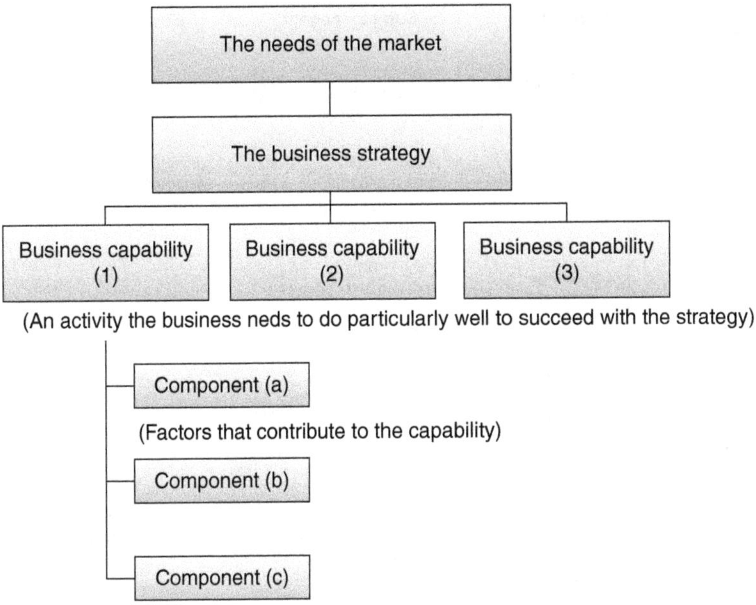

Figure 12.1 Capability tree
Source: The author.

performance. Advantage is gained by developing knowledge within these key components that is superior to competitors.

At this point, it is worth taking stock of the language we have developed to understand capabilities. It consists of 'business capabilities', 'components', 'sub-components', 'key components' and 'superior knowledge'. The last two terms need further explanation.

Key components are those components that are critical to the building of a superior capability. Key components are the components where the company has or can develop some proprietary knowledge that is not widely used by its competitors. Most competitors will perform most components of a business capability to a reasonable standard. For example, most family restaurants serve reasonably good food, on clean plates, on clean tables in a restaurant that is not overcrowded. The difference between unusual service and average service does not lie in these standard components. It is the key components, such as the behaviour of the waiter, that distinguish between average and excellent service.

Of course businesses can have weaknesses even in standard components, and part of the management task is to reduce the impact of weaknesses. However, weaknesses can be addressed by business divisions on their own: they do not need to coordinate with other divisions to succeed. This is

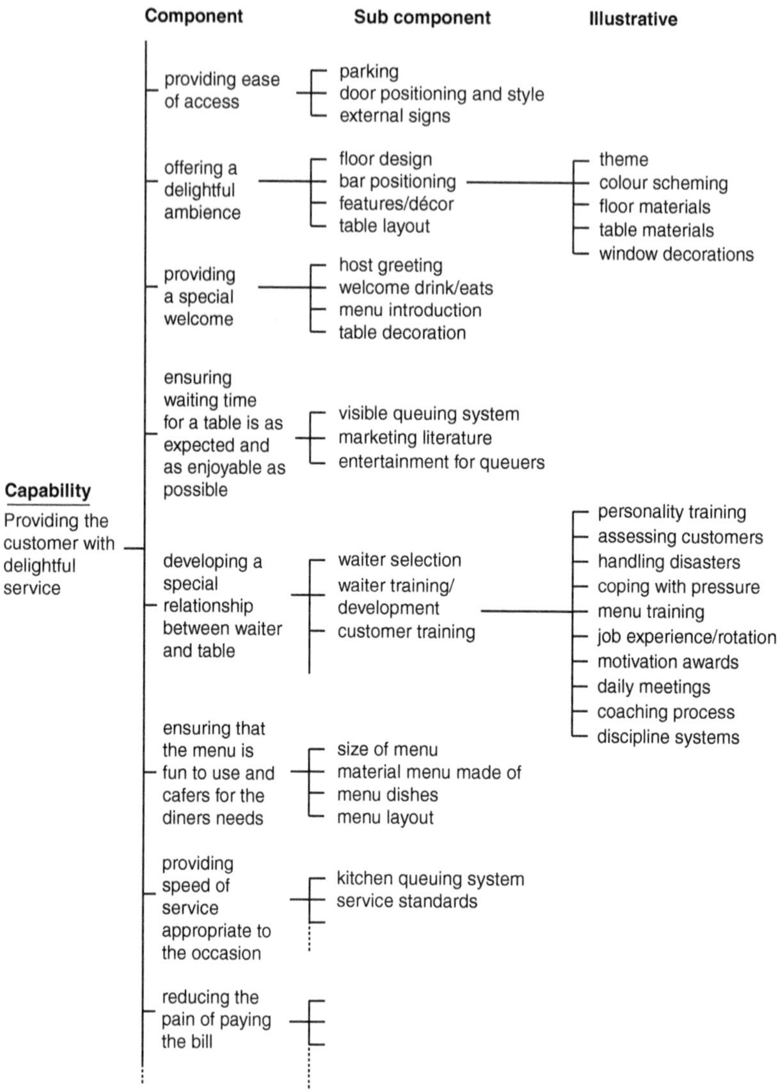

Figure 12.2 Capability component analysis
Source: The author.

because the knowledge needed to eliminate the weakness is likely to be commodity knowledge that can be acquired from a competent consultant or from hiring a capable executive into the business division.

Building a capability advantage, in contrast, requires developing superior knowledge' that is not readily available from a consultant or from external hires. While capability advantage often emerges in an unplanned way as businesses solve challenges they face (Toyota's just-in-time capability emerged from a lack of storage space), a planned approach involves identifying 'business capabilities', pinpointing the 'key components or sub-components' where 'superior knowledge' can give competitive advantage and then working to create the advantage.[10]

The roles of headquarters

Corporate headquarters has two roles with regard to the building of capabilities. The first role is to ensure that each business division has identified those capabilities that are important to its strategy and has a plan both for eliminating weaknesses and for building superior knowledge. In most companies, the strategic planning process is the main vehicle for doing this. It provides corporate headquarters with an opportunity to assess whether each business division is focusing on the right capabilities, and has plans in place to build these capabilities. Part of the planning process is often a strategic control system that measures the performance of a business division in areas that are critical to success.[11] Corporate headquarters can, therefore, use a combination of planning and control processes to make sure that the business divisions are devoting the necessary attention to their business capabilities.

The second role of corporate headquarters, and the focus of this chapter, is to promote, where appropriate, the building of capabilities across business divisions – core capabilities. This second role is only appropriate when multiple business divisions have business capabilities or key components in common. For example, in a company with multiple retail brands, each brand may have 'site selection and development' as a business capability. Because each brand is different, it is unlikely that the key components of this capability are identical across all brands. Some brands may require high traffic locations, while others are destination brands that can be in low traffic locations. Each will require specialist but different shop decors. However, some key components may be the same; for example, the capability of estimating the sales potential of a location or the capability of contracting with builders and fit-out specialists.

Where key components are common, corporate headquarters has a role in helping manage the development and transfer of knowledge. The headquarters role goes beyond just making sure that each business has a plan for keeping ahead of competitors. The centre has a role in helping the businesses work together to speed up the development of knowledge and in ensuring that the benefits are spread to all relevant business divisions.

Building core capabilities

Building core capabilities involves managing the development and transfer of knowledge across business units in selected key components. Success comes from focusing on transferable knowledge. Capability trees and component analysis are useful tools to help managers identify key components that involve transferable knowledge.

The management of these key components involves making choices about how to develop proprietary knowledge and how to transfer the knowledge across the business divisions. The fieldwork showed that successful companies chose different roles for different components and these different roles were based on different levels of involvement in both the *development process* and the *transfer process*. Using these two dimensions, five *generic approaches to managing key components* emerged from the research.

The development process

In a portfolio of business divisions with similar key components, knowledge is being developed simultaneously in different businesses. Headquarters, therefore, need to decide how to contribute to this decentralized knowledge development process.

At one extreme, headquarters can decide to remain detached from the development process allowing business units to carry out local development work against their local agendas and priorities. At the other extreme, headquarters can take charge of the development process with the aim of getting economies of scale, eliminating duplication or ensuring that sufficient investment is made in experiments and new ideas.

In between these extremes are many alternatives in which headquarters seeks to coordinate work being carried out in different businesses. For example, in a company with a portfolio of contracting businesses, development work on IT systems could be done by a lead business with the intention of transferring the developments to other businesses; it could be done by a combination of businesses working together; or it could be done by each business separately after agreeing a common plan.

Moreover, the people doing the development work could be located in headquarters, but the development projects could be commissioned and directed by the business divisions. Alternatively, the development work could be carried out in the businesses, but under the direction of a central development manager. By judging which manager, one at headquarters or one in the division, had final authority over both the size and direction of development work it was possible, in our research, to assess the degree of centralization of the development process.[12]

The transfer process

The way in which knowledge is transferred across business units depends upon the nature of the knowledge. If the knowledge is codified, it can be transferred by simple communication. If the knowledge is embedded in the innate skills of individuals or teams, it can be transferred by transferring skilled individuals or by transferring the know-how involved in selecting, training and developing the skilled individuals. Alternatively, it is possible to transfer the benefits of the knowledge rather than the knowledge itself.

This can be done by creating a central service built round the innate skills of a few people.

The main concern of the managers in headquarters is, therefore, not so much the choice of mechanism for transferring knowledge, but rather the degree of pressure they should exert to ensure that the transfer occurs. The minimum level of pressure is where headquarters assists with communication. Central managers make business divisions aware of the knowledge and skills available in other divisions, and let the business managers decide for themselves whether to and how to access the knowledge. To support this low level of pressure, headquarters may produce news letters, organize sharing forums, encourage managers to network with each other or offer support and services.

The maximum level of pressure is where headquarters demands that the business divisions use superior knowledge and acts quickly to discipline managers who are slow to respond. This is done by issuing policy instructions, insisting on performance standards, removing reluctant managers and setting up central functions to carry out some activities.

In between these two extremes, there are many alternatives. Headquarters can promote the transfer of knowledge by challenging the managers in business divisions to meet the standards set by other divisions. Headquarters can create peer pressure through committees or task forces. Headquarters can offer intermediate knowledge by supplying performance data and benchmarks that suggest where superior knowledge might exist.

Five generic approaches to managing core capabilities

Using these two dimensions, we were able to plot on a matrix the actual behaviour of the companies in our research with regard to different key components. One axis of the matrix represented the degree of central control in the development process. The other axis represented the level of pressure used in the transfer process (Figure 12.3).[13] Five generic roles emerged: 'stimulate the network', 'promote central developments', 'coordinate common solutions', 'impose best practice' and 'create a company way'.[14]

- *Stimulate the network* requires the least involvement from headquarters. Development is decentralized and uncoordinated. Headquarters may stimulate development by encouraging business divisions to spend money on development. But headquarters does not attempt to control either the size of expenditure or the direction of development. Knowledge is transferred between units through formal and informal networks. Headquarters stimulates these networks by sharing information and creating opportunities for managers to meet each other. But headquarters does not put pressure on businesses to use knowledge developed in other parts of the group. This role is the default role for all capability components that are not managed with one of the other roles. It is the 'share good practices' approach that is common in many companies.

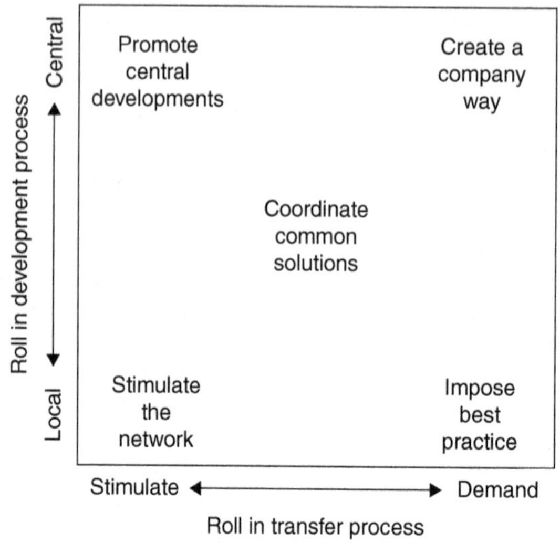

Figure 12.3 The role of headquarters in building core capabilities
Source: The author.

- Headquarters may decide to *promote central developments* in order to encourage the transfer of knowledge that has been developed centrally. Headquarters chooses to control the development process: deciding the size of the development budget and directing individual development projects. However, headquarters allows business divisions to make their own decisions about whether to use the knowledge in their own businesses. It is common for the centre to take on this role for components that involve scientific research and central laboratory work. For example, 3M has Technical Centres which are centrally controlled laboratories focusing on a technology with group-wide relevance. These laboratories have responsibility for advancing the technology. But they have no power to pressure divisions to use the technology they develop.
- *Coordinating common solutions* is a role that involves working closely with business units on both development and transfer. Many cases fit this middle ground, where development efforts are jointly conceived and directed, and the centre puts pressure on businesses that are slow to take up the new developments. An example is the development of the deodorant Axe in Unilever. The knowledge about the market opportunity was developed by the French subsidiary of Unilever Personal Products as a result of a product concept brief defined by global headquarters. Headquarters then worked closely with other European countries to roll out the benefits of this knowledge and encouraged countries to stick closely to the original Axe concept. Headquarters and the French subsidiary continued to work

together to refine the 'product guidance' based on experience and further knowledge developed throughout Europe.

It appears to be unusual for headquarters to attempt to coordinate development work without also seeking to pressure businesses to implement the results of the development. It is also unusual for the centre to pressure businesses to accept knowledge from other business units without also seeking to influence the development efforts. As a result, 'coordinating common solutions' is a role that covers all of the central ground in the matrix.

- *Imposing best practice* is not a common role. We did, however, identify a few cases where headquarters imposed knowledge even though it had not directed the development work. Companies adopt this approach when headquarters discovers big discrepancies in performance in a capability that is easy to document. For example, at Whitbread Restaurants, headquarters noted that its Pizza Hut subsidiary was benefiting from setting clear quality standards for customer service. So it imposed this practice on its other restaurant chains. Headquarters did not impose particular standards. It imposed an easy to document policy: that each restaurant should have defined standards. We have found that this role – imposing best practice – is most common in manufacturing and operating areas, particularly where the knowledge is codified.
- In the final approach, *creating a company way*, headquarters controls development work and imposes methods and standards on the businesses. It is a common role for the management of knowledge in the finance and HR functions, and it is also widely used on issues where there is an additional benefit from consistency and standardization. For example, the Shell logo is centrally controlled by managers in marketing. These managers issue policy guidelines on what is allowed and what is not allowed, and they control development work on how to improve the logo and the way it is used.

In many capabilities such as marketing or process engineering it is less easy to document knowledge. Nevertheless, we found examples even in these capability areas where headquarters had 'created a company way' of doing things. For example, in 3M one key component was the way managers bootleg resources to pursue projects that had not been funded in the development budget. This capability had not been documented in methods and standards. Yet it had become a 3M company way, jealously guarded by central management and symbolized by the 15 per cent rule, where managers are allowed 15 per cent of their time to pursue projects of their own choosing. The 'company way' had been created over many years by managing values and cultural norms, rather than through policy statements and documented knowledge.

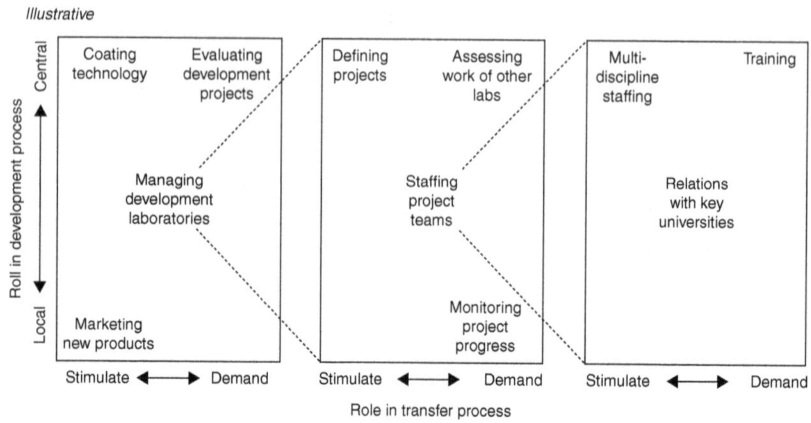

Figure 12.4 The role of headquarters in components and sub-components
Source: The author.

As we documented company examples, we noticed that headquarters can take on different roles for different capabilities and for different components and sub-components (Figure 12.4). At 3M, for example, there were significant differences. New product marketing was highly decentralized: the centre 'stimulates the network'. Coating technology was more centralized: headquarters 'promotes central developments' in areas where it has designated a Technology Centre. Even within a capability such as the management of development laboratories, headquarters took on a different role for different components. Knowledge involved with defining projects was managed by 'promoting central developments'. Knowledge involved in monitoring projects was managed by 'imposing best practice'. Moreover, at each further level of detail, the choice of how headquarters managed the knowledge differed by sub-component.[15]

Choosing a central role for each key component

Having identified the key components and the different roles that headquarters can play, managers need to be able to choose the most suitable role for each key component. Unfortunately, our research indicated that there is no stable link between the type of component and choice of headquarters role. The choice of role seemed to depend more on the culture of the company than the type component. Both Mars and Unilever had a core capability in brand management; yet they managed similar components in very different ways with equal effectiveness. In Mars, the knowledge involved in selecting advertising agencies was managed by 'stimulating the network'. In Unilever Personal Products, on the other hand, it was managed by 'creating a company way'. Both companies had found ways to make their own approach work effectively. We realized that each company had an established way of working and an established role for headquarters on most issues.

Therefore, we concluded in addition to the *commercial imperatives* that drive companies to look for advantage through core capabilities, companies also need to consider their established ways of working – what we have called *cultural realities*.

Cultural realities

The established roles of headquarters are influenced by the decisions that have been taken in the past on decentralization and involvement. These decisions create understandings between managers over time, and precedents about what is normal. When taken together, the centre's established roles amount to an informal 'decentralization contract'.[16] If it were possible to write down all these established roles, the document would define in detail the way headquarters is expected to get involved in or remain detached from all aspects of the business.

We observed that it is this decentralization contract that is the most potent force in the choices managers make about how to manage a particular knowledge component. Instinctively managers in Mars or Shell or Whitbread ask themselves 'if I interfere on this issue, will it contravene the principles of decentralization and autonomy we subscribe to?', or 'what is the usual way that we handle this kind of issue?'

Moreover, these established ways of working appear to make sense. From looking at cases of failure, where attempts to centralize development or impose knowledge transfer had failed, we noted that a major cause was resistance by unit managers who believed that headquarters was 'interfering'. The business divisions appear to hold an understanding of the decentralization contract in their minds, and, unless explicitly renegotiated, the existing contract acts as a barrier to changes in the role of headquarters. The current decentralization contract is a 'reality' of the organization that should be taken into account when choosing the appropriate headquarters role with regard to any capability component.

Commercial imperatives

We also noted the importance of commercial factors. These were influences relating to the requirements of the market place and technology and the actions of competitors. These 'commercial imperatives' are the commercial reasons that make it important for headquarters to take a particular role either in the development process or in the transfer process. For example, the cost of technology development is frequently greater than one business division can afford. By centralizing R&D, the company can afford bigger projects and gain from economies of scale.

Commercial imperatives can also exist for the transfer process. In situations where standardization is important to commercial success the transfer of knowledge must be imposed by the centre. Accounting firms, for example, need to be able to offer identical services from different country partnerships to large multi-national companies. Standardization is particularly important in the audit service. As a result, international accounting firms, such as Price Waterhouse Coopers, have standard audit manuals used by each of the different partnerships, and a central technical function whose role is to approve changes to the manuals and support development of methods and techniques. The central technical function imposes know-how transfer in order to ensure common audit standards in different partnerships.

Managing tensions

In many situations mangers at headquarters can choose a role that meets the needs of both the commercial imperatives and the cultural realities. In these situations, decisions about the headquarters role are easy to make.

But in some situations, the imperatives and the realities point towards different solutions – there is a tension between the role headquarters should take to maximise performance and the role headquarters should take to fit in with the established organization rules. The trite answer to this tension is for headquarters to change the rules. In practice, a much more politically astute solution needs to be found: one that requires the sort of 'practical wisdom' described by Nonaka and Takeuchi.[17] The solution must involve not only doing the right thing from a commercial perspective but also winning the support of leaders lower down (see Figure 12.5).

To illustrate the leadership challenge, we examine one situation in detail – product internationalization. In this situation, changes in technology or changes in customer preferences make international standardization more important and product, and marketing knowledge in one country more relevant to other countries.

Frequently, the established decentralization contract gives business divisions high levels of autonomy and allows headquarters only a minimal role in knowledge development or transfer. This is at odds with the growing commercial forces of internationalization that require standardized product features, centralization of some knowledge development and the transfer of knowledge from one division to another. The commercial forces suggest that headquarters should move from a role of 'stimulating the network' towards a role of 'creating a company way', at least for some key knowledge components. However, the cultural realities suggest that increases in central involvement will be resisted by the business divisions.

We noted three successful responses to this challenge. The first response is to avoid the problem by de-emphasizing or exiting that part of the business where the change in headquarters role is a commercial imperative. In many

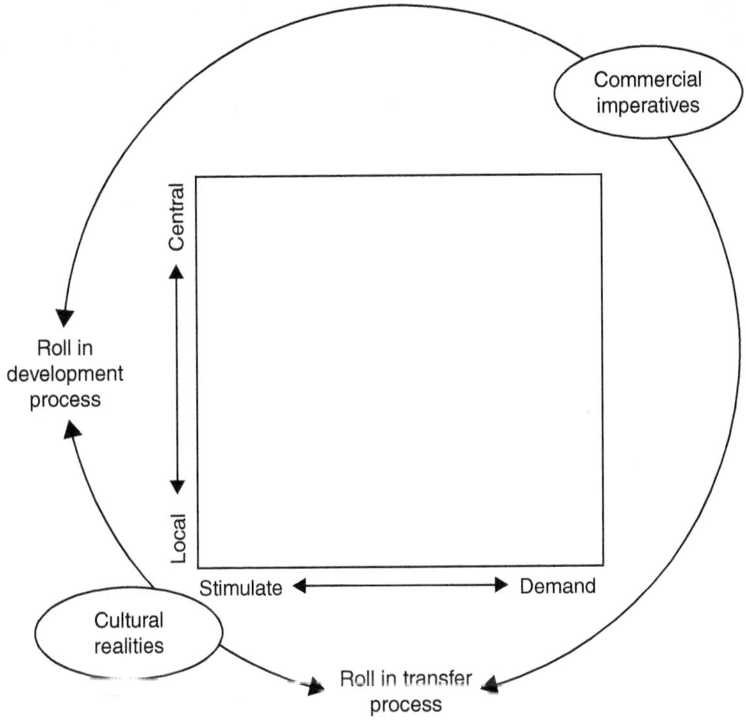

Figure 12.5 Choosing a management approach: imperatives and realities model
Source: The author.

cases, this is the rational response because, as the popular saying suggests, 'culture eats strategy for lunch'. If the dominant organization behaviour is one of high levels of decentralization, headquarters may not be able, even in the medium term, to win the support of business divisions to a change in behaviour within one product area. Rather than follow a second best solution, which could lead to loss of competitive position, the company might do better to de-emphasize or exit that product.

The second response is to make major changes in the existing decentralization contract by formulating a new strategy, changing the organization structure, renegotiating roles and changing managers who resist the new order. This solution can be effective, when it is done with determination and a grasp of the detail at the component level, and when the commercial logic for change is compelling. But it is risky and disruptive. Headquarters frequently does not have sufficient grasp of the detail, individuals with unique skills or knowledge can be side-tracked or sacrificed, and the organization can take some years before it settles into the new relationships. The track record for changes of this kind is poor.[18] While we were working with Unilever Personal Products, we were told that a major reorganization of the detergents businesses in Europe under the flag of 'Lever Europe' had been unsatisfactory, and a new attempt to coordinate the businesses in Europe was being made only 18 months after the first attempt was announced.

The third solution to the challenge is to change gradually. The initial step in gradual change is to identify the key components and start managing each component in the best way possible, given the restrictions of the existing decentralization contract. These 'toe-in-the-water' initiatives serve two purposes. They help to give focus on each key component so that its importance and the current decentralization contract can be assessed before major changes are made. They also help develop support from business divisions for more headquarters involvement, if it is needed. Because toe-in-the-water initiatives do not threaten the existing decentralization contract they do not attract the same political resistance, allowing managers in business divisions to make their own judgements about what is needed.

Headquarters can then increase involvement for key components where division managers can see the benefits. In Unilever Personal Products, we identified a groundswell of support from younger marketing directors and product managers for greater coordination by the centre of product and brand management. These managers could see the need to transfer knowledge quickly, to roll out new product ideas before competitors, and to standardize some product attributes to aid international recognition. This emerging support for a bigger headquarters role, made it possible to move from 'stimulate the network' to 'coordinate common solutions'.

As older managers more committed to the historic decentralization contract retired, it became possible to increase the headquarters role again. In selected areas headquarters moved from 'coordinate common solutions' to 'create a company way'.

The final step in gradual change is to pull together the many small changes that have taken place into a new statement of the centre's role and strategy: a new decentralization contract. In gradual change, the communication of the strategy and appropriate working relationships is best done towards the end of the change period rather than at the beginning.[19]

It is apparent that some situations do not allow managers time for gradual change. Major change or an exit from the business are the only choices. However, in many situations there is time: four or five years is not too long a period to make the changes. In these cases, an understanding of the existing decentralization contract and a sensitive attitude towards winning support from division managers will help avoid the expensive mistakes made by so many companies.

Conclusion

Many attempts by decentralized companies to build core capabilities have been disappointing. At Philips UK, for example, the Organisation and Efficiency (O&E) function set out to build capability in total quality management, just-in-time manufacturing and fast product development. These capabilities were clearly important to many of the business divisions in the UK. Yet little was achieved, despite the vigorous efforts of the O&E managers. Moreover, the failure resulted in the closure of the O&E function.

The reasons for this lack of success are not unusual. First, the O&E managers did not break down the capabilities into knowledge components at a low enough level of detail, nor did they pinpoint those components where it was most important to manage the knowledge across the businesses. Because the business units were diverse, ranging from consumer products to professional products and from high-tech areas like semi-conductors to mature areas like light bulbs, only a few key components were in fact relevant to the majority of business units.

Second, a cultural reality was working against the ambitions of the O&E function. Philips' was changing from a geographic structure to a global product structure. This made the role of the national organization, and hence the UK O&E function, less clear. It also sapped the determination of the UK headquarters to take an active role in managing knowledge. Without the determination of headquarters it was hard to discuss changes to the existing decentralization contract.

Finally, the O&E mangers were unable to win the attention of division mangers to their initiatives: the division managers were reluctant to commit time to working with UK-based functional managers as long as the degree of control likely to be exercised by the new global product area bosses was unknown.

The Philips example illustrates the three conditions necessary for success in building core capabilities: the effort must be focused on key components that are relevant across business units; headquarters must be determined to implement the role it has chosen with regard to each key component; division managers must have accepted the role that headquarters wants to play.

For companies wanting to invest more management time in building core capabilities, the best starting point is to analyse the components of those capabilities that appear to be common across business divisions. As a Senior Marketing Member of Unilever's Personal Products Coordination, said, 'The key is to decide which elements of the product package are critical and relevant across countries. Should we focus on the colour of the bottle, the shape of the label, the brand name, etc.? That is what we are trying to decide'.

Once key components have been chosen, headquarters needs to decide how much control to retain over the development of knowledge and how much pressure to apply to the transfer of knowledge. Heavy handed initiatives can be worse than inaction. By examining the commercial forces at work and remaining sensitive to the organization's natural ways of working, headquarters can choose a role that will speed the building of capability.

Notes

1. Gary, Hamel & C. K. Prahalad. (1990). The core competence of the corporation. *Harvard Business Review*. May/June, (3).
2. Alfred, D. Chandler (1962). *Strategy and Structure: Chapters in the History of the Industrial Enterprise*, Cambridge, MA, The MIT Press.
3. Robert M Grant. (1994). Nonaka's 'Dynamic Theory of Knowledge Creation': reflections and an exploration of the 'Ontological Dimension'. In Von Krogh, G., Kase, K., and G. Cantón, C. (eds). *Towards Organizatonal Knowledge: the Pioneering Work of Ikujiro Nonaka*. London: Palgrave Macmillan.
4. Rosabeth Moss Kanter was one of the most prominent recorders of the process of corporate headquarters slimming. In *When Giants Learn to Dance*, Simon and Schuster (1989), she described the jargon; 'Inside companies, downsizing (cutting employment), demassing (eliminating middle management positions), and decentralising corporate staff functions are among the tactics used by companies eager to be seeking and destroying wealth dissipators (improving profits)' (p. 57).
5. Rosabeth Moss Kanter was also in the forefront of academics studying the new mechanisms companies are using to replace the old central functions, Chapter 4, in *When Giants Learn to Dance*, titled 'Achieving Synergies: Value Added, Value Multiplied' describes many of the changes taking place. Michael Porters' (1985) book *Competitive Advantage*, New York, Free Press, which has a useful chapter on mechanisms. Finally, Free Press, 1985, also has a useful chapter on mechaniation – chapter 11 'Achieving Interrelationships'. The section from p. 393 – organisational mechanisms for achieving interrelationships – provides a useful classification. C. K. Prahalad & Yves Doz (1987) also describe horizontal mechanisms in *The Multi-National Mission*. New York, Free Press. In Chapter 11, 'Managing Interdependencies Across Businesses', they show how data management tools, manager management tools and conflict resolution tools, can be used to manage without central functions. Christopher Bartlett & Sumantra Ghoshal (1989), *Managing Across Borders*. Cambridge MA, HBS Press, describes the new style of management and coordination in an excellent chapter, entitled 'Managing Complexity: Developing Flexible Coordination'.
6. Michael Porter. (1985). *Competitive Advantage*. New York, Free Press, Chapter 10.
7. Many authors comment on the difficulty managers have had in making lateral mechanisms effective. Michael Porter opens his chapter on interrelationships with the sentence 'Achieving interrelationships has in practice proven to be extraordinarily difficult for many firms.' In the conclusion to *When Giants Learn to Dance*, Moss Kanter describes two 'principal problems' getting in the way of 'synergies'. The first is 'top management typically over estimates the degree of cooperation it will get and under estimates the costs' (p. 345). 'Bartlett and Ghoshal (1989) examine the successes and failures of the companies in their sample and conclude 'perhapgs the most difficult task is to coordinate the voluminous flow of strategic information and proprietary knowledge required to operate a transnational organization', p.170, *Managing Across Borders*. In the opening sentences of their

chapter on interdependencies, Prahalad and Doz (1987) comment 'few companies seem to have found an approach to manage the evolving interdependencies across businesses successfully'.*Synergy: Why links between business units often fail and how to make them work (1998)* by Andrew Campbell and Michael Goold describes four management mind sets that contribute to poor outcomes in coordination projects.

8. C. K. Prahalad and Gary Hamel (1990) have made this point in *Harvard Business Review*. May/June. (3). The point has also been made by Rosabeth Moss Kanter in her criticism of corporate headquarters slimming. Also the earliest writings of Chester Barnard and Kenneth Andrews clearly underlined the importance of building capability.
9. In essence this tool is identical to the value chain tool of Michael Porter, the business system tool of McKinsey & Co and the activity based analysis tool of Braxton Associates. It differs in being much more detailed than the value chain, and is focused on capability elements rather than activity elements.
10. A solid article on benchmarking as a tool of analysis is 'Benchmarking World Class Performance', Walleck, O'Hallaron, and Leader (1991) *McKinsey Quarterly*,. Another good piece is *The Power of Best Demonstrated Practice,* Bain & Co.
11. Michael Goold and John J. Quinn's (1993) *Strategic Control: Milestones for Long-Term Performance*. London: Financial Times/Pitman Publishing, describes best practice in this area.
12. All the authors who have researched interrelationships acknowledge the existence of strong barriers to accepting know-how from other parts of the organization. Michael Porter summarizes the 'impediments to achieving interrelationships' pp 385–393 of *Competitive Advantage*. The most interesting piece of direct research has been done by Tom Allen, an MIT professor who studied the degree of technical know-how exchanged within laboratories. He found that technicians preferred to go outside for information and know-how, even though it was more readily available inside the laboratory, because of the perceived costs of working with colleagues – Managing the Flow of Technology, Thomas Allen (1931).
13. Sumantra Ghoshal develops a categorization of innovation processes within multinational companies that is similar. He identifies central, local and global innovations, p. 47. 'The Innovative Multinational', unpublished PhD thesis, Harvard University No. 8617980. The same categorization is described in *Managing Across Boards* by Bartlett and Ghoshal.
14. Norman Blackwell, Jean-Pierre Bizet and David Hensley (1991) all of McKinsey & Co develop a similar categorization in "Shaping a Pan-European Organisation' *McKinsey Quarterly*, July. McKinsey & Co sponsored the research that this chapter is built on, and the exchange of thinking helped to bring our view and theirs into some proximity.
15. Christopher Bartlett and Sumantra Ghoshal produced an exhibit similar to Figure 12.4 in *Managing Across Borders*, p. 97. Our research has confirmed a conclusion of theirs that we were initially most uncomfortable with, namely that adjacent issues could be managed with different levels of coordination and differentiation.
16. Christopher Bartlett and Sumantra Ghoshal use the term 'administrative heritage', Chapter 3, *Managing Across Borders* to describe a concept similar to our decentralization contract. We have found the latter term more useful because the idea of a contract leaves managers more aware of their power to change the contract so long as they can persuade the division managers to agree to the changes. The

administrative heritage language is too passive because it implies that the past is a drag on the speed of change that is hard to manage.

17. Ikujiro Nonaka and Hirotaka Takeuchi, Hal use the term 'administrative heritage', chapter.
18. We collected a large number of the case studies produced by Harvard and Insead where major organization change was driven by a need for coordination or capability building. Only one (Henkel) was a story of success. The others either documented failed efforts or described bold changes, which, with the passage of time, proved not to work.
19. Work on mission and mission statements (*A Sense of Mission*, Andrew Campbell, Marion Devine and David Young, Hutchinson, 1990), demonstrates that written statements are most powerful after the change has been achieved rather than beforehand. Because change is a political process, clear statements of intention or vision can provide the ammunition needed for those managers determined to undermine the change. The authors observed that it is not unusual for the explanation to follow the action by months or even years.

References

Allen, T. (1931). *Managing the Flow of Technology*. Cambridge, MA: MIT Press.

Bain & Co. (n.d) *The Power of Best Demonstrated Practice*. Published booklet.

Bartlett, C.A., & Ghoshal, S. (1989). *Managing across Borders: The Transnational Solution*. London: Random House Business Books.

Campbell, A., & Goold, M. (1998). Synergy: *Why Links between Business Units often Fail and How to Make them Work*. Oxford: Capstone Publishing.

Campbell, A., Devine, M., & Young, D. (1990). *A Sense of Mission*. London: The Economist Books.

Chandler, A. D. (1962). *Strategy and Structure: Chapters in the History of the Industrial Enterprise*. Cambridge, MA: The MIT Press.

Goold, M., & Quinn, J. J. (1990). *Strategic Control: Milestones for Long-Term Performance*. London: The Economist Books.

Kanter, R. M. (1990). *When Giants Learn to Dance: Mastering the Challenge of Strategy, Management, and Careers in the 1990s*. New York: Routledge.

Nonaka, I., and Takeuchi, H. (2011). The wise leader. *Harvard Business Review*. May, Reprint RT1058.

Porter, M. E. (1985). *Competitive Advantage: Creating and Sustaining Superior Performance*. New York: The Free Press.

Prahalad, C. K., and Hamel, G. (1990). The core competence of the corporation. *Harvard Business Review*. May–June, 79–90.

Prahalad, C. K., & Doz, Y. L. (1987). *The Multinational Mission: Balancing Local Demands and Global Vision*. New York: The Free Press.

Grant, R. M. (1994). Nonaka's 'Dynamic Theory of Knowledge Creation': reflections and an exploration of the 'Ontological Dimension',

Walleck, O'Hallaron, & Leader. (1991). *Benchmarking World Class Performance*. McKinsey Quarterly,1.

Von Krogh, G., Takeuchi, H., Kase, K., and G. Cantón, C. (eds) (2013). *Towards Organizational Knowledge: the Pioneering Work of Ikujiro Nonaka*. London: Palgrave-Macmillan, pp. 77–95.

13

The Global Games Framework: Knowledge Creation through Strategic Interaction

Rodolfo G. Campos

Introduction

Game theory studies interrelated decision problems. When analysing a game, one is essentially trying to predict the outcome of these interrelated decision problems. This is done with the help of solution concepts, or equilibrium conditions. A set of equilibrium conditions are used to sift through all possible outcomes and find those that do conform to the definition of an equilibrium, usually a Nash equilibrium. A Nash equilibrium is a prediction of what will happen in that game. However, it is frequently the case that a game has more than one equilibrium, meaning that there is no clear prediction of what will happen. Multiple equilibria are particularly prevalent in a class of games called *coordination games*.

To overcome this multiplicity of equilibria, game theorists have devised more stringent definitions of what an equilibrium is. Still, some equilibria systematically refuse to be eliminated by these stronger conditions imposed on them. In recent years, advances in game theory made a step forward with the advent of a set of new techniques known under the header of *Global Games*.

The Global Games literature is technically demanding. As most frontier contributions to game theory, it exhibits a fairly high degree of mathematical sophistication. This is also true of game theory in general. This did not prevent game theory from being adopted in several disciplines. In particular, it has become widely used in the social sciences, mainly because it provides a versatile framework to think about human interaction. It is likely that the Global Games techniques may also find use in a wider community of social scientists who apply game theory to their research.

This text is a nontechnical exposition of the intuitions behind the extensive literature bundled together under the header Global Games. The intended audience consists of researchers who, while having been exposed to applications of game theory, do not follow the latest developments in game theory.[1] The last part of the chapter deals with the relationship between Global Games and Knowledge Creation Theory.

Coordination games and coordination failures

Games and Nash equilibrium

Game theory is a useful tool to study the behaviour of individuals involved in interdependent decision problems – not only to study the behaviour but also the outcomes generated by this behaviour. To do so, game theorists start by making an abstract representation of the decision problem. This representation is called a *game*. A game specifies who the players are, what actions or strategies are available to them, and how these actions or strategies map into outcomes or payoffs.

In a game, there is always more than one decision-maker. Otherwise, it would be a simple decision problem. The decision-makers are called the *players* of the game. A player may represent a person, a company, a nation or even a biological species. Each player has a number of possible courses of action, called *strategies*. The strategies chosen by all players jointly determine the *outcome* of the game. Associated to each outcome there are *payoffs*. Payoffs are used to provide a ranking over outcomes of the game for each player. This is usually done by assigning numerical payoffs to the different outcomes.

Once the game has been defined, the next step is to study what the likely outcomes of this game are. To select among outcomes, the game is analysed with the intent of identifying which individual choices are optimal according to some pre-specified criterion. The assumption is that players will select their strategies trying to reach the best possible individual outcome while rationally taking into account the strategies of others.

The most widely used solution concept is *Nash equilibrium* (Nash, 1950). Formally, in a Nash equilibrium each player plays a best response to other player's actual play. Stated colloquially, a Nash Equilibrium is a set of strategies such that everyone is doing as well as possible, given what everyone else is doing.

While a Nash Equilibrium can be defined as a situation in which each player plays a best response to other player's *actual* strategies, there is an alternative definition which makes use of *beliefs*. In this context, a belief is a forecast of what strategies are used by the other players. A Nash equilibrium can be defined as a set of strategies in which each player plays a best response to his or her *belief* while at the same time *making a correct prediction*. While it seems to be an unnecessary complication, defining a Nash equilibrium in such a way highlights the fact that players form beliefs about other players' strategies. Thus a Nash equilibrium can be thought of as consisting of two parts: a decision problem (choosing a best response given some beliefs) and a prediction problem (having correct beliefs, i.e., anticipating opponents' actual play).

Beliefs become a more important part of the analysis, if a game has more than one Nash equilibrium. If there is more than one Nash equilibrium, then even a player who is rational and who perfectly understands the game will be unable to solve for a unique course of action. There are various strategies that might be his or her best choices, which one to choose depends on what the other players will likely do. For certain beliefs among players, there will be one Nash equilibrium whereas for another configuration of beliefs the Nash equilibrium will be a different strategy profile.

Equilibrium multiplicity in coordination games

There is a class of games called *coordination games* which is riddled with equilibrium multiplicity. As an example of this type of game, consider the game with payoffs depicted in Figure 13.1. There are two players who have two strategies: A and B. If a players matches the other player's strategy, then the payoff is 1. Otherwise the payoff is zero. Therefore, in this game, players are interested in coordinating their actions. Not surprisingly, games with this characteristic are called *coordination games*. There are two pure strategy Nash equilibria in this game: in the first equilibrium both players play A and in the second both players play B.[2]

In the coordination game, players cannot deduce with certainty which equilibrium gets played. There is more than one candidate outcome that satisfies the conditions for a Nash Equilibrium.

A welcome coincidence in this first example of a coordination game is that both Nash equilibria yield the same payoffs. This means that if players somehow manage to play according to a Nash equilibrium, then it does not really matter whether it is the equilibrium in which A is played or in which B is played. They are equivalent in terms of payoffs.

In general, coordination games will have equilibria with payoffs which are not equivalent. It may also be the case that using one of the strategies is riskier than the other. Consider a second example of a coordination

		Player 2	
		A	B
Player 1	A	1,1	0,0
	B	0,0	1,1

Figure 13.1 A coordination game

Source: The author.

		Player 2	
		A	B
Player 1	A	1,1	−1,0
	B	0,−1	0,0

Figure 13.2 A coordination game with a coordination failure
Source: The author.

game with both of these features, and with the payoff matrix depicted in Figure 13.2.[3]

Like the game before, this game also has two pure strategy Nash equilibria. Again, in the first equilibrium both players play A and in the second equilibrium both players play B. The difference in this case is that both players prefer one equilibrium to the other. The first equilibrium, where both players play A, has higher payoffs for both players than the second equilibrium. There is something wasteful about the second equilibrium. If both players switched to playing A then both players would be better off.[4]

The equilibrium where both players play B is said to be a *coordination failure*. Players would like to always coordinate on the good equilibrium, but they may fail to do so. If they believe that others will play B then they are trapped in the relatively worse equilibrium.

There is another difference between the game in Figure 13.2 and the previous game in Figure 13.1. Both strategies do not involve the same risk. Playing B is safer. When playing B the player is certain to obtain a payoff of 0. When playing A the payoff might be either 1 or –1, depending on the other player's choice. There is a trade-off between high payoffs and safety.

Coordination failures in practice

The game with a coordination failure in Figure 13.2 fits a number of real-life situations. As an example, consider the case in which two people need to jointly invest (either money or effort) in a project in order for it to be successful. They might either invest (A) or not invest (B). The payoffs in Figure 13.2 provide a plausible reward structure in this case. If both investors decide to invest then the project succeeds and both of them get the highest possible payoff. If they both fail to invest then they get a lower payoff but not the worst possible payoff since, at least, they have not wasted their investment. The worst payoff accrues to a player who has invested whereas the other has not. The project does not succeed and the player has to pay the physical and psychological costs of having wasted his time or effort.

As shown before, the game has two equilibria. The good equilibrium is one in which both players exert effort and the project succeeds. The bad equilibrium has both players playing it safe and not exerting any effort. All that matters for which equilibrium is selected is what the beliefs of the players are. We could call the beliefs that the other player will invest (which leads to the good equilibrium) more optimistic and the beliefs that he will not (which leads to the bad equilibrium) more pessimistic. Optimism and pessimism in this case come out of thin air. There is nothing in the game which allows us to predict whether players will be optimistic or pessimistic.

Games with coordination failures, such as our example, have a long tradition in economics. The article by Cooper and John (1988) is the classical reference which applies game theory to the study of coordination failures in economics. They formalize previous insights by, for example, Bryant (1983), Diamond (1982), Hart (1982) and Weitzman (1982), and provide a unifying framework. In doing so, Cooper and John showed the importance of *strategic complementarities* in agents' payoff functions for delivering multiple equilibria in a macroeconomic game. A game with strategic complementarities is a game in which the optimal strategy of an agent depends positively upon the strategies of the other agents (Bulow, Geanakoplos, & Klemperer, 1985).

Cooper and John (1988) study the interaction of strategic complementarities and *spillovers*. Strategic complementarities are interactions at the level of strategies. Spillovers are interactions at the level of payoffs. They are otherwise known as externalities. The multiplicity arises from the presence of strategic complementarities: if the best response of all players is increasing in the strategy of others, then an increase of the strategy by all players may lead to a new equilibrium. The inefficiencies (meaning that equilibria can be characterized as 'good' or 'bad') arise because of externalities in the payoff functions, i.e., spillovers. The technical expression for the presence of 'good' and 'bad' equilibria is that equilibria can be ranked according to Pareto-dominance.[5]

When there are multiple Nash equilibria, some of which are Pareto-dominated by others, then this implies that a coordination failure is present. Even though there are mutual gains from moving to an alternative equilibrium, they may not be achieved because no individual player has incentives to unilaterally switch to another strategy.

The question of whether coordination failures arise in practice has also been tested in laboratory settings. The most well-known results are those of van Huyck, Battalio, & Beil (1990, 1991) and Cooper et al. (1990, 1992). These studies verified that coordination failures do arise in experimental settings. Human players playing in a laboratory sometimes settled on a Nash equilibrium which was worse than other Nash equilibria available to them.

Global games

The addition of more realism: dispersed knowledge

The existence of multiple equilibria in coordination games can be seen as the consequence of modelling assumptions introduced to simplify the theory, as argued by Morris and Shin (2001). One of the assumptions made is that the payoffs of players are assumed to be common knowledge. The assumption that a player is perfectly informed, not only about his or her own payoff, but about the payoffs of other players is clearly unrealistic in most real-world settings. It has been defended as an innocuous simplification, made for the sake of tractability, and which does not change the essential feature of the real-life situations that are modelled with a game.

Recent research has shown that the apparently innocuous assumption does have important implications on equilibrium multiplicity. The Global Games literature starting with Carlsson and van Damme (1993) shows that if the unrealistic common knowledge assumptions is relaxed then multiplicity gives way to a unique equilibrium. This result comes at a cost: games in which players are uncertain about the structure of payoffs, the *fundamentals* of the game, have a more complex structure and are more difficult to analyse. Accordingly, models in the Global Games literature have incorporated dispersed knowledge of fundamentals only in very stylized ways. They can be considered a first step in the direction of a more general theory of how uncertainty about fundamentals shapes equilibrium behaviour.

A key element in the study of Global Games is the concept of *higher-order beliefs*. Harsanyi (1967–1968) is an early contribution that shows that rational choice in an environment in which there is uncertainty about other players' actions depends on higher-order beliefs. Optimal strategies depend on a player's beliefs about the play of others, which in turn depends on the other player's beliefs. And the other player's beliefs depend on the first player's beliefs. Therefore, the optimal strategy depends on beliefs over beliefs, beliefs over beliefs over beliefs and so on. This is what is meant by *higher-order beliefs*.

This seemingly intractable problem can be tackled using a certain information structure, which is used in the global games literature. Rather than describing the technique in general, it is best to plunge directly into an example. As good example is the Investment Game taken from Morris and Shin (2003), and ultimately inspired by Carlsson and van Damme (1993).

The Investment Game in Figure 13.3 is a generalization of the coordination game with a coordination failure in Figure 13.2. The strategies have been renamed from A to 'Invest' and from B to 'Not Invest'. The game now

		Player 2: Invest	Player 2: Not-invest
Player 1	Invest	2c, 2c	2c–2, 0
	Not-invest	0, 2c–2	0, 0

Figure 13.3 The investment game

Source: The author.

has a parameter c, whose value is not common knowledge to the players. The variable c is called the *fundamental* variable. The game represents a situation in which players need to invest in a project. The project is successful if and only if both invest. The parameter c controls the payoff of Investing (good fundamentals make investing more profitable). A player who does not invest always receives a payoff of 0. Investing generates a payoff of 2c. If the other player does not invest, then the payoff from investing is reduced by 2.

The choice of numbers may seem strange, but notice that if c = 0.5, then the payoffs are exactly the same as in Figure 13.2, i.e., the game in Figure 13.2 is embedded in this game. However, the fact that the parameter c is unknown to players will prove important. Before describing how players learn about c, it is useful to solve for the equilibria of the game for all possible values for c (and assuming that the players know what the value is). The answers can be grouped into three cases: when c is negative, when c greater than one, and when c is between 0 and 1.

If c is negative, then playing Invest yields a negative payoff. It is obvious in this case that players are better off playing Not Invest which gives a certain payoff of zero. Hence, there is a unique equilibrium where both players do not invest. If c is greater than one, then playing Invest yields a payoff which is positive regardless of what the other player does. This is better than the certain payoff of zero from playing Not Invest. Hence, in this case the unique Nash equilibrium has both players investing.

For values of c between zero and one there are two Nash equilibria: one in which players invest and one in which they do not. The reasoning parallels the reasoning used to solve for the equilibrium in the game in Figure 13.2.[6] The Nash equilibrium in which players do not invest is a coordination failure. It is Pareto-dominated by the other Nash equilibrium in which players do invest.

Threshold strategies and uniqueness

Now consider the more realistic assumption that players do not know the value of c exactly although they have partial knowledge of what this value might approximately be. In the Global Games framework, they only know the value of c with error. The way this is modelled is that they observe a signal x which tells them the true value of the fundamental variable c plus some error: $x = c + e$. The error term is normally distributed with mean zero.

Players do not know the fundamental variable individually because they observe an imperfect signal. If they had access to everybody's signals they would collectively be able to increase their knowledge of c. But the signals observed are private information. Accordingly, the equilibrium concept that is used is a refinement of Nash equilibrium called *Bayesian Nash Equilibrium*. To solve for the equilibrium of this game is now more complicated. Because the other player faces uncertainty over c, each player has to rationally predict the beliefs of the other player before acting. This in turn involves predicting beliefs of the other player over one's own beliefs, beliefs over beliefs over beliefs and so on.

It turns out that, even though finding an equilibrium becomes technically more demanding, the actual equilibrium is very simple. Both players follow a threshold strategy in which the play Invest if they observe a signal which is higher than a certain threshold and play Not Invest if the signal is lower than this threshold. For this game the threshold can shown to be 0.5 (Carlsson & van Damme, 1993).[7]

The result is remarkable. There is only one equilibrium. Further, playing according to this unique equilibrium puts very simple cognitive demands on players. Because of the presence of higher-order beliefs, which require great powers of reasoning, the equilibrium should be expected to be very complicated. Contrary to this, the equilibrium of the game specifies that players use threshold strategies, which are very simple.

As shown by Carlsson and van Damme (1993) for a class of games to which the Investment Game belongs (symmetric binary action games) a player can always find the optimal action by using a simple heuristic. Rather than needing to solve a complicated computational problem, players can arrive at equilibrium play by holding diffuse beliefs about other players' behaviour. In particular, a player who is on the margin between the two actions should take the extremely agnostic view that the proportion of other players choosing each action is uniformly distributed to arrive at his or her best response.[8]

The use of threshold strategies has been verified with the use of experimental laboratory evidence. Heinemann, Nagel, & Ockenfels (2004, 2009) test the predictions of global games. They find that threshold strategies arise naturally in a laboratory setting in games of this kind. They also find that the global game with uncertain payoffs fits the data better than the multiple Nash equilibria in the related common knowledge game. This is further evidence which strengthens the case for using Global Games as a tool.[9]

Besides the result that players use simple threshold strategies, the main result in Global Games concerns the uniqueness of equilibrium. Dispersed knowledge about fundamentals is able to restore uniqueness. What is remarkable is that uniqueness is restored even though the error is extremely small. For an arbitrarily small variance in the error, the result that there is a unique equilibrium persists. What is done formally to prove this result is to consider the limit as the variance of the error in the signal goes to zero. The unique equilibrium persists as the error approaches zero. Only a small grain of doubt is necessary to move from equilibrium multiplicity in the case of common knowledge to equilibrium uniqueness in the case of dispersed knowledge of fundamentals.

More recently, the uniqueness result has shown not to be robust to some changes in the economic settings (Atkeson, 2001; Angeletos & Werning, 2006; Hellwig, Mukherji, & Tsyvinski, 2006). Rather than going deeper into this issue, I now turn to how the Global Games framework ties the likelihood of a given outcome to the value of fundamentals.

Outcomes

Previous attempts to reduce multiplicity in coordination games specified rules to decide which equilibrium is played that were external to the game. An example in this line is the literature on *sunspots*. Sunspots are defined as extrinsic random variable that does not directly affect economic fundamentals (Cass & Shell, 1983). The idea is that players observe this random variable and use it to coordinate on any given equilibrium. The sunspot literature has provided an important way of dealing with multiplicity in the past (see, for example, Guesnerie, 2006).[10] Absent by design in the sunspot literature is a direct relationship between the likelihood of reaching a certain outcome and the game itself. The selection of an equilibrium is external to the game.

In contrast, in the Global Games framework, the probability of arriving at the good (or bad) outcome is, in equilibrium, tied to the fundamental variable. The Investment Game can be used to illustrate this result. We know that players use threshold strategies which call to play invest whenever the signal is above 0.5. Suppose that players have very precise information. This means that their signals are very concentrated around the true value of c. For larger values of c, because signals are very close to this true value, the probability that players observe a signal above 0.5 is higher. This means that players are more likely to invest. The optimism or pessimism that lead to one outcome or the other have a real world counterpart, which is the true value of the fundamental variable.

Therefore, when the Global Games framework is applied to games with coordination failures, the likelihood of escaping the coordination failure is increasing in the fundamental variable. This stands in stark contrast to all previous attempts to deal with multiplicity in games with coordination failures where the probability of reaching a certain equilibrium was unrelated to anything specific to the game.

The best known example of how fundamentals affect the probability of a coordination failure is the article by Morris and Shin (1998) which popularized the use of Global Games to study economic problems. Morris and Shin (1998) dealt with currency crises.[11] The literature on currency crises had settled on a multiple equilibrium paradigm based on models such as the one by Obstfeld (1996). In these models, it was realized that countries defending a currency peg were exposed to an inherently fragile environment. It was possible that a country's currency peg could collapse if simultaneously attacked by a sufficiently large number of speculators. And, if a majority of speculators attacked it was optimal for the individual speculator to attack the currency as well. If, however, the attack could not muster sufficient support, then it was individually optimal to abstain from the attack. This implied that currency attack events were the bad equilibrium of a coordination game with multiple equilibria.

Morris and Shin (1998) showed that if individual speculators are not perfectly informed about the country's fundamentals (the amount of reserves available to defend the currency peg), then this uncertainty, however small, is enough to generate a unique equilibrium. Further, in the currency attack game, the probability of an attack can be tied to the amount of reserves (the fundamental variable).

Relationship to knowledge creation in firms

This chapter is a nontechnical account of how recent developments in game theory have shaped the way economists think about coordination failures. Given the ubiquitous nature of multiple equilibria and coordination failures, it is to be expected that the Global Games framework can be fruitfully employed in other areas of research.

The Global Games framework starts from the observation that knowledge is dispersed (Hayek, 1945). This dispersion of knowledge is also the starting point of a vast literature on knowledge creation in management science. In the knowledge-based view of the firm, a firm is viewed as an entity which creates knowledge, and for which this knowledge also functions as a competitive advantage (Nonaka, 1991, 1994; Nonaka & Takeuchi, 1995; Nelson, 1991, Kogut & Zander, 1996; Spender, 1996; Spender & Grant, 1996; Nahapiet & Ghoshal, 1998).

The main message of Hayek (1945) is that dispersed knowledge is aggregated through the price system. In contrast, in most applications of the Global Games framework, players are assumed not to have access to the price mechanism. In fact, the critique by Atkeson (2001) is that the standard global game by Morris and Shin (1998) ignores situations in which the existence of markets could be expected to coordinate individuals through the price system. With access to markets agents would have an additional channel to coordinate (by using the information contained in prices) and this could, in principle, overturn some of the results found in the Global Games literature.[12] Atkeson's critique is inapplicable when global games are used to model situations in which markets are absent. One such place is inside a firm.

In the theory of knowledge creation and its application to the theory of a firm, knowledge is defined as 'justified true belief' (Nonaka, 1994; Nonaka, von Krogh, & Voelpel, 2006). The truthfulness of beliefs is justified by individuals through their *interactions with the world*. In particular, as clarified by Nonaka and von Krogh (2009), the way to recognize whether someone has knowledge is through the *performance of a task*. The parallel with how an equilibrium is reached in a coordination game is extraordinary. In coordination games, the players form their beliefs based on the expectation of the actions of others (interactions with the world). Beliefs are instrumental in coordinating on an equilibrium (i.e., performing a task). The use of the Global Games framework revolutionized the take on coordination games by linking the likelihood of success of the task to the features of the game that is played (the state of the world).

In economics, after the article by Morris and Shin (1998), there was an explosion of research applying the global games technique to various topics in which previous literature had detected multiple equilibria in games with coordination failures. It remains to be seen whether this trend carries over to other disciplines and, in particular, whether it proves useful to study knowledge creation in firms.

Notes

1. The text presupposes only a basic knowledge of game theory. If needed, Gibbons (1992) is an excellent book to refresh or obtain a basic working knowledge of game theory.
2. If players are allowed to randomize over their strategies, then there is also a third Nash equilibrium (called a mixed strategy equilibrium) in which players choose each strategy with equal probability. In what follows, I will only consider pure strategy equilibria and disregard mixed strategy equilibria.
3. The game in Figure 13.2 is sometimes called the Stag-hunt game.
4. Notice that, in contrast to what happens in the well-known Prisoner's Dilemma, the outcome where both are better off is a Nash equilibrium of the game.
5. An equilibrium is Pareto-dominated by an alternative equilibrium if it yields a lower equilibrium payoff for one player and does not improve the equilibrium payoff for any other player.
6. The multiplicity result was to be unexpected. For c = 0.5 this game's payoffs coincide with those in Figure 13.2. Therefore, Nash equilibria must be the same for this value. What is said here is that the result carries over to other values close to 0.5.
7. This surprising result uses a technique which operates on the beliefs of the players in a way that is analogous to the elimination of strictly dominated strategies in games of complete information (Bernheim 1984; Pearce 1984).
8. Carlsson and van Damme (1993) link this result to the concept of risk-dominance (Harsanyi and Selten, 1988).
9. Experiments with global games are part of a rich research field. For example, more recently, Cabrales et.al. (2007) studied how players learn to play equilibria in the global game.
10. A good discussion on sunspots and fundamentals in the case of bank run models can be found in Ennis (2003).
11. Another example of the usefulness of the Global Games framework is in the bank-run literature. Goldstein and Pauzner (2005), for example, added noise to the classic bank runs model of Diamond and Dybvig (1983).
12. The problem of the coexistence of a global game and a market was studied by Angeletos and Werning (2006) and Hellwig et.al. (2006).

References

Angeletos, G.-M., & Werning, I. (2006). Crises and prices: information aggregation, multiplicity, and volatility. *The American Economic Review.* 96 (5), 1720–1736.

Atkeson, A. (2001). Rethinking multiple equilibria in macroeconomic modeling: comment. *NBER Macroeconomics Annual.* 15, 162–171.

Bernheim, B. D. (1984). Rationalizable strategic behavior. *Econometrica.* 52 (4), 1007–1028.

Bryant, J. (1983). A simple rational expectations keynes-type model. *The Quarterly Journal of Economics.* 98 (3), 525–528.

Bulow, J. I., Geanakoplos, J. D., & Klemperer, P. D. (1985). Multimarket oligopoly: strategic substitutes and complements. *Journal of Political Economy.* 93 (3), 488–511.

Cabrales, A., Nagel, R., & Armenter, R. (2007). Equilibrium selection through incomplete information in coordination games: an experimental study. *Experimental Economics.* 10 (3), 221–234.

Carlsson, H., & van Damme, E. (1993). Global games and equilibrium selection. *Econometrica.* 61 (5), 989–1018.

Cass, D., & Shell, K. (1983). Do sunspots matter? *Journal of Political Economy.* 91 (2), 193–227.

Cooper, R., DeJong, D. V., Forsythe, R., & Ross, T. W. (1992). Communication in coordination games. *The Quarterly Journal of Economics.* 107 (2), 739–771.

Cooper, R., & John, A. (1988). Coordinating coordination failures in Keynesian models. *The Quarterly Journal of Economics.* 103 (3), 441–463.

Cooper, R. W., DeJong, D. V., Forsythe, R., & Ross, T. W. (1990). Selection criteria in coordination games: some experimental results. *The American Economic Review.* 80 (1), 218–233.

Diamond, D. W., & Dybvig, P. H. (1983). Bank runs, deposit insurance, and liquidity. *Journal of Political Economy.* 91 (3), 401–419.

Diamond, P. A. (1982). Aggregate demand management in search equilibrium. *Journal of Political Economy.* 90 (5), 881–894.

Ennis, H. M. (2003). Economic fundamentals and bank runs. *Economic Quarterly.* 89 (2), 55–71.

Gibbons, R. (1992). *Game Theory for Applied Economists.* Princeton, NJ: Princeton University Press.

Goldstein, I., & Pauzner, A. (2005). Demand-deposit contracts and the probability of bank runs. *The Journal of Finance.* 60 (3), 1293–1327.

Guesnerie, R. (2006). General equilibrium, co-ordination and multiplicity on spot markets. In R. Aréna, & A. Festré (eds) *Knowledge, Beliefs and Economics.* Cheltenham, UK: Edward Elgar.

Harsanyi, J. C. (1967). Games with incomplete information played by "Bayesian" players, I-III: Part I. The basic model. *Management Science* 14 (3), 159–182.

Harsanyi, J. C. (1968a). Games with incomplete information played by "Bayesian" players, I-III. Part II. Bayesian equilibrium points. *Management Science.* 14 (5), 320–334.

Harsanyi, J. C. (1968b). Games with incomplete information played by "Bayesian" players, I-III. Part III. The basic probability distribution of the game. *Management Science.* 14 (7), 486–502.

Harsanyi, J. C., & Selten, R. (1988). *A General Theory of Equilibrium Selection in Games.* Cambridge, MA: MIT Press.

Hart, O. (1982). A model of imperfect competition with Keynesian features. *The Quarterly Journal of Economics*. 97 (1), 109–138.

Hayek, F. A. (1945). The use of knowledge in society. *The American Economic Review.* 35 (4), 519–530.

Heinemann, F., Nagel, R., & Ockenfels, P. (2004). The theory of global games on test: experimental analysis of coordination games with public and private information. *Econometrica*. 72 (5), 1583–1599.

Heinemann, F., Nagel, R., & Ockenfels, P. (2009). Measuring strategic uncertainty in coordination games. *The Review of Economic Studies*. 76 (1), 181–221.

Hellwig, C., Mukherji, A., & Tsyvinski, A. (2006). Self-fulfilling currency crises: the role of interest rates. *The American Economic Review.* 96 (5), 1769–1787.

Huyck, J. B. V., Battalio, R. C., & Beil, R. O. (1990). Tacit coordination games, strategic uncertainty, and coordination failure. *The American Economic Review.* 80 (1), 234–248.

Huyck, J. B. V., Battalio, R. C., & Beil, R. O. (1991). Strategic uncertainty, equilibrium selection, and coordination failure in average opinion games. *The Quarterly Journal of Economics*. 106 (3), 885–910.

Kogut, B., & Zander, U. (1996). What firms do? coordination, identity, and learning. *Organization Science.* 7 (5), 502–518.

Morris, S., & Shin, H. S. (1998). Unique equilibrium in a model of self-fulfilling currency attacks. *The American Economic Review.* 88 (3), 587–597.

Morris, S., & Shin, H. S. (2001). Rethinking multiple equilibria in macroeconomic modelling. *NBER Macroeconomics Annual*. 15, 139–182.

Morris, S., & Shin, H. S. (2003). Global games: theory and applications. In M. Dewatripont, L. P. Hansen, & S. J. Turnovsky (eds), *Advances in Economics and Econometrics: Theory and Applications, Eighth World Congress* (pp. 56–114). Cambridge, UK: Cambridge University Press.

Nahapiet, J., & Ghoshal, S. (1998). Social capital, intellectual capital, and the organizational advantage. *The Academy of Management Review.* 23 (2), 242–266.

Nash, J. F. (1950). Equilibrium points in n person games. *Proceedings of the National Academy of Sciences*. 36 (1), 48–49.

Nelson, R. R. (1991). Why do firms differ, and how does it matter? *Strategic Management Journal,* 12 (ArticleType: research-article/Issue Title: Special Issue: Fundamental Research Issues in Strategy and Economics/Full publication date: Winter, 1991/ Copyright © 1991 Wiley), 61–74.

Nonaka, I. (1991). The knowledge-creating company. *Harvard Business Review.* 69, 96–104, November–December.

Nonaka, I. (1994). A dynamic theory of organizational knowledge creation. *Organization Science*. 5 (1), 14–37.

Nonaka, I., & von Krogh, G. (2009). Tacit knowledge and knowledge conversion: controversy and advancement in organizational knowledge creation theory. *Organization Science.* 20 (3), 635–652.

Nonaka, I., & Takeuchi, H. (1995). *The Knowledge-Creating Company: How Japanese Companies Create the Dynamics of Innovation*. New York: Oxford University Press.

Nonaka, I., von Krogh, G., & Voelpel, S. (2006). Organizational Knowledge Creation Theory: Evolutionary Paths and Future Advances. *Organization Studies 27,* 1179–1208.

Obstfeld, M. (1996). Models of currency crises with self-fulfilling features. *European Economic Review.* 40 (3–5), 1037–1047.

Pearce, D. G. (1984). Rationalizable strategic behavior and the problem of perfection. *Econometrica*. 52 (4), 1029–1050.

Spender, J. C. (1996). Making knowledge the basis of a dynamic theory of the firm. *Strategic Management Journal*. 17 (Winter Special Issue), 45–62.

Spender, J. C., & Grant, R. M. (1996). Knowledge and the firm: overview. *Strategic Management Journal*. 17 (Winter Special Issue), 5–9.

Weitzman, M. L. (1982). Increasing returns and the foundations of unemployment theory. *The Economic Journal*. 92 (368), 787–804.

14

Knowledge after the Knowledge Creating Company: A Practitioner Perspective

Laurence Prusak and Thomas H. Davenport

In the early 1990s, the two authors of this chapter were busily engaged in trying to come up with new ideas about information for our then-employer, Ernst & Young. As researchers in the firm's newly-organized R&D Centre, established to create new ideas for its consulting business, we were focused on finding new approaches to the emerging practice of information management. We had developed a multi-client-sponsored research program consisting of about thirty organizations to work with us in exploring this subject. Out of that research, Tom – with some assistance from Larry – eventually published a book entitled *Information Ecology*.[1]

It was edited for Oxford University Press by their well-known business book editor, Herb Addison, whom we kept in touch with after the book was published. A year after *Information Ecology* came out, Herb mentioned to Larry that he was publishing a new book on knowledge in organizations by two Japanese professors and asked if we would like to see a proof copy. This came at an interesting time for us as we and some of our corporate research collaborators suspected that we were reaching the end of what could be usefully said about information management at that stage of its technical and functional development. Needless to say, we were eager to get our hands on this new book and welcomed the chance to read it ahead of the general public.

Even before Herb's most useful offer, we had begun to think of knowledge as something that might deserve of our attention. We had studied our Drucker and Bell as well as the rare economists such as Nelson and Winter, Arrow, and Teece, who wrote meaningfully about the subject. We even looked into those more common but not always rewarding sociologists who wrote about the sociology of knowledge. There were also a few management scholars doing work on this issue – Rob Grant, J-C Spender, Max Boissot come to mind – but their work was still pretty abstract for practitioners to work with directly. None of that gave us an explanatory handle or framework to make useful sense of the subject. Nor did we have a set of cases that could inform further research and analysis in this field.

Needless to say, reading *The Knowledge Creating Company*[2] (referred to as KCC for the rest of this essay) by Ikujiro Nonaka and Hirotaka Takeuchi (1995) proved a revelation to us. It gave us a viable framework, cases, many new references to other relevant research, and an illuminating and graceful way of speaking about this most elusive and valuable subject. We were excited and energized. KCC gave us just the push we needed to rebrand our multi-client research consortium and focus much more on knowledge and less on information. One of the first ways we marked that shift was to distribute KCC to all our members.

This program went on in one form or another for another ten years. When the Ernst & Young initiative ended, Larry recreated the program at IBM. Then Tom and Larry brought it to Babson College, where Tom was a professor. During that decade of research on organizational knowledge, we became familiar in one way or another with over 200 knowledge projects. Almost all of them were inspired in some ways by KCC.

One reason we were so taken by the book was that it took just the sort of hybrid approach we were seeking to use in our own writing, an approach warmly welcomed by our research collaborators, who wanted ideas they could act on in their organizations. Such books cite current academic research on their subjects when it is useful, but emphasize real-life cases and the useful practices and lessons that can be drawn from them. They are less common than one might expect because of the tendency in academia and in too much consulting to live in the world of abstraction and ideas about ideas. We were delighted to find that KCC was both intellectually sound and practical. The subsequent history of the book has surely ratified our initial judgment. Not only was KCC for a long time the most cited book in academic studies of organizational knowledge and learning, it was read by almost all the serious practitioners we have met in this field. It was to knowledge management what Michael Porter's books were to strategy – a thoughtful and vivid spur to action and further investigation.

What did our collection of practitioners get from our gift of KCC and the collective discussions and explications that followed? Looking back on those early pioneer efforts – starting say from 1995 – we think we can discern two major impacts on practice among many of our clients as well as in the general marketplace of business ideas. One was simply getting managers and executives to believe and accept that there was a separate thing called knowledge that was different from information, data and wisdom. The book put knowledge – not technology or information or human capital per se or data – on the management map. This development faced fierce resistance by many forces. Technology vendors were spending huge sums to convince firms that by managing an organization's data and information they would also be effectively managing many, if not all, of its knowledge resources.

They conflated the two subjects, as did most academics and economists who wrote and thought about it. There was little reference to knowledge as a distinct resource to be acted on in a distinct way in any of the major texts used to teach strategy, IT, HR or most other organizational functions. No wonder MBA-trained executives had trouble believing that this was a subject worth thinking about or funding. It was barely mentioned in the business press or practitioner journals and very rarely in the scholarly journals that were read exclusively by academics.

In these early years, it fell solely on the shoulders of managers who understood this new idea to make the case for knowledge. Organizations including Xerox, the World Bank, McKinsey and Co., Novartis, NASA, BP, 3M and Skandia took up this challenge with varying degrees of success. By the later 1990s, the idea that knowledge was a legitimate source of activities for organizations to work with was gaining traction around the world.

The second major impact of KCC, one that can be best seen in retrospect, was the introduction of tacit knowledge into the emerging global knowledge conversation and debate. The tacit dimension of knowledge had been a rich source of discussion and debate among philosophers at least as far back as Aristotle. It can surely be said, however, that it wasn't in any way a mainstay of social science or management thought before KCC. Nor was it mentioned by any of the more serious popularizers of 'the knowledge age' – for instance, Alvin Toffler and his imitators. When discussed at all by most commentators, knowledge was typically seen as a deeper type of information – perhaps richer and more detailed or action-oriented than other forms, but still fundamental information and therefore readily codified and easy and cheap to transfer and manipulate.

This changed when understanding of the concept of the tacit dimension of knowledge became widespread, thanks in significant measure to KCC. The book documented and discussed several cases of attempts to use the idea in practice. Nonaka and Takeuchi's (1995) SECI model, which charted the interaction of explicit and tacit knowledge through the processes of socialization, externalization, combination and internalization, was widely discussed, if not always faithfully adopted. It certainly spurred many discussions and attempts to work with this far richer understanding of what knowledge actually is. By enlarging the idea of knowledge to include non-documented and perhaps even non-documentable aspects, it gave a whole new perspective to the notion of what companies could do with knowledge. The cases and uses that were presented by KCC ranged far and wide and inspired a new cottage industry among consultants, software designers, writers and academics. It encouraged publishers to bring many of Michael Polanyi's books back into print because Polanyi's work on the tacit dimensions on knowledge had a powerful influence on KCC's authors.

It is a reasonable guess that this aspect of KCC was the one that caused the most excitement among practitioners in the early years of knowledge management. Having a new and exciting concept to work with is always catnip to idea practitioners looking for new arguments, tools and vocabulary. What is more, the book offered a ready-made model for exploiting tacit knowledge that seemed practical and productive. Tacit knowledge emerged as an idea that arrived at just the right time for the development of knowledge management.

From the mid1990s forward, the idea of explicitly working with organizational knowledge in its many forms slowly gained adherents throughout the world. New cases began to appear from leading business schools; academic and practitioner journals began to publish articles on knowledge strategies, technologies, organizational structures, human resource policies and organizational learning. Several new practitioner books and articles appeared (not excluding the book we wrote – *Working Knowledge*[3]!) that added new cases and some new ideas on how to best operationalize this still elusive resource. At the many, many conferences that took up the subject, oft-repeated stories were told about the success of this or that organizational knowledge effort. Chief Knowledge Officers were appointed. Executive Knowledge committees and other knowledge governance entities were created and budgets were approved to capture, develop, retain, analyse and transfer knowledge. By 2000, the *Financial Times* estimated that as many as 80 per cent of large firms had some sort of knowledge program underway. This did not include the knowledge activities of government agencies, NGOs and smaller enterprises. Almost all of this vibrant activity was strongly influenced by KCC, perhaps sometimes in ways unforeseen or even unbidden by the authors. But that is always the fate of new and consequential ideas.

Looking back from 2012, we can see three major directions that this movement has taken in the years since then. Depending on many and varied factors, organizations have tended to focus their activities on organizational structure and governance, technology and analytics, and knowledge services and integration. Let no one think these projects are mutually exclusive or even that they were consciously thought of in this particular way. And of course there are many projects that do not accord with this categorization. But it seems to work for the thousands of project we have been acquainted with, so we will stick to it.

In the earlier stages of the knowledge movement, when the focus was as much on information as it was on knowledge, the unit of analysis for many knowledge project was the individual. This trend was enhanced by the common idea of a kind of road warrior – the individual worker, armed with the newly available portable computers, roaming the earth with access to all the knowledge embedded in new technologies. This image was more powerful then we often assume and was reinforced by the usual combination of consultants, vendors, journalists, and even some academics. When it was examined a bit more closely, however, it proved of little use to those trying to take knowledge seriously. It failed to take into account any tacit dimensions of knowledge; it didn't allow for the learning and knowledge transfer that takes place between participating workers; and it surely didn't allow for the social nature of knowledge. KCC left no doubt that knowledge was essentially social, not solitary. This was not surprising. Coming from a culture that is far less individualistic then Anglo-American society, the authors emphasized throughout the volume the social and collaborative nature of knowledge development, processes, and productivity. Their explanation of the value of middle managers is a good example of this viewpoint.

At the same time, a different but related management 'fashion' was gaining currency and shaping many knowledge efforts, giving new life to many a fading knowledge drive in organizations. This was the new focus on networks and communities of practice. This unanticipated development seems to us to have had three causes. The first and simplest is that several of the major contributors to the most influential practitioner texts about networks and communities had a strong background in and understanding of knowledge issues and incorporated a knowledge perspective in their writings. Rob Cross, Andrew Parker, John Seely Brown, Paul Duguid, Etienne Wengner, Richard McDermott and several others focused on how these new forms of organization and communication were critically useful conduits for knowledge flow, transfer and development. A pattern quite similar to early KM efforts emerged in the later 1990s, with conferences and popular and academic writings devoted to this new perspective. As more and more practitioners recognized the social nature of knowledge, many, many knowledge projects began to take on a network or CoP component. This network emphasis brought with it a widespread recognition that new ways of organizing work needed to be established in order to best realize the true value of knowledge in the organization. Older, traditional forms of silo bureaucracies did nothing to enable cross-functional knowledge interactions and in fact may well have seriously impeded them. The organizational forms that had served industry so well for the past 170 years or so were seen as far less efficacious in providing a infrastructure for optimal knowledge use. Networks and CoPs provided an alternative. They have proven to be a durable contribution to both research and practice.

Inevitably, one branch of the networks and CoP movement developed a strong technology orientation. Just as businesspeople were beginning to become aware of 'social networks' in the organizational sense, social networking technologies hit the marketplace. Not surprisingly, there was confusion between actual social networks and social networking technologies. When the technology predominated, the emphasis on knowledge transfer was often lost. A few firms, including IBM and several large professional services organizations, viewed social networking technologies primarily in a knowledge management context. Most did not.

Another major direction knowledge practices took may best be described as knowledge integration. By this we mean the efforts of practitioners to establish knowledge processes and routines that make the best use of existing organizational knowledge and/or acquire or develop new knowledge. At the start of the period we are discussing, many thought that Peter Drucker's saying managing knowledge was everybody's business got managers off the hook – if knowledge was everyone's responsibility, they didn't have a particular responsibility to manage it. Of course, this was an illusion. When something is theoretically done by all, free riders come out of the woodwork and no one is accountable. And while social norms of collaboration are vital to a vibrant knowledge culture, they don't just spring from 'self-organizing free agents', as some utopians hoped. Within a few years, several models for 'managing' knowledge developed within organizations. At the time, we classified some of these by political terms including feudalism, federalism, enlightened despotism and some others not is current use. Many of these functions sat within technology departments and their knowledge concerns were quickly subsumed into the much larger and more expensive technology decisions that so dominated the hearts and minds of IT executives.

Two things happened next. One was that it became obvious to most practitioners that no department could actually 'manage' knowledge. One could manage 'around' knowledge by managing incentives, infrastructures of one kind or another, processes and all the other interventions or mechanisms in a manager's armoury. But managing knowledge per se either devolved into managing documents and systems (which could be managed) or embraced the fantasy that knowledge can all be made visible and therefore managed effectively. This was a wild distortion of what KCC was saying, but some SECI devotees were overwhelmed by their managers' need to measure and manage knowledge at the micro level. Of course all of this came to naught. On the positive side, several organizations did begin to define just what *could* be managed by a KM function and decide where that function should sit. Chief Knowledge Officers began to be seen by the later 1990s, as well as Executive Knowledge Committees, scaled-down knowledge divisions and departments and internal knowledge consultants.

Most of these later efforts were run by managers who now reported to quite a varied group of functions besides IT – perhaps the most common in larger organizations being Human Resources, Strategy and Communications. This helped reduce the tendency to look for technology 'solutions' to all knowledge issues, at least in part, and helped connect knowledge work to the aims and practices of the organization.

The idea that knowledge might be better understood as a verb then a noun – that it is an activity as well as a stock of valuable 'stuff' – also helped integrate knowledge efforts into the actual work of the organization. This led to a much stronger focus on processes and routines which could theoretically make knowledge activities more efficient and effective. One of the rallying cries for this approach was 'start with the practice – in other words, watch how work is actually being done and build up from there.

A value of doing knowledge work in this way is that, by providing methods, tools and encouragement to the knowledge worker at the 'coal face' or source of knowledge action, an organization has a better chance at both new knowledge creation and the more efficient use of knowledge by sharing throughout a global practice. IBM and McKinsey are exemplars of this approach.

The approach has paid dividends to organizations that have been willing and able to discern how and where knowledge actually flows. The World Bank, for instance, evaluates its degree of global knowledge integration by measuring and characterizing cross-sector and cross-functional knowledge interactions.

Another integration development is the rise of the term 'knowledge services'. After several bruising battles within firms as to what knowledge is and what should be managed by whom, something of a compromise was reached. Many types and categories of knowledge can be managed by a portfolio approach, giving funds and attention to different types of knowledge at different times, using the people and tools appropriate to each. In many of these efforts, technology focused initiatives co-exist with 'softer' human capital efforts. We see social media connectivity projects sharing the stage with new organizational learning ideas – all under a knowledge services banner. In some ways, this development can be viewed as an expansion of the corporate library idea; it is primarily oriented to explicit knowledge, but addresses broader topics than books and journal subscriptions.

There have also been a number of corporate and organizational knowledge activity directions that were not anticipated (or perhaps even approved of) by Nonaka and Takeuchi (1995), but are in our view consistent with the idea of a 'knowledge-creating company'. The shift toward analytics is one of these. Tom has pursued the idea of building analytical capabilities over the last decade or so, and these ideas have proven just as popular – if not more so – than knowledge management at its peak.

While not everyone in the analytics and big data movement sees it as closely related to knowledge management, Tom certainly does. He began to work on analytics as a form of 'data-derived knowledge' and pursued many of the ideas behind the KCC in an analytical context, including analytical culture, organizational models for analytics, relationships between analysts and decision-makers, and even the notion of a tacit familiarity with analytics. He co-authored an article (with Chuck Seeley, then an Intel knowledge manager) on 'Integrating KM and Business Intelligence at Intel'.

More recently, leading organizations in the analytics field are realizing that their analytical activities yield knowledge that needs to be managed. Some call it 'model management' or 'analytical asset management', but the fact is that knowledge management – with analytical models, insights, and assumptions as the key knowledge objects – is an important component of a successful analytics initiative.

Similarly, leaders in the KM field are considering the idea of 'knowledge analytics', discussed in an APQC research paper. The idea is that technologies make it increasingly easy to monitor who is producing and consuming explicit knowledge resources. Knowledge analytics should make it easier to focus interventions on the people and processes within an organization that are most in need of more knowledge. Of course, the fact that the use of explicit knowledge resources is more easily measured than tacit knowledge use should not mean that organizations emphasize one type of knowledge at the expense of the other.

While knowledge management within organizations has evolved in a variety of directions since *The Knowledge-Creating Company* was published, there is little doubt that the book has had a major and lasting influence on the work of practitioners. Without the ideas of Nonaka and Takeuchi (1995), it is likely that the technology-focused aspects of knowledge management would have received even more of the attention and resources of organizations than they have. KCC and its intellectual successors have been the primary factor in creating some sense of balance between tacit and explicit knowledge initiatives and have, therefore, in our opinion, given organizational knowledge activities much of their lasting power.

Notes

1. Davenport and Prusak (1997).
2. Nonaka and Takeuchi (1995).
3. Davenport and Prusak (2000).

References

Davenport, T. H., & Prusak, L. (1997). *Information Ecology: Mastering the Information and Knowledge Environment.* New York: Oxford University Press.

Davenport, T. H., & Prusak, L. (2000). *Working Knowledge* (2nd ed.). Boston MA: Harvard Business Review Press.

Nonaka, I., & Takeuchi, H. (1995). *The Knowledge-Creating Company: How Japanese Companies Create the Dynamics of Innovation.* New York: Oxford University Press.

15
Governing Knowledge Processes in Project-Based Organizations

Vesa Peltokorpi

Introduction

In addition to the rising importance of knowledge work (Nonaka, 1994), one of the most profound ongoing changes in organizations is the flattening of hierarchical bureaucratic structures in favour of teams and team-based arrangements (Child & Rodrigues, 2003; Peltokorpi, 2012). Unlike stable, rigid bureaucracies, flexible project-based organizations are ideal for consumer-focused knowledge creation and to manage cross-functional experience, product complexity, and technological uncertainty (Hobday, 2000). Despite the benefits, scholars have also identified problems with project-based organizations in terms of locating and sharing knowledge across projects and organization-wide learning because of loose connections among project teams and challenges in creating a balance between short-term project objectives and the long-term organizational learning (Prencipe & Tell, 2001).

To efficiently manage organizational knowledge processes (including the creation, retention, and sharing of knowledge), the knowledge governance literature maintains that project-based structures need to be aligned with appropriate governance mechanisms (Grandori, 1997, 2001; Foss, 2007, 2009; Foss, Husted, & Michailova, 2010). While providing important insights of why and how governance mechanisms motivate individual employees to contribute to knowledge processes, knowledge governance scholars often build their arguments on the behavioral assumptions of organizational economics (OE) (Williamson, 1985), especially to bounded rationality and opportunism, and focus only on 'hard' governance dimensions, such as compensation systems. Yet, knowledge processes are also dependent on individual voluntary contributions (Frost, Osterloh & Weibel, 2010). Adopting the view of benevolent and intrinsically motivated individuals, the knowledge management literature emphasizes the importance of 'soft' trust, community-based aspects in organizational knowledge processes (Kogut & Zander, 1992; Nonaka, 1994; Peltokorpi, Nonaka, & Kodama, 2007; Spender,

1996). Because both of these perspectives are equally important, I argue in this chapter that a more balanced account of knowledge processes in project-based organizations can be created by integrating the 'hard' dimensions of the knowledge governance literature with the 'soft' dimensions in the knowledge management (KM) literature.

The rest of this chapter is structured as follows. In the next section, I discuss basic features of project-based organizations and draw on the KM and knowledge governance literatures for an illustrative set of governance mechanisms that support knowledge processes in knowledge-intensive, project-based organizations. By the KM literature, I refer to publications describing organizations as knowledge creating communities (see Nonaka & Peltokorpi, 2006, for a review). Such descriptions are apparent especially in the knowledge-based views of the firm (e.g., Kogut & Zander, 1992). I then describe the method and the functioning of knowledge governance through a case study at a Japanese project-based organization, Mayekawa Manufacturing Ltd. I finish this chapter by discussing the contributions and limitations of the case study.

Project-based organizations

Project-based organizations (PBOs) consist of a variety of organizational forms that involve the creation of temporary systems for the performance of project tasks (Sydow, Lindqvist, & DeFillippi, 2004). Within a pure PBO, projects embody most, if not all, of the business functions normally carried out in departments of functional and matrix organizations. In PBOs, a project is also the primary mechanism for creating, responding to, and executing new business opportunities (Hobday, 2000). Projects include individuals working cooperatively together toward a common goal, within an established time frame and budget, to produce identifiable deliverables (Henrie & Sousa-Poza, 2005). Projects are often narrow, involving a specific, well-defined product and one or a few customers. Customers are often closely and directly engaged in projects because projects are critical to their business functioning, performance and profitability. Unlike the matrix structure, project networks can stretch beyond the boundaries of the firm, but do not dissolve fully into the market (Sydow et al., 2004). Instead, projects can take volatile positions in between, so that they allow for both short-term flexibility and long-term stability in allocating and coordinating human resources. The heavy reliance on projects suggests that a high degree of authority and responsibility is given to project teams in PBOs.

PBOs have distinctive advantages. For example, structural flexibility facilitates the timely, accurate allocation of physical and human resources to projects. Project-based structures further circumvent traditional barriers to organizational change and facilitate design optimization by enabling design cycles to be carried out effectively and efficiently by reducing the number of design and redesign cycles (and costs) associated with additional cycles, caused by backward feedback loops from later to early design stages. The PBO learns from the projects through an accumulation of experiences among the various project participants and project members. Small units and increased delegation of responsibility also increases local responsiveness and allows for the discovery and utilization of both local and dispersed knowledge. Work in cross-functional project teams and in close customer interactions is further proposed to increase innovativeness (Hobday, 2000). Projects can also increase product quality because they are based on the exact specification and needs of the buyer.

The advantages do not come without some weaknesses. For example, the project team autonomy tends to reduce knowledge sharing beyond the project team boundaries. While departments in functionally-based firms can act as isolated knowledge silos, the pure PBO lacks the mechanisms for cross-project knowledge transfer (Hobday, 2000). Employees can work well and learn a lot during projects, but care little about things outside their projects with a risk that the wheel is reinvented over and over again (Prencipe & Tell, 2001). Employees in fast-paced projects can also have little time to reflect on and document their experiences or lessons learned. If knowledge remains non-codified, organization-wide learning is reduced. In addition, PBOs often lack incentives and formal structures for intra- and cross-project learning. A study in a large German firm, for example, shows that technical managers had fewer incentives to mentor junior engineers after the firm reorganized from a functional matrix to a PBO (Hobday, 2000). To maximize the advantages of project-based structures PBOs, the knowledge governance literature maintains that adequate governance mechanisms need to be deployed (Grandori, 1997; Foss, 2007; Foss et al., 2010).

Knowledge governance

How then should organizational knowledge processes in PBOs be governed? A precise answer cannot be given because of the different rationales provided in the KM and knowledge governance literature. In contrast to the premises of individual opportunism in OE (Williamson, 1985), KM scholars (especially in the knowledge-based view of the firm) start their discussions with the assumption that firms as organizational forms exist to economize on the exchange of tacit knowledge rather than attenuate opportunism (Nickerson & Zenger, 2004). Placing emphasis on idiosynractic human actors and tacit knowledge, KM scholars further argue that organizations (like human actors) are presented in OE as homogeneous information-processing machines. The assumptions of information asymmetries between agents and principles hinder the ability to govern tacit knowledge within the organization. The OE governance spectrum, ranging from markets to hierarchies, is thus restricted to mechanisms geared to transfer of goods and services, not to transfer and share knowledge out of which they are produced. In summary, governance based solely on contracts is dysfunctional and limited to information-processing (Ghoshal & Moran, 1996).

Instead of the OE assumptions of opportunitist human actors who act in their self-interest and respond mainly to economic incentives, KM scholars describe the integration of activities within firm boundaries as a 'creator of a positive' rather than an 'avoider of a negative'. In this stream of literature, organizational actors are not opportunistic but intrinsically motivated to participate in and contribute to knowledge processes. An individual is intrinsically motivated if s/he performs an activity for no apparent reward except the activity itself (Deci, 1972). In the KM literature, intrinsic motivation has been attributed by individuals' attachment to trust and community-based organizations (Kogut & Zander, 1992). In contrast to the exercise of authority, KM scholars with the assumptions of intrinsically motivated 'social man' emphasize 'clan' and 'culture' modes of organizational control. While the positive aspects of group-based structures and soft coordination mechanisms have been emphasized, the KM literature is accused of being unable to develop comprehensive governance discussions since it disregards human opportunism, extrinsic motivation and hard governance dimensions (Foss, 2007; Nickerson & Zenger, 2004). Extrinsic motivation refers to the performance of an activity because it leads to external rewards (Deci, 1972). Further, the methodological collectivism (a collective or holistic approach to social phenomena) in the KM literature is problematic because it suppresses the level of individual action and interaction (Foss, 2009).

Disregarding the view of the benevolent social man in the KM literature, the knowledge governance literature (armed with the OE assumptions of human actors) starts with the premise that specific governance mechanisms can be used to influence and direct organizational knowledge processes (Grandori, 1997, 2001; Foss, 2007, 2009; Foss et al., 2010). Various governance mechanisms, such as training and development programs, organizational forms and compensation systems, thus influence individual ability and motivation, and provide individuals opportunities engage into organizational knowledge processes. In this stream of literature, governance choice is consistent with Friedrich Hayek's (1945) argument that the fundamental economic problem is determining the 'best way of utilizing knowledge initially dispersed among all people' (p. 520). While building their discussions on and being more sympathetic to the behavioural assumptions of OE, knowledge governance scholars also argue that OE is not able to provide full answers to all governance issues. For example, because OE assumes that all individual motives are rational and selfish, it neglects intrinsic motivation and important soft organizational dimensions (Osterloh & Frey, 2000).

The fundamental difference between the knowledge governance and KM literature is the assumptions of methodological individualism in the former and the methodological collectivism in the latter. Methodological individualism adopts the assumption that social phenomena can only be accurately explained by showing how they result from the intentional states that motivate individual actors (Hodgson, 2007). Knowledge governance scholars thus emphasize the need to build micro-foundations based on individual action and interaction for organizational-knowledge phenomena (Foss, 2007). Because governance mechanisms are classified according to the underlying cognitive models of organizational actors, decision makers are able to optimize knowledge processes by creating contingencies through a mixture of coordinating lateral interactions and governance mechanisms. In the KM literature, organizations are described as higher-order aggregates. KM scholars thus provide the perspective of the embedded, intrinsically motivated 'social man' whose actions are guided by organizational norms and culture. Shrinking does not occur because organizational actors are expected to contribute equally to organizational knowledge processes. Among the other related things, the KM literature has consequently neglected the well-established social psychological phenomena of social loafing (Lantane, Williams, & Harkins, 1979). Therefore, governance in organizations is not focused on the resolution of information asymmetries but on the coordination of distributed pieces of knowledge and distributed learning processes. On the other hand, it is also fair to argue that the knowledge governance literature has problems to provide coherent explanation of the collective phenomena on individuals.

The aim of this chapter is not to make 'either/or' choices and argue that the knowledge governance or KM literature provide the 'right' governance solution. Instead, this chapter seeks to illustrate the importance and complementary nature of these two streams of literature. In order to incorporate both the 'hard' dimensions of the knowledge governance literature and the 'soft' dimensions of the KM literature, knowledge governance is defined here as a set of formal and informal organizational mechanisms and practices used to influence and direct organizational knowledge processes. This definition goes beyond the restricted term used in OE in which governance is limited to the choice between the discrete structural alternatives hierarchy, hybrids, and markets (Williamson, 1985). Instead, price and authority can be treated as just two among several coordination mechanisms defining a space of governance possibilities. This definition also allows for a shift in analysis from the ideal types of structures to a variety of governance and coordination mechanisms and their possible combinations (Grandori, 1997).

Knowledge governance in project-based organizations

Knowledge governance seeks to maximize the distinctive benefits of project-based structures, including flexibility and innovation, and to minimize losses by making the behavioural options of the human actors more predictable and transparent. To successfully accomplish these objectives, knowledge governance needs to incorporate soft and hard dimensions. For this purpose, I draw from the KM and knowledge governance literatures for a non-exhaustive set of governance mechanisms expected to support knowledge processes in PBOs. These governance mechanisms are a consensus-based hierarchy, shared human resource management (HRM) practices, and performance and output control. These governance mechanisms, having non-causal relations with the project group- and organization-level outputs are complementary and can substitute for each other.

Consensus-based hierarchy

Consensus-based hierarchy, which emphasizes knowledge sharing and shared norms and values, has been identified in the KM literature as an important governance mechanism in group-based organizations because of its influence on collective monitoring, psychological contracts, trust and knowledge sharing and generation (Kogut & Zander, 1992; Grant, 1996; Spender, 1996). In such organizations, important top management duties are vision creation, resource allocation, and management through persuasion (Nonaka, 1994). Middle managers support knowledge creation, and combine ideas and link dispersed knowledge (Nonaka, 1994; Peltokorpi et al., 2007). Instead of top-down control, the management and employees decide and control collective action in a joint mode based on face-to-face interaction (Grant, 1996), as it strengthens trust and a sense of shared destiny–important preconditions for effective deployment of knowledge and collaborative team-work (Nahapiet & Ghoshal, 1998). Adler (2001) proposes joint decision-making in an official coordination mode with mutual persuasion and monitoring, using subjective judgments or clan control. These information sharing processes enable individuals to locate specialized knowledge sets within the organization (Kogut & Zander, 1992). In effect, while organizations act as distributed knowledge systems (Tsoukas, 1996), diverse and localized knowledge bases become connected.

Shared HRM practices

Shared HRM practices support lateral interactions and operational integration. For example, shared incentive and promotion schemes throughout the organization increase the sense of fairness and motivate individuals to share knowledge. Organizations are even argued to fail if incentives fail to motivate people to share knowledge (Foss, 2003). Because motivation is to a certain extent intrinsic (Deci, 1972), low-powered incentives facilitate knowledge sharing in group-based organizations (Nickerson & Zenger, 2004; Osterloh & Frey, 2000). The usage of high-powered incentives based on objective measures in knowledge-based organizations is difficult because of the problems of reliably measuring an employee's contribution to knowledge-sharing efforts. When knowledge is tacit and hard to transfer, job rotation is also argued to be an effective way to mobilize personal knowledge since it helps individuals to understand an organization's business from a variety of perspectives, accumulate expertise, develop social networks as well as locate distributed knowledge (Nonaka, 1994; Peltokorpi et al., 2007). Furthermore, Hansen, Northia, and Tierney (1999) propose that movement of people and knowledge sharing through person-to-person contacts is a KM strategy that does not require extensive knowledge codification. In such organizations, shared incentives enable people to be moved flexibly. Scholars also argue that internal and external training programs enhance knowledge creation and knowledge transfer as well as the creation of shared identity (Nonaka, 1994; Peltokorpi et al., 2007).

Performance measures and output control

Performance measures and output control, in turn, increase organizational transparency and collective monitoring. In a PBO, where employees are often involved in a number of projects and projects are treated as semi-autonomous units with their own resources and time schedules, shared performance and output measures increase transparency, enable units to compare their performance, and reduce the risk of opportunism (Foss, 2003). In group-based organizations and PBOs, the usage of group-based incentives has become more prevalent (Nickerson & Zenger, 2004). Group-based performance assessment and rewards are effective, as they make employees feel like owner-operators of small, internal subcontracting units (Nickerson & Zenger, 2004). Because this type of governance is partly based on codifying tacit knowledge, the ease of knowledge transfer will increase and costs associated with such transfer will decrease (Kogut & Zander, 1992). In order to determine 'what to do' rather than 'how to do it', the control criterion should at least partly exceed the traditional finance-oriented figures. Because intrinsic motivation is the foundation of knowledge creation (Nonaka, 1994), employees should be allowed to discuss and agree on criteria and methods to be applied in order to make them commitment to contribute to knowledge processes.

Method

Research design

I conducted a case study to explore how organizational knowledge processes are governed in PBOs. I used a qualitative case study method as the empirical basis because of limited research on knowledge governance and because of its advantages in improving contextual sense (Miles, 1979; Yin, 1994), deeper understanding (Geertz, 1973) and theory development (Van Maanen, 1979). In addition, Foss et al. (2010) recommended qualitative methodology in research on knowledge governance.

I conducted the case study at a Japanese PBO, Mayekawa Manufacturing Ltd (hereinafter Mayekawa). Established in 1924, Mayekawa is one of the world's leading industrial refrigeration system manufacturers. In 2000, the company had a 30 per cent share of the world's industrial refrigerator market. The most important market is North America. In 2000, Mayekawa employed 2500 people (2000 in Japan and 500 overseas), with overseas offices in 34 countries. Engineers consist of about 80 per cent of the employees. The manufacturing plants are located in Japan, Mexico, Brazil, and Korea. The main manufacturing facility is the Moriya Plant in Ibaraki Prefecture (close to Tokyo), which is comprised of the compressor and freezer manufacturing divisions, the after-service section, the electric and plant refrigerating division, and the technical research centre.

I conducted this study at Mayekawa for two reasons. First, Mayekawa provides an interesting research site due to its project-based structure in which financially independent, small companies (DOPPOs) coordinate their interdependent activities (Fojt, 1996). Second, while PBOs are hard to implement and govern because of limited inter-project interaction (Hobday, 2000), free-riding, and knowledge hoarding (Foss, 2003), the case shows that Mayekawa has successfully formed a PBO combining soft and hard governance dimensions, individual and group processes, flexibility and efficiency, and informal and formal relationships. The rationale behind the movement to the project-based DOPPO structure in 1980 was to stimulate entrepreneurial action and innovation. However, it should be noted that Mayekawa has recently announced that DOPPO units alone do not satisfy the needs of a growing and more complex global market. Consequently, DOPPO units are consolidated and reorganized based on industry sectors to meet the greater and deeper customer needs. The present analysis is limited to the DOPPO structure.

Data and data analysis

Data collected in collaboration with Ikujiro Nonaka and Emiko Tsuyuki consists of interviews, observations of Mayekawa operations and archival material. Most empirical data were collected through semi-structured interviews with 60 managers at Mayekawa between 2002 and 2009. The managers were working in the technical research centre (56 per cent), production (35 per cent), and other functions (9 per cent). Because interviewees can feel alienated and present themselves in a formal manner if unfamiliar language and complicated academic terms are used (Langdridge, 2004), the managers were asked open-ended questions about knowledge management processes at Mayekawa. Because Emiko Tsuyuki worked for Mayekawa for several years, we had relatively free access to internal documents. External documents, such as annual reports, web pages, and newspaper articles, were also analysed.

The study generated a large amount of data, largely in the form of transcribed interviews. The interview transcripts were analysed using the process of data reduction, display, conclusion drawing, and verification (Miles & Huberman, 1994). The initial categories were the DOPPO structure, shared HRM systems, small unit size, shared norms and visions, meetings, and shared operation standards. During the data display phase, the information was organized to draw conclusions. The regularities and patterns were used in the verification and conclusion drawing phase.

Knowledge governance at Mayekawa

The DOPPO structure

The DOPPO structure is based on self-organization, meaning that DOPPOs are in principle 'free' to arrange themselves based on environmental stimuli. The objective of the DOPPO structure is to empower employees, pushing decisions and actions to where relevant knowledge and information reside. To reach this aim, Mayekawa become almost entirely project-based and characterized by a substantial delegation of decision rights. The organizational structure is based on BLOCKs and independent, small companies called DOPPO. Consisting of several DOPPOs, BLOCKs are divided either functionally or regionally into technological development, manufacturing, energy management, food and meat, service industry, Western countries, Latin America and Asia. The Japanese market is divided into seven regional BLOCKs that consist of from five to ten DOPPOs. Basic research is conducted at the General Research Institute located close to headquarters. While each BLOCK has research units, they need to interact due to limited internal resources and technical competencies.

Within these BLOCKs, approximately 100 legally and financially independent DOPPOs operate with their own accounting statements. The word (独法 or DOPPO), not used in colloquial Japanese, consists two Kanji characters: (独 or DO means independent and 法 or HO/PPO) means law/method. While financially independent, DOPPOs' prosperity and survival depends on their existence as integrated parts of Mayekawa. In principle, all entities can draw on each other's resources based on customer needs. New DOPPOs are also established based on customer needs. One manager explained: 'When we find a potential market, we create a suitable DOPPO unit'. Projects usually evolve into new DOPPO and managers collaborate to staff new DOPPOs. As explained by another manager: 'Two relevant leaders start to discuss with one another. I don't know which starts out first, but anyway, one would tell the plan and ask the other to give appropriate people to compose a team'. Although employees identify with their DOPPOs, they share similar corporate values, vision, and beliefs. In this sense, Mayekawa exists as a collective entity.

In the DOPPO structure, inter-unit interactions are initiated mainly by projects, each often representing a custom-made product or system for a single customer. Project teams can arise anywhere within the organization, and project members can be drawn from several DOPPOs to combine skills and competencies necessary to provide the needed depth and spread of knowledge and experience for meeting complex project requirements. Projects link individual and collective knowledge. It is in these collaborative projects where the greatest interaction, learning and knowledge diffusion takes place. In order to execute the project successfully, it is imperative that the person who initiates the project (often a DOPPO leader) is able to identify either where the needed knowledge resources are located or the person who knows the location of the needed resources. Consequently, the DOPPO structure acts like organizational transactive memory systems in which employees in interdependent teams are aware 'who knows what' and 'who knows who', and able to use one another as external cognitive aids (Peltokorpi, 2012).

Small unit size

The small DOPPO size increases interdependency, specialization, and flexibility. Each DOPPO has on the average 15 employees. In principle, each DOPPO has responsibility for its own management and has its own consulting, marketing, sales, design, maintenance, general affairs, and accounting functions. Due to the limited number of employees within DOPPOs, each employee can be in charge of several work roles and functions. As DOPPOs grow, they break down into smaller entities. A manager explained: 'Big DOPPOs split into smaller ones as time passed. It happened naturally, not on purpose'. From an economic point of view, the small unit size creates costs in the form of redundancy and replication. While the combination of some functions could be economically rational, interviews show that the majority of managers believe that the small DOPPO size increases individual responsibility and enables a fast response to external stimuli. As reasoned by a manager: 'One of the best points of this system is that we can carry out our jobs very quickly. We can take quick actions and reactions. We can conduct business based on our own judgment and be responsible for everyday matters'.

The small DOPPO size naturally increases interdependencies among DOPPOs. For example, sales DOPPOs have to interact with technical DOPPOs to make product modifications and technical DOPPOs have to work with each other to combine complementary technologies. The interviews show that the more connections among DOPPO take place, the more DOPPOS became interdependent of one another. The need for inter-unit cooperation was described by a DOPPO leader: 'When you become a leader you realize the limitations of your DOPPO and start thinking about which other DOPPO(s) can complement your capabilities and try to cooperate to achieve your objectives'. Another manager explained: 'If a leader is searching for new employees, the others can suggest sending their members for some amount of money. Then they talk matters like how many days or how many people. It is very business-like'. At the individual level, small unit size encourages the formation of complementary skills and competencies, reflection, dialogues, and experimentation. At the DOPPO level, complementary competences and regional proximity further increase interaction. In some cases, cooperation has led to very strong interdependencies, as some DOPPOs share office space and work closely together.

Small DOPPO size and financial independence also facilitates close and synergistic customer interaction, especially during periods of market instability. For example, the Meat Processing System Engineering Division's survival strategy was based on close interactions with local meat centres in 2001. In Japan and other developed countries, major challenges for the food industry were to shoulder high labour costs and high sanitation requirements. Sales engineers persuaded several customers to engage in co-evolutionary development as new product innovations would help the customers to streamline their operations, and increased sales would enable the division to survive. A project team was formed and numerous meetings were held in the customers' facilities to find a way to provide benefits to both partners. The interactions enabled Mayekawa to create a total unmanned food processing and supply system based on increased automation. This example illustrates that instead of surviving as a profit-losing entity in the DOPPO system, financial independence forces small DOPPOs to innovate and survive through intense customer interaction.

Consensus-based hierarchy

The movement to the DOPPO structure in the 1980s was accompanied by a shift from top-down authority to a consensus-based hierarchy. The limited intervention capacity of Mayekawa headquarters is shown in its functions and responsibilities. Having only 70 employees, the main roles of the headquarters are to support synergies among the BLOCKs and DOPPOs, provide them with information and financial goals, as well as to articulate and instil the organizational philosophy and strategy. Taking into account the large number of entities, top executives are able to exert little direct influence over activities in BLOCKs and DOPPOs. The interviews also show that the former company president, Masao Mayekawa sought to provide advice more than to intervene in DOPPO processes. As explained by one manager: 'He [Masao Mayekawa] did not give specific orders or directions, but he gave us advice, such as "Why don't you ask Mr X of city Y? Maybe he could give you a good idea." We tried to handle problematic matters by ourselves'. The company president and Headquarters have not created any formal hierarchical distinction between DOPPOs and BLOCKs. These differences are created and recreated through social interactions and economic denominators.

The knowledge governance through consensus-based hierarchy requires frequent formal and informal social interactions at all organizational levels. For example, frequently occurring DOPPO and BLOCK level meetings serve as mechanisms to create, share and internalize a shared vision, discover market opportunities and combine resources. In addition to frequent meetings held at the DOPPO level, there are dozens of corporate planning meetings every year in which DOPPO leaders and top managers share their ideas about market changes. A manager explained: 'We talk about profits and losses, the business situation, market conditions, and so on [in BLOCK level meetings]'. Because the focus in these meetings is placed on customers and challenges in existing projects, the opinions of DOPPO leaders are valued. Open interaction increases system transparency. Individuals who do not contribute actively and share their experiences with others tend to develop a bad reputation and fail to secure resources from other entities in Mayekawa. Consequently, clan-based control is used to increase collaboration and decrease free-riding at Mayekawa.

Projects and resource transfer are decided in monthly steering committee meetings. In the meetings, DOPPO leaders identify customer needs and market trends, and 'sell' their ideas in a market-like fashion to start projects. As explained by one manager: 'DOPPO leaders get together and discuss new attractive business markets. In the meeting, they analyse the character of the market and try to find suitable partners'. In order to get started, projects need to be feasible and attractive to other DOPPOs. The final decision of new projects and resource transfer is made in the feasibility study meeting with the lead feasibility manager and people from the headquarters. As the combination of resources is based on a project's feasibility, overall operations are based on economic efficiency. In collaborative projects, requiring large amounts of resources and long-term commitment, DOPPO leaders consult with the headquarters and the company president. In collaborative projects, participating DOPPOs share profits. In large-scale collaborative projects, DOPPO leaders can also ask BLOCK leaders to help to coordinate activities. Headquarters further encourage DOPPOs to engage in long-term strategically important projects by taking part of the financial responsibility.

Because a weak point of the DOPPO structure is the emphasis placed on short-term gains at the DOPPO level, a headquarters orchestrated vision is used to govern operations by creating a sense of shared destiny and increasing unit interactions. Instead of trying to force visions through authority, visions at Mayekawa are co-created, discussed, and approved throughout the organization. The process through which implicit meanings are collectively converted to a shared corporate vision is called 'approaching the whole by working together'. In the process, employees at each DOPPO first summarize an annual business plan on a single sheet of paper. These plans are then distributed at a meeting where representatives of related DOPPO gather. They list the ideas they believe to exist behind the written words on additional sheets of paper. These ideas are then discussed and combined to create a shared vision for Mayekawa. Because basically all employees engage in the vision creation, the process increases their ownership and internalization of the corporate vision.

Shared HRM practices

Mayekawa has a number of shared HRM practices that guide knowledge processes. Some of the most important ones are skill development and knowledge transfer through on-the-job training (OJT) and job rotation, flexible movement of labour through standardized compensation systems and bottom-up promotion. Work-related skills are generated through OJT. Similar to many other Japanese companies, most employees at Mayekawa are recruited directly from schools. In entry-level recruiting, an emphasis is placed on the 'right' attitudes and values rather than on functional skills and competencies. The needed skills and competencies are developed internally. All entry-level recruits first go through two weeks of basic training, after which they receive three months of OJT. During the frequent *sempai* (senior) – *kohai* (junior) interactions, new employees learn the skills and knowledge needed in their tasks and internalize the corporate culture and norms. The emphasis paid on these practices are reflected in two managers' comments: 'It is considered very important and effective to learn by watching how experienced employees are working' and 'People don't get working skills by reading books. The only way is to work in the field, nothing else'.

The flexible movement of labour enables projects to be staffed with employees with the right skills. This increases the tasks, expertise and people alignment in projects. Because skillful employees are recognized as experts and in demand in projects, they are often motivated to develop their skills and competencies. While each employee is a member of a certain DOPPO, he or she is able to work semi-permanently in other DOPPOs or project teams. In either case, a standardized compensation system facilitates labour movement. The variable component in compensation is kept low to prevent large wage differences among employees across projects. This flexible mobility of labour helps employees to establish social networks, a broad awareness of company operations, awareness 'who knows what', and develop their skills and competencies. The ability of DOPPO leaders to jointly decide on the movement of labour guarantees that important employees are not pulled out of projects before their completion. This also ensures that employees do not join more projects than their time resources allow for, creating problems of coordinating schedules and work hours. While often initiated by DOPPO leaders, BLOCK leaders give final approval to all personnel transfers. A manager explained: 'Rather than initiating personnel movement, BLOCK leaders often accept them or sometimes give them back for further consideration'. This is used to ensure that the right people are sent to the right projects.

The standardized promotion system, in turn, ensures that skills and competences are more strongly linked with the formal position at Mayekawa. Power bases are earned, not given, and are based on skills and competencies, initiative and the capability to employ oneself and others. For example, BLOCK leaders are selected by DOPPOs based on their internal and external networks, functional knowledge, and personal characteristics. Sometimes, the same person can simultaneously be a DOPPO and a BLOCK leader. In principle, all managers possess the characteristics valued in Mayekawa. Taking into account the importance placed on customer interactions, an ideal manager was described in the interviews as having the ability to co-create new markets with customers. In other words, to make sure that DOPPOs have financially sound operations. Due to the importance placed on internal networks and knowing who knows what, Mayekawa relies on entry-level recruitment and internal promotion. As explained by a manager: 'When I look back, I don't know any DOPPO leaders who were employed mid-career'. Similar to other Japanese manufacturing organizations, the salary differences between employees and managers are rather small.

Shared performance standards and output control

Shared performance standards and output control reduce operational inconsistency and optimize inter-unit interactions. Shared performance standards, or what employees in Mayekawa call the 'induced fit', are created partly through collective evaluations and monitoring. All employees, DOPPOs and BLOCKs are evaluated periodically by a five-point grading system. Each employee is evaluated based on his or her individual ability, and communication and teamwork skills by DOPPO leaders. The evaluation system increases collaboration, as explained by a manager: 'to get your grade better, you need to work together with people around you'. Each DOPPO, in turn, is evaluated based on its profit and innovativeness by DOPPOs familiar with the business of the reviewed DOPPO. This increases inter-unit interactions because DOPPOs need to be familiar with one another's operations. As reasoned by a manager: 'They have to know what and how other units are doing. Without knowing, how they could grade each other?' The evaluation by profits keeps DOPPOs also focused and prevents them from stretching too far from their focal expertise area. A manager explained: 'One thing that we had to keep in mind that the project shouldn't stretch out like amoeba'. In addition, each BLOCK is evaluated by other BLOCKs based on their overall performance. The evaluation of research DOPPOs is based on their skills, knowledge and supporting research by related DOPPOs.

Standard operating procedures are also used to create shared performance standards and performance expectations at all organizational levels. In addition to means to convince external customers, the International Organization for Standardization (ISO) programs as shared quality standards are used to facilitate evaluation and interaction among the entities within and beyond the organizational boundaries. For example, Mayekawa obtained the ISO 9001 certification (international standard for quality management system) in 1994 and ISO 14001 certification (international standard for environmental management system) in 1996. These shared standards were initiated by the headquarters to exert control, maintain the Mayekawa group reputation and decrease coordination problems and other inefficiencies. The interviewees acknowledged that incompatible operational standards could dampen exploration and experimentation of new product opportunities. In addition to providing clear evaluation criteria and the basis for collective monitoring, these shared standards force DOPPOs and BLOCKs to benchmark their processes and performance. ISO guidelines create pressure for quality improvements especially for DOPPOs that are lagging behind.

Shared performance measures and output control are used to create the collective awareness that all entities at Mayekawa can exist only as an integrated part of the whole. Efficient interactions are possible only when all employees share the corporate philosophy and believe that they are an integral part of the DOPPO, and that each DOPPO is a constituent of Mayekawa. In order to be an integrated part of the Mayekawa Group, employees have to understand the importance of maintaining a balance between individual and collective needs and responsibilities. These tensions between autonomy and interdependence are captured in President Mayekawa's statements: 'realization of society with no competition' and 'doing business within one's territory'. Furthermore, a manager explained that 'the owner reminded us that our vision, our primary purpose should stand solid. Otherwise, we would not bind together as a team, and would eventually fall apart. Then, all our efforts would end up being a waste'. Emphasizing the importance of coexistence, another manager reasoned: 'We have to support each other to make the whole Mayekawa profitable'. While existing as integrated parts of the whole, all units are also responsible for their own operations. Because each DOPPO has responsibility for its own management and finances with the goal of responding to the needs of a given region, DOPPO operations are differentiated based on customer needs.

Discussion

The integration of the knowledge governance and KM literature and Mayekawa case were used in this chapter to demonstrate that both soft (e.g., communication, trust, management styles, and organizational culture) and hard (e.g., directives and rewards) dimensions are equally important used to govern knowledge processes in PBOs. Consequently, organizations can be understood as both 'creators of positive' through soft governance and 'avoiders of negative' through hard governance. In PBOs, such as Mayekawa, it is thus important for top managers to create and implement a coherent set of governance mechanisms that create a balance between control and autonomy, and to sustain that balance. In order for the Mayekawa's DOPPO structure to function efficiently, top managers work in close and frequent interaction with all organizational entities to create and maintain a corporate culture that is open, customer-oriented, innovation-oriented and performance-oriented.

The Mayekawa case also shows how a consensus-based hierarchy is used to create a shared direction and mind-set among the interdependent employees and units. Collaborative decision-making processes in inter-unit meetings functions as a coordination mode based on both persuasion and monitoring. Although all employees in principle are involved in the vision creation, top management orchestrates the articulation of visions. Instead of imposing visions and changes through authority, they are collectively created, installed and reformed through persuasion and dialogues. In PBOs like Mayekawa, there is high need for trust and an emphasis on the creation of a shared organizational mission. In inter-unit meetings, the bottom-up initiatives are taken into account, which facilitates the acceptance and internalization of shared visions. The meetings are used as institutionalized methods to internalize and develop shared norms. For example, DOPPO leaders learn what qualifications need to be taken into account when they sell projects in the steering meetings. In these meetings, DOPPO leaders act as 'knowledge brokers' integrating dispersed knowledge from all parts of the organization. They disseminate norms and visions in their respective units through interactions. Shared norms, values and knowledge in use, evolving through social interactions, are stored in the operating routines and in the networks of human relations.

While holding meetings is costly and the over-reliance on lateral interactions may delay decision-making, the managers interviewed were convinced that the benefits are greater than the associated costs. At the project level, brainstorming sessions, project reviews, ad hoc meetings, and so on, help employees to articulate and share knowledge systematically. These collective processes increase employee ownership to decisions made and increase their intrinsic motivation to contribute to organizational knowledge processes. Inter-unit meetings help to transform divergent interests into shared cognition and self-corrections. In meetings, employees acquire knowledge of task-related and organizational activities and learn how to interact in problem-solving processes, thereby internalizing and developing shared norms. These shared experiences are valuable because they result in the accumulation of a stock of collective knowledge, much of it tacit, helping to improve work processes and organization-wide performance. In addition, repeated interactions increase knowledge sharing and reduce the need for knowledge codification. Instead of spending time on writing formal reports, employees were explained to favour a more swift exchange of knowledge in meetings. From the top management point of view, an increased frequency of communication through lateral channels moves part of governance to lower levels. In summary, the findings suggest that intra- and intergroup meetings are integral to govern knowledge processes in PBOs.

The case also importantly helps to demonstrate that knowledge governance at Mayekawa consists of hard dimensions. Considering the large number of DOPPOs at Mayekawa, the shared performance measures and output control are important in creating transparent, unified standards and for measuring unit performance. Instead of hierarchical appraisal, there are open and visible peer review processes at all levels of the organization. In addition to reducing uncertainty caused by the lack of direct monitoring, the usage of transparent and shared evaluation criteria decreases possible conflicts created by system ambiguity. Standardized HRM processes facilitate learning, the combination and blending of specific skills, and the movement of labour. The work in various projects in the DOPPO structure enables employees to enlarge their interpersonal network, share ideas with others, gain responsibility and visibility, and utilize their interpersonal skills and general managerial competencies to a greater degree than in more hierarchically structured companies. The restricted size of DOPPO forces individuals from different units and projects to maintain close contact with others whose support they must rely on for the project's success as well as to start new projects. Mayekawa has developed project approval techniques to ensure that the right projects are started and the right mix of skills is available in projects to support the development and launch of innovative products.

Finally, the literature review and the case illustrate that organizations are able to use a mixture of governance mechanisms to manage knowledge processes. In the case of Mayekawa, knowledge is based more on soft rather than hard dimensions. Instead of relying on excessive measurement and seeking to codify knowledge, knowledge at Mayekawa is closely tied to an employee who developed it and is shared mainly through direct interpersonal contacts. The low reliance on hard governance dimensions at Mayekawa can be attributed partly to the 'clan-type' control in Japanese organizations (Ouchi, 1980). Based on Ouchi (1980), the Japanese model of employment relations – including long-term employment, non-specialized roles and career paths, implicit and internalized control mechanisms – provides the basis for the creation of informal control systems that rely on the socialization of employees and their internalization of company norms and values. The strong organizational culture provides an environment free from ambiguity and uncertainty, as long as all employees internalize norms and values grounded in the organizational ideology. Occasionally, social control can be considerable to ensure that employees internalize their roles. At Mayekawa, corporate values and norms make entrepreneurial activity and knowledge generation both a possibility and a duty for individual employees. It should be noted that over-reliance on shared norms can lead to normative fixation and group-think, which are detrimental rather than conducive to knowledge creation (Grandori, 2001).

Limitations and suggestions for future research

The case study has some limitations that should be taken into account in future research. First, the qualitative methodology used cannot establish causal claims of knowledge governance. Clearly, the present study, as well as the KM and knowledge governance literature would benefit from quantitative analyses. Further, while case studies provide important insights, they do not always generalize to population phenomena. Because a set of shared beliefs, language, and agreed-upon behaviour constitutes an important part of governance and coordination, the DOPPO-like forms can be most suitable to organizations with a homogeneous labour force. In particular, scholars have pointed out that governance in Japanese organizations is based on clan-type control (Ouchi, 1980) and that Japanese and Western organizations differ in the coordination of knowledge creation through organizational forms (Hedlund & Nonaka, 1993). However, I believe that similar effects can also be found in other national settings and hope that the proposed governance mechanisms and findings promote more research on knowledge governance in PBOs. In any case, more research is needed to understand governance of knowledge processes in PBOs. The future research could compare governance mechanisms in different PBOs, such as Danish Oticon (Foss, 2003) and Brazilian Semco (Killian, Perez, & Siehl, 1998).

Conclusion

By integrating the literature on knowledge governance and KM and through a qualitative case study, this chapter shows that knowledge governance, consisting of soft and hard dimensions, facilitate knowledge processes in PBOs. These dimensions should be used simultaneously to create an optimal balance of control and trust, efficiency and innovation, and intrinsic and extrinsic motivation. While soft dimensions tend to increase motivation, trust and shared norms and vision, hard dimensions promote transparency and collective monitoring. The shared corporate identity and project-based organizational structure, where entities exist in the long-run only as integrated parts of an interdependent whole, ensure a balancing between self and whole at the individual, project and organizational levels, and that interdependences develop beyond arms-length transactions.

References

Adler, P. S. (2001). Market, hierarchy, and trust: the knowledge economy and the future of capitalism. *Organization Science*. 12 (2), 215–234.

Child, J., & Rodrigues, S. B. (2003). Corporate governance and new organizational forms: issues of double and multiple agency. *Journal of Management and Governance*. 7, 337–360.

Deci, E. L. (1972). Intrinsic motivation, extrinsic reinforcement, and inequality. *Journal* of Personality and Social Psychology. 22, 113–120.

Fojt, M. (1996). Managing change in the work place. *Management Decision*. 34 (5): 1–68.
Foss, N. (2009). Alternative research strategies in the knowledge movement: from macro bias to micro-foundations and multi-level explanation. *European Management Review*. 6, 16–28.
Foss, N. (2007). The emerging knowledge governance approach: challenges and characteristics. *Organization*. 14 (1), 29–52.
Foss, N. (2003). Selective intervention and internal hybrids: interpreting and learning from the rise and decline of the oticon spaghetti organization. *Organization Science*. 14: 331–349.
Foss, N., Husted, K., & Michailova, S. (2010). Governing knowledge sharing in organizations: levels of analysis, governance mechanisms, and research directions. *Journal of Management Studies*. 47 (3), 455–482.
Frost, J., Osterloh, M., & Weibel, A. (2010). Governing knowledge work: transactional and transformational solutions, *Organizational Dynamics*. 39 (2), 126–136.
Geertz, C. (1973). *The Interpretation of Cultures*. Basic: New York.
Ghoshal, S., & Moran, R. (1996). Bad for practice: a critique of transaction cost theory. Academy of Management Review. 21 (1), 13–47.
Grandori, A. (1997). Governance structures, coordination mechanisms and cognitive models. Journal of Management and Governance. 1, 29–47.
Grandori, A. (2001). Neither hierarchy nor identity: knowledge governance mechanisms and the theory of the firm. *Journal of Management and Governance*. 5, 381–399.
Grant, R. (1996). Toward a knowledge-based theory of the firm. *Strategic Management Journal*. 17, 109–122.
Hansen, M.T., Norhia, N., & Tierney T. (1999). What's your strategy for managing knowledge? *Harvard Business Review*. 77 (2), 106–116.
Hayek, F. (1945). *Individualism and Economic Order*. Chicago: University of Chicago Press.
Hedlund, G., & Nonaka, I. (1993). Models of knowledge management in the West and Japan. In P. Lorange, B. Chakravarthy, J. Roos, & A Van de Ven (eds) *Implementing Strategic Processes: Change, Learning, and Cooperation* (pp. 117–144). Oxford: Blackwell.
Henrie, M., & Sousa-Poza, A. (2005). Project management: a cultural literature review. Project Management Journal. 36 (2), 5–14.
Hobday, M. (2000). The project-based organization: an ideal form for managing complex products and systems? *Research Policy*. 29, 871–893.
Hodgson, G. M. (2012). The mirage of microfoundations. *Journal of Management Studies*. 49 (8), 1389–1394.
Hodgson, G. M. (2007). Institutions and individuals: interaction and evolution. Organization Studies. 28 (1), 95–116.
Killian, K., Perez, F., & Siehl, C. (1998). Richardo Selmer and Semco S.A. *Thunderbird Case* #A15–98–0024.
Kogut, B., & Zander, U. (1992). Knowledge of the firm, combinative capabilities, and the replication of technology. *Organization Science*. 3, 383–397.
Langdridge, D. (2004). Introduction to Research Methods and Data Analysis in *Psychology*. Prentice-Hall: Harlow.
Lantane, B., Williams, K., & Harkins, S. (1979). Many hands make light the work: the causes and consequences of social loafing. *Journal of Personality and Social Psychology. 37*, 822–832.
Miles, M. B. (1979). Qualitative data as an attractive nuisance: the problem of analysis. Administrative Science Quarterly. 24, 590–601.

Miles, M. B., & Huberman, A. M. (1994). *Qualitative Data Analysis*. Sage: London.
Nahapiet, J., & Ghoshal. S. (1998). Social capital, intellectual capital, and the organizational advantage. *Academy of Management Review*. 23 (2), 242–266.
Nickerson, J. A., & Zenger, T. R. (2004). A knowledge-based theory of the firm: the problem- solving perspective. *Organization Science*. 15 (6), 617–632.
Nonaka, I. (1994). A dynamic theory of organizational knowledge creation. Organization Science. 5 (1) 14–37.
Nonaka, I., & Peltokorpi, V. (2006). Objectivity and subjectivity in knowledge management: a review of 20 top articles. *Knowledge and Process Management*. 13 (2), 73–82.
Osterloh, M., & Frey, B. (2000). Motivation, knowledge transfer and organizational form. *Organization Science*. 11, 538–550.
Ouchi, W.G. (1980). Markets, bureaucracies, and clans. *Administrative Science Quarterly*. 25, 120–142.
Peltokorpi, V. (2012). Organizational transactive memory systems: review and extension. *European Psychologist*. 17 (1), 11–20.
Peltokorpi, V., Nonaka, I., & Kodama, M. (2007). NTT DoCoMo's launch of i-mode in the Japanese mobile phone market: a knowledge creation perspective. *Journal of Management Studies*. 44 (1), 50–72.
Prencipe, A., & Tell, F. (2001). Inter-project learning: processes and outcomes of knowledge codification in project-based firms. *Research Policy*. 30, 1373–1394.
Spender, J-C. (1996). Making knowledge as the basis of a dynamic theory of the firm. Strategic Management Journal. 17, 45–62.
Sydow, J., Lindqvist, L., & DeFillippi, R. (2004). Project-based organizations, embeddedness, and repositories of knowledge: editorial. *Organization Studies*. 25(9): 1475–1489.
Tsoukas, H. (1996). The firm as a distributed knowledge system: a constructionist approach. Strategic Management Journal. 17, 11–25.
Van Maanen, J. (1979). Reclaiming qualitative methods for organizing research: a preface. Administrative Science Quarterly. 24, 520–526.
Williamson, O. E. (1985). *The Economic Institutions and Capitalism*. New York: Free Press.
Yin, R. (1994). *Case study research: Design and Methods* (2nd ed.). Beverly Hills, CA: Sage.

16

Knowledge-Based Marketing: Fostering Innovation through Marketing Knowledge Co-Creation

Florian Kohlbacher

Introduction

'In an economy where the only certainty is uncertainty, the one sure source of lasting competitive advantage is knowledge' (Nonaka, 1991, p. 96). This statement was the starting point of Ikujiro Nonaka's seminal article on the knowledge-creating company in 1991. Dealing with knowledge creation, transfer and exploitation will be more and more critical to the survival and success of corporations, and of societies (Hedlund & Nonaka, 1993). This ever increasing importance of knowledge for organizations has raised – and actually still raises – 'questions about how organizations process knowledge and, more importantly, how they create new knowledge' (Nonaka, 1994, p. 14). Indeed, as Ichijo and Nonaka (2006, p. 3) note, 'the success of a company in the twenty-first century will be determined by the extent to which its leaders can develop intellectual capital through knowledge creation and knowledge-sharing on a global basis' as knowledge constitutes a competitive advantage in this age.

What followed was a knowledge and knowledge management boom. As a matter of fact, knowledge management has not only become a ubiquitous phenomenon both in the academic as well as in the corporate world, but has also turned into one of the most prominent and widely discussed management concepts of the post-modern era. Publications on knowledge management are legion, and business practitioners do not fail to stress its importance for the competitiveness of their corporations. Prusak (2001, p. 1002) – who sees the year 1993 as the beginning of knowledge management – argues that knowledge management is 'a practitioner-based, substantive response to real social and economic trends', with the three most important ones being globalization, ubiquitous computing, and the knowledge-centric view of the firm. Even though knowledge management has also been analyzed and discussed as a management fad and within the framework of management fashion models (cf. e.g., Scarbrough, Robertson, & Swan, 2005; Scarbrough & Swan, 2001; Skyrme, 1998) to explain its diffusion and 'strong rhetorical appeal' (Alvesson, Kärreman, & Swan, 2002, p. 282), no management scholar or practitioner is likely to disagree with Newell and fellow researchers' (2002, p. 2) pronouncement to the effect that '[m]anaging knowledge and knowledge workers is arguably the single most important challenge being faced by many kinds of organizations across both the private and public sectors in the years to come'. Indeed, it is now widely recognized that the effective management of knowledge assets is a key requirement for securing competitive advantage in the knowledge economy (Boisot, 1998).

Ikujiro Nonaka's publications (e.g., Nonaka, 1991, 1994, 2005; Nonaka & Takeuchi, 1995; Nonaka, Toyama, & Hirata, 2008) have drawn the attention to Japanese firms as – particularly effective – knowledge-creating companies, a feature that supposedly has helped them to create the dynamics of innovation and to become world leaders in the automotive and electronics industries, among others, in the 1980s and the beginning of the 1990s. The difference, it was argued, between Japanese and Western firms, lies in the focus on tacit knowledge of the former and explicit knowledge of the latter (& Nonaka, 1993; Nonaka & Takeuchi, 1995; Nonaka, von Krogh, & Voelpel, 2006; Takeuchi & Nonaka, 2000), and this Japanese firms' particular ability for knowledge creation and harnessing tacit knowledge has also been received and credited by Western scholars (e.g., Baumard, 1999; Cohen, 1998; Davenport & Prusak, 2000; Holden, 2002; Leonard, 1998).

In recent years, knowledge management has also become a dominant area in strategic management and has increasingly been adapted to the global context. Especially the capability of multinational corporations (MNCs) to create and efficiently transfer and combine knowledge from different locations around the world is becoming more and more important as a determinant of competitive advantage and has become critical to their success and survival (cf. e.g., Asakawa & Lehrer, 2003; Bartlett & Ghoshal, 2002; Doz, Santos, & Williamson, 2001; Gupta & Govindarajan, 2000; Kohlbacher, 2007). However, despite the strong interest in and the large number of publications on the issue of knowledge flows within MNCs, the literature is 'still in the early stages of understanding the central aspects, mechanisms, and contextual factors in the process of managing knowledge in MNCs' (Foss & Pedersen, 2004, p. 342). In fact, 'rather little is known about the determinants of intra-MNC knowledge flows in spite of their obvious importance to theoretical arguments about the MNC' (Foss & Pedersen, 2002, p. 52). So far, the extant literature has mainly focused on the issues of transferring knowledge between different units in MNCs – i.e., the knowledge flows within MNCs – and factors influencing it (e.g., Foss & Pedersen, 2002; Gupta & Govindarajan, 2000; Martin & Salomon, 2003; Mudambi, 2002). However, research on the process of knowledge creation within MNCs is still scarce, despite the crucial importance of the cross-border synergistic process of joint knowledge creation, i.e., 'global knowledge creation' (Nonaka, 1990).

Despite the fact that the theory of organizational knowledge creation has been applied to numerous fields (cf. e.g., Nonaka, von Krogh, & Voelpel, 2006), this does not seem to be the case for marketing and marketing research. Indeed, even though 'marketing functions lend themselves particularly well for an investigation of knowledge transfer within MNCs', 'there is a dearth of research on knowledge transfer in the field of marketing' and 'it is high time to include marketing into the research agenda for knowledge management and to overcome the paradox that marketing functions are neglected in the discussion on knowledge transfer' (Schlegelmilch & Chini, 2003, pp. 220–221, 226). Yet, in an increasingly global business environment, the creation and transfer of marketing knowledge and intra-firm collaboration through knowledge-based approaches to marketing will become more and more crucial as a determinant for corporate competitive advantage and survival of firms (Kohlbacher, 2007).

Despite the obvious importance of knowledge to the marketing discipline, the marketing literature has struggled for more than 10 years to come to an understanding of the nature of marketing knowledge and there does not seem to be a common ground unifying scholars (Kohlbacher, Holden, Glisby, & Numic, 2007). Indeed, even though 'marketers have been using knowledge management long before this latter phrase began to be popularised in the management literature' (Chaston, 2004, pp. 22–23) there has to date been 'no clear statement about the forms that marketing knowledge can take, or its content' (Rossiter, 2001, p. 9) and Chaston's (2004) book on knowledge based marketing is one of the few works – if not the only one – that shows how knowledge can be utilized to underpin and enhance the marketing management function within organizations.

My work (Kohlbacher, 2007; Kohlbacher & Mukai, 2007; Kohlbacher & Kraehe, 2007; Kohlbacher, 2008a, 2008b; Ichijo & Kohlbacher, 2008; Kohlbacher, 2009a, 2009b; Wilhelm & Kohlbacher, 2011) has been inspired and influenced by the previously mentioned major themes of knowledge as an important source of competitive advantage, of managing knowledge, global aspects of managing knowledge and – most importantly – the role of knowledge and knowledge management in marketing management. Building from a comprehensive empirical study and the state-of-the-art literature in the field, I introduce and define the concept of knowledge-based marketing and propose a shift towards a new dominant logic – namely a knowledge-based one – for marketing (see also Kohlbacher, 2007; Kohlbacher, 2009a, 2009b).

Objective of the chapter

This chapter is essentially about knowledge and knowledge creation in a global context. Its aim is not only to illustrate, analyze and discuss knowledge-related processes in organizations but also to create new knowledge, i.e., amend and extend existing theory and even build new theory. Based on the assumption that marketing affairs are one of the most knowledge-intensive parts of a company, the focus lies on a particular type of knowledge, marketing knowledge, which has been widely neglected in past research. The objective of this research is to analyze the role of knowledge in marketing, and the way it is created and managed, and develop a conceptual framework and model of knowledge-based marketing.

Scholars and practitioners around the globe have identified the capability of multinational corporations (MNCs) to create and efficiently transfer and combine knowledge from different locations worldwide as an increasingly important determinant of competitive advantage, corporate success and survival (cf. e.g., Asakawa & Lehrer, 2003; Doz et al., 2001; Gupta & Govindarajan, 2000). However, even though 'marketing functions lend themselves particularly well for an investigation of knowledge transfer within MNCs', 'there is a dearth of research on knowledge transfer in the field of marketing' (Schlegelmilch & Chini, 2003, pp. 220–221). Yet, in an increasingly global business environment, the creation and transfer of marketing knowledge and intra-firm collaboration through knowledge-based approaches to marketing will become more and more crucial as a determinant for corporate competitive advantage and survival of firms. Based on a review and evaluation of the extant literature on knowledge management (KM), organizational learning and marketing, this chapter applies the concepts of KM and knowledge creation to marketing. Based on Nonaka's theory of organizational knowledge creation (e.g., Nonaka, 1994, 2005; Nonaka & Takeuchi, 1995; Nonaka et al., 2008), a conceptual framework of knowledge-based marketing is developed and the essential processes of marketing knowledge co-creation with the main actors in the business ecosystem of global firms – customers, suppliers, competitors, business partners – are analyzed. Traditional marketing approaches have focused overly on explicit knowledge and neglected the important role of tacit knowledge, specifically in international (cross-cultural) settings. This paper aims to adjust this imbalance in the extant literature, and – drawing on real-life examples of knowledge-based firms – makes a call for a new knowledge-based marketing paradigm, with knowledge and knowledge co-creation being the key to sustainable competitive advantage in the global knowledge economy. In proposing a shift towards a new dominant logic – namely a knowledge-based one – for international marketing, this paper extends the knowledge-based view of the firm and thus contributes both to the field of KM as well as to the field of (international) marketing. While opening up a new area of application for KM concepts and tools it also helps to close the disconcerting gap in the marketing literature pointed out by Schlegelmilch and Chini (2003) previously mentioned, and thus explores a 'new frontier of KM' (Desouza, 2005). Finally, this paper is meant to provide marketing scholars and practitioners with a conceptual framework for preparing marketing for the challenges of the knowledge economy of the twenty-first century and for analyzing and deploying knowledge and value co-creation through marketing activities.

Theoretical foundation: previous research

The overall theoretical framework of this paper is the knowledge-based view of the firm, which sees knowledge and competencies as decisive foundations for the performance and abilities of organizations (Foss, 2005; Grant, 2002; Nonaka & Toyama, 2005; Spender, 1996). Given this epistemological basis, this paper builds its theoretical foundation on two broad fields of research, namely (global) KM and (international) marketing. The main pillar for constructing a theory of knowledge-based marketing is Ikujiro Nonaka's theory of organizational knowledge creation (e.g., Nonaka, 1994, 2005; Nonaka & Takeuchi, 1995; Nonaka et al., 2008) and its focus on the process of knowledge creation and the importance of tacit knowledge. The KM aspects of the theoretical foundation are complemented by a review of the relevant literatures on communities of practice, global knowledge-based management – i.e., the creation, transfer and management of knowledge across borders/in an international context – and inter-organizational knowledge-based management. Subsequently, the paper reviews and summarizes the literature on marketing knowledge and the state-of-the-field in knowledge-based management and organizational learning in marketing (functions) and their building blocks.[1] Particularly relevant research streams in this context proved to be 1) 'market orientation' (e.g., Day, 1994; Deshpandé & Webster, 1989; Kohli & Jaworski, 1990; Narver & Slater, 1990), which frequently explicitly or implicitly refers to and/or draws from the organizational learning and learning organization literature and 2) relationship marketing (e.g., Grönroos, 1994; Gummesson, 2002; Tzokas & Saren, 2004).

The literature review revealed that – even though different streams of research have contributed to the field – all in all research on knowledge-based approaches to marketing is still rather in its infancy. However, according to Schlegelmilch and Chini (2003, p. 226) 'it is high time to include marketing into the research agenda for KM and to overcome the paradox that marketing functions are neglected in the discussion on knowledge transfer'. Despite the obvious importance of knowledge to the marketing discipline, the marketing literature has struggled for more than 10 years to come to an understanding of the nature of marketing knowledge and there does not seem to be a common ground unifying scholars. Indeed, all in all, it may not be outlandish to suggest that the marketing discipline is tying itself up in semantic knots while it struggles to create consensus on an agreed definition of the term marketing knowledge, its practical scope and supporting constructs (Kohlbacher, 2007; Kohlbacher et al., 2007).

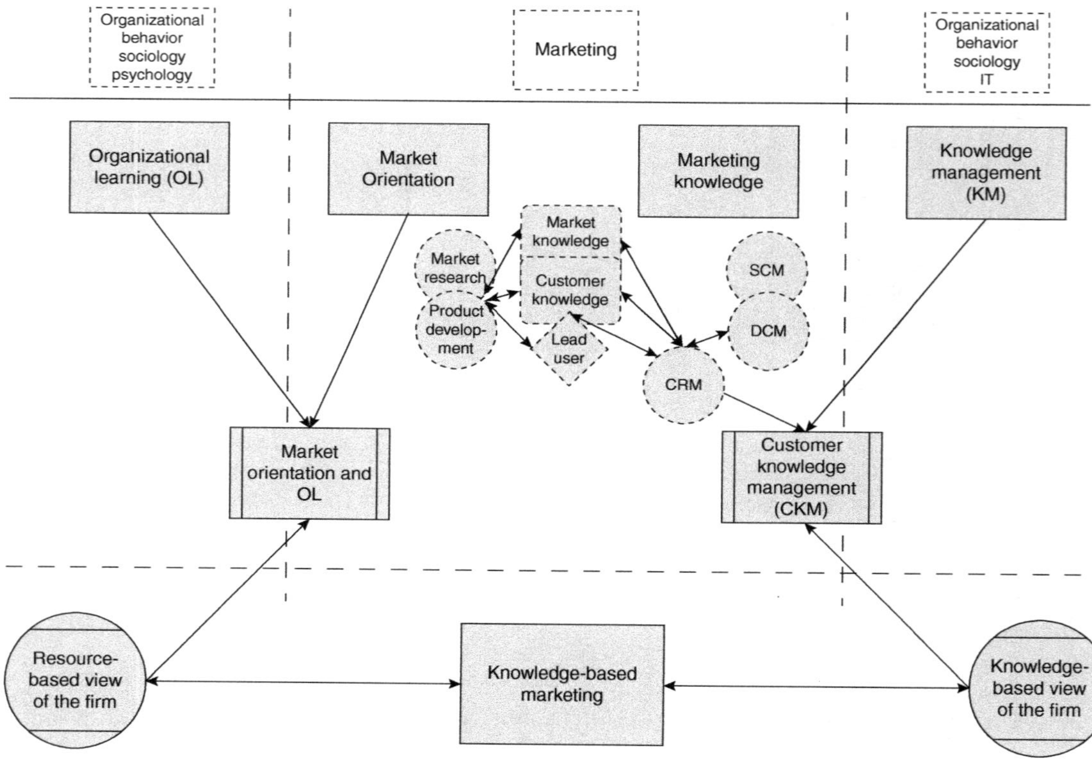

Figure 16.1 Related concepts and antecedents of knowledge-based marketing

Source: The author.

Finally, the literature reviews on market orientation and organizational learning, marketing knowledge and areas of marketing knowledge creation and application have shown that there are many research streams contributing to the field and that there many different angles, processes and functions from which one can take a knowledge-based view of marketing. However, most of the time, these streams are independent of each other and there is no comprehensive framework integrating the different approaches and areas of research. Figure 16.1 gives an overview of the related research streams, concepts and antecedents of a knowledge-based view of marketing and illustrates their theoretical/conceptual affiliations and inter-relations. It demonstrates how scattered and heterogeneous the state-of-the-field of knowledge-based marketing is and how many different streams of research have to be considered. The dashed line above knowledge-based marketing is meant to emphasize that although all of the preceding research streams and areas contribute, there is no theory that links and integrates the different approaches to and into knowledge-based marketing (see also Kohlbacher, 2007).

Last but not least, there is a good deal of hypothesizing about marketing as a knowledge-based activity, but a dearth of studies about how firms consciously develop and apply a knowledge-based approach. The literature is correspondingly short of case material and completely silent about the application of a knowledge-based approach to marketing as in explicitly international pace cross-cultural contexts.

Conceptual model of knowledge-based marketing

As the literature review revealed, the current marketing literature does not offer one satisfactory definition of marketing knowledge which is also amenable to the investigation of international marketing interactions. However, providing a clear definition of the term marketing knowledge is absolutely essential for the development of a knowledge-based theory of marketing and for any discussion of knowledge-based marketing. I am proposing the following definition of marketing knowledge:

> Marketing knowledge is all knowledge, both declarative as well as procedural, concerning marketing thinking and behavior in a corporation.

The previous definition includes both tacit as well as explicit knowledge about products, markets, customers, competitors, partners, marketing processes and marketing strategy. It includes also experiences of past marketing efforts such as new product introductions and so on as well as future expectations. This is obviously a very broad concept of marketing knowledge and a finer and narrower definition leads to each of the subunits of marketing knowledge, such as customer knowledge, competitor knowledge and so on.

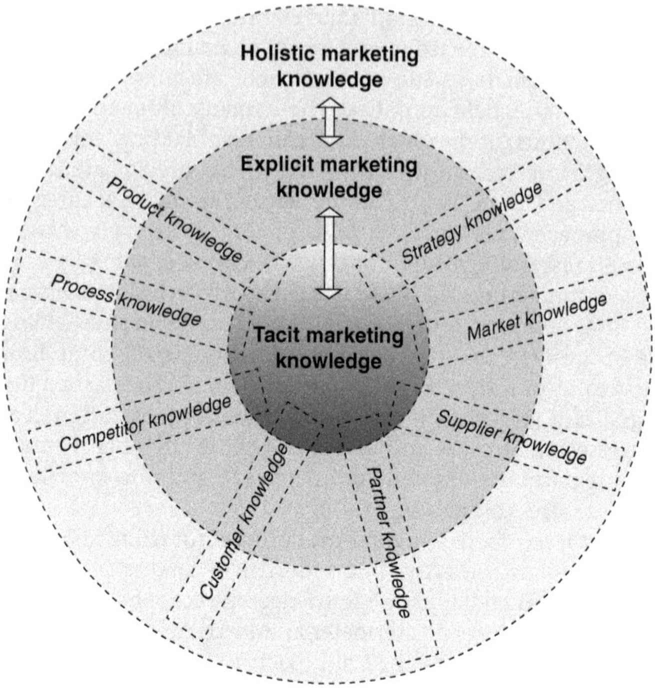

Figure 16.2 A holistic view of marketing knowledge
Source: The author.

Marketing knowledge itself is a holistic concept and has deliberately been defined in such a broad way.

Given the significance of tacit knowledge, it is important to note that the expression 'all knowledge' in the previous definition of marketing knowledge actually refers to a concept I would like to term 'holistic knowledge'. This 'holistic marketing knowledge' is a combination and synthesis of both tacit and explicit marketing knowledge (cf. Figure 16.2).

As Gummesson (2001, p. 29, added emphasis) notes, '[s]ervices and B-to-B (business-to-business) marketing, relationships, networks, quality, *knowledge management*, brand equity, green marketing, information technology and other developments have had some impact but have not made marketing theorists bake a cake according to a new recipe, just to add decorations on the glazing of the old cake'. This chapter is therefore an attempt to engage in the first steps of building a knowledge-based framework for marketing and build theory. I have obliged myself to use – or actually create – a new recipe but the challenge will be to successfully bake the new cake.

As a result, I developed the following definition of 'knowledge-based marketing':

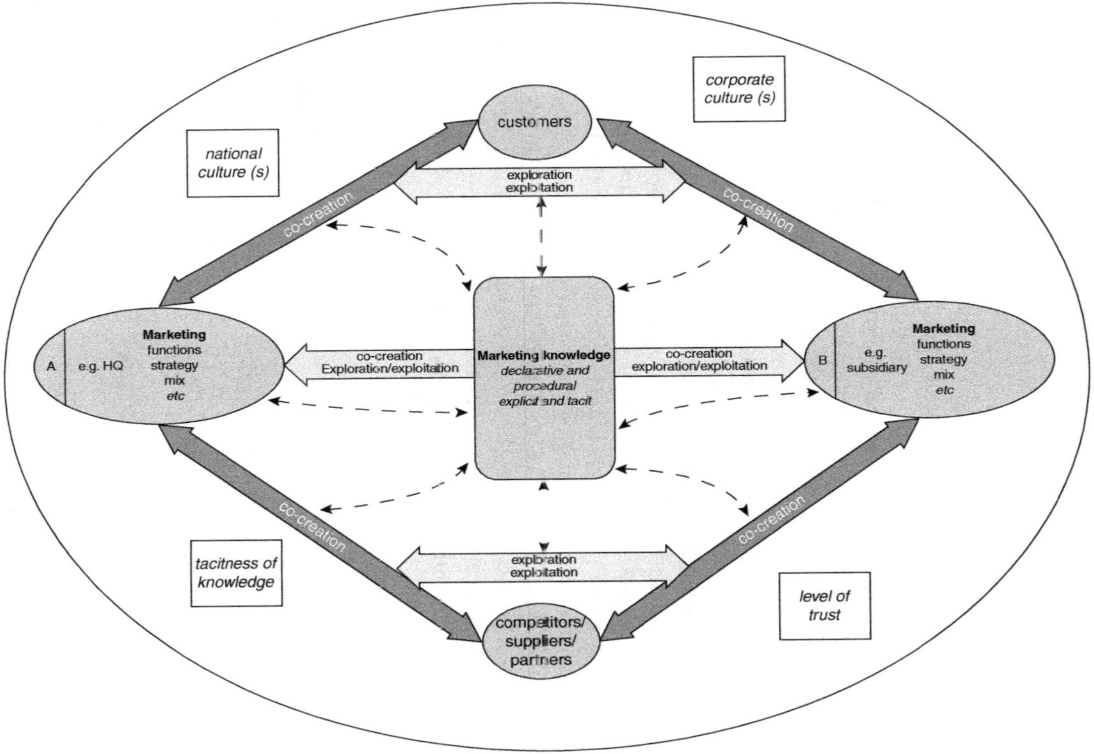

Figure 16.3 Knowledge-based marketing

Source: The author.

> Knowledge-based marketing is a KM approach to marketing that focuses both on the exploitation (sharing and application) and exploration (creation) as well as the co-creation of marketing knowledge from contexts, relations and interactions in order to gain and sustain competitive advantage.

Note that – even though the term is not mentioned in the definition – the (co-) creation of value is an essential prerequisite for gaining and sustaining competitive advantage. Often, the (co-) creation of knowledge goes hand in hand with the (co-) creation of value, but sometimes it can also be an antecedent. Following the previous definition of marketing knowledge, I stress that knowledge-based marketing involves stakeholders such as customers, competitors, suppliers, partners and so on, and is influenced by certain factors, such as national and corporate culture, tacitness of knowledge and the level of trust (Figure 16.3).

Firms generate, collect and analyze knowledge about customers, customers' needs, competitors, suppliers and so on. But the real challenge and source of essential knowledge for competitive advantage might be to go beyond knowledge creation and application as a unilateral concept. In fact, interactions and knowledge co-creation might become more and more crucial. Indeed, nowadays companies can hardly be viewed as single, independent and isolated beings any more, and business networks have become ubiquitous in our economy (e.g., Iansiti & Levien, 2004). Therefore, knowledge and value co-creation with customers – but also with suppliers and other business partners – has also received significant attention recently (e.g., Prahalad & Ramaswamy, 2004; Thomke & von Hippel, 2002, 2003). Indeed, as Nonaka (2007, p. xiv) puts is, '[f]irms and managers have to take the standpoint of

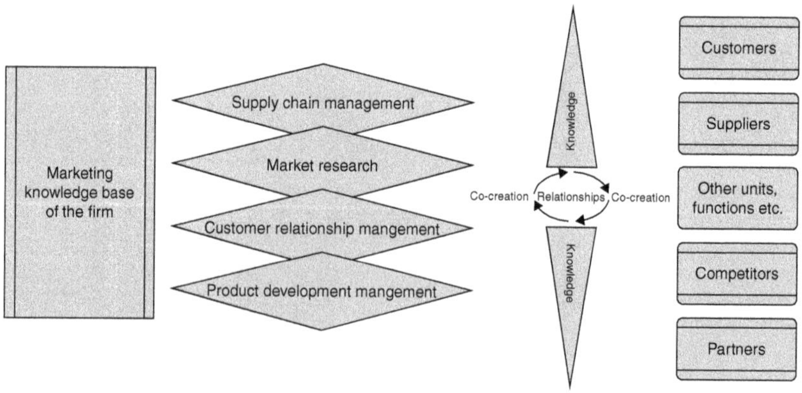

Figure 16.4 Knowledge-based marketing processes
Source: The author.

the customer, and collaborate with them and dwell in them to share and co-create tacit knowledge'.

Figure 16.4 illustrates these relationships and the knowledge-based marketing processes along the value chain and shows that a knowledge-based approach to marketing asks for the co-creation of knowledge – and subsequently the co-creation of value – with a variety of key players and actors in the business ecosystem as well as other units and functions within an MNC. These four marketing processes have been identified from the literature review, but they are mainly meant to represent certain key processes and I acknowledge that many more such processes exist and could be analyzed from a knowledge-based perspective.

Research methodology

Both the shortage of research on the organizational creation of marketing knowledge and the dearth of studies about how firms consciously develop and apply a knowledge-based approach as well as the corresponding shortage of case material have prompted the empirical research project.

This paper is the result of a continuous and reiterative research process over two and a half years (April 2004–October 2006). Literature review, empirical data collection, theoretical reasoning, paper writing and discussion with scholars and practitioners constantly alternated and overlapped in the process. As previously discussed, the literature review revealed there is no accepted theory of marketing knowledge and knowledge-based marketing. There being no theory to test, this particular contribution can do no more than attempt to generate theory from the explorative empirical study and the six case investigations that are introduced in this paper. Indeed, 'before a theory can be validated, it must be constructed' (Patton & Appelbaum, 2003, p. 65). I recognize the limitations of building theory from case studies, but take heart from Eisenhardt's (1989, p. 536) encouragement that breakthroughs can be possible if one proceeds as if there is 'a clean theoretical slate'. As I hope to show, the particular cases represent a 'real-life method of inquiry ... [which] ... may be a nouveau solution' (Patton & Appelbaum, 2003, p. 69). This paper is an attempt to break away from this rather tricky stranglehold and to attain 'a nouveau solution' for marketers who, like myself, are engaged in the quest of developing a knowledge-based concept of international marketing. Indeed, I conceive of this work as theory-building and theory-extending and therefore have chosen a qualitative research approach to explore my assumptions and examine new relationships, concepts, and operational definitions (e.g., Eisenhardt, 1989; Flyvbjerg, 2006a; Weick, 1996). According to Yin (2003b, p. 2) 'the distinctive need for case studies arises out of the desire to understand complex social phenomena' because 'the case study method allows investigators to retain the holistic and meaningful characteristics of real-life events', such as organizational and managerial processes. In fact, '[o]rganizations constitute an enormously complex arena for human behavior' (Dubin, 1982, p. 379) and case studies seem to be the preferred strategy when 'how' or 'why' questions are being posed when the investigator has little control over events, and when the focus is on a contemporary phenomenon within some real-life context (Yin, 2003b). In such a setting, case studies are explanatory ones, i.e., they present data on cause-effect relationships, explain how events happened and extend theoretical understandings (Yin, 2003b, 2003a) and make use of the 'power of example' (Flyvbjerg, 2006b).

To illustrate and explain my concept of knowledge-based marketing, I triangulate from a variety of data sources, from qualitative interviews to archival materials such as company documents, articles in the business media, existing case studies and other relevant literature (Yin, 2003b). For specifically critical cases, participant observation and action research were also used. As for sampling, I opted for purposive sampling (purposeful sampling) and theoretical sampling (e.g., Glaser & Strauss, 1967; Gummesson, 2001). Companies to study for this research project have been selected purposefully by choosing firms and cases that seemed to be most appropriate to provide insights into knowledge-based management processes and specifically knowledge-based approaches to international marketing. Of the 35 companies where I conducted research, nine were purposefully selected to conduct in-depth case studies. Of these nine, six were purposefully selected to serve as explanatory cases studies of knowledge-based marketing in this paper. In total, 118 qualitative interviews with top executives, middle managers and selected employees in 35 different companies have been conducted in 2005 and 2006 mainly in Japan but also including supplementary interviews – where appropriate and necessary – in selected countries.

Findings

In the process of conducting and analyzing the expert interviews and the in-depth case studies of the empirical study, thoughts, ideas and insights from the literature review became interwoven with each other and initiated the development of some sort of grounded theory, not unlike the grounded theory described by Glaser and Strauss (1967) and Strauss and Corbin (1990). Thus, a – still somewhat vague and multi-faceted – picture of knowledge-based approaches to marketing has been shaping up. But despite the growing recognition of the need for knowledge-based approaches marketing, my research revealed that there are only few pioneer firms that are already taking or trying to take such an approach. However, there are already some firms that face the challenge of an increasingly global business environment with fierce competition and take up and master the challenge with the help of knowledge-based marketing. The most outstanding example is probably Toyota. Indeed, Toyota has often been found to be very strong at organizational learning and knowledge creation and sharing. Toyota learns from its stakeholders and partners in the business ecosystem, such as suppliers and competitors and co-creates new knowledge with them. The case study here shows how Toyota has established an international joint venture between with PSA Peugeot Citroën in Kolín, Czech Republic (Toyota Peugeot Citroën Automobile Czech, TPCA) and discusses the process of mutual learning and knowledge co-creation there.

Swiss-based Schindler Elevator's knowledge-based marketing strategy for the market introduction of a new escalator product into Asian markets showed that even for a large MNC with its vast network of subsidiaries that are well connected by e-mail, intranet, databases, telephone and video conferences, the sharing of tacit knowledge on a personal level is still a very reasonable or even indispensable approach. In fact, a combination of both a codification and a personalization strategy for marketing KM in order to leverage both tacit and explicit knowledge proved highly successful. Similarly, Hewlett Packard (HP) Consulting and Integration leverages both tacit and explicit marketing, sales and application knowledge from its field people – consultants and system engineers – through communities of practice. Last but not least, German conglomerate Siemens – like HP frequently featured as a company with a strong background in KM – leverages competitive advantage and new business opportunities through a cross-selling and knowledge sharing project that spans the boundaries of its different business divisions.

As for knowledge-based new product development management, the Mazda case showed how to enable 'empathic design' and leveraging tacit knowledge in developing the third generation Roadster Miata that won the Japan Car of the Year Award 2005/2006. The product development team was indeed able to capture customer needs and translating them into a successful product concept because of their capacity to leverage even tacit customer needs and knowledge and achieve a high level of experience co-creation between the customers and the product. Finally, Maekawa Manufacturing Ltd – famous for its decentralized structures and project-based management approach – found that producing and selling industrial parts is not enough any more. Through co-creation of common contexts and knowledge with its customers it was able to combine its products with its process knowledge to offer an integrated service including consulting. However, they do not simply offer pre-defined process and manufacturing models, but actively co-create the solutions together with their customers, an achievement that helped them to escape the red oceans of cutthroat competition and create new market space (blue ocean), yet 'untainted by competition' (Kim & Mauborgne, 2004, p. 77).

Finally, the six explanatory case studies of knowledge-based approaches to marketing show how things could and can be done differently in two senses: First, the six companies have consciously opted to pursue knowledge-based approaches to marketing and thus act differently from many of their competitors. And second, the approaches of the six companies – despite some similarities – also differ from each other and thus offer insights on different knowledge-based strategies. This can be summarized as follows:

1) The HP CI case vividly illustrated the significance of tacit knowledge from *gemba* or the front-line of the company. Knowledge is shared and co-created in a shared context or *ba*, in this case the so-called learning communities. It highlighted also the importance of knowledge from, about and to support customers as a sine qua non to provide superior service and value propositions.
2) The Schindler case illustrated the case of exploitation and exploration of marketing knowledge by combining both a personalization and a codification strategy in a new product market introduction project. The focus is here on the collaboration and effective communication – but also the co-creation – of both tacit and explicit marketing knowledge between headquarters (i.e., the competence centre escalators in Vienna and the headquarters Asia Pacific in Hong Kong) and subsidiaries (e.g., Japan, China, other Asian countries etc.) and between subsidiaries and thus goes far beyond what Dixon (2000) has termed 'strategic transfer'.
3) In a similar vein, the Siemens case showed how important (marketing) information and knowledge is collected, co-created, shared and applied both across business units but also across subsidiaries or regions/countries. It takes the approach yet a step further through its customer focus and KAM approach, which includes direct interaction and co-creation of knowledge with customers. As previously mentioned, it is therefore a very comprehensive case of knowledge-based marketing which actually goes far beyond the focus on marketing knowledge co-creation within the firm presented in this paper.
4) The Toyota case has illustrated the importance of the co-creation of knowledge with competitors, especially when entering new and yet rather unexplored markets. Here mutual learning and knowledge co-creation do not only boost the performance of the strategic alliance, but lessons learned can also be transferred and implemented at the respective headquarters and other subsidiaries
5) The Mazda case has depicted the necessity to empathize with customers and to directly 'experience' their needs. This gained tacit knowledge then needs to be translated or externalized into explicit knowledge and product concepts e.g., with the help of metaphors. Thus, this case has also shown the importance of language for knowledge creation as well as the critical issue of re-creating and refining tacit knowledge over time. Last but not least, it also highlighted the significance of value co-creation with customers.
6) The Maekawa case showed the importance of co-creating shared contexts or *bas* with customers and of establishing and nurturing long-term

Table 16.1 Summary: A taxonomy of knowledge-based marketing

Informant company	Approach	Main co-creator(s)	Classification
HP CI	Intra-firm knowledge co-creation and sharing: CoPs	Local staff/ front-line employees	Intra-firm co-creation
Schindler Elevator	Intra-firm knowledge creation and sharing: inter-subsidiary	Local staff	Intra-firm co-creation
Siemens	Intra-firm knowledge creation and sharing: inter-divisional and inter-regional	Local staff (in different countries and different business divisions)	Intra-firm co-creation
Toyota/ TPCA	Inter-organizational knowledge creation and sharing	Competitor	Competitor co-creation
Mazda	Intra-firm knowledge creation and sharing; Value co-creation with customers	Local staff (product development team members)	Intra-firm co-creation; Customer co-creation
Maekawa	Inter-organizational knowledge creation and sharing	Local staff/ front-line employees	Customer co-creation

Source: The author.

relationships with them. Consequently, the mutual understanding and co-creation of tacit knowledge is crucial for creating superior solutions and value jointly in the business ecosystem of a firm.

Table 16.1 summarizes the main points of the six approaches in a table.

To sum up, this chapter has identified three different basic patterns – co-creation within the MNC, co-creation with competitors, suppliers and partners, and co-creation with customers – and has provided six different exemplifying case studies for these. The important results here are not necessarily the ways of co-creation and how they can be compared, but rather the fact that co-creation of knowledge and value in the business ecosystem is crucially important, with the identified cases serving as guiding real-life examples of how knowledge-based firms do it in practice.

As Hansen and Nohria (2004, p. 22) correctly note, the ways for MNCs to compete successfully by exploiting scale and scope economies or by taking advantage of imperfections in the world's goods, labour and capital markets are no longer profitable as they once were, and as a result, 'the new economies of scope are based on the ability of business units, subsidiaries and functional departments within the company to collaborate successfully by sharing knowledge and jointly developing new products and services'. This statement strongly supports my call for knowledge-based marketing. At the same time, '[m]anagers and executives must strive towards meeting the slogan, 'think globally and act locally' to be truly successful in managing knowledge across borders' (Desouza & Evaristo, 2003, p. 66), as in the era of globalization, 'a firm has to achieve global integration and local adaptation at the same time' (Nonaka & Toyama, 2002, p. 998).

The following five key conclusions can be drawn from this chapter:

- In an increasingly global business environment, the creation and transfer of marketing knowledge and intra-firm collaboration through knowledge-based approaches to marketing will become more and more crucial as a determinant for corporate competitive advantage and survival of firms.
- As marketing affairs are one of the most knowledge-intensive parts of a company, applying KM concepts and practices to the field of marketing and to marketing functions will prove especially efficient and effective.
- As large parts of marketing knowledge are tacit and hard to codify, face-to-face communication and the integration of local staff into marketing processes and decision-making will be a critical factor for global marketing knowledge sharing that leads to successful marketing and sales achievements.
- As no firm can be seen as isolated in the global network economy, relationship marketing and the co-creation of knowledge and value with other entities in the business ecosystem are increasingly important.
- Given the broad marketing concept underlying this paper, findings not only contribute to the fields of global KM and international marketing, but also international business in general; indeed the business ecosystem is by no means confined by national boundaries, but on the contrary is an international, cross-cultural network.

This paper presented a conceptual framework of knowledge-based marketing and highlighted essential processes of marketing knowledge co-creation with the main actors in the business ecosystem of global firms – customers, suppliers, competitors, business partners. As shown, traditional marketing approaches have focused overly on explicit knowledge and neglected the important role of tacit knowledge, specifically in international (cross-cultural) settings. This chapter's aim was to adjust this imbalance in the extant literature and – drawing on real-life examples of knowledge-based firms – makes a call for a new knowledge-based marketing paradigm, with knowledge and knowledge co-creation being the key to sustainable competitive advantage in the global knowledge economy. In fact, facing the current global business environment and fierce competition, knowledge-based marketing has already become crucial as a determinant for corporate competitive advantage and as such a sine qua non for firms like Toyota, Mazda, Schindler, Siemens, HP and Maekawa. Especially when introducing new products or when entering new markets, knowledge creation and transfer and intra- as well as inter-firm collaboration prove critical for the success of the projects. Therefore, applying knowledge management concepts and practices to the knowledge-intensive field of marketing and to marketing functions bears out particularly efficient and effective. Besides, as large parts of marketing knowledge are tacit and hard to codify, face-to-face communication and the integration of local staff into marketing processes and decision-making is an important factor for global marketing knowledge sharing that leads to successful marketing and sales achievements. Finally, all of the previously mentioned companies can be seen as firms with a strong market orientation, possessing 'the basis for rapid adaptation to customers' manifest and latent needs, which may translate into superior new product success, profitability, market share, and, perhaps, sustainable competitive advantage' (Baker & Sinkula, 2005, p. 483). Even though it might be too early to identify and present real best practices, the 'next practices' (Prahalad & Ramaswamy, 2004) previously quoted show that some global leading companies are on their best way to successfully implement and leverage knowledge-based marketing for competitive advantage.

Limitations and implications for further research

Although carefully researched, documented and analyzed, the findings from the empirical study are subject to some limitations. First of all, the insights gained were derived and concluded from an exploratory study adopting a case study research design and are thus based on single – each probably rather unique – cases, even if this is exactly what case study research is all about (Stake, 2000). Indeed, the common limitations of generalizability of such field research are well documented (e.g., Eisenhardt, 1989; Hartley, 2004; Yin, 2003b), though analytic generalization – in contrast to statistical generalization – is possible (Hartley, 2004; Numagami, 1998; Yin, 2003b). Therefore, it would prove helpful to conduct further case studies of the companies presented in this paper – longitudinal case studies (Leonard-Barton, 1990; Yin, 2003b) – but also of other firms in order to analyze knowledge-based approaches to international marketing in different environments and under different conditions. I have used case studies and argued that they might not necessarily be seen as best practices but rather as next practices (Prahalad & Ramaswamy, 2004). They were explanatory ones that used 'the force of example' but were probably not (yet?) what Flyvbjerg (2006a, p. 232) terms paradigmatic cases.

Furthermore, the marketing knowledge co-creation framework is based on and grounded in Nonaka's theory of organizational knowledge creation. However, despite its development and advances over more than 20 years now, even Nonaka and Toyama (2003, p. 2) still conclude that 'it seems that we are still far from understanding the process in which an organization creates and utilizes knowledge' (also Nonaka & Toyama, 2002) and the theory has also frequently been criticized in various aspects (e.g., Glisby & Holden, 2003; Gourlay, 2006; Gueldenberg & Helting, 2007; Zhu, 2006). However, Gummesson (2002, p. xiii) is certainly right when he states that '[k]nowledge development in practical work in learning organizations as well as scholarly research can only humbly report progress and should not boast about conclusive results'. Besides, viewing all knowledge as tentative, however, researchers have to train themselves to listen to reality without preconceived ideas. At a later phase, the results can be compared with existing concepts and theory and will thus proceed as an interplay between the inductive and the deductive (Gummesson, 2005, pp. 322–323).

Next, there are a couple of important issues I have not been able to discuss but which should definitely be included in future research: the role of power and value in knowledge-based management, the issues of motivation and incentives to create and share knowledge, micropolitical issues and research on social capital.

But finally I take heart from Gummesson (2001, p. 44): 'To generate new knowledge in marketing, scholars should be guided by curiosity and the search for truth. Science must take risks and make mistakes; it must be entrepreneurial, not bureaucratic'. In researching and writing this paper, I was certainly guided by curiosity and the search for truth, a new truth for international marketing. I have probably also made mistakes along the way and this paper cannot provide a final answer. But it is my sincere hope that it provides us with the opportunity to discuss, learn and co-create a new dominant logic for doing business in the knowledge economy of the 21st century.

Acknowledgements

This paper is a summary of the findings from my doctoral research on 'Knowledge-based Approaches to International Marketing: Creation and Transfer of Marketing Knowledge in Multinational Corporations' carried out at Hitotsubashi University Tokyo and Vienna University of Economics and Business. A revised version of my dissertation has been published as *International Marketing in the Network Economy: A Knowledge-Based Approach* by Palgrave Macmillan in 2007. The interested reader may find the book helpful as a detailed follow-up on this paper.

This chapter and the book would never have been possible without the help, advice and support of many people. I am most greatly indebted to Jiro Nonaka for his guidance and kind support of my work, not least the Mazda and Maekawa case studies. I learned a lot from working with him and he gave invaluable feedback on my research and the manuscript of my book. I am also grateful to Nigel Holden and Charles Savage for the many insightful discussions and their many insightful comments on my work and the manuscript of my book. I would also like to thank the following people (in alphabetical order): Atsushi Degawa for his invaluable feedback, especially in the early stages of the research project in 2004 and 2005; Jeff Funk who made the research stay at Hitotsubashi University in Tokyo possible in the first place; Marcus Heuberger as well as my former colleagues at Schindler Japan for their kind support and adivce with the Schindler case study, Kaz Ichijo for his kind support of my work, especially concerning the Toyota case study and Japanese transcriptions; Yoshio Iwasaki for his support and advice with the Maekwa case study; Kazuo Mukai for the many interesting discussions and his kind support with the HP case study; Hiroyuki Ogamoto for his helpful suggestions and his kind support with the Siemens case study; Alfred Taudes for his feedback, advice and support. All mistakes are solely mine.

Note

1. A detailed outline and discussion of the literature review I conducted would go beyond the scope of a single paper. I refer the inclined reader to the full treatment of the literature in my book (Kohlbacher, 2007) as well as related papers (Kohlbacher & Mukai, 2007; Kohlbacher & Kraehe, 2007; Kohlbache, 2008a, 2008b; Ichijo & Kohlbacher, 2008; Kohlbacher, 2009a, 2009b; Wilhelm & Kohlbacher, 2011).

References

Alvesson, M., Kärreman, D., & Swan, J. (2002). Departures from knowledge and/or management in knowledge management. *Management Communication Quarterly*. 16 (2), 282–291.

Asakawa, K. & Lehrer, M. (2003). Managing local knowledge assets globally: the role of regional innovation relays. *Journal of World Business*. 38 (1), 31–42.

Baker, W. E. & Sinkula, J. M. (2005). Market orientation and the new product paradox. *The Journal of Product Innovation Management*. 22 (6), 483–502.

Bartlett, C. A. & Ghoshal, S. (2002). *Managing across Borders: The Transnational Solution* (2nd ed.) Boston: Harvard Business School Press.

Baumard, P. (1999) *Tacit Knowledge in Organizations*. (S. Wauchope, Trans.) London: Sage.

Boisot, M. H. (1998). *Knowledge Assets: Securing Competitive Advantage in the Information Economy*. New York: Oxford University Press.

Chaston, I. (2004). *Knowledge-based Marketing: The Twenty-first Century Competitive Edge*. Thousand Oaks: Sage Publications.

Cohen, D. (1998). Toward a knowledge context: report on the first annual university of California Berkeley forum on knowledge and the firm. *California Management Review*. 40 (3), 22–39.

Davenport, T. H. & Prusak, L. (2000). *Working Knowledge: How Organizations Manage What They Know*. Boston: Harvard Business School Press.

Day, G. S. (1994). The capabilities of market-driven organizations. *Journal of Marketing*. 58 (4), 37–52.

Deshpandé, R. & Webster, F. E. (1989). Organizational culture and marketing: defining the research agenda. *Journal of Marketing*. 53 (1), 3–15.

Desouza, K. C. & Evaristo, R. (2003). Global knowledge management strategies. *European Management Journal*. 21 (1), 62–67.

Desouza, K. C. (2005). The new frontiers of knowledge management. In K. C. Desouza (ed.) *New Frontiers of Knowledge Management.* (pp. 1–10) Basingstoke: Palgrave Macmillan.

Dixon, N. M. (2000). *Common Knowledge: How Companies Thrive by Sharing What They Know.* Boston, MA: Harvard Business School Press.

Doz, Y., Santos, J., & Williamson, P. (2001). *From Global to Metanational: How Companies Win in the Knowledge Economy.* Boston: Harvard Business School Press.

Dubin, R. (1982). Management: meaning, methods, and moxie. *Academy of Management Review.* 7 (3), 372–379.

Eisenhardt, K. M. (1989). Building theories from case study research. *Academy of Management Review.* 14 (4), 532–550.

Flyvbjerg, B. (2006a). Five misunderstandings about case-study research. *Qualitative Inquiry.* 12 (2), 219–245.

Flyvbjerg, B. Making organization research matter: power, values, and phronesis. In S. R. Clegg & C. Hardy & T. Lawrence & W. Nord (eds) (2006b). *The Sage Handbook of Organization Studies* (2nd ed.) (pp. 370–387) Thousand Oaks: Sage.

Foss, N. J. (2005). *Strategy, Economic Organization, and the Knowledge Economy: The Coordination of Firms and Resources.* New York: Oxford University Press.

Foss, N. J. & Pedersen, T. (2002). Transferring knowledge in MNCs, the role of sources of subsidiary knowledge and organizational context. *Journal of International Management.* 8 (1), 49–67.

Foss, N. J. & Pedersen, T. (2004). Organizing knowledge processes in the multinational corporation: an introduction. *Journal of International Business Studies.* 35 (5), 340–349.

Glaser, B. G. & Strauss, A. (1967). *The Discovery of Grounded Theory: Strategies for Qualitative Research.* Chicago: Aldine.

Glisby, M. & N. Holden. (2003). Contextual constraints in knowledge management theory: the cultural embeddedness of nonaka's knowledge-creating company. *Knowledge and Process Management.* 10 (1), 29–36.

Gourlay, S. (2006). Conceptualizing knowledge creation: a critique of nonaka's theory. *Journal of Management Studies.* 43 (7), 1415–1436.

Grant, R. M. (2002). The knowledge-based view of the firm. In C. W. Choo & N. Bontis (eds) *The Strategic Management of Intellectual Capital and Organizational Knowledge.* (pp. 133–148) New York: Oxford University Press.

Grönroos, C. (1994). From marketing mix to relationship marketing: towards a paradigm shift in marketing. *Management Decision.* 32 (2), 4–20.

Gueldenberg, S. & H. Helting. (2007). Bridging 'the great divide': Nonaka's synthesis of 'western' and 'eastern' knowledge concepts reassessed. *Organization.* 14 (1), 99–120.

Gummesson, E. (2001). Are current research approaches in marketing leading us astray? *Marketing Theory.* 1 (1), 27–48.

Gummesson, E. (2002). *Total Relationship Marketing.* Oxford: Butterworth-Heinemann.

Gummesson, E. (2005). Qualitative research in marketing: road-map for a wilderness of complexity and unpredictability. *European Journal of Marketing.* 39 (3/4), 309–327.

Gupta, A. K. & V. Govindarajan. (2000). Knowledge flows within multinational corporations. *Strategic Management Journal.* 21 (4), 473–496.

Hansen, M. T. & N. Nohria. (2004). How to build collaborative advantage. *MIT Sloan Management Review.* 46 (1), 22–30.

Hartley, J. (2004). Case study research. In C. Cassell & G. Symon (eds) *Essential Guide to Qualitative Methods in Organizational Research.* (pp. 323–333) London, Thousand Oaks, New Delhi: Sage Publications.

Hedlund, G. & I. Nonaka. (1993). Models of knowledge management in the West and Japan. In P. Lorange, B. Chakravarthy, J. Roos, & A. Van de Ven (eds) *Implementing Strategic Processes: Change, Learning and Co-operation.* (pp. 117–144) Oxford: Basil Blackwell.

Holden, N. J. (2002). *Cross-cultural Management: A Knowledge Management Perspective.* Harlow: Financial Times/Prentice Hall.

Iansiti, M. & R. Levien. (2004). *The Keystone Advantage: What the New Dynamics of Business Ecosystems Mean for Strategy, Innovation, and Sustainability.* Boston: Harvard Business School Press.

Ichijo, Kazuo & Florian Kohlbacher. (2008). Tapping tacit local knowledge in emerging markets – the Toyota way. *Knowledge Management Research and Practice.* 6 (3), 173–186.

Ichijo, K. & I. Nonaka. (2006). Introduction: knowledge as competitive advantage in the age of increasing globalization. In K. Ichijo & I. Nonaka (eds) *Knowledge Creation and Management: New Challenges for Managers.* (pp. 3–10) New York: Oxford University Press.

Kim, W. C. & R. Mauborgne. (2004). Blue ocean strategy. *Harvard Business Review.* 82 (10), 76–84.

Kohlbacher, F. (2007). *International Marketing in the Network Economy: A Knowledge-based Approach.* Basingstoke: Palgrave Macmillan.

Kohlbacher, F. (2008a). Knowledge-based marketing – building and sustaining competitive advantage through knowledge co-creation. *International Journal of Management and Decision Making.* 9(6), 617–645.

Kohlbacher, Florian (2008b). Knowledge-based new product development: fostering innovation through knowledge co-creation. *International Journal of Technology Intelligence and Planning.* 4 (3), 326–346.

Kohlbacher, Florian. (2009a). Strategic knowledge-based marketing. *International Journal of Knowledge Management Studies.* 3 (1–2), 154–175.

Kohlbacher, Florian (2009b). Leveraging organizational capital for innovation: the process of marketing knowledge co-creation. In Ahmed Bounfour (ed.) *Organizational Capital: Modelling, Measuring and Contextualising.* (pp. 234–257) Abingdon, Oxon: Routledge.

Kohlbacher, Florian & Michael O. B. Kraehe. (2007). Knowledge creation and transfer in a cross-cultural context – empirical evidence from Tyco flow control. *Knowledge and Process Management.* 14 (3), 169–181.

Kohlbacher, F., N. J. Holden, M. Glisby, & A. Numic. (2007). Knowledge-based approaches to international marketing: unleashing the power of tacit local and global knowledge to create competitive advantage. *Paper presented at the 49th Annual Meeting of the Academy of International Business (AIB), Indianapolis.*

Kohlbacher, F. & K. Mukai. (2007). Japan's learning communities in Hewlett-Packard Consulting & Integration: challenging one-size fits all solutions. *The Learning Organization.* 14 (1), 8–20.

Kohli, A. K. & B. J. Jaworski. (1990). Market orientation: the construct, research propositions, and managerial implications. *Journal of Marketing.* 54 (2), 1–18.

Leonard, D. (1998). *Wellsprings of Knowledge: Building and Sustaining the Sources of Innovation.* Boston: Harvard Business School Press.

Leonard-Barton, D. (1990). A dual methodology for case studies: synergistic use of a longitudinal single site with replicated multiple sites. *Organization Science*. 1 (3), 248–266.

Martin, X. & R. Salomon. (2003). Knowledge transfer capacity and its implications for the theory of the multinational corporation. *Journal of International Business Studies*. 34 (4), 356–373.

R. Mudambi. (2002). Knowledge management in multinational firms. *Journal of International Management*. 8 (1), 1–9.

Narver, J. C. & S. F. Slater. (1990). The effect of a market orientation on business profitability. *Journal of Marketing*. 54 (4), 20–35.

Newell, S., M. Robertson, H. Scarbrough, & J. Swan. (2002). *Managing Knowledge Work*. Basingstoke: Palgrave Macmillan.

Nonaka, I. (1990). Managing globalization as a self-renewing process: experiences of Japanese MNEs'. In C. A. Bartlett & Y. Doz, & G. Hedlund (eds) *Managing the Global Firm*. (pp. 69–94) London: Routledge.

Nonaka, I. (1991). The knowledge-creating company. *Harvard Business Review*. 69 (6), 96–104.

Nonaka, I. (1994). A dynamic theory of organizational knowledge creation. *Organization Science*. 5 (1), 14–34.

Nonaka, I. (2007). Foreword. *International Marketing in the Network Economy, Florian Kohlbacher*. (pp. xi–xv) Basingstoke: Palgrave Macmillan.

Nonaka, I. & H. Takeuchi. (1995). *The Knowledge-creating Company: How Japanese Companies Create the Dynamics of Innovation*. New York: Oxford University Press.

Nonaka, I. & R. Toyama. (2002). A firm as a dialectical being: towards a dynamic theory of a firm. *Industrial and Corporate Change*. 11 (5), 995–1009.

Nonaka, I. & R. Toyama. (2003). The knowledge-creating theory revisited: knowledge creation as a synthesizing process. *Knowledge Management Research & Practice*. 1 (1), 2–10.

Nonaka, I. (2005). Managing organizational knowledge: theoretical and methodological foundations. In K. G. Smith, & M. A. Hitt (eds) *Great Minds in Management: The Process of Theory Development*. (pp. 373–393) New York: Oxford University Press.

Nonaka, I. & R. Toyama. (2005). The theory of the knowledge-creating firm: subjectivity, objectivity, and synthesis. *Industrial and Corporate Change*. 14 (3), 419–436.

Nonaka, I., G. von Krogh, & S. C. Voelpel. (2006). Organizational knowledge creation theory: evolutionary paths and future advances. *Organization Studie.s* 27 (8), 1179–1208.

Nonaka, I., Toyama, R., & Hirata, T. (in collaboration with Bigelow, S., Hirose, A., & Kohlbacher, F.) (2008). *Managing Flow: A Process Theory of the Knowledge-based Firm*. Basingstoke, UK: Palgrave Macmillan.

Numagami, T. (1998). The infeasibility of invariant laws in management studies: a reflective dialogue in defense of case studies. *Organization Science*. 9 (1), 2–15.

Patton, E. & S. H. Appelbaum. (2003). The case for case studies in management research. *Management Research News*. 26 (5), 60–71.

Prahalad, C. K. & V. Ramaswamy. (2004). *The Future of Competition: Co-creating Unique Value with Customers*. Boston: Harvard Business School Press.

Prusak, L. (2001). Where did knowledge management come from? *IBM Systems Journal*. 40 (4), 1002–1007.

Rossiter, J. R. (2001). What is marketing knowledge? Stage I: forms of marketing knowledge. *Marketing Theory*. 1 (1), 9–26.

Scarbrough, H., & J. Swan. (2001). Explaining the diffusion of knowledge management: the role of fashion. *British Journal of Management*, 12 (1), 3–12.

Scarbrough, H., M. Robertson, & J. Swan. (2005) Professional media and management fashion: the case of knowledge management. *Scandinavian Journal of Management.* 21 (2), 197–208.

Schlegelmilch, B. B. & T. C. Chini. (2003). Knowledge transfer between marketing functions in multinational companies: a conceptual model. *International Business Review.* 12 (2), 215–232.

Skyrme, D. J. (1998). Fact or fad? Ten shifts in knowledge management. *Knowledge Management Review.* 1 (3), 6–7.

Spender, J. C. (1996). Making knowledge the basis of a dynamic theory of the firm. *Strategic Management Journal.* 17 (Winter Special Issue), 45–62.

Stake, R. E. (2000). Case studies. In N. K. Denzin, & Y. S. Lincoln (eds) *Handbook of qualitative research.* (pp. 435–453) Thousand Oaks: Sage.

Strauss, A. & J. M. Corbin. (1990) *Basics of Qualitative Research: Techniques and Procedures for Developing Grounded Theory.* Newbury Park: Sage.

Takeuchi, H. & I. Nonaka. (2000). Reflection on knowledge management from Japan. In D. Morey, M. Maybury, & B. Thuraisingham (eds) *Knowledge Management: Classic and Contemporary Works.* (pp. 183–186) Cambridge, Massachusetts: The MIT Press.

Thomke, S. H. & E. von Hippel. (2002). Customers as innovators: a new way to create value. *Harvard Business Review.* 80 (4), 74–81.

Tzokas, N. & M. Saren. (2004). Competitive advantage, knowledge and relationship marketing: where, what and how? *The Journal of Business & Industrial Marketing.* 19 (2), 124–135.

Weick, K. E. (1996). Drop your tools: allegory for organizational studies. *Administrative Science Quarterly.* 41 (2), 301–313.

Wilhelm, Miriam M., & Florian Kohlbacher. (2011). Co-opetition and knowledge co-Creation in Japanese supplier-networks: the case of Toyota. *Asian Business & Management.* 10 (1), 66–86.

Yin, R. K. (2003a). *Applications of Case Study Research* (2nd ed.).Thousand Oaks: Sage.

Yin, R. K. (2003b). *Case Study Research, Design and Methods* (3rd ed.). Thousand Oaks: Sage.

Zack, M. H. (2003) Rethinking the knowledge-based organization. *MIT Sloan Management Review.* 44 (4), 67–71.

Zhu, Z. (2006). Nonaka meets giddens: a critique. *Knowledge Management Research & Practice.* 4 (2), 106–115.

17
Judgement-Making in the Face of Contingency

Kimio Kase and César G. Cantón

Introduction

Uncertainty is a fact of life, of which there is no denying. Accordingly, it has been studied by a wide range of disciplines, including physics, philosophy, statistics, economics, finance, insurance, psychology, sociology, engineering and information science. It may be defined as the lack of certainty owing to having limited knowledge where it is impossible to exactly describe the existing state, a future outcome or more than one possible outcome.

Management practices and their studies are no exception and faced almost everyday and at every moment with the need to take decisions in the teeth of uncertainty.

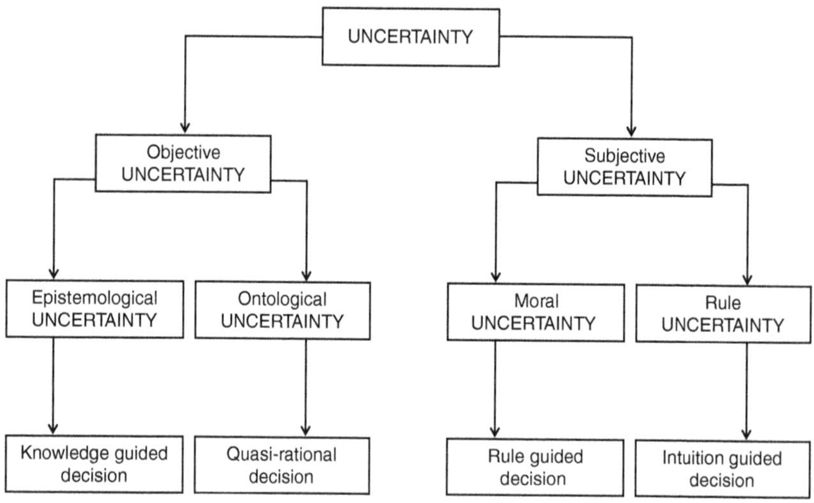

Figure 17.1 Taxonomy of uncertainties and decisions
Source: Tannert et al. (2007), p. 894.

The taxonomy of uncertainty proposed by Tannert, Elvers, and Jandrig (2007, p. 893) is shown in Figure 17.1.

Of these uncertainties,[1] what concerns us is epistemological and ontological uncertainties (especially the latter) defined, respectively, as '[the one] caused by gaps in knowledge… [for which] decision-makers must both rely on existing knowledge' and '[the one] caused by the stochastic features of a situation… characterized by non-linear behaviour, which makes it impossible to resolve uncertainties by deterministic reasoning and/or research' (Tannert et al., 2007, p. 893).

Uncertainties are derived from contingency and from among different relationships among events (Gigerenzer, Hoffrage, & Kleinbölting, 1991; Hitchcock, 2011; Jung, 1967; 1973; Pearl, 2009; Tannert et al., 2007; Van Asselt & Rotmans, 2002). This chapter focuses on the relevant survey of literature on contingency, synchronicity and probabilistic causality as shown in Figure 17.2, which illustrates the relationships among two or more events. The section numbers refer to the sections that deal with each relationship.

Accordingly, this chapter starts by reviewing the existing thought about contingency and related areas (Sections 1a and 1b).

Synchronicity as a kindred but recondite concept to contingency is discussed based on Jung's works (Section 2); Probabilistic causality, perhaps a more exoteric concept, is reviewed afterwards (Section 3), supplemented with the analysis of a survey concerning the degree of conviction or credence

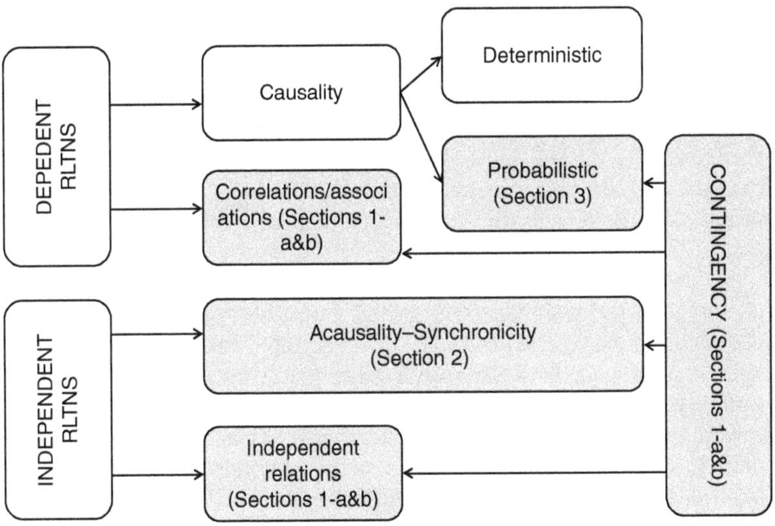

Figure 17.2 Illustration of the relationships among two or more events

Source: Authors.

and a good guess. Propositions based on the literature survey are enunciated (Section 4).

In order to round our argument off and to apply the propositions formulated, we analyse in the last Section 5, an actual empirical example concerning the development of blue LED in which two different streams of technology were initially pursued with the result that ultimately one of them were advanced by two different groups of researchers.

Section 1a: Contingency

The concept of contingency is central to this paper. As such and to give due shades of meaning to it our construal is split in two sections. In Section 1a, the general structure and connotation/intension are set out; in Section 1b, more detailed exposition is focused on empirical contingency as the core notion of contingency relevant to the theme of the paper.

Fear and insecurity surrounding human life is derived from uncertainty about what will happen, which we may tackle by breaking it down into probability, a quantitative representation of contingency, and ambiguity or contingency (Ichinose, 2011, pp. vi–ix).

Prior to analysing contingency, we review major concepts related to it including certainty, truth concepts, the contingency-necessity binomial and the *de re/dicto distinction*.

Certainty, a concept similar to incorrigibility, is 'the property a belief has of being such the subject is incapable of giving it up' (psychological kind of certainty) or 'a belief is certain when it has the highest possible epistemic status (epistemic kind of certainty)' (Reed, 2011).

Various lines of thought have been formulated around truth including correspondence theory, coherence theory, constructivist theory, consensus theory and pragmatic theory within the category of substantive theory; performance theory and redundancy theory within the category of deflationary theory; and pluralist theory (Lowe, 2005b).

A survey result reveals the degree of acceptance of various theories of truth:

> [a] survey of professional philosophers and others on their philosophical views which was carried out in November 2009 (taken by 3226 respondents, including 1803 philosophy faculty members and/or PhDs and 829 philosophy graduate students) 44.9 percent of respondents accept or lean towards correspondence theories, 20.7 percent accept or lean towards deflationary theories and 13.8% epistemic theories (http://en.wikipedia.org/wiki/Truth#Most_believed_theories accessed on August 2nd, 2012).

Accordingly, we focus our literature review on the deflationary and the correspondence theories.

Davidson (2005, p. 195) enunciates that 'a theory of truth is deflationary if it declares that truth is a concept that is easily shown to be dispensable, or is no more than technically useful'. Its simplest form is the redundancy theory that 'draws on the apparent equivalence between asserting a proposition p and asserting that p is true to claim that the truth-predicate "is true" is redundant, in the sense that it is, in principle, always eliminable without loss of expressive power' (Lowe, 2005a).

The correspondence theory is the view that truth is correspondence to a fact, which embraces the idea that truth consists in a relation to reality or to some portion of reality (Marian, 2009). It differs itself from the coherence theory in that it states that 'the truth conditions of propositions are not (in general) propositions, but rather objective features of the world', whereas the coherence theory states that 'the truth conditions of propositions consist in other propositions' (Young, 2008).

In this work, we accept the idea of truth as correspondence, in a very broad sense, between the mind and some kind of reality's objective features. That means that excellent managers, by turning contingency into necessity, have a privileged, practical access to reality.

The distinction between *de re* and *de dicto* refers to that between necessity of things versus necessity of words (Macintosh, 2005). 'The literal translation of the phrase "*de dicto*" is "of (the) word," whereas "*de re*" translates to "of (the) thing"'.[2] Because of the difference between *de re/de dicto*, '[b]elieving, of God, that he is benevolent is different from believing that God is benevolent' (Macintosh, 2005). It means that 'the view one takes on the nature of propositional attitudes [differs from] one's conception of the *de re/de dicto* distinction' (McKay, 2010).

Regarding contingency Aristotle asserts:

> Most of the things about which we make decisions, and into which we inquire, present us with alternative possibilities. For it is about our actions that we deliberate and inquire, and all our actions have a contingent character; hardly any of them are determined by necessity (Aristotle, 2001b, p. 1357ª1323–1327).
>
> The enthymeme[3] and the example must, then, deal with what is for the most part capable of being otherwise, the example being an induction and the enthymeme a deduction. The enthymeme must consist of few propositions, fewer often than those which make up a primary deduction (Aristotle, 2001b, p. 1357ª1314–1318).

Thomas Aquinas affirms that chance is a real component of human life, but is overruled by divine providence, although this instance may be both invisible and incomprehensible to humans (1965, p. I, q. 22, art. 22). Nevertheless, his interpretation of Aristotle infers that contingent things, understood as universal and immutable concepts (*rationes*), belong to the knowledge handled by the demonstrative sciences, but, understood in the concrete, they are variable, 'do not fall under the intellect except by sensitive powers' to which particular reason or the sensory power of judgement is applied, and are objects of counsel and operation (Aquinas, 1993, p. 1123). 'For this reason [Aristotle] says that necessary and contingent things, like speculative universals and individual operable things, belong to different parts of the rational soul' (Aquinas, 1993, p. 1123).

Our main source on contingency analysis is Shuzo Kuki, a Japanese philosopher about whom Heidegger (1982), his master, said he had 'a lasting memory'. Maraldo (n.d.) enumerates four features of Kuki's work on contingency that set him apart: (1) the systematic treatment of contingency in the 'entire history of philosophy'; (2) his evaluation of contingency as a reality to be appreciated, not to overcome; (3) his consideration of metaphysics as the only discipline thematizing contingency as such, viewing it as the primary problem of metaphysics; and (4) his treatment of the triangle formed by the contingency of the absolute, the contingency of the natural world, and the contingency of individuals and their fortuitous encounters. Likewise, Maraldo (n.d.) stresses Kuki's awareness that a theory of contingency is self-negating, since by nature 'contingency refers to the factors that do not fall under the general plan or rule or law'.

Kuki (2011f, pp. 29–30) argues that contingency is the negation of necessity whereas necessity is a manifestation of the identity from the viewpoint of modality, where the law of identity expressed as 'A (concept) is A (mark)' describes the most precise and basic modality of necessity, namely, (1) the categorical necessity in which a concept and its mark coincide by being A and therefore by being identical; but this proposition may develop into another – 'if A (cause) then A (consequence)', in which the cause (A) and the consequence (A) are related through 'if' or (2) the hypothetical necessity; and furthermore may develop into the proposition 'A is either "A" or A"' or (3) the disjunctive necessity, since the first proposition "A is A" may contain the statement "'if A, then A'" and "if A, then A" and therefore "A is either A' or A"'.

Kuki (2011f) holds that contingency is the negation of necessity and therefore there are necessity-contingency correspondences such as categorical necessity and categorical contingency, etc. Accordingly, Kuki (1966, p. 2011g, 15) asserts that there are three types of contingencies: (1) logical or catégorique; (2) empirical or hypothétique; and (3) metaphysical or disjonctive. According to Maraldo's (n.d.) interpretation, Kuki considers these three types as being interrelated insofar as they have each a core meaning that is rooted in one another.

Logical or categorical contingency

Logical contingency occurs when the relationships between the concept and non-essential characteristics are not bound by necessity but by contingency

(Kida, 2001; Kuki, 2011a). For Kuki (1966, p. 8), the construction of a concept is founded on the observation of a general identity shared among a number of representations and its *structural* content is composed of a set of essential characteristics (or marks) abstracted from this identity, while its *possible* content depends on the access given to unessential characteristics. Therefore, the relation of the concept and unessential characteristics is the relation of contingency where the unessential characteristics are called contingent characteristics in contrast to the essential characteristics that are called necessary characteristics (Kuki, 1966).

Kida (2001) contends that Kuki considers accidental attributes and characteristics of individual objects as representing the logical contingency. Plato's idea is, therefore, a concept that is eternally unchangeable unlike each object that, though it participates in the idea, realizes the *eidos* or form derived from the idea by means of matter signifying that the combination of the *eidos* and the form is accidental or contingent (Kida, 2001, p. 63).

Aristotle's statement that 'accidents do not belong to things in virtue of their own nature' (Aristotle, 2001a, p. 1018a 1011–1012) and 'the matter, which is capable of being otherwise than as it usually is, must be the cause of the accidental' (Aristotle, 2001a, p. 1027a 1013–1014) refers to this. That the skin be white or black, the health be good or bad is accidental characteristic for a man seen as each individual and does not apply to the man as the general concept (Kida, 2001, p. 63). The contingent or accidental characteristic of individuals is interpreted to be a variation of logical contingency (Kida, 2001).

As a consequence Kuki's logical contingency refers, as set out in the following subsection, to the contrast of individual thing's specificity to the concept's generality (where it seems to be different from the contingency related to fate or destiny) (Kida, 2001, p. 63).

Empirical or hypothetical contingency

Kida (2001, p. 64) construes Kuki's (2011f) statement on *principium rationis sufficientis* and its concretion *qua* causality and final cause as referring to the cause-effect relations and objective-means relations. In other words, any event can be justified in terms of a causal relationship to a prior (either temporarily or logically) event. Objective-means relationships, namely, 'for A to be achieved, B must be done' presupposes cause-effect relationships, namely, 'if B is done, then A must necessarily be achieved' (Kida, 2001). Accordingly, empirical or hypothetical contingency empirically presents itself either as (a) causal contingency or (b) final or purposeful contingency.

Causal contingency is observed if a tile falls from a roof and squashes a balloon that was underneath (Kuki, 2011g, p. 110). There are two different streams of cause-effect flows: (1) the tile may have fallen because the roof was in a bad state or a strong wind blew causing it to fall and (2) by some reason a balloon abandoned by a child may have come to stop under the roof; however, that these two different flows of cause-effect relations meet is thought to have been due to contingency (Kida, 2001, p. 65).

Final contingency refers to a chance finding of a treasure trove in the ground and, 'l'enchaînement des actes du pépiniériste qui plante un arbre, d'une part, et celui des actes du voleur qui cache un trésor dans la terre, d'autre part, étant indépendants, la relation de quelque espèce qui s'établit positivement entre eux est autre que finale'[4] (Kuki, 1966, p. 54). It refers to the contingency arising from the fortuitous encounter of two or more purposeful actions.

Metaphysical or disjunctive contingency

Kuki (1966, p. 111) asserts the following,

> La contingence disjonctive relève de la relation existant entre le tout et les parties. Le tout possède l'identité absolue, de par sa nature même de tout. Pour autant qu'il est détermine comme être achevé, le tout est définitivement identique à soi; son existence s'accompagne donc de nécessité. Au contraire, la partie, de par sa nature même de partie, manqué de l'identité absolue à soi: n'étant que partie, elle suppose les autres parties... La partie possède en elle-même la nature de pouvoir être aussi bien une partie autre que la partie qu'elle est: en cela consiste la contingence de la partie.[5]

Kida (2001, p. 67) starts his explanation of metaphysical contingency by referring to empirical contingency. As illustrated in Figure 17.3 chain of events, empirical contingency occurs when more than two independent cause-effect chains cross each other, namely, at the point C, A and B meet apparently by chance; however, going back in the cause-effect chains A and B can be traced back to A" via A' and B" via B', respectively, and ultimately both of them may have been derived from O, which means that the crossing of A and B may not be by chance at all (Kida, 2001, p. 67; Kuki, 2011f, p. 44).

Even if O is a consequence of a chance encounter of M and N, these events may be finally traced back, as shown in Figure 17.3 causal chain to a common event P, which may mean that O was after all necessary happening and if we generalize it we may have to follow what Spinoza dictates, namely, 'all things follow from God's eternal decree by the same necessity as it follows from the essence of a triangle that its three angles are equal to two right angles' as quoted by Jarret (2009).

```
     ↗ M" → M' →     →    ↗ A" → A' → A ↘
P                       O                   C
     ↘ N" → N' →     →    ↘ B" → B' → B ↗
```

Figure 17.3 Chain of events, empirical contingency occurring when more than two independent cause-effect chains cross each other

Source: Kida (2001), p. 67.

Kida (2001) concludes that metaphysical necessity is thus the necessity that governs the relations among events regardless of whether we can recognize them or not. However, the world as a whole, that immediately follows from God or metaphysical necessity, is identified by Kida with Kuki's (1966, 2011a, 2011c, 2011d, 2011e, 2011f) metaphysical contingency or ultimate cause of natural things X, as shown in Figure 17.3. The ultimate cause of natural things can be reached by means of infinitely tracing back all events, signifying that X will not have any other cause than itself, namely, Schelling's primal contingency or *Urzufall*[6] (1996) cited by Saito (n.d., p. 69).

We will now attempt to further our understanding of the notion of empirical contingency because managers operate in the real world and it is the kind of contingency that they are able to turn into necessity.

Section 1b: Further discussion on empirical contingency

Delving into the notion of empirical contingency

As previously discussed in relation to disjunctive contingency, 'natural laws necessitate what will happen once certain initial conditions are given, but whether a certain set of conditions obtains or not is a matter of chance' (Maraldo, n.d., p. 42), in which these conditions may depend on primary contingency.

Maraldo (n.d., pp. 43–44) adds three more cases in which empirical contingency is at work in the realm of natural laws or necessities. First, contingent factors may affect a causal sequence with such factors being unpredictable not merely due to a lack of possible knowledge. In a mutation in DNA caused by random radiation, the radiation, once emitted, might be predicted how it could affect the cells, but if the radiation particles are emitted at random without determinate causes, the occurrence of the mutation is ultimately contingent, which is a 'microcosmic version of primal contingency' (Maraldo, n.d., pp. 43–45).

Second, some physicists and philosophers assert that natural laws are 'inductive generalization with probable, not necessary outcomes', where contingency might have a relevant role. Smolin (2007), cited by Maraldo (n.d.), argues that 'fundamental physics – the search for the laws of nature – is losing its way' because there might be hidden variables that determine the course of any natural event. The chance of happening to know all the relevant variables would be contingent and 'the more hidden variables the more room for the contingency of any particular natural event' (Maraldo, n.d., p. 44).

Third, empirical reality can be seen as implying an 'intention by a knowing, planning and scheming mind', namely, the divine plan as the free intention of a divine power. 'If God designs freely, the God's particular plan is contingent upon what God happens to choose'. Then, it is God's choice whether or not to create the world. And '[t]he principle of sufficient reason, i.e., the thesis that for every state of affairs that obtains there must be a sufficient reason why it obtains...implies that God must have a sufficient reason for creating just this world...given God's moral perfection...the world selected must be the best possible' (Sleigh, 2005, p. 510). Therefore, there is no contingency in God's existence and in how the world happens to be (Maraldo, n.d., p. 45).

However, two questions ought to be begged: (1) 'if it is necessary that God be perfect, does it follow that it is necessary that God create a world? If a perfect, necessary being does not have to create a world at all, then the fact of creation is contingent'; and (2) 'how necessary is this definition of God? Is this definition necessary for intelligent design theory? Does an intelligent designer have to be a perfect, necessary being?' (Maraldo, n.d., pp. 45–46). After raising these questions Maraldo (n.d., p. 46) contends that the ultimate contingency of the designer's choice and nature may possibly be supposed.

On the other hand, Spinoza (2002, p. I.33. Schol 31) sustains that:

> a thing is termed 'contingent' for no other reason than the deficiency of our knowledge...we still cannot make any certain judgement as to its existence because the chain of causes is hidden from us, then that thing cannot appear to us either as necessary or as impossible. So we term it either 'contingent' or 'possible'.

Empirical contingency and cognition

Another important point to be clarified before moving ahead in our exposition is whether empirical contingency is due to objective features of the world or to human cognitive constraints.

Kuki (2011b) might think the imperfection of knowledge at human beings introduces a 'genuine' contingency (1) because the possibility of any human knowing more than he happens to know would result in contingency; and (2) because God's perfect knowledge and human imperfect knowledge, namely, the duality that for Kuki gives rise to contingency, 'implies the possibility of an other to each' (Maraldo, n.d., p. 46).

Our stance is to accept contingency as both existing in reality in itself and due also to the imperfection of our knowledge. This can be also seen from the perspective of the *de re/de dicto* distinction: contingency can be predicated from things and from what it is affirmed from things.

Empirical contingency and fate

Kuki (n.d., pp. 43–44) argues:

> ...la contingence se définit comme une rencontre, une conjoncture. En japonais, le *gū* 偶de *gūzen*, contingence, a la sens de 'doublé', paire, couple, réunion, le même sens est le nombre fondé sur la rencontré de 1 et 1 qui font deux. Le *gū* de *gūzen* (contingence), est le *gū* de *gūza*, (face-à-face), le *gū* de *haigū* (mariage). Le sens de la contingence se noue en profondeur

> autour de la rencontre de A et de B où se nie le principe d'identité A est A. Nous pourrions définir la contingence comme 'la rencontre de deux éléments indépendants'.[7]

Kuki (1966, pp. 86–87) points out that σύμ-πτωμα, συμ-βεβηκός, con-tingens, ac-cidens, Zufall are all of them terms that mark the encounter of two elements by a prefix. Also, chance is derived from *cadentia* coming from *cadere*. Thus for Kuki, contingence is related to encounter or chance meeting.

Kuki (1966, pp. 86–87) enumerates three characteristics of empirical contingency: (1) a situation that may or may not exist; (2) the encounter of a thing or situation with another; and (3) something that may only exist in a very rare occasion.

First, contingency occurs when an object or situation may exist or take place not on account of necessity, while, if it does not exist or take place, it is not because of the absolute impossibility of its existence or taking place. For example, like in the case when a dice is rolled over and shows a three though there is no necessity that it be so nor there is no probability that three won't turn up – this is a case of contingency (2011c, p. 17).

Second, however, as the first characteristic is only a necessary, not a sufficient condition for contingency to occur insofar as that a thing or situation may occur or may not occur only shows a possibility, the encounter between two objects or situations comes up as a condition for contingency to take place like in the case in which a visit to a hospital to see a sick friend gives rise to a chance encounter with another friend (Kuki, 2011c, p. 17).

Third, that an object or situation is produced only on rare occasions enhances the contingent character of contingency as it constrains the occurrence with the first characteristic like in the case in which six consecutive throwing of dice shows a three six times, which may be considered a rare occurrence (Kuki, 2011c, pp. 19–20). Kida (Kuki, 2011c, p. 22) cites Kuki as having affirmed that 'contingency turns its back to necessity but turns its face to impossibility'.

As previously suggested, fate fulfils all of these three criteria. For Kuki (2001, p. 75) fate is contingency that carries a very significant meaning for the existence of human beings. It can be of internal or external significance, but, as a powerful occurrence that may shake the very existence of a human being is usually of internal nature, fate may be defined as internalized contingency (2011c, p. 23). Contingency referred to in this definition is empirical contingency, whose characteristic of being contingent is intensified when viewed from the standpoint of fate (Kuki, 2011c, p. 24).

Contingency and time

Kuki (Kida, 2001, p. 85) sustains that, as the theory of modalities has a deep relation with the temporality, it is important to elucidate the temporal nature of contingency, especially when by examining the relations with other modalities in the context of time the structure of contingency may be clarified.

Modality means, 'the classification of propositions on the basis of whether they assert or deny the possibility, impossibility, contingency, or necessity of their content' (American Heritage Dictionary). Kida (1966, p. 155) interprets that Kuki's reference to modalities includes possibility, contingency and necessity and that it concerns the conception of things as being possible, contingent or necessary.

Possibility possesses the future temporality and is related to the Heiddegerian project (*Entwurf*), since the mode of being in existence as possibility lies in the concern by way of project for future (2001, p. 77).

Necessity is, following Aristotle's analysis that the essence of necessity is 'the being of what was', 'de même que la possibilité est toujours munie d'une anticipation du future, de même la nécessité doit toujours garder un regard en arrière sur le passé' (Kuki, 1966, p. 155).

The temporality of contingency is, unlike possibility's future temporality and necessity's past temporality, is the present; and the occurrences of the possible in the face of the reality are contingency in a broad sense (Kuki, 1966, p. 156).

Kida (Kuki, 1966, p. 157) argues that, when Kuki takes up the issue of time, he refers to Heiddegerian 'temporalisation', namely, the basic behaviour of human beings that develops in the context of time divided into the future, the present and the past; and therefore that the existence of human being is, according to Kuki, characterized by subjecting itself to the future, the and the present in an integrative manner.

The argument bears significantly upon our study, since excellent managers seem to be able to put together events from different positions in time in order to reach better decisions.

Discussion

Empirical contingency's basic elements, along with important related concepts, such as cognition, fate, and temporality have so far been discussed. In the following Sections 2 and 3, we explore the main three forms in which empirical contingency can face the manager: (1) fate; (2) synchronicity for final contingency; and (3) causal probabilism, for causal relationships.

After a review of Kuki's analysis of contingency, Kida (2001, p. 68) contends that what we call destiny or fate is related to empirical contingency. Fate makes an excellent case of final empirical contingency, because: (1) It is revealed through an event that is contingent in a necessary and sufficient way; (2) This event is also extremely unique and rare. As we will in the following, those are the main three features of empirical contingency. To this, it must be added that the agent experiences it through events that seem to hint at a cosmic 'message' or purpose for him or her; that is what makes it an example of final, and not causal, contingency.

Causal probability is characterized by quantification of contingent phenomena, drawing on the law of large numbers, central limit theorem[8], and statistical hypothesis testing Takeuchi (2010, passim). It embodies the core of mainstream decision-making theory and, hence, holds a paramount place among the tools managers use to tackle empirical contingency

However, a concept which we should not omit in discussing contingency or chance occurrences is synchronicity, because it shows a case of empirical contingency that is not, however, causality based. Synchronicity has been defined as 'the simultaneous occurrence of two meaningfully but not causally connected events' (Jung, 1973, p. 25). Causal connections here refer to Aristotelian efficient cause (Aristotle, 2001a, p. V 2), namely, 'the primary source of the change or rest', e.g., the artisan, the art of bronze-casting the statue, the man who gives advice, the father of the child.

Excellent managers make use of all three in their judgment-making activities.

Section 2: Synchronicity

Jung (1973) calls into question the validity of natural laws to explain the connection between two events, since, for him, underlying the conception of natural laws is causality, which, however, could be only statistical truth and could not be relied on in the 'realm of very small quantities'.

Jung (1973, pp. 5–6) defends the scientific validity of the study of synchronicity by arguing that the connection between cause and effect can turn out to be only statistically valid and may depend in certain circumstances on other than causal relations requiring another principle of explanation. Furthermore, the experimental method of inquiry to establish causal relations is aimed at repeated events and therefore unique or rare events, such as those habitually featured as synchronic, are ruled out (Jung, 1973, p. 6).

Kammerer's law of series

Jung (1973, pp. 7–8) holds that 'there may be some general field where acausal events are found to be actual facts'. Kammerer's law of series points to the cases of the coincidence of events among which there does not exist 'the remotest probability of a causal connection' (Jung, 1973, p. 8).

Kammerer (1919) cited by Diaconis and Mosteller (1989) enumerates as such some examples:

> My brother-in-law E. V. W. attended a concert in Bosendorfer Hall in Vienna on 11 Nov. 1910 he had seat #9 and also coat check #9.
>
> On the walls of the Artist's Cafe across from the University of Vienna hang pictures of famous actors, singers, and musicians. On the 5th of

> May 1917, I noticed for the first time a portrait of Dr Tyvolt. The waiter brought me the New Free Press, in which there was an article on the crisis in the German Popular Theatre, with Dr Tyvolt as the author.

Meaningfully but not causally connected events

Jung (1973, pp. 8–10), however, contends that chance grouping or series fall within the realm of probability. In lieu of the law of series, Jung (1973, p. 25) proposes the term 'synchronicity' defined as 'the simultaneous occurrence of two meaningfully but not causally connected events'. It relates to 'a certain psychic state with one or more external events which appear as meaningful parallels to the momentary subjective state'.

Synchronicity designates the meaningful coincidence or equivalence of (a) a psychic and physical state or event without any causal relationship to one another and (b) similar or identical thoughts, dreams occurring at the same time at different places (Jaffé, 1983).

Epiphanies, paradox, form and patter; and time, space and causality

For Peat (n.d.), synchronicity is the bridge between the inner world of our experiences, dreams, memories and so on. (inscape), and the world of matter, space, and causality (landscape) and he links it to (1) epiphanies; (2) the paradox; (3) form and pattern and (4) time, space and causality.

First, epiphany occurs when 'the world, our thoughts and memories...becomes integrated and charged in a numinous fashion...as if the things around us, the significance of what we are about to do and the pattern of our life becomes unified within a field of meaning...at one and the same time universal, yet highly specific to the details of our own particular history and character' (Peat, n.d.).

Peat (n.d.) argues that epiphany is the essence of synchronicity in that 'sense of a unifying pattern of meaning brings together in a perfectly seamless way of the unfolding movement of inner and outer events'.

Second, the paradox regarding synchronicity concerns the acausality and the unfolding of causally unconnected events in time and space. A point in case of paradox in this sense is the problematic outcome of quantum theory, that particles may be in two different places at the same time (Peat, n.d.). The question is what kind of connection could exist that lies beyond or outside causality (Peat, n.d.). Unitary transformations understood as 'the particular state of the present being totally determined as being a function of a state in the past' leads to the belief that 'every event in the physical world is the end point of a causal chain' and therefore, consequently 'the implications of the future are causally and completely contained within the present' (Peat, n.d.).

Peat (n.d.) sustains that the occurrence of related dreams, memories and visions are left out in this perspective at a pattern of events in the physical world and insists that, unlike some who argue in favour of the possibility that in the quantum theory the measurement problem may hint at the involvement of human consciousness, Schrodinger's Equation is as much governed by unitary transformations as the Newtonian laws of planetary motion. Accordingly, 'quantum theory cannot provide us with a convincing explanation for synchronicity' (Peat, n.d.)

Jung and Pauli (2012), according to Zabriskie (1995, p. 540), sustain the synchronicity principle:

> [w]hich presumes that indestructible energy has a dual relationship to the space-time continuum: on the one hand there is the constant connection through effect, that is, causality, and, on the other, an inconstant connection through contingence, equivalence, or meaning that is synchronicity.

Third, the notion of pattern and form through the Pauli Exclusion Principle (Pauli, 1973) is relevant to the discussion on synchronicity where as such it is understood that 'systems spontaneously fall towards their lowest energy state by getting rid of any excess energy ... [and] ... no two electrons can possess the same value for all their quantum numbers ... [thanks to which] the variety and distinction of the different chemical elements become possible ... ' (Peat, n.d.).

Peat (n.d.) further elaborates on the importance and implications of the Exclusion Principles for synchronicity:

> [t]he wave function that describe the quantum system of electrons must have a particular global form – called anti-symmetry ... something seems to be correlating the dynamics of each individual electron by keeping them apart in their different energy levels, or quantum states ... the mutual exclusion of electrons is truly 'acausal' ... the internal correlation of the electrons'' dynamics is not brought about by any physical force ... it is the direct manifestation of the global form of the wave function of the whole system ... therefore ... the dynamics of the electrons are the manifestation of a global, non-local pattern, or form – a true expression of synchronicity (Peat, n.d.).

The global form referred to above implies the 'non-separability' because of which 'the form of the wave function cannot be broken down into contributions localized at different points in space and time' (Peat, n.d.). The non-separability results in Bell Inequalities or Bell Theorem (Mermin, 1981) to the effect that:

> [t]he results predicted by quantum mechanics could not be explained by any theory which preserved locality. In other words, if you set up an experiment like that described by Einstein, Podolsky, and Rosen, and you

> get the results predicted by quantum mechanics, then there is no way that locality could be true. Years later the experiments were done, and the predictions of quantum mechanics proved to be accurate (Felder, 1999).

The locality is:

> [t]he principle that an event which happens at one place can't instantaneously affect an event someplace else. For example: if a distant star were to suddenly blow up tomorrow, the principle of locality says that there is no way we could know about this event or be affected by it until something, e.g., a light beam, had time to travel from that star to Earth (Felder, 1999).

The existence of the global form means that of dynamical patterns of form underlying all of nature material, energetic and mental – and speculatively we may imagine a 'coherent dance of form, pattern, meaning and information' in matter as well as in mind (Peat, n.d.).

Finally, Peat (n.d.) discusses the question of time, space and causality and call into question the existence of non-unitary processes signifying that 'while the present enfolds the past is not totally determined by it' wherefore the present is converted into an inscape and thanks to it 'within the present are, contained and enfolded, the orders of time'.

As an illustration of the foregoing review of literature on synchronicity, we analyse below a book of Chinese origin that may be founded on synchronicity rather than on causality, the Book of Changes.

Along with the thesis expounded by Kase, Slocum, and Zhang (2011) that Westerners and Asians may hold different views about temporality (Adam, 2006; Hall, 1976), predictability (Chermack & van dr Merwe, 2003), materiality (Leonardi & Barley, 2008; W. J. Orlikowski, 2006), falsifiability and proof (Hume, 1969a, 1969b; Popper, 1957, 2002), recursivity (W. J. Orlikowski & Gash, 1994; W. J. Orlikowski & Yates, 1994), approach to learning (Mayer, 1992a, 1992b), approach to thinking and restructuring of problems (Mayer, 1992a, 1992b), and approach to categorization (Mervis & Rosch, 1981), the causality/synchronicity binomial may be one issue worthy of more attention.

Book of Changes and synchronicity

In line with Bright's (1997, p. 613) statement that synchronicity's unique contribution is to hermeneutics, Jung (1967) observes that the Chinese mind as reflected in I Ching or the Book of Changes seems to be exclusively preoccupied with the chance aspect of events or coincidence and disfavours the Western causalistic procedures.

In the belief that 'whatever happens in a given moment possesses inevitably the quality peculiar to that moment', I Ching deems the hexagram worked out in a given moment is an indicator of the essential situation prevailing in the moment of 'its origin (Jung, 1967, p. xxiv).

Accordingly, I Ching stands on the same ground as the principles of synchronicity, as the latter takes the coincidence of events in space and time as something more than mere chance and underscores 'a peculiar interdependence of objective events among themselves as well as with the subjective (psychic) sates of the observer or observers' (Jung, 1967, p. xxiv).

Parallel to the causal chain A → B→ C→ D, it may happen that A', B', C' and D' appear in the same moment and in the same place because 'the physical events A' and B' are of the same quality as the psychic event C' and D' and all of them are the exponents of one and the same momentary situation' (Jung, 1967, pp. xxiv–xxv).

The sixty-four hexagrams that I Ching may produce reflect the meaning of sixty-four different but yet typical situations and, with situations being unique and not repeated, the only criterion of the validity in synchronicity regarding I Ching's hexagrams is the observer's opinion that 'the text of the hexagram amounts to a true rendering of his psychic condition' (Jung, 1967).

The Chinese believe that 'spiritual agencies' or *shen* acts in a mysterious way that makes the yarrow stalks produce a meaningful answer (Jung, 1967, p. xxv).

> The I Ching does not offer itself with proofs and results; it does not vaunt itself, nor is it easy to approach. Like a part of nature, it waits until it is discovered. It offers neither facts nor power, but for lovers of self-knowledge, of wisdom – if there be such – it seems to be the right book. To one person its spirit appears as clear as day; to another, shadowy as twilight; to a third, dark as night. He who is not pleased by it does not have to use it, and he who is against it is not obliged to find it true. Let it go forth into the world for the benefit of those who can discern its meaning (Jung, 1967, p. xxxix).

Discussion

We reviewed synchronicity concept in this section and are inclined to accept Boutroux's (2010, pp. 25–32) dictum that 'there is no equivalence, no relation of causality, pure and simple, between a man and the elements that gave him birth, between the developed being and the being in process of formation' when the principle of causality is understood as to indicate that 'any change that occurs in things is invariably connected with another change, as a condition, not with any change, but with a fixed one, of such a nature that there is never anything more in the conditioned than in the condition... [and] any change is the correlative of another change that has come about under the conditions in which it happens, and... the relation between such change and some other is an invariable one'.

If so and if causality is not, often times, the relations that helps understand how relata[9] are connected (see Figure 17.2), then, managers and executives or any person facing the need to take some kind of decision will have to cope with the uncertainty derived from contingencies with some kind of criterion.

However, a balanced view of the synchronicity suggests that:

- To the takers of management judgement, synchronicity may sound too removed a concept for their tasks in that it may strikes them too esoteric to be taken seriously into consideration.
- Compared with probabilistic causality, it may be less open to the sharing of a view in an organization.
- The thrust of synchronicity, though, is that there can be different ways to connect (if only in mind) relata with causality not being the only and exclusive one.

We analyse in the next Section 3 the concept of probabilistic causality, another kind of relations linking relata, along with causality and synchronicity.

Section 3: Probabilistic causality, Simpson's Paradox and causality

Probabilistic causality according to Reichenbach (1991, p. 161) is expressed as follows:

$$P(E \mid C) > P(E \mid \sim C)$$

which means that:

- the understanding that C is the cause of E comes from the comparison of two sets of probabilities obtains depending on (2), (3) and (4);
- the probability that when C occurs, E will occur;
- the probability that E will occur, even when C does not;
- if the probability (2) is larger than the probability (3), then C is likely to be the cause of E.

It is long believed that causes raise the probability of their effect expressed as:

$$(PR1) P(E \mid C) > P(E)$$

In words, 'the probability that E occurs, given that C occurs, is higher than the unconditional probability that E occurs' (Hitchcock, 2011).

Or, expressed alternately,

(PR2) P(E | C) > P(E | ~C).

Hitchcock (2011) explains that "(PR) C is a cause of E just in case P(E | C) > P(E | ~C)."

Citing Reichenbach (1991) Ichinose (2011: 43) underlines the possibility of event A may be 'screened off' by even C in the establishment of causal relations with B:

P(B | A) > P(B | ~A), but
P(B | A&C) = P(B | C).

Event A is called 'spurious cause' (Ichinose, 2011, p. 43), because, given the occurrence of C, B occurs without need for A to occur.

Therefore, in order to eliminate the spurious causes, upon establishing probabilistic causality a systematic handling of the relations among variables must needs be invented, and thus Bayesianism came to the forefront in the 1950s (Ichinose, 2011, p. 44).

Bayesian Conditionalisation (Williamson, 2007, p. 7) contends that, if $P_{pos}(h) > P_{pri}(h)$, then e is confirmed by e, whereas, if $P_{pos}(h) < P_{pri}(h)$, then h is disconfirmed by e, when h stands for a hypothesis, e for proofs, pri for the probability prior to the obtaining of proofs e, and post for the probability after the obtaining of proofs e (Ichinose, 2011, p. 48).

This conditionalization was qualified by Jeffrey (1990) on the ground that $P_{pos}(h \mid e)$ may not be 1 since, even with proofs e, some ambiguity always lingers on. For this reason, Jeffrey Conditionalisation was proposed in its place:

$$P_{pos}(h) = P_{pri}(h \mid e) = P_{pri}(h \mid e)\ P_{pos}(e) + P_{pri}(h \mid {\sim}e)\ P_{pos}(\ \mid e).$$

This conditionalization coincides with Bayesian Conditionalisation when $P_{pos}(e) = 1$ (Ichinose, 2011, p. 49).

Ichinose (2011, pp. 56–57) goes on to enumerate reservations on probabilistic causality such as (1) Rosen's puzzle (event α may be considered as the cause of β even if α may reduce the chance of β's occurrence); and (2) Humphrey's Paradox (i.e., backward causality allowing an effect to occur before its cause), but insists that the most difficult reservation to ignore is Simpson's Paradox.

Simpson's Paradox

Simpson's Paradox refers to a statistical phenomenon in which a correlation present in different groups is reversed when the groups are combined (Simpson, 1951), namely, there are examples of 'an association between a pair of variables that can consistently be inverted in each subpopulation of a population when the population is partitioned' (Malinas & Bigelow, 2009).

Table 17.1 Simpson's Paradox

	Male		Female		Sum male and female	
	Recovered	Not recovered	Recovered	Not recovered	Recovered	Not recovered
Therapy	20	40	20	10	40	50
Non therapy	15	40	90	50	105	90

Source: Ichinose (2011), p. 59.

As cited by Malinas and Bigelow (2009), Cohen and Nagel (1993) reported tuberculosis death rates in 1910 in Richmond and New York and found that (1) 'the death rate for African American was lower in Richmond than in New York'; (2) 'the death rate for Caucasians was lower in Richmond than in New York'; but (3) 'the death rate for the total combined population of African American and Caucasians was higher in Richmond than in New York'.

Malinas and Bigelow (2009) attribute this to Simpson' Reversal of Inequalities and give the following example:

- $a/b < A/B$
- $c/d < C/D$, and
- $(a+c)/(b+d) > (A+C)/(B+D)$

$1/5 < 2/8$
$6/8 < 4/5$
$7/13 > 6/13$.

Ichinose (2011, pp. 59–60) takes the following table (Table 17.1 Simpson's Paradox) from Malinas and Bigelow's article in Stanford Encyclopedia of Philosophy published in 2004.

The purpose of Malinas and Below's is to show how Simpson's Paradox works on the following propositions:

- the male patients may have a higher rate of recovery when they receive therapy than when they may not;
- the female patents may have a higher rate of recovery when they receive therapy than when they may not;
- by consequence, the patients, both male and female, may have a higher rate of recovery when they receive therapy than they may not.

1. obtains because $20/(20+40) > 15/(15+40)$
2. obtains, too, because $20/(20+10) > 90/(90+50)$

3. does not fulfil because 40/50 < 105/(105+90).

Ichinose (2011, p. 60) represents the propositions (1) to (3) as follows:

- $p \supset r$
- $q \supset r$
- $(p \vee q) \supset r$

Although the propositions (1) to (3) follow the classical inferential form and seem to be quite right, Ichinose (2011) sustains that the fore-going illustration going counter to the propositions demonstrates the possible failure of probabilistic causality if it continues to believe in the possibility-raising theories of causation (Hitchcock, 2011).

Probabilistic causality after its 'quietus'

Ichinose (2011, pp. 70–71) surmises that the way to continue with the probabilistic causality could result in two outcomes: (1) the mystification; or (2) the endless pursuit. First, understanding that the problem of Simpson's Paradox is how to discern how the population and reference class work out may lead to the belief that all of a sudden and without our realization of how it occurs the adequate population presents itself, a pure mystery (Ichinose, 2011).

Second, efforts may be deployed to discern the relationships based on probabilistic causality and those that are not based on such causality by means of empirical verification of adequate populations for probabilistic causality, which, after all, will lead us to the 'darkness of infinity' (Ichinose, 2011). It is a kind of St. Petersburg Paradox (Bernoulli, 1954), namely, 'a particular (theoretical) lottery game that leads to a random variable with infinite expected value, i.e., infinite expected payoff, but would nevertheless be considered to be worth only a very small amount of money'.[10] And as Hájek (2003, p. 273) points out, 'every probability assignment has uncountably many '"trouble spots"'.

In order to avoid the afore-mentioned outcomes, Ichinose (2011, p. 71) advises us to adopt the stance that causality is something that one has to assume as a norm, even if one not be aware of it as such, instead of continuing to believe that causality can be verified and confirmed.

Discussion

Takeuchi (2010: passim) asseverates that probability as quantification of contingent phenomena, drawing on the law of large numbers, central limit theorem,[11] statistical hypothesis testing, cannot make inference of people's behaviour because of their internal necessity based on their free will. He also insists that 'Quetelet's dogma', with its belief in the normal distribution of all the social phenomena, is out of phase with the reality and that the present-day society is dominated less and less by the law of large numbers, which signifies the end of an era in which attempt was made to 'domesticate' contingency.

Takeuchi (2010) sustains the idea that in such a circumstance we have to learn to live with contingency and design new behavioural criteria such as (1) to ignore events of minimum probability (e.g., the collision of earth with another heavenly body), to become aware of that the social phenomena like the financial market are dominated by the mutual and self-fulfilling enforcement of market opinions (e.g., bubbles and their bursts); and (2) to realize that there can be a different kind of contingency that cannot be put under control by the law of large numbers (e.g., biological mutations, contingencies in the historical events, good and bad lucks). Chaos may, for Takeuchi (2010), be an example of the combination of necessity and contingency, since chaos in short term may be explained by differential equations as events dominated by necessity, but chaos in long term is determined by its initial conditions as events dominated by contingency. Takeuchi (2010) contends that this is further enhanced by the fact that the operating forces on the present-day society are the law of increasing entropy and at the same time the law of increasing information. The former operates for the increase in chaos and therefore contingency, while the latter brings about the increase in order (Takeuchi, 2010, pp. 73–74).

Takeuchi's (2010) argument rounds up the arguments exposed in Section 3 and shows the shortcomings of an excessive reliance upon probabilistic causality as deliberated in relation to the synchronicity concept. Whereas the objections raised in the synchronicity section were of external nature to the logical structure, this section has dealt with the difficulties that emerge from the very centre of causal probabilism (internal to the logical structure).

In concluding this section, we render complete our review of different literature survey fields related to contingency by exploring the linkage between the degree of conviction or credence and the probability of good guess, based on Ariño survey {Ariño, 2012 #4460}. In brief, its findings contend (1) that a subjective assessment of one's decision may always be affected by contingency; and (2) that the conviction can be quite an illusory phenomenon until one is almost firmly confident of one's 'correctness'. Overall, the survey results point to the possibility that good guess or hit rate may be anticipated by the degree of conviction or credence, namely, the more convinced a person is, the better he 'hits the bull's eye'. This is relevant, as far as we are concerned, to the elucidation of P_1 and P_2 regarding the contingency/necessity binomial.

Before moving on to the analysis of an empirical case of judgement-making in a situation of uncertainty in Section 5, we summarise our findings by way of propositions in the next Section 4.

Section 4: Propositions

On the basis of the literature survey we carried out in the previous sections on contingency, synchronicity and probabilistic causality, and an empirical survey on the linkage between the degree of credence/conviction and right guess, we offer below our propositions regarding the way executives and 'actors' cope with contingency.

P_1 the phenomena we are dealing with fall into final contingency under the category of empirical contingency

Related to this proposition is the causal judgement literature. Contingency information is defined as 'information about the occurrence or non-occurrence of a certain effect in the presence or absence of a certain causal candidate' (White, 2000, p. 415).

Two dominant accounts of how people make these judgements are (1) the use of rules of inference; and (2) associative-learning mechanisms (White, 2000, p. 415). For the former, Δ P rule is proposed which involves 'subtracting the proportion of occasions on which the effect occurs in the absence of a causal candidate from the proportion of occasions on which the effect occurs in the presence of that candidate' (White, 2000, p. 415). This is pretty much the way probabilistic causality has been described to work in the preceding section. The model's heuristic value with regard to human contingency judgements is important (Allan, 1993, p. 446)

Associative-learning approach considers that 'the judgement follows the accumulation of a record of experiences, forming an association between mental representations of a cue (or an action) and an outcome' (White, 2000, p. 415). Associative-learning principles are also useful in understanding human contingency judgement (Allan, 1993, p. 446).

White (2000, p. 416) adds one more account called idiosyncratic that refers to reports or uses of a single type of information and does not imply that the person in question avails himself from models (e.g., Δ P rule) of all types of information.

The four types of contingency information are CO (candidate cause present, outcome occurs), C-O (candidate present, outcome does not occur), -CO, and –C-O (White, 2000, p. 416).

P_2 the final contingency is handled as if it were the final necessity by the protagonists

This is the reason why fate seems to entail an element of necessity in the way the agent feels about it. The event or events that triggers the recognition of one's own fate may look contingent at first sight, but the idea of fate implies that, somehow, the agent will necessarily get at it at some point of his or her lifetime. Thus, if fate was described above as 'internalised contingency',

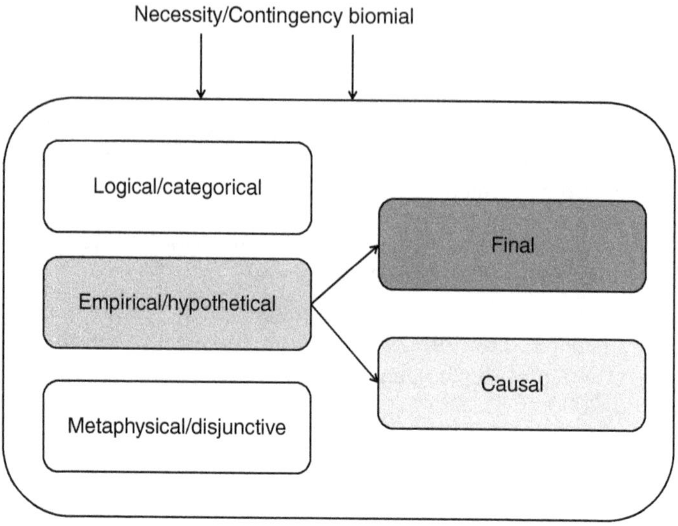

Figure 17.4 Necessity and contingency categories
Source: Authors based on Kuki (1996, etc.).

it also can be called 'internalised necessity' (see Figure 17.4 necessity and contingency categories).

P_3 the shift from contingency to necessity is supported by the protagonists' expertise, knowledge, degree of credence, insofar as they reduce the level of uncertainty derived from contingency

Keynes (1957, p. 148) underscores the reasonableness of being guided 'by the facts about which we feel somewhat confident'.

This stands on reason since without previous experience there is no intuition, as 'usually, many trials are needed to acquire procedural knowledge, although one-trial learning does occur' (Ten Berge & van Hezewijk, 1999, p. 607), in particular when it is dealt with synchronic or fateful events. Likewise, in experiments where subjects were repeatedly exposed to cards recognition, 'the means indicate an effect of training, because in each subject, response latency decreased over the segments, reaching asymptote between sessions 33 and 40' (Lewicki, Czyzewska, & Hoffman, 1987, p. 526). And also 'by about card 50, all normal participants began to express a "hunch" that decks A and B were riskier and all generated anticipatory SCRs whenever they pondered a choice from deck A or B' (Bechara, Damasio, Tranel, & Damasio, 1997, p. 1293). Causal probabilism is the base of knowledge it is usually drawn upon when exposed to scientific or technical knowledge.

The emotional oracle effect may explain part of this proposition since it points out that 'individuals who have higher trust in their feeling can predict the outcomes of future events better than individuals with lower trust in their feelings' (Pham, Lee, & Stephen, 2012).

P_4 chance factors may occur in aid of the protagonists

Besides sheer chance, we argue that this can also be related to the occurrence of synchronicity, that is, the meaningful happening of unrelated events which advances the purposive actions taken by the agent.

P_5 the protagonists live in a present that embraces past and future

The protagonists or agents are able to build upon past events to take action in the present that includes an evaluation or innovation of possible future states of events. As Schopenhauer (2007, pp. 85–86) stated, 'in the daily affairs of life, you will have very many opportunities of recognizing a characteristic difference between ordinary people and people of prudence and discretion; in estimating the possibility of danger in connection with any undertaking, an ordinary man will confine his inquiries to the kind of risk that has already attended such undertakings in the past, whereas a prudent person will look ahead, and consider everything that might possibly happen in the future...'.

In the next Section 5, these propositions are verified with a case of technology development in the face of uncertainty resulting from the existence of several optional technology streams. Comparison of Akasaki's and Nakamura's trajectories will be made to substantiate these propositions. For the convenience of explanation the order of exposition will not follow. $P_1 \rightarrow P_4$.

Section 5: Judgement-making vis-à-vis contingency, example of blue light-emitting diode development

We have reviewed literature on judgement-making (Nonaka & Konno, 2012) in the light of contingency, probabilistic causality and synchronicity and have also analysed an empirical survey report to see the relations between the conviction or degree of credence and the probability of right answers.

Our interests now lie in integrating the information and insight garnered from the previous sections. Basically, we hypothesise that at the moment of judgement-making the actors (or those with success) configure their decision and undertake their actions by coping with the degree of uncertainty surrounding the decision, which is usually done by 'good' actors by considering it as dependant on contingency-necessity category, specifically, within the subcategory of empirical contingency/final contingency. In this process, final contingency comes to be deemed rather to be final necessity, namely, if event A occurs event B also occurs. Such shift from contingency to necessity that takes place in the mind of the actors is aided and supported by the past experience, expertise, knowledge, etc., since they would lessen the degree of uncertainty at least in the sphere of the actor's mind.

To have a view of judgement-making in the round we proceed to review and analyse an empirical example in this section. The development of blue diode by two groups of Japanese researchers will be described below. These groups opted for one of the two method to develop diode, though the rest of researchers followed the other method.

Shinagawa research

This section therefore largely draws on the research conducted by Shinagawa, Gemba, and Abe (2012) on the development of blue LED (light emitting diode) during the last thirty years mainly in Japan, which focuses on process innovation rather than on product innovation.

Shinagawa et al. (2012) justify their selection of process innovation instead of product innovation on the following reasons:

- Economies of scale for cost reduction and productivity increase by process innovation.
- More chance to exploit new process technology in high-technology industries.
- Cases of Kuhnian normal scientific progress (1996) more frequent than 'extraordinary science' events with process innovation representing more of normal science.
- Limited research conducted on process innovation so far.

Shinagawa et al. (2012) compare the development of two streams of research and development on blue light-emitting diodes (blue LEDs), namely, gallium nitride (GaN) and zinc selenide (ZnSe) and propose a new theory named scientific seed theory that explains how 'new process technology is established [and]...accelerates scientific progress in specialized applied science that leads to the development of new technologies'. The implications of blue LED development are that it could quadruple the amount of data that could be read and stored on a compact disc, digital video disc (DVD), etc., and also that, combined with red and green the blue can produce white light (Science Watch, 2000).

Shinagawa et al (2012, pp. 4–5) contend (1) that, when basic product concepts are still in development, opportunities for product innovation are higher than for process innovation; (2) that, on the one hand, process innovation has more chance of success when a dominant design emerges that reduces uncertainty in developing process technology; (3) that, on the other, process technology gains importance in the growth of new industry (e.g., electronic devices, nano-technology, bio-based products) since it needs that uncertainty be eliminated by radical process innovation; and (4) that superior process technology comes to dominate by means of a 'contagion' effect based on 'cognition occurring as part of the application of the scientific progress'.

Shinagawa et al. (2012, p. 6) observe that the number of accumulated papers on GaN development initially grew gradually but its pace of publication rapidly increased whereas its rival technology ZnSe did not catch up with GaN's publication rhythm.

Shinagawa et al. (2012) trace the evolution of the publications on each one of the two streams by using bibliometrics, 'a technique that arose from the practice of bibliography to identify trends in scientific research' (Shinagawa et al., 2012, p. 3). The commercial bibliography database Scopus was made use of, because it covers 80 per cent of the approximately 23,000 peer-reviewed journals in the field (Shinagawa et al., 2012, p. 7). They use the logistic equation to model the diffusion of innovation to see how 'contagion' effect occurs, namely, the adoption of a stream of technology by others.

Figure 17.5 the Evolution of research and development on GaN and ZnSe between the 1960s and 2011 graphically represents the evolution of research and development on the two streams between the 1960s and 2011.

Our observations of Figure 17.5 run as follows:

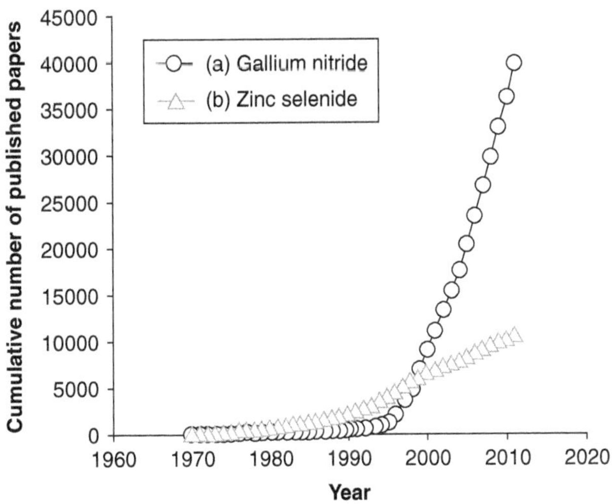

Figure 17.5 Evolution of research and development on GaN and ZnSe between the 1960s and 2011

Source: Shinagawa, Gemba, & Abe (2012), p. 8.

- according to Figure 17.1 until 2000 the cumulative number of articles was bigger in the case of ZnSe;
- it took thirty years (1970–2000) for the trend to become more favourable to GaN;
- the change in the trend may seem to have happened around the beginning to mid1990s to the end1990s with the publication of some import articles.

Related to the observations, some questions crop up such as:

- Before the contagion takes place, do some epoch-making papers (perhaps only a few of them) have to be produced that change the research atmosphere?
- During the thirty year take-off period (1970–2000) did researchers think their options (ZnSe and GaN) better? No awakening of awareness that theirs is a losing option?
- Does point 1 mean that the change in the trend appear all of a sudden thanks to the publication of a very few number of ground-breaking papers?

Table 17.2a The top three most frequently cited papers

	No of Citation	Sources
1	1,041	Amano, H.N. Sawaki, I. Akasaki, & Y. Toyoda. (1986). Metalorganic vapor phase epitaxial growth of a high-quality GaN film using an AIN buffer layer. *Applied Physics Letters*. 48 (5), 353–355.
2	699	Nakkamura, Shuji. (1991). GaN growth using GaN buffer layer. *Japanese Journal of Applied Physics Part 2: Letters*. 30 (10A), L1705–L1707.
3	534	Nakkamura, Shuji, Naruhito Iwasa, Masayuki Senoh, & Takashi Mukai (1992). Hole compensation mechanism of p-type GaN films. *Japanese Journal of Applied Physics, Part 1: Regular Papers and Short Notes and Review Papers*. 31 (5A), 1258–1266.

Source: Shinagawa et al. (2012), p. 12.

Table 17.2b High-impact papers by Shuji Nakamura published since 1994

High-Impact Papers by Shuji Nakamura, Published Since 1994 (Ranked by average citations per year)			
Rank	**Paper**	**Total citations**	**Average cities per year**
1	S. Nakamura et al. (1996). InGaN-based multi-quantum-well-structure laser diodes. *Japan J. App!. Phys.* 2, 35 (1B), L74-L71.	601	172
2	S. Nakamura, T. Mukal, & M. Sengh. (1994). Candela-class high-brightness InGan-AlGan double heterostructure blue light-emitting diodes. *App!. Phys. Lett.* 64 (13), 1687–1689.	572	104
3	Nakamura et al. (1995). Superbright green InGaN single-quantum-well structure light-emitting diodes. *Japan J. Appl. Phys.* 2, 34 (10B), 1332–1335.	207	59
4	Y Narukawa et al. (1997). Role of self-formed InGaN quantum dots for exciton localization in the purple laser-diode emitting at 420 nm. *Appl. Phys.* Lett. 70 (8), 981–983.	142	57
5	S. Nakamura et al. (1995) High-brightness InGan blue, green and yellow light- emitting diodes with quantum-well structure. *Japan J. Appl. Phys.* 2, 34 (7A), 797–799.	238	53

Source: ISI's Science Indicators Database, 1981–June 1999 cited by Science Watch 2002.

So no prediction can be made of this sudden change? How fast can you detect this sudden change? How can you provide a warning system to change research trend?

- In case the change takes place very gradually, it will be very difficult to predict it; even after the epoch-making articles (Amano, Akasaki & Nakamura articles as shown in Table 9.2a the top three most frequently cited papers and other articles as shown in Table 9.2b High-impact papers by Shuji Nakamura published since 1994) ten more years were needed for the clear bifurcation of the trends (1991–2000)?
- If ten years were needed for the above change, a long latency period existed so that some kind of SECI process (i.e., socialization, externalization and internalization) (Nonaka et al., 2008) occurs slowly?

In summary, we are discussing the key issues of concern (1) if the trend is changed by some small number of articles; and (2) how and why the proponents of these articles take up the stream of development that may or may not belong to the main stream. If not main stream, then they must have been prepared to assume more risk or at least the risk subjectively felt, being a minority in the research trend. As shown in Fig. 17.5 and analysed before, ZnSe held more sway than GaN until the 1990s, but the trend was inversed by more articles on GaN that started to be published around that period.

Comparison of GaN and ZnSe: trend-setting by Akasaki, Amano and Nakamura

Shuji Nakamura is cited by Science Watch (2000) as asserting as follows:

> The crystal quality of zinc selenide is very good. The dislocation density, which is a measure of the number of defects in the crystal, was less than 10^3 per cubic centimetre. Gallium nitride was more than 10^{10} per cubic centimetre. And when people wanted to make reliable LEDs and laser diodes, they knew that the dislocation density has to be lower than 10^3 or even 10^2. This is just physics.

GaN, on the contrary, had two hurdles to overcome, according to Mizobuchi (n.d., pp. 7–8; Takeda Foundation, 2005a, p. 3): (1) the difficulty to obtain a uniform quality of film on sapphire substrate; (2) the difficulty in forming p-type film on the device; and (3) dislocation or irregular density problem.

The pioneer in GaN research is Isamu Akasaki whose achievement in collaboration with Amano is described as follows:

> [Akasaki] started working on GaN-based blue LEDs in the late 1960s. Step by step, he improved the quality of GaN crystals and device structures at Matsushita Research Institute Tokyo, Inc.(MRIT), where he decided to adopt metal organic vapour phase epitaxy (MOVPE) as the preferred growth method for GaN. In 1981 he started afresh growth of GaN by MOVPE at Nagoya University, and in 1985 he and his group succeeded in (1) growing high-quality GaN on sapphire substrate by pioneering the low-temperature (LT) buffer layer technology. This high-quality GaN enabled them; (2) to discover p-type GaN by doping with magnesium (Mg) and subsequent activation by electron irradiation (1989); (3) to produce the first GaN p-n junction blue/UV LED (1989); and (4) to achieve conductivity control of n-type GaN (1990) and related alloys(1991) by doping with silicon (Si),enabling the use of heterostructures and multiple quantum wells in the design of more efficient p-n junction light emitting structures. They achieved stimulated emission from the GaN firstly at room temperature in 1990, and developed in 1995 the stimulated emission at 388nm with pulsed current

> injection from high-quality AlGaN/GaN/GaInN quantum well device. They verified quantum size effect (1991) and quantum confined Stark effect (1997) in nitride system, and in 2000 showed theoretically the orientation dependence of piezoelectric field and the existence of non-/semi-polar GaN crystals. (http://en.wikipedia.org/wiki/Isamu_Akasaki accessed on 30 July, 2012).

By the time Akasaki and Amano managed to produce the first GaN p-n junction blue/UV LED in 1989, Nakamura's effort[12] to develop two-flow MOCVD[13] was under way (Mizobuchi, n.d., p. 8).

Nakamura cited by *Science Watch* (2000) asserts:

> Usually a MOCVD has only one gas flow [which] is a reactive gas that blows parallel to the substrate… [by adding] another subflow with an inactive gas blowing perpendicular to the substrate [which] suppressed the large thermal convection you get when you're trying to get a crystal at 1,000 degrees.

Nakamura conjectured that the production of p-type by electron radiation would not be amenable to mass production and succeeded to make p-type using a thermal annealing technique in 1992 (Science Watch, 2000).

The dislocation density problem was also sorted out by Nakamura using the two-flow MOCVD at the end of 1995 (Science Watch, 2000).

Contingency and management judgement: why did Akasaki, Amano and Nakamura choose GaN process in lieu of ZnSe?

For the analysis of why Akasaki, Amano and Nakamura stuck to GaN technology despite the fact that their technology of choice did not form the main stream of the two rivalling alternatives, we make use of the propositions enunciated in Section 5.

Akasaki and Amano case[14]

Isamu Akasaki, born in 1928, started his life as researcher in 1952 upon graduating from Kyoto University and joining the present-day Fujitsu. His first research was on the development of fluorescent material for cathode tubes. After a stint at Nagoya University between 1959 and 1964, where he successfully contributed to the development of high quality germanium transistor using epitaxial growth, Akasaki joined Matsushita Electrics' research centre. In the belief that compound semiconductors would have a great future as light device, he carried out research on the production methods of compound semiconductors epitaxial film using arsenic gallium, phosphorus gallium, and gallium nitride. ⇐ P_3, P_4 (these numbers correspond to the proposition numbers in Section 5).

Ever since Akasaki joined Matsushita, he had keen interest in gallium nitride semiconductor but was aware that due to its large energy gap it was not appropriate for electronic devices. However, in 1971 it was published that a blue-green light emitting diode had been developed using gallium nitride, which gave rise to a surge of GaN research, though ended up by losing its momentum because of the difficulty to produce uniform film without cracks. ⇐ P_3

Akasaki cherished a strong interest in blue light diode even before GaN research became popular because of 1971 surge and in 1973 took up three alternatives for consideration for his research, namely, silicon carbide (SiC), zinc selenide (ZnSe) and gallium nitride (GaN). From among these three alternatives GaN was the least favourite on account of the difficulty to produce uniform filming. Other researchers considered in order of preference SiC and ZnSe rather than GaN. ⇐ P_1, P_2, P_3

Akasaki decided in favour of GaN, (1) because he believed that epitaxial growth technology in which he excelled would lead to the success in producing uniform GaN filming; (2) because he considered ZnSe too bland for a stable electronic device based on his experience of handling various compound semiconductors; (3) because GaN is more solid and has better heat-conductivity, albeit less open to be converted into p-type on account of higher band gap for pn junction. Akasaki likewise reckoned that GaN, along with its similar materials such as AlN and InN, promised more as semiconductor and that, even if its crystallization offered more technical difficulties due to nitride's high steam pressure, it would be sorted out by using epitaxial growth method. ⇐ P_1, P_2, P_3

For three years, starting from April 1975, Akasaki spent his effort on testing GaN device using sapphire substrate and produced thousands of trial units of MIS-structured blue diodes with the average and maximum luminous efficiency of 0.03 per cent and 0.12 per cent, respectively, figures too distant for practical use. Instead of thinking better of abandoning the project Akasaki newly brought himself to believe in GaN option on the ground that even if the film was not uniformly formed there were spots where the surface was even and neat, therefore it was the question of finding a way to extend these spots to the rest. ⇐ P_3, P_4

Akasaki reconsidered the GaN film-forming methods. Until then, he used hydride chemical vapour deposition method but its film growth rate seemed to be too fast, whereas molecular beam epitaxial method (MBE) was too slow. Accordingly, he settled on Metal Organic Chemical Vapour Deposition (MOCVD). ⇐ P_3, P_4

In 1981, Akasaki moved to Nagoya University and in the following year he met his future research partner, Hiroshi Amano, who would collaborate with Akasaki for the next twenty-one years. ⇐ P_4

Akasaki was convinced that his research would almost be successful if he managed to obtain the forming of uniform filming without cracks.

He also undertook to restudy crystal growth process. Sapphire substrate would continue to be used. Various combinations of substrate temperature, quantity of trim ethyl gallium and ammonia gas, nitride, hydrogen were tried, but no uniform and transparent filming without cracks was beyond reach. ⇐ P_2, P_3

Akasaki came to adopt the idea that changing only the combination of different conditions would not lead him anywhere and hit upon the idea that he might put buffer layers between a sapphire substrate and GaN film. Four candidate materials were proposed to Amano: zinc oxide, aluminium nitride, GaN and SiC. Amano took up aluminium nitride but could not produce any good results; Akasaki insisted on it, however, based on his hunch feeling and asked Amano to continue to prove it. ⇐ P_3, P_4

In 1986, Amano under Akasaki's supervision chanced to try to treat aluminium nitride at 500 degree centigrade in view of an electric furnace not working properly that day (as it only needed that level of temperature) and, after the furnace being fixed, produced GaN film at 1000 degrees. At first, upon inspecting the output Amano suspected that the process had not got through on account of usual opaque film not being observed, but actually found that GaN film was successfully formed and it was as transparent as sapphire substrate. Thus the introduction of a buffer layer was a breakthrough in the development of blue light-emitting diode. ⇐ P_4

Apart from the forming of uniform film there was one more obstacle for blue diode to come into being: p-type GaN film carrying a positive charge. The film so far obtained was of n-type semiconductor property.

Based on his experience Akasaki knew that, adding a small quantity of zinc to gallium nitride, blue luminescence would be obtained and thought zinc additive might help to produce p-type property. The test results did not turn to be positive, but in 1987 Amano happened to read in J. C. Philips's book on bonds and bands in semiconductors that magnesium tended to produce p-type better than zinc. Though test results did not show the formation of p-type film even with magnesium, Akasaki and Amano saw that the device, exposed to electric voltage, emitted blue light stronger than in previous tests. ⇐ P_3, P_4

Amano also happened to observe in an experiment that gallium nitride to which zinc was added, when exposed to electron beam, increased cathode luminescence as the electron beam was intensified. Akasaki suspected that this phenomenon might signify the formation of p-type film thanks to electron beam, though later experiments did not confirm this suspicion. ⇐ P_3, P_4

In 1989, Akasaki and Amano decided to combine the results of the two findings, namely, (1) GaN with magnesium additive emitting a stronger luminescence; and (2) gallium nitride with zinc additive emitting stronger cathode luminescence, exposed to electron beam. Accordingly, gallium nitride doped with magnesium was exposed to electron beam and as a result electric resistance went down by two digits and p-type formation was confirmed. A trial piece of pn diode was immediately manufactured by putting alternately p-type and n-type gallium nitride films. They discovered that the emission of blue-colour luminesce was ten times stronger than the previous records. The results were reported in 1989 in Japanese Journal of Applied Physics. ⇐ P_3

Drawing on the success on two fronts, namely, the obtaining of uniform gallium nitride without cracks using low-temperature buffer layers, on the one hand, and the manufacturing of p-type film with electron exposure, on the other, Akasaki and Amano succeeded in producing a trial piece of blue light-emitting diode with one percent luminescence efficiency in 1992 and by 1995 they developed gallium nitride blue colour semiconductor laser using pn multi-quantum well structure device.

Akasaki's success as researcher comes from his work done between 1986 and 1989 when he was 58 and 61 of age, respectively, despite his fifty years' dedication to research. He attributes it to his perseverance around his main field of specialization in GaAs, aluminium gallium arsenide, and solid solutions (Akasaki, 2002).

Nakamura case[15]

Nakamura joined Nichia Chemical after his graduation from Tokushima University in 1979. During the first ten years in the company, he succeeded in launching three compound semiconductors, which, though a remarkable achievement for one man, could not be considered as commercial success and felt in the need of demonstrating to the company what he could contribute.

In 1988, Nakamura directly pleaded for the president's support to start the development of blue light-emitting diode in the light of the refusal from his direct superior. The budget assigned by the president amounted as much as to ¥ 300 million, which, for Nichia with the yearly turnover of ¥ 20 billion, was a huge amount. ⇐ P3, P_4

Nakamura chose GaN despite the technological difficulties it implied. He reminisces as follows:

> At that time, 1989, there were two materials for making blue LEDs: zinc selenide and gallium nitride. These had the right brand gap energy for blue lasers. But everybody was working on zinc selenide because that was supposed to be much better. I thought about my past experience: if there were a lot of competition, I cannot win. Only a small number of people at a few universities were working with gallium nitride so I figured I'd better work with that. Even if I succeeded in making a blue LED using zinc selenide, I would lose out to the competition when it came to selling it (Science Watch, 2000). ⇐ P_3

Another decision Nakamura had to take concerned the production method: MBE or MOCVD. Nakamura opted for MOCVD because of its appropriateness for mass production. In order to learn about MOCVD Nakamura went to Florida State University as visiting researcher for a year from April 1988. He found there two units of MOCVD but with everybody trying to use them it was impossible for Nakamura to make use of neither of them, which forced him to use a third, broken-down unit. He had to spend nine months to bring it to a working condition. This experience, though, helped him back in Japan to handle the unit he had ordered for Nichia from the US prior to his stay in Florida. $\Leftarrow P_4$

The MOCVD at Nichia was of one flow type. Nakamura tried for three months to get uniform film combining different temperatures, gas flow quantity, etc., in vain. It was generally believed that gallium compound, nitrogen, and other gas should be injected as laminar flow from one direction in parallel currents, but gallium nitride film thus obtained lacked uniformity nor nitrogen fixed was scarce. Nakamura undertook to modify the unit on his own, which allowed him to save a long waiting time for modification works done outside. $\Leftarrow P_2$

In February 1990, Nakamura hit upon the idea that gallium compound and other source gases be injected to the substrate horizontally while nitrogen and hydrogen gas be injected to it vertically (two-flow method), but in March that year the new Nichia president instructed him to halt the development of blue LED and to produce gallium arsenic for mobile phones HEMT (high electron mobility transistor). Nakamura decided to continue to work on his original project risking his dismissal from the company. The two-flow method made it possible to produce transparent and uniform gallium nitride film and it was awarded a patent (so-called Patent No. 404). In 1991, it produced a sample with Hall coefficient[16] of 200 cm^2 in excess of Akasaki's with 90 cm^2. $\Leftarrow P_2, P_4$

Another important technical problem was the difficulty in forming p-type film because the light-emitting device needs both n-type and p-type gallium nitride film. As mentioned before, Akasaki and Amano team succeeded in 1989 in making p-type film by exposing it to electron beam.

However, Nakamura thought better of it and conjectured that the manufacturing of p-type film by electron beam might not be amenable to mass production and started to work on a different and new method. Akasaki and Amano attributed their success to some kind of thermal effect by electron beaming and added magnesium to gallium nitride to administer annealing effect but did not gain much success. Nakamura, therefore, theorized that the thermal effect could be enhanced by treating gallium nitride in an atmosphere containing nitrogen but devoid of hydrogen, which would activate magnesium additive and help the formation of p-type film. His theory is based on the proposition that hydrogen atoms bond with acceptor impurities. As a matter of fact, gallium nitride film heat-treated in an atmosphere not containing hydrogen showed resistivity five digits lower with 2Ùcm and as a consequence p-type film with 10 $cm^2/V.s$ electron electron mobility was made in 1992. Amano, in contrast, failed to produce p-type film because of his heat-treatment of gallium nitride being done in an atmosphere containing ammonium. To clarify this failure Nakamura submitted p-type samples obtained by heat-treatment in nitrogen atmosphere to the heat-treatment in an atmosphere with ammonium and discovered that the heat-treatment in high temperature made them lose p-type property because of the formation of compounds from hydrogen and magnesium atoms. He also discovered that the use of ammonium gas in making gallium nitride resulted in the loss of p-type activation. Nakamura applied on behalf of Nichia for a patent in December 1991. The difference between Nakamura and Akasaki/Amano lay in the use of different atmospheres, which favoured in Nakamura's case. $\Leftarrow P_1, P_2, P_3, P_4$

In the development of blue light-emitting diode itself, too, Nakamura took the shine out of his rivals.

Gallium nitride emits 360 to 390 mm wavelength and its colour is rather violet than blue for which the wave length must be changed to around 420 mm. Akasaki and Amano tried to mix indium and gallium nitride but failed to produce a satisfactory result despite their infinitude of experiments. Amano is reported to have admitted in later years that in the bottom of his heart a doubt had crossed his mind that it could be impossible to produce a film based on the combined crystallization of gallium nitride and indium[17]. $\Leftarrow P_1, P_4$

By contrast, Nakamura never lost his heart and pushed on using the same idea and in 1991, he reported his success in producing 420 mm wave length, blue diode using gallium nitride and indium compound. Amano immediately replicated Nakamura's experiment and succeeded without any problem. $\Leftarrow P_1, P_4$

Takeda Foundation's report (2005b, p. 9) cites this case as an example of situations in which nobody stakes their bet on the success of an idea but somebody may cherish a strong belief in it and persevere in its achievement and attain the desired goal; and, on the contrary, if somebody pushes on half-heartedly because of lack of conviction, no positive result comes out of his effort. In our propositions this can be interpreted as an illustration of the success because the protagonist is capable of turning the final contingency into necessity. $\Leftarrow P_1$

Discussion

The propositions enunciated in Section 4 are below construed in the light of the fore-going example.

> P_1 the phenomena we are dealing with fall into final contingency under the category of empirical contingency and P_2 the final contingency is handled as if it were the final necessity by the protagonists.

From the foregoing description and comparison of Akasaki, Amano and Nakamura rivalry in developing blue light-emitting diode, we can infer that in the mind of these researchers who separated themselves from the rest of the pack there does not seem to exist any concern about a possible failure in the pursuit of their objective. Therefore final contingency looks to be handled as if it were final necessity, even as fate.

The characteristics of chemical field may give some part of explanation[18]. The elimination of technological certainty may be in place because of a relatively small number of technology alternatives. And exhaustion of possible combinations of elements leading to a solution may be more relevant in this field than mere inspiration, namely, perseverance rather than the sharpness of intelligence, which may work out in favour of people of unfailing 'optimism'.

> P_3 the shift from contingency to necessity is supported by the protagonists' expertise, knowledge, degree of credence, insofar as they reduce the level of uncertainty derived from contingency.

Nakamura's success in using nitrogen atmosphere comes as a result also of his constant research effort, supported by his competence. Such effort may fail when the constancy that may bring about the conversion of final contingency into final necessity works in the wrong direction, as is the case with Amano when he tried to combine gallium nitride and indium to obtain blue colour. Minimum hesitation and minimum doubt seem to operate against the contingency-necessity binomial.

> P_4 chance factors may occur in aid of the protagonists.

Chance played an important role as in the case of Amano's finding of treating aluminium nitride at 500 degrees centigrade or of the use of electron beam on gallium nitride with zinc additive. It may also be conjectured that these chance happenings were a result of constant and thorough-going research effort.

> P5 the protagonists live in a present that embraces past and future

In this sense, also the experience, accumulated in the past, more often than not allows researchers to extrapolate with relative ease towards the future.

Further study is required to see if the propositions we hazard are a universal phenomenon across different industries, management echelons, different stage of economic progress, etc. The capturing of the quiddity of the situation will very much bear on the handling of contingency, since the contingency construed as necessity requires the capturing of quiddity. That will be studied and discussed in another paper in preparation.

Section 6: Conclusions

Uncertainty is a fact of life. Both in their day-to-day operations and at a critical moment managers have to find a way to equip themselves with some manner of coping with it. Drucker's theory of business (1994) is one such example of behaviour for a manager to make sense out of the events at the surrounding environment and the situation facing him. A human being, faced with a world out of which he cannot make any sense, might end up by perishing powerless (Weick, 1995, 1996).

Uncertainty resulting from the possible existence of different outcomes, namely, contingency may be better dealt with, if some kind of explanation is put in place. Reduction of uncertainty may be achieved, or even if not achieved, at least a guiding principle facilitating the passage through it may be discerned.

In this chapter, we focused on the contingency-certainty binomial. In the example we analysed in the previous section, we saw that the protagonists never failed to believe in their effort leading them to a way-out from the difficulties. Credence or conviction was a force on which they counted. Past experience, knowledge, skills, will not to fail, etc., guided them through. The remarkable thing is that they did not seem to care about the competition pushing onward through a different technological stream; they stuck to the technology of their choice. Trials and experiments were exhausted. Not any eventuality or contingency was left to luck. Theorizing each step, both successful and failed, they reduced ambiguity and contingency. Perseverance and chance factors are the order of the day: for one of them the successful achievement took fifty years, while for the other it came in two decades.

Faced with contingency, to take some stance is important. Be it intuition, or be it some kind of risk reduction measure. Schopenhauer (2007, pp. 85–86) alludes to the taking of stance by affirming that 'in the great moments of life, when a man decides upon an important step, his action is directed not so much by any clear knowledge of the right thing to do, as by an inner impulse – you may almost call it an instinct – proceeding from the deepest foundations of his being'.

Kida (2001, pp. 106–107) refers to Schopenhauer's opinion about people's belief in transcendental theory of fate that dictates the existence of events in people's life which, despite their seemingly fortuitous occurrence, fit marvellously their objectives. This theory, if it takes a firm hold in a person's mind, may help him not to falter in his endeavours.

Though synchronicity may be a concept very much removed from management field it still may be relevant for our pursuit of contingency and taking of stance in that the Book of Change stresses the importance of actions because 'his actions intervene as determining factors in world events, the more decisively so, the earlier he is able with the aid of the Book of Changes to recognize situations in their germinal phases' (Wilhelm, 1967, p. liii).

As we have cited before, Takeuchi (2010) sustains the idea that we have to learn to live with contingency and design a new behavioural criteria such as to ignore events of minimum probability (e.g., the collision of earth with another heavenly body), to become aware of that the social phenomena like the financial market are dominated by the mutual and self-fulfilling enforcement of market opinions, and to realize that there can be a different kind of contingency that cannot be put under control by the law of large numbers (e.g., biological mutations, contingencies in the historical events, good and bad lucks).

The whole thrust of this paper is that the coping with contingency is essential for managers, not only for survival, but also it can be turned into a competitive advantage. The turning of contingency into necessity is a vital means by which managers make sense of the situation and in which they may seek guidance (with the shift from contingency to necessity perhaps taking place without the person being even aware of it occurring). It could have a high explanatory power of many successes in managerial history. It may deal, therefore, more with behavioural criteria than actual, scientific analysis.

Be that as it may, contingency is here to stay and we will have to take a stance towards it, like it or not. Needless to say that honing one's skills, expertise, etc., to build up a conviction about one's course of action and judgement making is of significant import.

Notes

The authors wish to express their deep gratitude to IESE Business School's IRCO (International Research Centre on Organisations) for its financial support to carry out this research, especially Professor José Ramón Pin and Angela Gallifa for their help. Our thanks go to International Research Centre on Organisations at IESE Business School for financing part of this Project.

1. '[T]he second form of uncertainty in our taxonomy is subjective uncertainty ... characterised by an inability to apply appropriate moral rules [that] can lead to societal anxiety ... which Emile Durkheim called "anomie"' (Tannert et al., 2007, p. 894), therefore it is out of our purview that is concerned with management judgement and judgement-making.
2. http://en.wikipedia.org/wiki/De_dicto_and_de_re accessed on 2 August 2012.
3. 'A syllogism in which one of the premises or the conclusion is not stated explicitly', American Heritage Dictionary.
4. 'The sequence of acts of a nurseryman who plants a tree, on the one hand, and the acts of a thief who hides a treasure in the earth, on the other hand, being independent, the relationship of any kind that is positively established between them is less than final'.
5. 'Contingency is the disjunctive relationship between the whole and the parts. The whole has the absolute identity by its very nature of whole. As much as it is determinate as being complete, the whole is definitely identical to itself and therefore its existence is accompanied by necessity. The part is, on the contrary, by its very nature of being part, lacks the absolute identity to itself: being only part, it

presupposes the existence of other parties...The part has in itself the nature of being able to be the part it is or another part: in this consists the contingency of the party of the game. In itself the nature of being both a party other than the part it is: in this consists the contingency of the part'.

6. '[I]t has no cause outside itself...from which everything else that is accidental derives'. However, urzufall seems to refer to the world of sense that came into existence as a consequence of the original sin. Therefore, it cannot be identified with God nor with Spinoza's God. That is why it can be contingent, while Spinoza's God is necessary.
7. '...contingency is defined as an encounter, a situation. In Japanese, the gu 偶 of gūzen, contingency, has the meaning of "double," pair, couple, meeting, the same as its homonym signifies reencounter. The gu 偶 of gūzen (contingency), is the gu of Guza, (face to face encounter), the gu haigū (marriage). The meaning of contingency is closed related to the meeting of A and B which denies the principle of identity A is A. We could define contingency as "the encounter of two independent elements"'.
8. 'Given certain conditions, the mean of a sufficiently large number of independent random variables, each with finite mean and variance, will be approximately normally distributed' (http://en.wikipedia.org/wiki/Central_limit_theorem accessed on 3 August 2012).
9. Relatum, pl. relata, is 'each of two or more objects between which a relation subsists'. Shorter Oxford Dictionary, 6th Edition.
10. http://en.wikipedia.org/wiki/St._Petersburg_paradox accessed on 27 July 2012.
11. 'Given certain conditions, the mean of a sufficiently large number of independent random variables, each with finite mean and variance, will be approximately normally distributed' (http://en.wikipedia.org/wiki/Central_limit_theorem accessed on 3 August 2012).
12. Shinagawa brings to our notice in a personal communication (an email message dated 6 August 2012) that about that time a group of researchers were developing a similar two-flow type device (Matloubian & Gershenzon, 1985, p. 640), and attributes it to the possibility that among researchers similar ideas might tend to crop up. Shinagawa does not know if Nakamura was aware of the competing research and took a hint from it.
13. MOVPE (or alternatively metal-organic chemical vapor deposition, MOCVD)l (Kakanakova-Georgieva, Ciechonski, Forsberg, Lundskog, & Janzén, 2009, p. 880), namely, MOVPE and MOCVD are the same device.
14. Based on Takeda Foundation (Akasaki, 2002, 2005a, 2005b).
15. Based on Mizobuchi (n.d.) and Science Watch Science Watch (2000) and Johnstone (2004).
16. Hall effect is defined as 'generation of an electric potential perpendicular to both an electric current flowing along a conducting material and an external magnetic field applied at right angles to the current upon application of the magnetic field' (American Heritage Dictionary).
17. (Takeda Foundation, 2005b: 9)
18. In his personal communications with the authors of this article during June and July 2012 by means of email messages and a PowerPoint presentation, Shinagawa contends that the following circumstances may intervene in the researchers' decision-making:
    - The experience, accumulated in the past, more often than not allows researchers to extrapolate with relative ease towards the future.

- The elimination of technological certainty may be in place because of a relatively small number of technology alternatives.
- Exhaustion of possible combinations of elements leading to a solution may be more relevant in this field than mere inspiration, namely, perseverance rather than the sharpness of intelligence, which may work out in favour of people of unfailing 'optimism'.

References

Adam, B. (2006). Time. *Theory, Culture and Society.* 23 (Special Issue on Problematising Global Knowledge), 119–126.

Akasaki, I. (2002). The development of gallium nitride blue light-emitting device – insight, challenge and success (chikka gallium aoiro hakko device kaihatsu – dosatsu, chosen to seiko) *The Takeda Award Forum 2002*. http://www.takeda-foundation.jp/award/takeda/2002/forum/01a.html accessed on July 2nd 2012: Takeda Foundation.

Allan, L. G. (1993). Human contingency judgments: rule based or associative? *Psychological Bulletin.* 114 (3), 435–448.

Aquinas, T. (1965). *Summa Theologiae: Cura Fratrum eisudem Ordinis* (Vol. I–V). Madrid: Biblioteca de Autores Cristianos.

Aquinas, T. (1993). *Commentary on Aristotle's Nicomachean Ethics* (C. I. Litzinger, Trans.). Notre Dame IN: Dumb Ox Books.

Ariño, M. A. (2012). *10 Principles to Make Effective Decisions*. Barcelona: IESE Business School.

Aristotle. (2001a). Metaphysica. In R. McKeon (ed.) *The Basic Works of Aristotle* (pp. 689–934). New York: The Modern Library.

Aristotle. (2001b). Rhetoric. In J. Barnes (ed.) *The Complete Works of Aristotle* (pp. 2152–2269). Princeton, NJ: Princeton University Press.

Bechara, A., Damasio, H., Tranel, D., and Damasio, A. R. (1997). Deciding advantageously before knowing the advantageous strategy. *Science.* 275 (28 February), 1293–1294.

Bernoulli, D. (1954). Exposition of a new theory on the measurement of risk. *Econometrica: Journal of the Econometric Society.* 22 (1), 22–36.

Boutroux, É. (2010). *The Contingency of the Laws of Nature*. Forgotten Books.

Bright, G. (1997). Synchronicity as a basis of analytic attitude. *Journal of Analytical Psychology.* 42 (4), 613–635.

Chermack, T., and van dr Merwe, L. (2003). The role of constructivist learning in scenario planning. *Future.* 35 (5), 355–369.

Cohen, M. R., and Nagel, E. (1993). *An Introduction to Logic* (2nd ed.). Indianapolis, IN: Hackett Publishing Company.

Davidson, D. (2005). Deflationary theories of truth. In T. Honderich (ed.) *The Oxford Companion to Philosophy* (pp. 194–195). Oxford: Oxford University Press.

Diaconis, P., and Mosteller, F. (1989). Methods for studying coincidences. *Journal of the American Statistical Association.* 84 (408), 853–861.

Drucker, P. F. (1994). The theory of the business. *Harvard Business Review* (September–October), 95–107.

Felder, G. (1999). Spooky action at a distance: an explanation of Bell's Theorem http://www4.ncsu.edu/unity/lockers/users/f/felder/public/kenny/papers/bell.html accessed on 26 July 2012.

Gigerenzer, G., Hoffrage, U., and Kleinbölting, H. (1991). Probabilistic mental models: a Brunswikian theory of confidence. *Psychological Review.* 98 (4), 506.

Hájek, A. (2003). What conditional probability could not be. *Synthese.* 137 (3), 273–323.

Hall, E. T. (1976). *Beyond Culture.* New York NY: Anchor Publishing.

Heidegger, M. (1982). *On the Way to Language.* New York NY: HarperOne.

Hitchcock, C. (2011). Probabilistic causation. In E. N. Zalta (ed.) *The Stanford Encyclopedia of Philosophy* (Winter, 2011 ed.). http://plato.stanford.edu/archives/win2011/entries/causation-probabilistic/ accessed on 27 July 2012.

Hume, D. (1969a). *A Treatise of Human Nature.* London: Penguin Books.

Hume, D. (1969b). *A Treatise of Human Understanding.* Harmondworth: Penguin Books.

Ichinose, M. (2011). *Probability and Philosophy of Uncertainty (kakuritsu to aimaisei no tetsugaku).* Tokyo: Iwanami Shoten.

Jaffé, A. (1983). Glossary. In A. Jaffé (ed.), *Memories, Dreams, Reflections* (pp. 411–421). London: Fontana Press.

Jarret, C. (2009). Spinoza on necessity. In O. Koistinen (ed.) *The Cambridge Companion to Spinoza's Ethics.* http://cco.cambridge.org/extract?id=ccol9780521853392_CCOL9780521853392A007 accessed on 10 July 2012, Cambridge University Press.

Jeffrey, R. C. (1990). *The Logic of Decision* (2nd ed.). Chicago: University of Chicago Press.

Johnstone, B. (2004). Shuji Nakamura – Inventor of blue laser diodes *Fighting 44s.* http://www.thefighting44s.com/forum accessed on 1 July 2012.

Jung, C. G. (1967). Foreword. *I Ching or Book of Changes: The Richard Wilhelm Translation* (pp. xxi–lxii). London: Penguin Books.

Jung, C. G. (1973). *Synchronicity: An Acausal Connecting Principle* (R. F. C. Hull, Trans.). Princeton, NJ: Princeton University Press.

Jung, C. G., and Pauli, W. E. (2012). *The Interpretatio of Nature and the Psyche.* Tokyo: Ishi Press.

Kammerer, P. (1919). *Das Gesetz der Serie: Eine Lehre von den Wiederholungen in Lebens–und im Weltgeschehen.* Suttgart: Deutsche Verlags-Anstalt.

Kase, K., Slocum, A., and Zhang, Y. (2011). *Asian versus Western Management Thinking: Its Culture-Bound Nature.* Hampshire: Palgrave Macmillan.

Keynes, J. M. (1957). *The General Theory of Employment Interest and Money.* Tokyo: Maruzen Co.

Kida, G. (2001). *Contingency and Fate (guzensei to unnmei).* Tokyo: Iwanami Shoten.

Kuhn, T. S. (1996). *The Structure of Scientific Revolutions.* Chicago: Chicago University Press.

Kuki, S. (1966). *Le Problème de la Contingence* (H. Omodaka, Trans.). Tokyo: University of Tokyo Press.

Kuki, S. (2011a). The contingency – a conference (guzensei – koen). *The Complete Works of Kuki Shuzo Volume 2 (Kuki Shuzo Zenshu Dai Ni Kan)* (pp. 324–351). Tokyo: Iwanami Shoten.

Kuki, S. (2011b). The contingency – his PhD dissertation (guzensei – hakushi ronbun). *The Complete Works of Kuki Shuzo Volume 2 (Kuki Shuzo Zenshu Dai Ni Kan)* (pp. 269–319). Tokyo: Iwanami Shoten.

Kuki, S. (2011c). Contingency and fate (guzen to unnmei). *The Philosophy of Contingency and Amazement (guzen to odoroki no tetsugaku)* (pp. 15–26). Tokyo: Shoshi Shinsui.

Kuki, S. (2011d). An inquiry into the basic character of contingencies (guzensei no kisoteki seikaku no ichi kosatsu). *The Complete Works of Kuki Shuzo Volume 2 (Kuki Shuzo Zenshu Dai Ni Kan)* (pp. 375–384). Tokyo: Iwanami Shoten.

Kuki, S. (2011e). A logic informed by contingencies (guzenka no ronri). *The Complete Works of Kuki Shuzo Volume 2 (Kuki Shuzo Zenshu Dai Ni Kan)* (pp. 354–373). Tokyo: Iwanami Shoten.

Kuki, S. (2011f). Modalities of contingency (guzen no shoso). *The Philosophy of Contingency and Amazement (guzen to odoroki no tetsugaku)* (pp. 27–48). Tokyo: Shoshi Shinsui.

Kuki, S. (2011g). The problems of contingency (guzensei no mondai) *The Complete Works of Kuki Shuzo Volume 2 (Kuki Shuzo Zenshu Dai Ni Kan)* (pp. 9–261). Tokyo: Iwanami Shoten.

Leonardi, P. M., and Barley, S. R. (2008). Materiality and change: challenges to building better theory about technology and organizing. *Information and Organization.* 18 (3), 159–176.

Lewicki, P., Czyzewska, M., and Hoffman, H. (1987). Unconscious acquisition of complex procedural knowledge. *Journal of Experimental Psychology: Learning, Memory, and Cognition.* 13 (4), 523–530.

Lowe, E. J. (2005a). Deflationary theories of truth. In T. Honderich (ed.) *The Oxford Companion to Philosophy* (p. 195). Oxford: Oxford University.

Lowe, E. J. (2005b). Truth. In T. Honderich (ed.) *The Oxford Companion to Philosophy* (pp. 926–927). Oxford: Oxford University Press.

MacIntosh, J. (2005). de re and de dicto. In T. Honderich (ed.) *The Oxford Companion to Philosophy* (p. 201). Oxford: Oxford University Press.

Malinas, G., and Bigelow, J. (2009). Simpson's paradox. In E. N. Zalta (ed.) *The Stanford Encyclopedia of Philosophy* (Fall, 2009 ed.). http://plato.stanford.edu/archives/fall2009/entries/paradox-simpson/ accessed on 27 July 2012.

Maraldo, J. C. (n.d.). The Contingencies of Kuki Shuzo. http://nirc.nanzan-u.ac.jp/publications/EJPhilosophy/ accessed on 11 May 2012.

Marian, D. (2009). The correspondence theory of truth. In E. N. Zalta (ed.) *The Stanford Encylopedia of Philosophy* (Fall, 2008 ed.). http://plato.stanford.edu/archives/fall2009/entries/truth-correspondence/ accessed on 6 July 2012.

Mayer, R. E. (1992a). *Gestalt. Thinking, Problem Solving, Cognition.* Cranbury NJ: W. H. Freeman and Co.

Mayer, R. E. (1992b). *Thinking, Problem Solving, Cognition* (2nd ed.). Cranbury NJ: W. H. Freeman and Company .

McKay, T. (2010). The de re/de dicto distinction. In E. N. Zalta (ed.) *The Stanford Encylopedia of Philosophy.* http://plato.stanford.edu/entries/prop-attitude-reports/dere.html accessed on 2 August 2012.

Mermin, N. D. (1981). Bringing home the atomic world: Quantum mysteries for anybody. *American Journal of Physics.* 49 (10), 940–943.

Mervis, C. B., and Rosch, E. (1981). Categorization of natural objects. *Annual Review of Psychology.* 32, 89–115.

Mizobuchi, Y. (n.d.). The putting to practical use of the blue colour diode-semiconductor laser (aoiro hakko diode-handotai laser no jitsuyoka) *Research report.* Tokyo: The Takeda Foundation.

Nonaka, I., and Konno, N. (2012). *The Grammar of Knowledge Creating Management for Prudent Capitalism (chishiki sozo keiei no principles: kenryo shihonshugi no jissenron).* Tokyo: Toyo Keizai.

Nonaka, I., Toyama, R., and Hirata, T. (2008). *Managing Flow: A Process Theory of the Knowledge-Based Firm*. London: Palgrave Macmillan.

Orlikowski, W. J. (2006). Material knowing: the scaffolding of human knowledgeability. *European Journal of Information Systems*. 15 (October), 460–466.

Orlikowski, W. J., and Gash, D. C. (1994). Technological Frames: Making Sense of Information Technology in Organizations. *ACM Transactions on Information Systems*. 12 (2), 27.

Orlikowski, W. J., and Yates, J. (1994). Genre repertoire: the structuring of communicative practices in organizations. *Administrative Science Quarterly*. 39, 33.

Pauli, W. (1973). Exclusion principle and quantum mechanics – Nobel Lecture. *Physics Today*, 26, 53.

Pearl, J. (2009). Causal inference in statistics: an overview. *Statistics Surveys*. 3, 96–146.

Peat, F. D. (n.d.). Synchronicity: the speculum of inscape and landscape. http://www.fdavidpeat.com/bibliography/essays/synch.htm accessed on 25 July 2012.

Pham, M. T., Lee, L., and Stephen, A. T. (2012). The emotional oracle effect. *Journal of Consumer Research*. 39 (October), Electronically published 12 January 2012.

Popper, K. (1957). Science: conjectures and refutations (pp. http://cla.calpoly.edu/~fotoole/321.321/popper.html accessed on June 318, 2008) Cal Poly State University.

Popper, K. (2002). *The Logic of Scientific Discovery*. Abington Oxon: Routledge.

Reed, B. (2011). Certainty. In E. N. Zalta (ed.) *The Stanford Encylopedia of Philosophy* (Winter 2011 ed.). http://plato.stanford.edu/cgi-bin/encyclopedia/archinfo.cgi?entry=certainty accessed on 22 July 2012.

Reichenbach, H. (1991). *The Direction of Time*. Mineola NY: Dover Publications.

Saito, T. (n.d.). The human and the absolute in the writings of Kuki Shuzo. nirc.nanzan-u.ac.jp/publications/EJPhilosophy/PDF/EJP3-Saitoh.pdf accessed on 10 July 2012.

Schelling, F. W. J. (1996). *Philosophie der Mythologie*. Paderborn: Wilhelm Fink GmbH.

Schopenhauer, A. (2007). The worldy fortune. *Parerga and Paralimpomena* (pp. 83–94). New York: Cosimo Classics.

Science Watch. (2000). Nichia's Shuji Nakamura: dream of the blue laser diode. 11 (1), http://www.sciencewatch.com/jan-feb2000/sw_jan-feb2000_page2004.htm accessed on July 30, 2012.

Shinagawa, K., Gemba, K., and Abe, A. (2012). *The Role of a "scientific seed theory" in Scientific Innovation*. Paper presented at the The XXIII ISPIM Conference – Action for Innovation: Innovating from Experience Barcelona.

Simpson, E. H. (1951). The interpretation of interaction in contingency tables. *Journal of the Royal Statistical Society*. Ser. B (13), 238–241.

Sleigh, R. C. (ed.). (2005). *Leibnitz, Gottfried Wilhelm*. Oxford: Oxford University Press.

Smolin, L. (2007). *The Trouble with Physics: The Rise of String Theory, the Fall of a Science, and What Comes Next*. Boston: Houghton Mifflin.

Spinoza, B. (2002). *Ethics* (S. Shirley, Trans.). Indianapolis/Cambridge: Hackett Publication.

Takeda Foundation. (2005a). Akasaki Isamu: the development of galium nitride blue light-emitting device – a challenge in the fronteer of the electronics (chikka galium aoiro hakko device no kaihatsu – fronteer electronics heno chosen) *Entrepreneur retsuden 2*. http://www.takeda-foundation.jp/reports/pdf/ant0202.pdf accessed on 29 July 2012.

Takeda Foundation. (2005b). Amano Hiroshi: the passion, struggle and triump in the development of gallium nitride (GaN) blue LED device (chikka galium aoiro hakko device no kaihatsu ni okeru jonetsu, kuto soshite kokufuku) *Entrepreneur retsuden 2*. http://www.takeda-foundation.jp/reports/pdf/ant0203.pdf accessed on 29 July 2012.

Takeuchi, K. (2010). *What is Contingency?: Its Positive Meaning (Guzen to wa nanika: sono sekkyokuteki imi)*. Tokyo: Iwanami Shoten.

Tannert, C., Elvers, H.-D., and Jandrig, B. (2007). The ethics of uncertainty. *EMBO reports*. 8 (10), 892–896.

Ten Berge, T., and van Hezewijk, R. (1999). Procedural and declarative knowledge – an evolutionary perspective. *Theory and Psychology*. 9 (5), 605–624.

Van Asselt, M. B. A., and Rotmans, J. (2002). Uncertainty in integrated assessment modelling: from positivism to pluralism. *Clim Change* 54 (1–2), 75–105.

Weick, K. E. (1995). *Sensemaking in Organzations*. Thousand Oaks, CA: Sage Publications.

Weick, K. E. (1996). Prepare your organization to fight fires. *Harvard Business Review* (May–June), 143–148.

White, P. A. (2000). Causal judgment from contingency information: relation between subjective reports and individual tendencies in judgment. *Memory & Cognition*. 28 (3), 415–426.

Wilhelm, R. (1967). Introduction (C. F. Baynes, Trans.). In R. Wilhelm (ed.) *I Ching or Book of Changes* (pp. xlvii–lxii). London: Penguin Books.

Williamson, J. (2007). Motivating objective Bayesianism: from empirical constraints to objective probabilities. In W. L. Harper & G. R. Wheeler (eds) *Probability and Inference: Essays in Honor of Henry E. Kyburg Jr* (Draft of 8 August 2006 ed., pp. 155–183). London: College Publications.

Young, J. O. (2008). The coherence theory of truth. In E. N. Zalta (ed.) *The Stanford Encyclopedia of Philosophy* (Fall, 2008 ed.). http://plato.stanford.edu/archives/fall2008/entries/truth-coherence/ accessed on 6 July 2012.

Zabriskie, B. (1995). Jung and Pauli: a subtle asymmetry. *Journal of Analytical Psychology*. 40 (4) 531–553.

Index

www.ingramcontent.com/pod-product-compliance
Lightning Source LLC
Chambersburg PA
CBHW060749150926
51501CB00004B/137
9781137024954